Music and the Elusive Revolution

CALIFORNIA STUDIES IN 20TH-CENTURY MUSIC

Richard Taruskin, General Editor

1. *Revealing Masks: Exotic Influences and Ritualized Performance in Modernist Music Theater*, by W. Anthony Sheppard

2. *Russian Opera and the Symbolist Movement*, by Simon Morrison

3. *German Modernism: Music and the Arts*, by Walter Frisch

4. *New Music, New Allies: American Experimental Music in West Germany from the Zero Hour to Reunification*, by Amy Beal

5. *Bartók, Hungary, and the Renewal of Tradition: Case Studies in the Intersection of Modernity and Nationality*, by David E. Schneider

6. *Classic Chic: Music, Fashion, and Modernism*, by Mary E. Davis

7. *Music Divided: Bartók's Legacy in Cold War Culture*, by Danielle Fosler-Lussier

8. *Jewish Identities: Nationalism, Racism, and Utopianism in Twentieth-Century Art Music*, by Klára Móricz

9. *Brecht at the Opera*, by Joy H. Calico

10. *Beautiful Monsters: Imagining the Classic in Musical Media*, by Michael Long

11. *Experimentalism Otherwise: The New York Avant-Garde and Its Limits*, by Benjamin Piekut

12. *Music and the Elusive Revolution: Cultural Politics and Political Culture in France, 1968–1981*, by Eric Drott

Music and the Elusive Revolution

Cultural Politics and Political Culture
in France, 1968–1981

Eric Drott

UNIVERSITY OF CALIFORNIA PRESS
Berkeley · Los Angeles · London

University of California Press, one of the most
distinguished university presses in the United States,
enriches lives around the world by advancing
scholarship in the humanities, social sciences, and
natural sciences. Its activities are supported by the UC
Press Foundation and by philanthropic contributions
from individuals and institutions. For more
information, visit www.ucpress.edu.

University of California Press
Berkeley and Los Angeles, California

University of California Press, Ltd.
London, England

Library of Congress Cataloging-in-Publication Data

Drott, Eric, 1972– .
    Music and the elusive revolution : cultural politics
and political culture in France, 1968/1981 / Eric Drott.
       p.   cm.—(California studies in 20th-century
music ; 12)
    Includes bibliographical references and index.
    ISBN 978-0-520-26896-8 (cloth : alk. paper)—
    ISBN 978-0-520-26897-5 (pbk. : alk. paper)
    1. Music—Political aspects—France—History—
20th century.   2. France—History—1958–   I. Title.
    ML3917.F8D76 2011
    780.944'09046–dc22

                                          2010052459

Manufactured in United States of America

20 19 18 17 16 15 14 13 12 11
10 9 8 7 6 5 4 3 2 1

In keeping with a commitment to support environmen-
tally responsible and sustainable printing practices, UC
Press has printed this book on Rolland Enviro100, a
100% post-consumer fiber paper that is FSC certified,
deinked, processed chlorine-free, and manufactured
with renewable biogas energy. It is acid-free and
EcoLogo certified.

To Marianne

Contents

List of Illustrations — *ix*

Acknowledgments — *xi*

Introduction — *1*

1. Music and May '68 — *21*

2. Genre and Musical Representations of May — *70*

3. Free Jazz in France — *111*

4. *La Cause du Pop* — *155*

5. Contemporary Music, *Animation,* and Cultural Democratization — *203*

Conclusion — *268*

Notes — *275*

Select Bibliography — *317*

Index — *329*

Illustrations

FIGURES

1. Poster of Daniel Cohn-Bendit / *33*
2. Cartoon by Siné published in *Le Point* / *35*
3. The Paris Opéra on strike / *51*
4. Cover art for Dominique Grange, *Chansons de mai–juin 1968* / *73*
5. Cover art for Dominique Grange, *Nous sommes les nouveaux partisans* / *76*
6. A map of the musical field published in *Jazz-Hot*, May 1970 / *88*
7. Cover art for Evariste, "La Révolution / La Faute à Nanterre" / *108*
8. Death notice for French pop concerts / *198*

MUSIC EXAMPLES

1. Dominique Grange, "Les Nouveaux partisans," first half of verse / *78*
2. Dominique Grange, "Les Nouveaux partisans," second half of verse / *78*
3. Dominique Grange, "Les Nouveaux partisans," chorus / *79*
4. Léo Ferré, "L'été 68," first climax / *99*

5. Léo Ferré, "L'été 68," final climax and close / 99

6. Evariste, "La Révolution," opening verse / 109

7. François Tusques, "Intercommunal Music," opening rhythmic motto / 145

8. François Tusques, "La bourgeoisie périra," opening and continuation / 147

9. François Tusques, "Portrait d'Erika Huggins," opening / 149

10. François Tusques, "Portrait d'Erika Huggins," failed trumpet entry / 149

11. Yves Prin, *L'Ile de la vieille musique,* scene 7 / 247

12. Yves Prin, *L'Ile de la vieille musique,* final scene / 250

13. Yves Prin, *L'Ile de la vieille musique,* final chorus / 250

14. Georges Aperghis, *Exercices, variants, musiques de la Bouteille à la mer,* "La fanfare des phrases," opening / 254

Acknowledgments

This book would never have been written without the assistance I received from countless individuals and institutions. Initial research for the project was made possible by a Summer Research Award from the University of Texas at Austin. A College of Fine Arts Research Grant and a University of Texas Research Grant funded subsequent research trips to France. A Dean's Fellowship from the College of Fine Arts in spring 2007 provided the opportunity to begin drafting the first portions of the manuscript. A fellowship from the National Endowment for the Humanities gave me much-needed time to complete the manuscript, though any views, findings, conclusions, or recommendations expressed in this publication do not necessarily reflect those of the National Endowment for the Humanities.

While in France I benefited greatly from the kind assistance I received from a number of librarians, archivists, and scholars. Their knowledge, patience, and professionalism greatly facilitated the hard slog through the archives: Sonia Popoff and Marie-Jo Blavette at the Médiathèque Mahler Musicale; Corinne Monceau at the Centre de documentation de la musique contemporaine; Annelore Veil at the archives of the Institut national de l'audiovisuel; Marie Lakermance and Claire Vidal at the Centre de documentation of the Délégation au développement et aux affaires internationales in the Ministère de la Culture; Rosanna Vaccaro at the Centre d'histoire sociale (Université de Paris I); and Françoise Burg at the Archives départementales de Seine–Saint Denis. I would also like to thank Scott Kraft at the McCormick Library at Northwestern University, who was extremely helpful as I sifted through the wonderful collection of *gauchiste* journals housed there.

I am particularly grateful to the numerous friends and colleagues whose insights, ideas, and feedback were a source of both inspiration and encouragement through every stage of this book's development, from its first vague glimmerings to its very last revisions: Robert Adlington, Amy Beal, Georgina Born, Ben Givan, Sumanth Gopinath, Roman Ivanovitch, Beate Kutschke, Tamara Levitz, David Metzer, Karl Miller, Ben Piekut, Jann Pasler, Philip Rupprecht, and John Turci-Escobar. Among these I must single out for special mention my academic "fellow travelers," Robert Adlington and Beate Kutschke. To have two colleagues working on musical life in Holland and Germany during the '68 period has been tremendously stimulating. I have benefited immensely from the various panels, forums, and publications on which we have collaborated.

I have also had the good fortune to have colleagues at the University of Texas at Austin as supportive as mine have been and continue to be. I am greatly indebted to Byron Almén, Jim Buhler, David Neumeyer, Edward Pearsall, and Marianne Wheeldon for all that they have done to make our department a warm and welcoming place to pursue my research.

For their generosity in permitting me to reproduce samples of their creative work, I owe a debt of gratitude to Siné, Michel Baron, Dominique Grange, Joël Sternheimer, Georges Wolinski, and Yves Prin. Thanks are due as well to Matthieu Ferré for granting me permission to reproduce some of his father's music and poetry. Renaud Gagneux was gracious enough to share his recollections of the student occupation of the Paris Conservatoire. I would also like to thank Brunhild Ferrari for speaking with me about her husband's music, life, and politics.

I benefited greatly from Clifford Allen's knowledge and passion for French free jazz, and I truly appreciate the information, insights, and recordings he shared with me. I am also very much indebted to Diane Gervais, not just for the help she provided in dealing with some of the trickier twists and turns of the French language, but for the numerous enjoyable conversations we have had concerning the peculiar pleasures of French pop.

For her role in ushering this book through the publication process, I am extremely grateful to Mary Francis. From start to finish, her guidance and unflagging enthusiasm for the project have been a great boon.

Eric Schmidt also deserves great thanks for his tireless work in preparing the manuscript, as well as answering my endless stream of questions. And it has been a great pleasure to work with series editor Richard Taruskin. His comments and criticisms have greatly improved the quality of both the writing and the arguments contained in this volume (though, to be sure, whatever faults remain are mine and mine alone).

Finally, to have Marianne Wheeldon as both wife and colleague has been a blessing beyond measure. This project would not have come to fruition without her unflagging support through every step of the long process. It is to her that I dedicate this book.

Portions of chapter 3 were first published as "Free Jazz and the French Critic," *Journal of the American Musicological Society* 61, no. 3 (December 2008): 541–81. © University of California Press.

Portions of chapter 5 were first published as "The Politics of *Presque rien*," in Robert Adlington, ed., *Sound Commitments: Avant-garde Music and the Sixties* (Oxford: Oxford University Press, 2009), 145–66. © Oxford University Press.

Introduction

On 13 May 1968 nearly one million people marched through the streets of Paris to protest the brutal police response to recent student unrest. The same day, Pierre Boulez gave a lecture on the state of contemporary music in the city of Saint-Etienne. The talk was the high point of the Semaine de la musique contemporaine, a one-week new music festival organized by critic Maurice Fleuret. Fleuret conceived the festival as a way of bringing recent developments in avant-garde music to a community cut off from the major centers of artistic creation, explaining that "there was no reason why the populace of a large city does not have the right . . . to live in unison with its time."[1] Boulez's talk summarized what had been accomplished in the world of contemporary classical music during the past twenty years and outlined what remained to be done.[2] This last question was critical. To ensure the continuing viability of new music, Boulez asserted, it was necessary to develop a general solution to the contemporary crisis of musical language. Rehearsing an argument he had made many times before, he assured his audience that only a comprehensive approach, one that overhauled instruments and institutions as well as compositional techniques, would shore up the uncertain position of new music. He set this totalizing vision against that of other, unnamed figures in the musical field, whom he characterized as pursuing limited, partial solutions to the problems confronting contemporary music. Such musicians were "scattered, isolated searchers," trapped in "small ghettos."[3] To underline the low esteem in which he held these putative adversaries, Boulez drew from the language of contemporary political discourse, using the pejorative term *groupuscule* to describe his rivals. An epithet that had gained currency as a way of denigrating extreme left-wing organizations was thereby enlisted to settle aesthetic scores: "Everyone defends his own small piece of territory and regards himself, in the fashionable jargon, as a *groupuscule*. This really is the death of music in the wider sense and of expression as such."[4]

A very different scene was playing out in Paris the same evening. Following the afternoon's march through the city's streets, a group of young demonstrators descended upon the Sorbonne. The university had already been closed for ten days on account of student unrest, its buildings cordoned off by the police. In the face of mounting criticism of the government's security measures, Prime Minister Georges Pompidou announced on 11 May that the government would henceforth adopt a softer line with regard to student protestors. He ordered the police to withdraw from the university on 13 May. It took little time for protestors to take advantage of this opportunity. By 6 P.M. the Sorbonne had been seized, a red flag raised to signal that control of the institution had changed hands from the police to the protestors.[5] For the rest of the night and into the following morning, the courtyard of the Sorbonne was the site of a euphoric celebration. Militants soon found themselves joined by curious onlookers who were drawn by the carnivalesque atmosphere of the "liberated" Sorbonne. "The occupied Sorbonne is 'Paris by Night'—something to visit after dinner," one observer remarked.[6] Animating the impromptu fête were the sounds of music. Within hours of the occupation's beginning a grand piano had been dragged from a lecture hall into the courtyard. Other instruments soon joined what had turned into an impromptu jam session. Not everyone present was pleased, however, by music's intrusion into the symbolic center of the students' protest movement. In a news report broadcast on the radio station RTL the night of 13 May, an exasperated militant can be heard trying to put an end to the performance: "Go and talk instead of playing this shit music!"[7] Straining to make himself heard over the sounds of stride piano, the unidentified militant harangued those who had come to the Sorbonne simply to take in the scene. "You are real dogs," he yelled at them. Driving the militant's tirade, it would seem, was a fear that political discourse was being drowned out by music, just as political action was at risk of being confused with the spectacle of revolution.

Musical performances elicited a very different response in occupied factories once the student protests of the first half of May gave way to the general strike in the second half. Although the major labor federations (the Confédération générale du travail and the Confédération française démocratique du travail) had been caught off guard by the sit-down strikes that spread across France, they quickly adjusted to the new realities. In many factories a new, provisional order was quickly established. In the Renault plant in Boulogne-Billancourt, for instance, union officials organized security details, press departments, and food services in addition to picket lines.[8] Union officials also made provisions for entertainment. Singer Francesca Solleville was one of those called on to help distract striking workers. Performing in factories was nothing new to Solleville. She had already collaborated with the association Travail et Culture, an organization whose mission was to broaden access to culture by bringing it to people's places of work.[9] However, the situation that Solleville encountered in the factories during May and June 1968 was a far cry from anything she had previously experienced. What stood out to her above all was the undercurrent of tension present in the picket lines between those who wished to maintain the strike action and those, occupying a more precarious social position, who wished to see it end quickly: "When all the factories went on strike, I discovered what picket lines really meant, the strikes in the factories, the fear that workers would come back on Monday, immigrant workers above all, the wretched ones who wanted to resume work because, for them, the stakes were enormous."[10] In these circumstances, performing music took on a completely different significance. The need to provide striking workers with some form of diversion assumed an urgency missing in routine concert settings. That Solleville and other singers lacked the customary equipment—microphones, backing musicians, and the like—seemed unimportant: "Our working conditions, they weren't really working conditions, [we sang] on a kind of dolly, in the corners of the factory, without any amplification."[11] Solleville shrugged off such inconveniences: "It was necessary to forget all about the professional side of things, that is to say singing with lighting, a sound system, it was necessary to sing out in the open, in the noise."[12] A sense of political duty outweighed any concerns she might have had about artistic standards. The demands of the movement superseded those of the métier.

Circumstance and theme bind these three episodes together. Each took place during the tumultuous months of May and June 1968, when the combined pressure of student demonstrations and a nationwide strike came close to toppling the French government. In addition, all three unfolded at the point where music and politics meet, although the nature and meaning of this meeting was different in each case. Boulez's use of political language in the context of a talk on musical aesthetics was *performative*: political antagonisms were mapped onto musical ones in order to legitimize Boulez's own position within the musical field.[13] The intervention of the militant in the courtyard of the Sorbonne, by contrast, evinced a *conflictual* understanding of the relationship between music and politics. Instead of putting one domain at the service of the other, the militant appeared more concerned with monitoring the relationship between the two. It was crucial that the line separating the pleasures of music from the patient work of politics was not transgressed. Finally, Solleville's performances in occupied factories assumed a *sacrificial* conception of music's relation to politics. Engaged singers such as herself were obliged to subordinate artistic prerogatives for the good of the strike movement.

I begin with these three episodes because they illustrate the central concern of this book: how the May '68 uprising and its memory reverberated through the French musical field during the "long 1970s," a period that stretched from the failed revolution of May 1968 to the electoral victory of the Socialist Party in May 1981.[14] But I have chosen to begin with these incidents not simply because each, in its own way, exemplifies the fact that May '68 and its aftershocks provoked a politicization of musical life in France. Rather, I have chosen them because they exemplify the diverse forms that this politicization assumed. This, if anything, is the guiding premise of this book: that different kinds of music, performed or conceptualized in different social contexts, engage politics in different ways. The uses and meanings ascribed to a chanson are distinct from those ascribed to a piece of avant-garde classical music, which are distinct from those assigned to a jazz improvisation. To flesh out this argument, subsequent chapters examine different music scenes affected by contemporaneous political movements: those of free jazz, rock *français,* and contemporary classical music. But even in the brief episodes with which I began, distinctive patterns of politicization are apparent. The framing of aesthetic oppositions in Boulez's lecture responded to the exigencies of the world of contemporary music, namely the priority it accords to aesthetic discourse. The need to carve out a niche within the musical field makes critical discourse an almost obligatory supplement to composition, with political analogies a well-mined

resource in this continuous labor of position taking. In the case of Solleville, the image of the chanson as a realist genre, rooted in French
working-class culture, made it the obvious musical candidate for entertaining striking workers. In this sense, the appropriateness of the chanson in the context of the factory occupation was not just a question of
the music's appeal to the workers but a function of the perceived fit
between genre and identity. And the perception that the boogie-woogie-
tinged jazz being played in the Sorbonne the night of 13 May was a
form of "light" entertainment inappropriate to the gravity of the moment no doubt informed the militant's hostility. It is doubtful that he
would have had the same reaction had the musicians opted to play
"The Internationale" or "The Carmagnole" instead.

If the theoretical proposition that different musical genres—rock,
jazz, avant-garde, or folk—afford different political functions seems
straightforward, the practical implications that follow from this proposition are anything but. Perhaps it is because of the self-evidence of the
thesis that scholars have paid scant attention to the myriad ways in
which genre mediates political expression. Although there is an exten-
sive literature on the topic of music and politics, for the most part
scholarly writing on this subject has explored this relationship in the
context of individual genres: hence the numerous books exploring such
subjects as the politics of opera, the politics of pop, or the politics of
rap. When other musical traditions are evoked in the course of such
studies, more often than not they form an undifferentiated background
against which the genre in question can better come into focus. Or—
more problematically still—these traditions are used as foils, handy figures of an ideologically benighted mainstream. This is particularly the
case when the desire to demonstrate the political efficacy of a given type
of music shades into advocacy on its behalf. Defining a musical subculture in terms of its symbolic resistance to mainstream culture requires
that another genre play the part of its (denigrated) other. A similar phenomenon plays out in writing that treats the transgressions of avant-
garde music as political gestures. Again, the existence of some vilified
musical other—in this case, a genre that embodies conventions instead
of repudiating them—is the condition that makes such political readings
possible.

For its part, scholarly work addressing the interplay of different
music genres has focused mainly on cultural hierarchies: how divisions
between "high" and "low" genres are established, reproduced, and (on
occasion) overturned. This, to be sure, is itself a political issue in that it

involves competition over a resource, prestige, that is no less scarce for being intangible. But contests over legitimacy are just one way that the system of musical genres interacts with the political sphere. At a more practical level, differences in how genre organizes musical activities shape the kinds of uses to which these activities may be put. Distinctions based on musical style, performance practices, modes of production and distribution, performance venue, institutional frameworks, and funding sources structure the space in which debates about music's political utility take place. For example, the fact that rock music is typically produced and distributed by commercial firms is more than just a distinguishing mark of the genre. It is at the same time a stake in disputes about rock's relation to progressive politics. Does the music's mode of production and distribution disallow it from adopting an antisystemic stance? Or does it still allow for the possibility—as many enthusiasts in the 1960s hoped—for subverting from within the system that supported it? In tracing such lines of conflict, genre delimits, but does not determine, the meanings and uses music can accommodate. To take another example, the heavy reliance of contemporary classical music on state subsidies (in Europe at least) shapes the political significance attributed to it. For some, such support is what enables the avant-garde's critical, contestatory ethos because it exempts composers from the demands of the marketplace. For others, such support undercuts the music's claim to radicalism, transforming it into the very image of a state-backed "official" music. The point is not that such debates can be decided one way or the other; the point is that distinctive funding patterns structure the field of political possibility inhabited by any genre.

As the foregoing indicates, the definition of genre I am employing in this book is an expansive one, encompassing parameters often placed under the heading of the "extramusical." Thus my discussion of various music scenes in Part II focuses less on how the upheavals of May '68 and *l'après-mai* found themselves reflected in new sounds, styles, or musical structures, and more on how they affected a variety of activities and institutions (festivals, music criticism, pedagogies, cultural policies, professional organizations, and distribution networks). In this regard, the term "genre culture" coined by Keith Negus might be more apt. As Negus notes, a genre culture is defined not solely in terms of a repertoire's musical characteristics, its "melodies, timbres and rhythms," but also by such criteria as "audience expectations, market categories and habits of consumption."[15] Conceiving of genre in this way places social determinants on an equal footing with musical ones.

I will return to this approach and explore some of its implications in chapter 2, but for the moment I would like to highlight one factor crucial to the political work of musical genre: specifically, the association that binds genres and social groups together. This circuit flows in two directions. On the one hand, genres help forge communities, bringing musicians, fans, critics, and support personnel together around a set of shared musical interests. Genre, in other words, organizes the forms of collective activity that constitute different "art worlds."[16] On the other hand, these communities, to the extent that they overlap with extant demographic groups defined in terms of race, class, age, or nationality, themselves function as a way of distinguishing one genre from another. That is, the correlation of certain patterns of taste with certain communities gives rise to idealizations regarding the social identity of a genre. To take one example, certain kinds of pop music, being consumed by a predominantly youthful audience, come to be defined in terms of this identity—defined, in other words, as youth music. The ethnic, generational, and class divisions that exist between different genre cultures become essentialized, treated as inherent to the genre itself. In this way, terms like black music, white music, working-class music, or elite music cease being descriptive and instead become normative. They do not describe a situation where all (or even a majority of) participants within a genre culture necessarily belong to a particular social category. Rather, such labels are the product of ideological work. They privilege some participants within a genre culture over others, some musical and extramusical traits over others.

Genres, in short, both constitute social groups and are constituted by them. In addition, such identifications mediate musical and political fields. Political ideologies, after all, are shaped in accordance with the constituencies to whom they are designed to appeal and on whose behalf they purport to act. Every ideology constructs a hierarchy of social actors, with some groups elevated to the status of protagonists: the industrial working class of orthodox Marxism, the colonized subject of national liberation movements, the *Volk* of right-wing nationalisms, or the rational, self-interested agents of classical liberalism. How musical genres are evaluated, what kind of utility political movements find in them, depends on whether the identity associated with a particular genre is valorized or denigrated within its ideological matrix. Furthermore, it is not just the position identities occupy within an ideology that affects how a political formation will view associated genres. If it is true that genre cultures involve more than just a collection of shared stylistic conventions, it is no less true that political groups require more than just an adherence to shared principles. Rather, political formations are as much a product of a common culture, of the practices, customs, and rituals that provide the affective base of solidarity. Such formations, in other words, possess a distinctive political culture, which not only helps to forge an otherwise disparate group of individuals into a collectivity but enables the transformation of abstract ideals into lived experience.[17]

A principal aim of this volume is to explore what happens when political cultures and genre cultures intersect. That they should intersect stands to reason. Both genre cultures and political cultures mobilize individuals around a common cause, one artistic, the other ideological. Both summon forms of collective action that foster a sense of shared identity, hence the claim of philosopher Boris Groys that "both are realms in which a struggle for recognition is being waged."[18] Yet it is precisely because of such similarities that the various points of contact between these two domains can easily turn into points of rivalry. A recurrent theme in the study that follows is the fragility of musical and political alliances. Efforts to bring the interests of the two spheres into alignment more often than not encounter resistance, typically on the grounds that such endeavors undermine the principles of a political movement or the putative autonomy of a music scene. As we will see in chapter 3, the attempt by certain critics to tie free jazz to *tiers-mondiste* ideologies met with hostility among other members of the French jazz community, who saw this maneuver as compromising the genre's claim to the status of the universal. What certain enthusiasts advanced as a means of legitimizing a musical genre was received by other enthusiasts as an unthinkable breach of the genre's integrity. Similarly, the introduction of music into the spaces reserved for politics was often rejected as an unwanted distraction, as borne out by the fulminations of the militant in the courtyard of the Sorbonne on 13 May.

Yet such spectacular moments of contention should not blind us to the existence of less dramatic—but no less vital—ways in which musical and political formations interact. Music has often been called upon in the elaboration of political cultures, as is readily apparent in the case of anthems. Along with the raised fist and the red flag, "The Internationale" (whose role in May '68 is discussed in chapter 1) forms a central element in the symbolic repertoire of the French workers' movement. Conversely, the rhetoric of political movements has long furnished a vocabulary for artists seeking to justify their aesthetic positions. From specific instances of appropriation (like Boulez's derogatory use of the term *groupuscule*) to more general borrowings (like the term *avant-garde* itself), political discourse provides a medium for articulating aesthetic ideals.

. . .

Besides being about the relations between music and politics, this book is also about May '68 and the long shadow it cast over French culture and society. It is hard to overstate the impact of what came to be known as *les événements*. This is above all due to the scope of the movement, as the protests and general strike touched every corner of French society. The months of May and June 1968, it is often remarked, bore witness to the largest work stoppage in the history of the country. But just as significant as the number of individuals involved (estimates put this figure between seven and nine million) was the heterogeneity of the movement. Students and industrial workers may have been the dominant figures in media representations of the May events, but they were hardly the only participants in the movement. Farmers, white-collar employees, football players, department store clerks, journalists, actors, artists, clergy, scientific researchers, and musicians were just some of the groups that joined the strike action as it spread from one sector of the economy to another. Even those hostile to the revolt could not escape the disruptions the work stoppage imposed, or the anxieties that the political vacuum induced. Few could avoid being caught up in the events of May, a point that singer Dominique Grange underlined when she sang "Even if your car wasn't burned/even if you don't give a damn/each one of you is concerned."[19]

If there is little question about the significance of May '68, what this significance consists in is far from being settled. Nor is there any sign that debates about May's legacy will abate any time soon. Even to this day, May '68 has the power to arouse passions and prejudices. This fact was underscored by the controversy that erupted during the presidential elections of 2007, when then-candidate Nicolas Sarkozy declared that it was necessary to "liquidate" the memory of the uprising. "May 1968," he proclaimed, "imposed intellectual and moral relativism upon us. The heirs of May 1968 have imposed the idea that everything was equal to everything else, that there was no longer any difference between good and bad, true and false, beautiful and ugly. They sought to make [us] believe that there existed no hierarchy of values. What is more, that there were no longer any values, any hierarchy. There was no longer anything at all!"[20] The Parti socialiste and their left-wing allies were quick to denounce Sarkozy's remarks. Aging *soixante-huitards* were among the most vocal of those contesting the conservative candidate's version of history. Henri Weber, leader of the Jeunesse communiste révolutionnaire in 1968 and socialist MP in the European Parliament in 2007, retorted that the May movement was not opposed to "all forms of authority," only "the most authoritarian forms of exercising power."[21] Daniel Cohn-Bendit, the public face of the Mouvement du 22 mars during the May events, was more pointed in his rhetoric, accusing Sarkozy of a "Stalinist" desire to erase the historical record.[22] It would appear that Sarkozy's diatribe, far from blunting the memory of May '68, had the opposite effect, reaffirming its continuing significance. Cynical observers might even say that this was precisely the point of his discourse: by invoking the specter of May '68, Sarkozy was able to drive a powerful cultural wedge through the electorate. But far more interesting than the actual positions staked out by either Sarkozy or his adversaries was the fact that all felt obliged to take a position on May '68—obliged, that is, to either repudiate or defend an event that had transpired thirty-nine years earlier. There is no better indication that the significance of 1968 has scarcely diminished with time. As the May events recede into the past, the list of social ills for which they are blamed—as well as the advances for which they are credited—grows ever longer.

That May '68 should continue to occupy such a central place in French public life is all the more curious considering that the revolt was, by most accounts, a failure. The fact that the government did not topple, that power was not seized, deprived the event the satisfying—if ultimately illusory—sense of conclusiveness that "successful" revolutions possess. This has given rise to two broad approaches to assessing May's impact. From one perspective, the failure of the movement to enact sweeping political change is equated with failure *tout court*. As Peter Starr has noted, this way of reading the May movement is informed by an absolutist understanding of political revolution: the transformation of society must be complete and irrevocable or it will not be.[23] At the same time, this reading conceives political action narrowly, as a struggle for the levers of state power.[24] The notion that the May movement never really engaged in the "serious" work of insurrection, the kind that might have led to an overthrow of the government, has led some to deny that May '68 was a political event at all. Raymond Aron was one of the first to maintain this position, famously declaring that May was nothing more than a "psychodrama" in which different parties to the events acted out pre-established roles: "I played the part of Toqueville . . . others played Saint-Just, Robespierre or Lenin."[25] The protests and factory occupations are thus reduced to an empty miming of historical models, scripted in advance and sustained by a collective suspension of disbelief. Conceived in this way, May '68 was a purely symbolic revolt, having little direct impact on the real world.

Even those more sympathetic to the movement could be dismissive when it came to its political consequences. Hardened militants chided their peers for their strategic and organizational shortcomings: the lack of a political structure to coordinate actions, the refusal of protestors to move past symbolic gestures, and the reluctance of students to stray from the familiar confines of the Latin Quarter. Pierre Goldman, a militant who had gained firsthand experience in guerrilla combat during a sojourn to Venezuela in the late sixties, recalled his incredulity when faced with the methods of *soixante-huitard* demonstrators: "I was excited but I cannot hide the fact that I sensed in that revolt obscene emanations. It seemed to me that the students spreading out onto the streets, in the Sorbonne, represented the unhealthy tide of an hysterical symptom. They were satisfying their desire for history using ludic and masturbatory forms. I was shocked that they were seizing speech and that they were happy with that. They were substituting speech for action. The seizure of power was an imaginary power."[26]

The notion that the May revolt was imaginary—or, in Aron's phrase, "elusive" *(introuvable)*—was further supported by its rapid dissipation after President de Gaulle's radio broadcast of 30 May 1968. In virtually every history of the uprising, this short declaration to the nation is treated as the pinprick that burst the insurrectionary bubble. Such was the case with both Aron and Goldman. Kristin Ross has pointed out the curious symmetry that exists in the attitudes of these ideological opposites: "In each of these accounts [Aron's and Goldman's], de Gaulle returns to the source of his strength, the army, the threat of a military situation is evoked, and the students evaporate into the thin air of the imaginary."[27] May is thus cast as politically impotent, so insubstantial that a speech sufficed to bring it to an end. May, in short, comes to be seen as a revolt in word but not in deed.

A second line of interpretation picks up where the first leaves off. This way of reading May accepts its political failure on its face but places the movement's true import elsewhere, in the domains of culture, personal behavior, and social norms. In its crudest applications, this interpretive tradition ascribes to the "spirit" of May a whole range of subsequent transformations that took place in culture and society. Quite a few histories of rock in France, for example, use 1968 as a dividing line separating the emergence of a (purportedly) authentic rock scene from the commercialized *yéyé* style that had hitherto dominated youth culture.[28] More sophisticated treatments read the cultural repercussions of the events as a response to the movement's shortcomings, a kind of psychic compensation for political disappointment. Revolutionary energies, thwarted at the level of the real, are channeled into the task of "revolutionizing" the spaces of everyday life and artistic expression. This premise underlies Starr's argument that, in the early 1970s, intellectuals associated with the poststructuralist movement found an outlet for frustrated political desires in the notion of *écriture:* "Writing served as the vehicle for a compensatory utopianism, for the dream of voyage *ailleurs* (elsewhere), to utopian . . . spaces."[29] For others, the cultural turn was not so much a response to May as the revelation of its underlying truth. From this perspective, the workerist rhetoric that figured prominently in the tracts, posters, and slogans of May did not reflect the real aspirations of the movement but were simply the jargon that activists fell back on for lack of a more appropriate mode of expression. The real meaning of May '68 was instead to be found in the call to "liberate expression" or the dictum that it was "forbidden to forbid."

Viewing the May events as an eruption of hedonistic individualism gained even more traction in the 1980s. This was particularly evident in the writings of Gilles Lipovetsky, Luc Ferry, and Alain Renaut. For Ferry and Renaut, the violence witnessed during May was the product of clashing sensibilities, as an emerging ethos of unconstrained individualism ran up against the values of restraint and self-mastery that had long underpinned "the classical idea of the subject."[30] For Lipovetsky, this new political style was already evident in May '68. The "revolution" of May was not "a question of seizing power, of singling out traitors, in drawing lines separating the good from the bad," but of "free expression, . . . liberating the individual from the thousand alienations that weigh upon him daily, from having to work at the supermarket, from television, and [from] the university."[31] As this new individualism overtook the traditional model of subjectivity after 1968, the latent ambitions of the movement, ambitions masked by the *marxisant* rhetoric of the period, were at once revealed and realized.

What ties these various readings of the May events together is a tendency to prioritize the cultural at the expense of the political. Yet, as

Kristin Ross has argued in her study of May's "afterlives," the "official story" that has developed to explain (or explain away) the political dimension of the May '68 events involves a series of problematic moves. To begin with, it requires that the movement's parameters be truncated, historically, geographically, and sociologically. Historically, by omitting from consideration both the roots of the social conflict in the divisions wrought by the Algerian War and its prolongations in the social movements of the 1970s. Geographically, by characterizing the movement as an essentially Paris-centered rather than a nationwide phenomenon. And sociologically, by emphasizing the role of students (and generational conflict) at the expense of the workers' movement (and class conflict).[32] With the scope of the events thus whittled down, all that remains is a self-gratifying image of May '68 as a harmless and healthy release of accumulated social tensions. Such exclusions, Ross concludes, are nothing more than "the price that must be paid for 'saving' May as a happy month of 'free expression.'"[33]

At the same time, this rewriting of May is erected on the basis of a number of uninterrogated binarisms: culture versus politics, self-expression versus self-renunciation, individualism versus collectivism, pleasure versus political struggle. These oppositions are embodied in the cast of clichéd characters that populate histories of '68: "Figures of populist abjection or masochistic self-denial, the stereotype of the *curé rouge* (militant priest) stands at the opposite end of the pole from that other equally stereotyped figure of May, the libertarian hedonist. The two stereotypes rely on each other to exist, like reflections in a funhouse mirror."[34] But for Ross, such dichotomous representations belie a more complex reality, where categories thought to oppose one another actually interpenetrated, their boundaries blurred in the heat of protests and factory occupations. Rather than being divorced from militancy, the pleasures of May '68 were inseparable from political agitation. The heady atmosphere of the moment emerged out of, and not in spite of, the marches, meetings, and picket lines: "The 'festival' or pleasure of the climate of those days was not the residue that remains when politics has been subtracted, but is in fact part and parcel of concrete political action itself."[35] Yet in deconstructing the binarisms that underpin depictions of May as an essentially cultural phenomenon, the moment when "poetry ruled the streets," Ross stops just short. Her aim, it would seem, is not so much to dismantle such dualisms as to invert the hierarchies they establish. To the extent that culture figured prominently in the events of May (in posters, slogans, chants, and various forms of "cultural agitation"), it was subordinated to the political demands of the moment. What May represented was not the triumph of "free expression," understood as a curative for social ills, but the opposite, "the failure of cultural solutions to provide an answer, the invention and deployment of political forms in direct contestation with existing cultural forms, the exigency of political practices over cultural ones."[36] The ascendancy of such "cultural solutions" in the years that followed thus represents for Ross a degeneration of the movement, seen most clearly in the emergence of the counterculture in France: "In England or the United States . . . one could conceivably become initiated into a political culture by creeping through the back door of the counterculture; in France or Italy, on the other hand, the 'counterculture' of the 1970s mostly represented the waning of what had been a much more vibrant and forceful political militancy than had been generated in the United States."[37] The border between culture and politics is opened up in Ross's account, but traffic is only allowed to flow in one direction: politics invests the cultural field, but movement in the opposite direction is not admitted.

It is not my intention in this book to carry the dismantling of the culture/politics divide through to its logical conclusion. Nor do I intend to adjudicate between "culturalist" interpretations of May and those, like Ross's, that seek to reinstate the primacy of politics. Rather, my aim is to resituate these alternatives by locating them in a broader range of possible articulations, examining how different historical actors conceived of the relation between the cultural and the political. Doing so reveals that the binarisms offered up in subsequent representations of May did not exhaust the range of possible relationships between culture and politics that were imagined, advocated, and put into practice in the years around 1968. Far from it. A remarkable diversity of positions existed among those who concerned themselves with the problem of music's relation to political action. For some, music was a distraction from properly political work or a displacement of revolutionary impulses. For others it represented a site where the unrealized aspirations of politics could be fulfilled, if only symbolically. Still others saw in politics an outlet for the utopian longings to which art gives voice. What is vital to recognize is that assertions about how culture and politics interact were themselves stakes in contemporary struggles. Claims about what constitutes the proper relation between music and the political were not just descriptive but performative, reshaping how people perceived social realities and how they acted upon these perceptions.

In acknowledging the variety of positions different agents adopted regarding the music/politics interface in the years around 1968, it is necessary to avoid equating diversity with mere eclecticism. The positions individuals espoused and the meanings that accrued to such positions varied in accordance with the aesthetic, ideological, and professional affiliations of different individuals and groups. Where the line separating music and politics was drawn depended, among other things, on whether one was a professional musician or a political militant. Which is not to say that one's location within the musical or political fields wholly determined how one imagined this relationship. Rather, the political uses attributed to music—and, more importantly, the significance these uses acquired—were inflected by the context in which they were enunciated. To say that music should be subordinated to political demands meant something entirely different depending on whether this claim was made by a militant or a musician. The stakes and interests of the one were only rarely in alignment with those of the other.

Such divergences, which were in full view during the months of May and June 1968, form the focus of chapter 1. For militants marching through the streets of Paris, the only music that really mattered was the revolutionary chanson, "The Internationale" above all. Singing "The Internationale" became a way of performing a number of tasks simultaneously: contesting political authorities, fostering a sense of common purpose, and, most significantly, identifying with the workers' movement. For musicians and others implicated in the cultural field, the exigencies imposed by the political movement were of an entirely different order. For all those who, like Solleville, were ready and willing to put their music into the service of the movement, there were others for whom the events compelled a reexamination of what it meant to be an engaged artist. In certain cases this led to a reconceptualization of the musician as worker. In other cases it led to a questioning of the status of the artist as a privileged, specialized social category. Uniting these and other points of intersection between music and the May events was the question of identity: at the same time that the appropriation of songs like "The Internationale" helped certain agents fashion themselves as revolutionary subjects, musicians were compelled to reframe their professional identity as artists as pressure mounted to contribute directly to the social movement.

The uses ascribed to music during May and the *après-mai* period varied not only across musical and political formations but also from one musical genre to another. Chapter 2 examines this topic in greater detail and provides a framework for understanding how genre mediates political expression. The norms, ideologies, and discourses that govern different genres play a decisive role in determining what can or cannot be said through music, what uses a song can or cannot afford. Of particular importance is the correlation of genre and identity, inasmuch as the political agency imputed to a given social group conditions what functions will be attributed to the music(s) associated with this group. To flesh out this thesis, chapter 2 examines how the events of May were represented in different types of popular song. By examining songs drawn from the genres of the literary *chanson* (Léo Ferré's "L'été 68"), the revolutionary *chanson* (Dominique Grange's "Les nouveaux partisans") and contemporary French pop music (Evariste's "La révolution"), I show how the conventions governing subject matter, rhetoric, imagery, and musical style in each influenced their depictions of May '68.

While chapters 1 and 2 focus on the immediate impact that May '68 exercised on French musical life, chapters 3 through 5 take a broader view, examining how the politicization of musical life continued to reverberate through various genre communities during the course of the "long 1970s." And while the case studies in chapter 2 focus on how generic constraints shaped musical responses to May '68, the more expansive case studies in chapters 3 through 5 take a broader perspective on the question of genre. Here the emphasis turns away from the impact the upheavals of the *après-mai* period had on musical texts and toward that which it exercised on the practices, discourses, and institutions of different genre communities. Chapter 3 examines the reception of free jazz in France in the years before and after 1968, paying particular attention to the debates that erupted in the jazz press regarding the music's relation to African-American political movements. The identification of the genre with the romanticized figure of the black revolutionary subject, itself seen as an embodiment of a broader, transnational figure—the third-world revolutionary—triggered a heated back-and-forth within the jazz community. For certain critics, this identification threatened to undermine the claims made on behalf of jazz's universality, a cornerstone of postwar attempts to valorize the genre in the French cultural sphere. Yet the identification of free jazz with African-American political radicalism also posed challenges for the music's proponents. By constructing an image of free jazz that stressed its irremediable alterity, writers and musicians alike were compelled to find alternative ways of relating it to contemporary French concerns.

Similar issues arise in chapter 4 in connection to the arrival of rock music and the counterculture in the years following 1968. Efforts at bringing the latest British and American styles to France confronted a number of obstacles. The close association of rock with American youth culture may have offered an appealing alternative to both a stifling parent culture and a highly commercialized French youth culture, but it also raised doubts about the local scene's legitimacy. At the same time, the suspicions of a resurgent *gauchisme,* which viewed the counterculture as a distraction at best and a means of depoliticizing youth at worst, presented another set of challenges to the genre's viability in France. Chapter 4 examines how the relationship between the nascent rock community and left-wing groups evolved in the late 1960s and early 1970s, focusing on the institution of the rock festival, viewed as a site of contention between different political and musical communities. While rock enthusiasts viewed festivals as a vehicle for propagating rock culture within France, certain segments of the extreme left saw them instead as occasions for inciting youth revolt—and thereby reigniting the revolutionary impulses dormant since May '68.

Chapters 3 and 4 are primarily concerned with how genres associated with social identities privileged in left-wing discourse made them ripe targets for politicization in the wake of May '68, when *gauchisme* was in its ascendancy. In chapter 5, attention turns to another legacy of May: namely, the desire to open up the field of cultural production. Specifically, chapter 5 traces the influence that the discourse on cultural democratization exerted upon the world of contemporary classical music during the 1970s. No less than its counterparts in popular music and jazz, avant-garde classical music witnessed a surge in popularity in the months and years following May '68. Yet the renewed interest in the avant-garde proved short-lived, and by the early 1970s commentators were virtually unanimous in describing a state of crisis within the new music scene. The drop-off in attendance at concerts of new music, the failure of any significant new movement to emerge at the beginning of the 1970s, and the growing competition presented by popular music led a number of observers to argue that the avant-garde had reached an impasse. Exacerbating this situation was the genre's identification with cultural elites, an association that was toxic in the charged political atmosphere of *l'après-mai.* Chapter 5 explores the various ways musicians responded to this crisis and how these responses coincided with government-sponsored initiatives aiming to democratize access to cultural life. In particular, I examine the emergence of novel forms of cultural mediation after '68—which went by the general name of *animation musicale*—that offered members of the contemporary music community new professional opportunities as well as a way of legitimizing their activities.

Finally, the conclusion reconsiders the links connecting music, politics, and identity in light of the changing political culture of the later 1970s and early 1980s. With the socialists' electoral victory in 1981, there was a sense that many of the aspirations of May '68 might be realized at last. But this hope was offset by the sense that the socialists' victory foreclosed the utopian dreams that May had kindled, dreams in which the identifications and symbolic investments afforded by music had played a key role.

. . .

Two final points: First, this book does not seek to provide a comprehensive history of the genres discussed in its pages. My aim is more narrowly focused. The studies that follow are better understood as snapshots than as fully fleshed-out narratives, vignettes that illustrate the configuration of musical and political forces at a given moment in time. What is more, some aspects of French musical life are necessarily omitted from consideration: neither the music of immigrant communities nor the popular traditions resuscitated by the regional folk revivals of the 1970s figure prominently in the stories that I relate—which is not to deny their importance within the broader cultural landscape. More striking, perhaps, is the relatively limited space devoted to the *chanson,* the dominant and most identifiably French of musical genres. This absence is all the more notable since the *chanson* has long been characterized as the quintessential form of French popular music, "popular" not just in commercial terms but in a more fundamental sense—as a form of musical expression bound up with the mythic figure of *le peuple.*

To a certain extent these omissions are borne of necessity: unless a book aspires to the condition of the Borgesian map, whose exactitude is such that it is coextensive with the territory it describes, relationships must be condensed, lines drawn, and topics excluded. This is particularly true in the case of *chanson;* given the genre's dominant position in the French musical field, an examination of the changes it underwent in the post-May period would require a book-length study all its own. But aside from the mere question of scope, there is the simple fact that the place the *chanson* occupied in French cultural life was several orders of magnitude greater than any of the other genres examined here.

Because of this centrality within the system of genres, the *chanson* acted in a manner analogous to that of an unmarked term in linguistics: as the horizon against which other, minority tastes stood out. Indeed, one of the main factors driving the choice of genres treated in this book is precisely their markedness, their relative salience as novel developments in the musical field during the period under consideration. Rock and free jazz both emerged as distinct genre communities in the years around 1968. This chronological proximity to the May events led contemporary observers to tie the emergence of these genres to the social upheavals of the period. In the case of contemporary music, the sudden if short-lived success that avant-garde composers like Iannis Xenakis and Pierre Henry experienced after 1968 likewise encouraged observers to connect this changing status to the political situation in France. By contrast, the *chanson,* being such a well-established genre, did not lend itself to such (admittedly simplistic) narratives. While it was true that a number of engaged or "alternative" artists either emerged in the years following May (François Beranger, Brigitte Fontaine, Jacques Bertin, Claire, and Maxime Le Forestier, to name a few) or else saw their public profile transformed as a result of the events (as was the case with Colette Magny or Léo Ferré), it is nevertheless hard to identify a single, coherent movement in this tangle of consequences.[38] Rather, these developments within the *chanson* appear more as a disparate collection of individualized trajectories, at times convergent, but more often than not following their own unique paths.

The second point I would like to make has to do with my use of the word "elusive." As mentioned above, the description of May as an "elusive revolution" derives from Raymond Aron. For Aron the phrase was meant pejoratively, the "elusive" quality of May '68 being a matter of its fundamental unreality. What students were searching for—Aron rarely alludes to workers in his reflections on the events—was a phantom, the myth of revolution that haunts the French imagination. This is not the sense in which I use the word. Rather, in borrowing the phrase from Aron I am engaging in a *détournement* of its meaning. It is my contention that the elusiveness of the May events did not reside in their ludic, delirious quality, in their alleged status as a "psychodrama." This was not an attribute of the events as they unfolded so much as one that emerged after the fact, as May '68 entered into collective memory. For one thing, this memory was quickly buried under a welter of interpretation, lost within a forest of signs. To a certain extent this fate was inevitable, since history must pass through the filter of language. And while this is true of all historical events, few have been so thoroughly worked over as May '68. Michel de Certeau was one of the first to take note of the "tidal wave" of books to which the events had given rise: "Everywhere there is a vital need to understand what happened. It aims at overcoming the irrationality of the event; to defend oneself from it, for some; to defend it, for others; for all, no doubt, [a need] to make sense of and repair the tear that it has produced in the system of social relations."[39]

To the extent that May '68 has indeed become elusive, it is in no small part for the reasons outlined by de Certeau. The event has disappeared behind all that it has come to symbolize: modernization, generational conflict, the rise of individualism, the disruption of social positions, the emergence of postindustrial society, and (perhaps most importantly) the enduring possibility that such an event can take place at all. This last point suggests another sense in which the May '68 events have, with the passage of time, grown elusive. Even as their memory has been absorbed in a proliferating web of discourse, the simple fact that (as Ross puts it) "something . . . indeed happened" during May and June 1968 has sustained the hope that something similar may yet happen again.[40] It was this hope that fueled the actions of militants during the *après-mai* period, those for whom the memory of May provided a tangible reminder of what was possible. But it was the same hope that fueled interest in rock festivals and *fêtes* in the years that followed 1968, conceived as a way of re-creating the same break in the march of everyday life that May afforded. It was the same hope that fed the more radical attempts at democratizing cultural production that took root in the decade after May, seen as a way of revivifying the liberation of expression, the *prise de parole* effected during the uprising. In this sense, May '68, rather than receding into the past, has been continually projected into the future. Or, as one of the more memorable slogans of May put it, "Ce n'est qu'un début, continuons le combat"—"This is only a beginning, let's continue the fight." Neither a bounded event in the past nor a cul-de-sac having no outlet on the present, May '68 becomes instead an opening, a horizon that, however distant it may appear, still stretches before us.

CHAPTER I

Music and May '68

Our October Revolution was a night in May, comrades
A night in May when we built barricades
To fight repression and cultural degradation,
And to create a new society.

—Anonymous, "Le chant des barricades" (May–June 1968)

Knowledge is finished. Culture today consists of speaking out.

—Striking worker outside the department store La Samaritaine
(May 1968)

On Friday, 3 May 1968, at one o'clock in the afternoon, approximately four hundred students gathered in the courtyard of the Sorbonne in Paris. They had come to protest the closure of the Nanterre campus of the Université de Paris following a series of disturbances, as well as the threatened expulsion of Daniel Cohn-Bendit and seven other members of the Mouvement du 22 mars group for their role in stoking student unrest. The gathering in the Sorbonne followed a well-rehearsed pattern, another in the series of political rallies staged by student militants in recent months, protesting everything from American involvement in Vietnam to the government's planned restructuring of the French university system. After speeches condemning the administration's actions, the meeting drew to a close, its organizers announcing that another demonstration would take place the following Monday.[1] The crowd began to disperse. But by 2 P.M. a few hundred students had reassembled in the courtyard, spurred by rumors that the neofascist youth group Occident was planning to confront the students as they left. With far-right students marching in the streets just outside the Sorbonne, and an assortment of anarchist, Trotskyist, and Maoist militants milling about inside its walls, the university administration feared a violent clash was imminent.[2] Jean Roche, the rector of the Sorbonne, decided to cancel courses for the rest of the day and to call in security forces. By 4:30 P.M. the police had arrived and began forcing students off the premises, ushering them onto the rue de la Sorbonne. The students had been assured that they would be able to leave freely, but upon exiting the university, they found themselves shepherded into police vans.[3] The actions of the police only served to inflame an already fraught situation. Incensed by the sight of their peers being led away en masse by the police for no apparent reason, students and other bystanders on the streets outside the Sorbonne grew agitated. Shouts of "free our comrades" and "the Sorbonne to the students" welled up from the crowd. Some tried to bar the way of the vans; others started to hurl loose paving stones at the police. The police responded by charging the assembled crowd and throwing canisters of teargas into their midst. By 8 P.M. the situation had exploded, as approximately two thousand students flooded the boulevard Saint Michel to protest the police's "occupation" of the Latin Quarter.[4]

The drama that unfolded over the next four weeks marked the most serious political crisis that the French Fifth Republic has faced. Within a week protests against police repression had grown in both size and intensity. On 7 May, some twenty thousand protestors marched through the streets of Paris. By 10 May, the "Night of the Barricades," the Latin Quarter had turned into a site of low-level street fighting between police and youth, with barricades erected in the streets across the fifth arrondissement. Parallels began to be drawn in the media to other flashpoints in French history, most notably 1789 and the Paris Commune.[5] These parallels were strengthened by the exponential growth of the movement. A one-day strike called by the major trade unions swelled the ranks of protestors. One million people were alleged to have participated in the march through Paris that took place on 13 May, the day of the strike and, ironically, the tenth anniversary of de Gaulle's accession to power. But the most remarkable development came during the second week of the uprising, when wildcat strikes broke out across France. Inspired by the students' occupation of the Sorbonne (itself precipitated by the government's decision to withdraw police from the university on 13 May), workers seized control of factories throughout the country.

By the beginning of the third week of May, the country's economy had come to a virtual standstill. Public transport, telephone services, gasoline and food deliveries, and other critical services functioned sporadically, if at all. Although estimates vary, around nine million people were reported to have gone on strike, making it the largest work stoppage in France's history. The sense that the country was teetering on the brink of revolution was made all the more palpable on 27 May by the refusal of the union rank and file to accept the Grenelle accords, the wage and workplace concessions that trade unions had extracted from government and industry representatives. Not only had de Gaulle's government been overtaken by events; so too had the nominal representatives of the working classes. In less than a month the field of political possibility had opened up in a way that would have been inconceivable just four weeks earlier. Doubts that de Gaulle's government would survive were widespread. And if it did fall, what would take its place? A new government, led by a coalition of left-wing parties? A new constitution and a new republic, the third in two decades? The replacement of a Republican system of government with one based on the principles of direct democracy? Or the imposition of Communist rule?

That none of these outcomes came to pass has done little to rob the memory of May '68 of its force. That de Gaulle managed to hold onto power in spite of everything has only served to mythologize the May events. Unburdened by the consequences that would have ensued had the government actually toppled, the student-worker uprising of 1968 has been able to retain the magical allure of pure possibility. Yet there were other peculiarities that explain the continuing fascination that the May events exercise. Among these was the fact that such a sweeping challenge to the status quo could have materialized in conditions that, by all appearances, were hardly conducive to social unrest. France at the beginning of 1968 was, in the eyes of most observers, a peaceful and prosperous country, in the midst of an unprecedented economic expansion. *Les trente glorieuses*—the thirty years of growth that extended from the end of World War II to the oil shock of 1973—had promised to bring to an end the gaping disparities that had long fueled social strife in France.[6] Increasing disposable income, the spread of credit, and an influx of consumer goods had improved the standard of living for a sizable fraction of the French populace.[7] Politically, the country seemed to be moving past the bitter conflicts of the 1950s and early 1960s. The cold war tensions that had brought about the dismissal of the Communist ministers from the government in 1947 and that had led to the marginalization of the Parti communiste français (PCF) during the 1950s had receded. More significantly, the wounds opened by decolonization—and by the Algerian War of Independence in particular—seemed more or less healed by the late 1960s. The Battle of Algiers, the collapse of the

Fourth Republic, the generals' putsch of April 1961, the massacre of Algerian nationals in October 1961, the death of antiwar demonstrators at the Charonne métro station in February 1962—such painful memories could now be forgotten. Or, if not forgotten, then at least repressed.[8]

By contrast, France in 1968 appeared tranquil, perhaps even a little "bored," as one commentator famously put it.[9] Within this context, the uprising of May and June 1968 could only have seemed an unanticipated event, an explosion without cause or explanation. This, to be sure, was a misrepresentation, one that ignored signs of growing disaffection in the months leading up to May. As Kristin Ross has observed, May "was not . . . a kind of meteorological accident arising out of unforeseen planetary conjunctures or, as in the oft-heard cliché, 'the thunderclap in the middle of a serene sky.' "[10] University students, for their part, had legitimate complaints about the state of the French educational system. The postwar baby boom had increased the student population faster than institutions could keep pace, leading to overcrowding, a high student-to-teacher ratio, and dissatisfaction with outdated teaching methods. Making matters worse was the government's proposal to render university admissions more selective in an effort to reduce the pressure on an already overburdened system. To many, such measures represented a step backward, a return to the bad old days when a university education was the preserve of a social elite.[11] For members of the working class, the principal grievance lay in the inequitable distribution of France's postwar prosperity. Despite claims that France was on its way to becoming a "consumer society," this was true for only certain strata of French society. Most members of the working class remained trapped in low-wage jobs with little hope of social advancement. As of 1967, 40 percent of the population made 1,800 francs a year or less.[12] The situation was even worse for the immigrants who made up the bulk of the unskilled and semiskilled workforce. They had to contend not only with low wages but also with shockingly poor living conditions: many still lived in *bidonvilles,* ramshackle shantytowns, while others took shifts renting out beds from so-called *marchands de sommeil* (sleep merchants).[13] Such inequalities in education, income, and life chances provided the fuel that would feed the protests and general strike of May and June 1968.

Yet if the belief that May '68 came out of nowhere was not entirely accurate, it has proven durable, firing the imagination of the left in the decades since 1968. For if such a revolt could arise in an advanced capitalist economy, during a period of economic expansion and full employment, it could occur at anytime, anywhere. At the same time, the fact that the revolt spread from the university milieu to the industrial sector set May '68 apart from other social movements of the same period. Unlike contemporaneous upheavals sweeping the United States, Japan, Mexico, and Germany, the uprising of May '68 was not strictly a youth phenomenon. On the contrary, a common front emerged uniting French students and workers, fragile and short-lived though it may have been. Indeed, it was the conjunction of these previously separated sites of social struggle, the university campus and the factory shop floor, that was the most destabilizing aspect of the May movement. The one seemed to feed off the other, with students borrowing tactics from past labor struggles (most notably that of workplace occupation), which were then revived by striking workers in turn.

But while the explosive character of May '68 explains much of its continuing fascination, one must look elsewhere, to the domain of culture, to fully comprehend the mystique that suffuses its memory. The conjugation of the political and the cultural took two contrasting forms. On the one hand, culture and creativity were conceived as resources that the movement could draw upon in refashioning social relations. It was not just that various artistic media were put to work by the movement for the purposes of propaganda (though this was certainly the case: the posters produced by the students at the Atelier populaire in the Ecole des Beaux-Arts were but the most notable examples of this tendency). Rather, the slogans, chants, wall inscriptions, and tracts that proliferated during the events bore witness to a belief that creative expression possessed a more profound function, that of nourishing the movement's utopian aspirations. Graffiti declaring "all power to the imagination," that "poetry is in the streets," concisely expressed the role accorded to cultural production as a force for personal and social liberation. On the other hand, culture itself became the object of contestation. The function of art in modern society was indicted on a number of counts: for its role in perpetuating social divisions, in transmitting hegemonic values, and in distracting individuals from political activism. Such polemics at their most virulent echoed avant-gardiste calls to eliminate art as a separate category of social life. It was here that the influence of the situationist movement was most clearly felt during May. For every inscription extolling the power of the imagination, one could find others that warned against the distortions wrought by art: "Culture is the inversion of life," "Art is dead, let us free our daily life," or, blunter still,

"Art is shit."[14] It was not the content of art that was challenged so much as its very existence.

No less than other art forms, music was drawn into debates about culture's role in political struggle. But music's engagement in the movement took more prosaic forms as well. As the scope of the work stoppage widened during the second half of May, musicians of all stripes joined the strike. Just as factories and universities had been occupied by workers and students, so too were concert halls and conservatories. And, as in the case of so many professions, the musical field undertook a thoroughgoing self-examination during the course of the revolt. General assemblies were held at which the role of music in society was debated, professionals and nonprofessionals exchanged ideas on what its function in the new society should be, and proposals for the democratization of musical culture were advanced. And yet for all this ferment, music remained strangely at the margins of *les événements*. Compared to the theater, cinema, and visual arts, the sites of dramatic and widely publicized interventions such as the États généraux du cinéma and the occupation of the Odéon theater, the actions undertaken within the musical sphere unfolded in the background, more or less invisible in accounts of the uprising. To a certain extent this was due to the nature of musicians' participation in the movement: by going on strike, performers brought musical production to a standstill, silencing their voices at the precise moment when others were clamoring to be heard. But music's marginal position in the May events was also due to the equivocal manner in which performers and composers responded to the crisis. Musicians' unions were particularly susceptible to the sort of charges *gauchistes* leveled at the institutional left: that far from wishing to bring about radical change to French society, they were chiefly concerned with furthering their own interests.

Yet to say that music's place within the May movement was marginal, especially relative to other forms of "cultural agitation," is not to say that it was either absent from or irrelevant to the events. As noted in the introduction, benefit concerts were held in occupied factories to entertain striking workers, the sounds of jazz (and free jazz in particular) accompanied the uprising at key moments, and, most notably, "The Internationale" was embraced by students as a symbol of their political aspirations. But even here, what might be described as the "problem" of music's role in May '68 is evident. Although the appropriation of "The Internationale" by young protestors was a multivalent gesture, its meaning dependent upon one's social position, it nonetheless signaled a significant lack within the political culture of the left, as well as French youth culture. Without a repertoire of contemporary political songs that they could draw upon, without a defined sub- or counterculture by means of which they could signify their resistance to dominant culture, French youth had to reach back to a century-old mainstay of the workers' movement to voice their opposition. "Clearly the movement was a little short on songs," music critic Jacques Vassal observed a few years afterward, noting that it was thus "reduced to pulling out the 'classics' of previous insurrections."[15] Even if the adoption of "The Internationale" represented what Ron Eyerman and Andrew Jamison call the "mobilization of tradition"[16]—a way of using song to link past and present struggles—the fact that a song dating back to the Paris Commune, rather than something more current or topical, became the primary musical touchstone for the movement demands reflection.[17] The same holds for the ambiguous role played by musicians in the movement. Their marginal position within the uprising and general strike not only reveals something about the place that music occupied in the French cultural and social landscapes during the late 1960s; it also points to the endurance of longstanding beliefs concerning the relationship between art and society, and the role of these beliefs in enabling—or disabling—musicians' ability to conceive of themselves as political actors.

This chapter examines the curious place music and musicians occupied in the May uprising. Here as elsewhere, a principal concern is the reciprocal relation that exists between musical practices and social identity. Like Eyerman and Jamison, I am interested in how traditions were mobilized and used as a resource in individuals' self-fashioning as political actors. What I would stress, however, is the heterogeneity of traditions that were available to individuals during May and June of 1968. It was in large part the multiplicity of available political identities that led to conflicts within the musical field, and within the larger social movement that emerged during May '68. Three traditions stand out in particular: those of working-class culture, as embodied in the students' embrace of "The Internationale" and other tokens of the French revolutionary heritage; the historical avant-garde, evinced in the utopian calls of "cultural agitators" to radically reconfigure the artistic sphere, leading ultimately to its reintegration with everyday life; and what might best be referred to as trade union culture, which acted as a critical resource in enabling the musicians' participation in the strike movement. As these three instances make clear, the symbolic repertoires that individuals could draw upon went beyond the purely musical plane and embraced a range of extra- or para-musical practices. By this I mean that in fashioning themselves as political actors, individuals utilized not only music, but an array of discourses, rhetorical stances, and self-representations historically associated with "movement cultures," whether musical, artistic, or social. To take one example, the most significant aspect of the musicians' participation in the strike is that it entailed a radical refiguring of their self-identity, requiring a temporary abandonment of the role of artist—romantically conceived as a person set apart and above economic and political concerns—in favor of that of (culture) worker. Here as elsewhere, the refashioning of identity functioned as a means of breaking out of habituated routines, enabling forms of action that one's established social role did not readily accommodate.

DEBOUT LES DAMNÉS DE NANTERRE!

Musical life in France went about normally during the first weeks of May 1968. In Paris, the protests taking place in the Latin Quarter did little to disturb the nightly rituals acted out in concert halls. On Friday, 10 May, the night of the barricades, concert life continued without interruption: Yehudi Menuhin appeared at the Salle Pleyel as part of a concert of Schubert's chamber music, Verdi's *Rigoletto* was performed at the Paris Opéra, and a concert of new music was put on at the American Center on the boulevard Raspail.[18] Even singer-songwriter Léo Ferré's appearance at the annual meeting of the Fédération anarchiste, held at La Mutualité in the heart of the Latin Quarter, unfolded uneventfully. It was not until the following Monday, 13 May, that the events of the preceding ten days began to have an impact on the musical sphere, with concerts being canceled or postponed on account of the one-day general strike.[19] There were other signs that the musical community was beginning to take notice of the turmoil unfolding around it. According to critic Maurice Fleuret a new slogan, intoned by the students of the Paris Conservatoire, could be heard during the demonstrations of 13 May, one that demanded "Xenakis, pas Gounod!"[20]

As singers, bands, orchestras and ensembles played on during the first weeks of May, outside the concert hall a different kind of music could be heard. The demonstrations of the preceding week had given birth to an array of slogans and chants, whose rhythmic mottos defined the soundscape of May: "C.R.S.—S.S.," "A bas l'état policier," or "Ce n'est qu'un début, continuons le combat," among others. Indeed, this last slogan became so pervasive, so familiar, that one author described it as having given the movement its distinctive "acoustic code."[21] More conventional musical resources were also marshaled during May '68. Principal among these were a pair of heavily freighted anthems, "La Marseillaise" and "The Internationale," more often than not opposed to one another during protests. Both carried in tow a host of associations, many of them contradictory, accumulated over long histories of reception and use. It was this polysemy that made both songs such powerful, and attractive, vehicles of political expression. But it was this same quality that made both the object of intense contest during May–June 1968, as different political factions struggled to lay claim to the songs and impose a certain conception of their proper use and meaning.

"La Marseillaise" was composed in 1792 by Claude-Joseph Rouget de Lisle, a captain in the French army. The song was the product of a brief moment of national consensus, as France's declaration of war against Austria in 1792 fostered a fragile sense of solidarity among liberal elites and the revolutionary masses.[22] However, its subsequent adoption by the Fédérés of Marseille solidified the song's revolutionary credentials, henceforth linked in the collective imagination with the monarchy's overthrow.[23] As a result of these overlapping and multivalent associations, "La Marseillaise" has been able to function throughout its history as both an expression of patriotic sentiment *and* an emblem of revolutionary fervor. The prevalence of one or the other function at any given time has depended in large part on who was singing the song, and to what end. Over the course of the nineteenth century, the fate of "La Marseillaise" was tied to that of Republicanism as an ideology and political movement. For monarchists, "La Marseillaise" was anathema, a token of the forces that had brought down the *ancien régime*. For those dedicated to fulfilling the unkept promise of 1789, workers and liberal Republicans alike, the song became on the contrary a galvanizing force. In 1848, and again during the Paris Commune, it was sung along with "Ça ira," "La Carmagnole," and other songs of the revolutionary period.[24] It was only in the decades after the institution of "La Marseillaise" as the national anthem of the Third Republic in 1879 that large swaths of the French left began to express disenchantment with the song.[25] While the chauvinism of "La Marseillaise" had discomfited earlier generations of utopian socialists, the antimilitarism of the workers' movement in the latter half of the nineteenth century, along with its growing commitment to the ideal of international solidarity, made the song appear increasingly ill-suited to the ideological desiderata of the French left.[26]

Into this breach came "The Internationale," written by Eugène Pottier in the aftermath of the Paris Commune and set to music by Pierre Degeyter in 1888.[27] Although "The Internationale" was slow to gain traction, over the course of the 1890s and 1900s the song was adopted by the majority of socialist, syndicalist, and anarchist organizations in France. Over the decades that followed, "The Internationale" and "La Marseillaise" performed a complex counterpoint, at times set against one another, at other times conjoined. In the early years of the twentieth century the songs were more often than not opposed, with Republicans and the nationalist right championing "La Marseillaise" and the socialist and anarchist left embracing "The Internationale."[28] With the onset of World War I, the demands of national unity in the face of external threat led many on the left to abandon "The Internationale" in favor of its erstwhile rival. This in turn discredited "La Marseillaise" after 1918 for certain segments of the French left, especially members of the newly formed Parti communiste, as the song was now identified with the kind of blind nationalism that had provoked the Great War.[29] The fortunes of the two anthems changed once again beginning in the 1930s. With the accession of the Popular Front to power in 1936 and the revival of patriotic sentiments engendered by the Second World War, all but the most intransigent elements of the French left again came around to embracing "La Marseillaise."[30] The identification of "La Marseillaise" with the resistance to German occupation meant that by 1945 it could serve effectively as a signifier of French national unity.[31] At the same time, the waning of the socialists' influence in the decades that followed the end of the war, coupled with the waxing strength of the Parti communiste, meant that "The Internationale" increasingly came to be viewed in partisan terms. Even as other factions on the far left (anarchists, Trotskyists, and Maoists) continued to stake their claim to "The Internationale," it was the Parti communiste that was most closely identified with Pottier and Degeyter's paean to working-class struggle.

Given this context, the fact that students embraced "The Internationale" during May '68, its strains accompanying every major demonstration, was noteworthy. Even if many of those singing did not know all the song's verses—a situation that the satirical journal *L'Enragé* sought to rectify by publishing its lyrics in its inaugural issue—the ubiquity of "The Internationale" attested to both the students' awareness of its potency as a symbol of working-class struggle and their desire to lay claim to this legacy.[32] Meanwhile, counterdemonstrations staged by Gaullists and extreme right-wing *groupuscules* such as Occident typically looked to "La Marseillaise" as a way of mobilizing their own nationalist traditions.[33] The two anthems did more, however, than simply distinguish left from right. How the anthems were deployed and what they signified varied widely. It was not just a matter of who sang "The Internationale" and where, but also who recounted the details of its performance after the fact, in what circumstances, and for whom. Still, one can identify at least three broad functions that "The Internationale" assumed during the uprising: signaling a generalized sense of oppositionality; interpellating the working class as a political actor; and traversing the various barriers that separated different social groups from one another.

In an interview published in the Communist literary review *Lettres françaises,* an anonymous student in literature explained what singing "The Internationale" meant for him and his peers. Describing the protests of 6 May, he remarked that "For us singing the *Internationale* was in any case a sign of revolt, more a song of opposition *[un chant contre]* than a Communist hymn, strictly speaking. It's a song everyone knows, a song of revolt. That's the meaning it had when we sang it."[34] What immediately stands out in the student's comments is his characterization of the song's meaning in negative terms. The specific ideals articulated by its text do not figure prominently in his description, nor do the political ideologies with which the anthem has been historically associated. "The Internationale" serves, within this account, as an abstract signifier of revolt, a way of gesturing one's rejection of authority. Furthermore, the fact that he *does* underline that the song was "more" than "a Communist hymn" points to a fundamental ambiguity in the way he and his peers employed "The Internationale." This ambiguity derived from the fact that the song was claimed by all the various factions that made up the left-wing universe of the time, Communists, socialists, syndicalists, anarchists, Trotskyists, and Maoists alike. While the broad appeal of "The Internationale" could serve as a vehicle for uniting a fractured left, it also became an object over which various political rivals vied. The remarks of the anonymous student testify to its ambiguous status, at once acknowledging the song's identification with communism (and, by extension, with the Parti communiste) and refusing to allow it to be reduced to this narrow, partisan association. In this sense, his comment is symptomatic of the uncertain and often openly antagonistic relationship that existed between student militants and the PCF. For radicalized elements within the student movement—members of the Trotskyist, Maoist, and anarchist *groupuscules* active in the university milieu—the PCF was as much an adversary as de Gaulle's regime. The party's disavowal of revolutionary action, its willing participation in the parliamentary system of the Fifth Republic, its troubled association with Stalinism, its highly bureaucratized structure—these were but some of the factors that explained the hostility that *gauchistes* and other members of the non-Communist left exhibited toward the Parti communiste. Within the extreme left in particular, the PCF's readiness to play the "electoral game" was seen as a clear sign that it was more interested in exploiting working-class disgruntlement than in fundamentally transforming the class structure of French society.

The recruitment of "The Internationale" as "un chant contre" was manifest at a number of junctures in May and June. One of the most notable instances came on 6 May, when it was sung by Daniel Cohn-Bendit and other members of the Mouvement du 22 mars on their way into the disciplinary council that had been convoked to decide the matter of their expulsion. This impromptu performance was immortalized when students in the occupied Ecole des Beaux-Arts created an iconic poster using a press photograph of Cohn-Bendit singing the refrain of "The Internationale" in front of an agent of the Compagnie républicaine de sécurité (CRS) (figure 1). The image of this confrontation between Cohn-Bendit and a helmeted figure of state authority captured the oppositional dynamic at play in this and other renditions of the song.

An even more flagrant use of "The Internationale" to express opposition to the symbols of authority occurred the following day, 7 May, during the course of the first truly sizable student demonstration in Paris. That afternoon at least twenty thousand protestors wended their way through the streets of the capital, their march capped by a procession down the Champs-Elysées. Exactly how the demonstrators ended up on this iconic boulevard, in the heart of bourgeois Paris, sheds light on the power ascribed to cultural and historical symbols as instruments of political contest. An account of the march given by Daniel Bensaïd and Henri Weber, leaders of the Trotskyist student group Jeunesse communiste révolutionnaire (JCR), describe how the protestors, having been prevented from entering the Latin Quarter by a cordon of CRS officers, were forced to change the direction of their demonstration.[35] Disputes broke out among various left-wing factions as to where the protestors should head. Certain students affiliated with "pro-Chinese" (Maoist) groups argued that the assembled forces should make for the working-

FIGURE 1. "Nous sommes tous indésirables" (We are all undesirable); poster of Daniel Cohn-Bendit singing "The Internationale." Courtesy Bibliothèque nationale de France.

class districts on the outskirts of Paris to signal their solidarity with "the people." Others (and here Bensaïd and Weber take credit for the initiative) agitated for the mass of students to double back and descend upon the Right Bank. Against Maoist charges that the Trotskyists wanted to "lead the protestors to the *beaux quartiers* of their brethren, the bourgeoisie," Bensaïd and Weber responded that marching through working-class neighborhoods would be symbolically impotent, bereft of imagination or impact.[36] Such a course of action would represent a retreat, a return to territory traditionally conceded to the left. But should the mass of young demonstrators process down the boulevard des Champs-Elysées—the symbolic center of wealth, prestige, and power in the capital—this would mark a conspicuous break with the established conventions of political engagement.

In the end the protestors opted for the Right Bank, and the provocation that Bensaïd and Weber hoped the gesture would have was borne out. The crowning moment of this act of transgression came when the marchers, having reached the Arc de Triomphe, sang "The Internationale" before the Tomb of the Unknown Soldier. Here, the act of signaling opposition involved the conflict between symbol and setting: an anthem celebrating international solidarity is intoned at the site that commemorates the virtue of sacrifice on behalf of the French nation. This inversion of values sent an unequivocal message, at least if we are to believe Bensaïd and Weber: "To walk up the Champs-Elysées while singing 'The Internationale,' to hoist red flags on the Arc de Triomphe, has the same meaning as the occupation of a faculty or the forceful riposte to police charges. It signifies that one refuses to respect any longer the rules of the institutional game according to which the system maintains itself."[37]

For Bensaïd and Weber, the march down the Champs-Elysées marked a turning point in the May uprising. By striking at the heart of bourgeois Paris, the demonstration revivified, as if by magic, a moribund left. Standing behind this interpretation of the function of "The Internationale" was the Trotskyists' longstanding hostility toward the Parti communiste, which they saw as an obstacle to revolutionary action. Bensaïd and Weber contrast this demonstration to the rallies staged by the PCF in preceding years, in which participants acted out well-rehearsed roles in an empty spectacle of contestation: "What a difference with the foot-dragging processions that the blue-collar bureaucrats have accustomed us to! In the ranks of the PCF people are passive, limp, nonchalant. They go to a protest like one goes to the movies, between 6 and 8 o'clock in the evening."[38] Although the account given by Bensaïd and Weber was hardly impartial, their portrayal of the student protests was not exceptional. Contemporary accounts refer to the sincerity and authenticity evident among younger militants, and more often than not point to their spirited renditions of the "The Internationale" as proof of a rejuvenated sense of political engagement.[39] The satirical cartoonist Siné, whose work had graced the pages of *Jazz Hot*, *L'Enragé* and *Charlie-Hebdo*, described the demonstration of 7 May in a letter to the editor of the newspaper *Le Point* in precisely these terms. He singled out the rendition of "The Internationale" sung at the Tomb of the Unknown Soldier not just for its political impact but for its emotional force: "To

FIGURE 2. "Debout les damnés de Nanterre" (Arise ye wretched of Nanterre); cartoon by Siné published in *Le Point*. Used by permission of Siné.

hear twenty thousand youths singing 'The Internationale,' I had never seen something so moving."[40] To illustrate his point, he included a cartoon that was published alongside his letter. Its caption ("Debout les damnés de Nanterre!") played upon the opening line of "The Internationale" ("Debout les damnés de la terre!"), substituting the student demonstrators of Nanterre for the oppressed masses of the song's original lyric (see figure 2).

The belief that the singing of "The Internationale" by students signaled a reawakening of the previously dormant left leads to a second function that was ascribed to the song during May '68, that of interpellating the working class as a political actor. As noted above, how and what the anthem signified depended in large part on the particular ideological investments of observers, so that the same rendition might afford multiple, and at times incompatible, interpretations. Such was the case with the 7 May march. What appeared to many as a simple affront to state authority was viewed in an altogether different light by those for whom the primary axis of social conflict did not oppose students and the Gaullist state, but workers and the forces of capital. In a tract published by the Fédération des étudiants révolutionnaires (FER), a more orthodox Trotskyist rival to Bensaïd and Weber's JCR, the demonstration is again cast as a pivotal event in the nascent uprising. But here it is treated as the point when the momentum generated by the student protests of the preceding days had to be transferred to the working class if the revolutionary potential of the moment was to be realized. The mobilization of key symbols of working-class agitation—the red flag and "The Internationale"—are, from this perspective, means of recalling workers to their historic role: "Together with the UNEF leaders, the FER . . . led the demonstration to the Champs-Elysées, where 50,000 young people and workers, red flags waving, sang the *Internationale*. The situation was becoming clear: it was the workers' turn to act."[41] Within the Trotskyist scheme at play in this reading of the event—according to which the student movement functioned as a kind of vanguard group, incapable of effecting revolutionary change by itself, but charged with the mission of impelling the working class to action—cultural icons like "The Internationale" functioned as a conduit through which the revolutionary impulse could pass. "The Internationale" and the red flag became forms of address, by means of which one group (students) was able hail another (workers).

With the onset of the general strike after the middle of May, a third, related use of "The Internationale" may be identified. Just as the song's history permitted it to serve as a means of hailing the working class in the weeks prior to the strike, during the period when the latter had yet to join the protest movement, the significance of such acts of musical interpellation was transformed after the first wave of factory occupations. Now singing "The Internationale" could be seen as a way of symbolically traversing social barriers, not as a vague gesture of sympathy or solidarity, but to affirm that students and workers were engaged in the same struggle. If Kristin Ross is correct in asserting that May was "a crisis of functionalism," a vast experiment in "*de*classification, in disrupting the natural 'givenness' of places"[42] in society, then the intoning of "The Internationale" can be understood as one way of dissolving the fixed social positions that kept students and workers isolated from one another. Whereas the use of "The Internationale" to interpellate the working class in the 7 May march assumed an irreducible difference between the two social identities—such that the students, themselves unable to enact revolutionary change, had to call out to workers, who *did* possess this capacity—the use of the song to surmount social boundaries made the opposite assumption. What was highlighted instead were the points of contact, the links binding these two groups together.

At times the barriers that separated students and workers, and that "The Internationale" was called upon to transcend, were not just social but physical. This was the case on the night of 17 May, when a contingent of students set out from the Sorbonne in order to march to the recently occupied Renault factory in Boulogne-Billancourt, just outside Paris. Their goal, by all accounts, was to make contact with the workers there, though it is not entirely clear what they hoped would come out of this meeting. A banner carried by a band of Maoists cast the procession as signaling the transfer of political initiative from the students to the "true" agents of historical change: "The workers will take from the fragile hands of the students the torch of revolt against the antipopular regime of unemployment and misery."[43] But it is unlikely that this self-sacrificing conception of the student movement, figured as a weak link that must yield to the strength of the industrial proletariat, was shared by others. No doubt most came with no other aim in mind than to assert, as one marcher put it, that "the students' ideal is your ideal, it's the same."[44] This understanding of the students' march was not shared by the leadership of the Confédération générale du travail (CGT), the main labor federation aligned with the Communist Party. For them, the crowd of students making their way to the factory gates represented a risk. Given the events of recent days, there was a concern that student militants might stir up trouble for the striking workers. In a communiqué, the union contended that the "adventurism" of left-wing groups endangered the strike movement and warned against any provocations that might draw out the forces of order: "We appreciate the solidarity of the students and teachers . . . but are opposed to any ill-judged initiative which might threaten our developing movement. . . . We strongly advise the organizers of this demonstration against proceeding with their plans."[45] But for most *gauchistes* the reluctance of the trade union leadership to welcome their support suggested an ulterior motive: namely, that the CGT and their allies in the PCF wished to use the strike as a way of shoring up their position as brokers of the workers' movement.

Arriving at the Renault factory toward midnight, the students were greeted by gates that had been locked and barricaded. On a truck parked in front of the factory a CGT official addressed the crowd. After thanking them for their show of support, he entreated those present to forbear approaching the gates, lest the management "use it as an excuse to call the police."[46] Confronted with these physical barriers separating them from the union rank and file, the marchers resorted to song as a way of both demonstrating their good faith and making contact across the factory walls. One eyewitness recounted the scene: "We wave. They wave back. We sing the *Internationale*. They join in. We give the clenched fist salute. They do likewise. Everybody cheers. Contact has been made."[47] In this portrayal the singing of "The Internationale" functions along with other gestures (like the raised fist) as a perlocutionary act, which in eliciting a response from the factory workers persuaded them at the same time of the students' shared ideals. The workers' reciprocation indicates that the gesture tendered by the students has been accepted. Thus commenced, the symbolic transaction continues with a proposed inversion of the position occupied by the two groups:

> A group of demonstrators starts shouting *"Les usines aux ouvriers"* (The factories to the workers). The slogan spreads like wildfire through the crowd. . . . *"Les usines aux ouvriers"* . . . ten, twenty times the slogan reverberates round the Place Nationale, taken up by a crowd now some 3,000 strong.
>
> As the shouting subsides, a lone voice from one of the Renault roofs shouts back: *"La Sorbonne aux Etudiants."* Other workers on the same roof take it up. Then those on the other roof. By the sound of their voices they must be at least a hundred of them, on top of each building. There is then a moment of silence. Everyone thinks the exchange has come to an end. But one of the demonstrators starts chanting: *"La Sorbonne aux ouvriers."* Amid general laughter, everyone joins in.[48]

That the logical continuation of this exchange was not forthcoming—there is no record of any factory worker crying out *"Les usines aux etudiants"*—points to the limitations of such symbolic transactions. Even if the singing of "The Internationale" represented an attempt on the part of the students to adopt a different political identity, one that would afford contact across physical and social boundaries, the entrenched divisions such a gesture had to overcome were so deep that it is doubtful that song itself, no matter how great its symbolic weight, would be sufficient to bridge them. As a more cynical observer noted, the working class was "more inclined to listen to the CGT than to the students, who were viewed with an instinctive suspicion," adding that if workers bore a grudge against "consumer society," it was because "it did not allow [them] to consume enough."[49] Images of burned-out cars and uprooted trees piled to form barricades, broadcast on state-run television and reproduced in newspapers and magazines, played into the union's charge that the student radicals only wanted to come to this and other factories in order to "break everything."[50] The existence of such broad, class-based differences in perception meant that attempts to traverse social boundaries confronted considerable obstacles.

Students' deployment of certain charged cultural symbols also had to account for the fact that these signified differently according to one's subject position. "The Internationale" may have seemed the perfect vehicle for expressing student-worker solidarity, but it was precisely the capaciousness of its meaning that made the song too fluid, too mutable to ensure unambiguous communication. Such distinctions were in full force during an episode that took place toward the end of May, an exchange between a high-school student and a CGT member *(un cégétiste)*.[51] When asked if he preferred the *tricolore,* the French flag, over the black flag of the anarchists, the *cégétiste* answered in the affirmative: "But naturally, it's the flag of France."[52] This reflexive expression of national sentiment led the student to ask in turn why he and other union members continued to sing "The Internationale." To which the *cégétiste*'s only response was: "stupid idiot" *(pauvre con)*.[53] There is no better illustration than this of how the different meanings ascribed to "The Internationale" could accentuate, rather than overcome, social divisions. While it may have been self-evident to the high-school student that the song espoused a principle of transnational solidarity, one whose logic demanded the renunciation of patriotic sentiment, the same could not be said for the *cégétiste,* for whom the song functioned primarily as a marker of group identity.

Episodes like these point out some of the difficulties students encountered in appropriating the artifacts of working-class culture in fashioning themselves as political militants. They may have sought to perform a different identity or role than that which was assigned to them, but intent alone could not guarantee success: to be effective, this performance had to win over an audience, to persuade others of their legitimacy. Failure to do so would leave students open to the charge of "posing" or playacting. Indeed, this was a charge leveled against them from the beginning of the uprising, when Communist Party leader Georges Marchais attacked what he called the "false revolutionaries" of the extreme left: "For the most part they are the sons of rich *bourgeois* . . . , who will quickly snuff out their revolutionary flame in order to go manage daddy's business."[54] Ridicule was also leveled at student militants from the opposite side of the political spectrum. In one tract, the extreme-right group Mouvement jeune révolution attacked those "who have nothing to suggest to this society but archaic formulas: the red flag and the *Internationale,* expressing only a *caricature of revolution.*"[55] In both cases there is the suggestion that an act like singing "The Internationale" was inauthentic: in doing so students were guilty of exploiting a song, a culture, that did not rightfully belong to them. Of course the disjunction between the perceived class position of students and the cultural symbols they deployed could have the effect of defamiliarizing the latter, reinvesting them with a force that had ebbed over the years. Such was the case in the enthusiastic reactions that the 7 May march elicited from older *gauchistes* like Siné. But it appears that both the affirmative and negative aspects of this disjunction were bound together. The transcendence of social positions that the appropriation of "The Internationale" promised could not be separated from the risk that it would have the opposite effect, that of reinforcing these positions in the eyes of others.

CULTURAL AGITATION

If any single event precipitated the wave of sit-down strikes that spread across France in the second half of May, it was the students' occupation of the Sorbonne on the evening of 13 May. From the very beginning of the uprising, the Sorbonne had represented the symbolic center of the conflict between the students and the French state. A turning point in this dispute came on 11 May, when Prime Minister Georges Pompidou announced that he would grant amnesty to jailed students and reopen the Sorbonne in an effort to quell the rising tide of protest. Yet, as noted in the introduction, Pompidou's gesture of goodwill backfired, offering students an opportunity that they wasted little time in seizing.[56] As the crowd that had marched through Paris on 13 May dispersed, young demonstrators flooded into the Sorbonne, now emptied of police. Within days militants had instituted a rudimentary form of governance in the Sorbonne. Tasks were divided among a variety of ad hoc organisms: *commissions,* charged with analyzing specific issues such as educational reform or political strategy; *comités,* which oversaw the day-to-day operation of the occupied Sorbonne; and the *assemblée générale,* open to all, which voted on proposals put forward by the *commissions* and *comités.*[57]

One of the committees founded in the days after 13 May was the Comité révolutionnaire d'agitation culturelle (CRAC), which took upon itself the task of organizing artists within the movement.[58] The group comprised a heterogeneous mix of students, intellectuals, and professional artists, counting among its members sociology professor Georges Lapassade, credited with being the driving force behind the group, as well as the musicians Renaud Séchan, Dominique Grange, and Evariste.[59] A document dating from the early days of the Sorbonne's occupation suggests that the impetus behind the creation of CRAC lay in the casual way in which the arts, and music in particular, had been deployed in the protests to that point. This theme was picked up in another tract, apparently the group's founding statement, which announced that "certain recent incidents concerning jazz in the Sorbonne oblige us to recollect our line of action."[60] While such spontaneous acts may have had some benefit as a source of relaxation or release, they did little to advance the movement's agenda. But what the music played in the courtyard of the Sorbonne on 13 May lacked in terms of political value it possessed in terms of diagnostic value. It bespoke a broader, untapped reservoir of creative energy that might be turned to political advantage, if only it were channeled properly. To this end CRAC urged that cultural producers and intermediaries "organize themselves into action groups" and use the specific means at their disposal to help further the students' protests.

The establishment of CRAC serves as a useful landmark in the evolving relationship between cultural and political action within the May movement. Whereas the protests of the first two weeks had drawn from revolutionary traditions and working-class culture in an ad hoc manner, the formation of organizations devoted to questions of cultural agitation transformed art and culture into sites of political intervention. At least two broad approaches to the "cultural question" can be discerned within this discourse, the anti-elitist and anti-aesthetic critiques of art. In anti-elitist discourse, art's perceived class character becomes the principal target of critique, both in terms of its role as a marker of social distinction and as a vehicle for promoting dominant values. Attacks on the antipopular character of bourgeois culture were rife during May (especially following the occupation of the Sorbonne), as were condemnations of artists who sought out the patronage of social and economic elites.[61] Yet even if the anti-elitist critique cast culture as something suspect, besmirched by its historic complicity with power, it at least held out the promise that this taint might be washed away, if only the barriers impeding access to culture were dismantled. The same could not be said for the anti-aesthetic critique of art, which was less sanguine about the possibility of redeeming art. Rooted in the legacy of the historical avant-gardes and their postwar avatars (in particular situationism), this school of thought held that art was a symptom of the alienation of creative powers under capitalism. Or, as a slogan scrawled on the walls of the Sorbonne put it, "Culture is the inversion of life." Unlike anti-elitist discourses, there was no possibility of salvaging a use for art within this conception: it had to be done away with as such, integrated into everyday life.

In addition to transforming culture into a site of political intervention, the advent of cultural agitation also marked the entry of artists in large numbers into the May events. Although motives for participation varied widely, the significance militants themselves attached to culture, creativity, and the imagination was likely an important factor. At the same time, the prominence of anti-elitist and anti-aesthetic discourses within the movement created a treacherous environment for artists to navigate. Both posed fundamental questions artists had to confront in imagining a constructive role for themselves. What constituted revolutionary art? How were cultural forms to be incorporated into protest? And beyond producing "engaged" works, was there anything artists could do *as* artists that would have a tangible impact?

In responding to these and other questions, artists were able to avail themselves of a number of proven strategies. The long tradition of artistic and intellectual engagement in France provided a repertoire of actions artists could draw from: benefit concerts could be organized, pressure groups formed, petitions signed, and so forth.[62] Such established forms of political intervention enjoyed some favor but were far from universally embraced. To a certain degree this was due to the fact that such forms of intervention appeared to stand outside political action proper. Benefit concerts and petitions may have provided material support and demonstrated artists' good faith, but they had little direct bearing on the movement itself. Especially given the privilege accorded to direct action during May, traditional forms of rhetorical support lost much of their appeal. The declaration that announced the founding of the Union des écrivains on 21 May foregrounded this devaluation of traditional forms of engagement: "The writers who have come together in this place, on this morning, have concluded that it was no longer the time to be present simply in the form of a press communiqué, or as joint signatories."[63] The pressure to find a more immediate form of engagement was also exerted on artists from without by militants who expected something more of their artist-comrades. Léo Ferré, for one, found himself criticized for not having passed from the stage to the street following his concert at La Mutualité the night of 10 May, the night of the barricades, this in spite of his longstanding affiliation with the anarchist movement. Or perhaps it was *because* of this affiliation: "At La Mutualité this evening there's Léo Ferré. We shout: 'Ferré, come with us!', 'Léo, in the street!' He won't come. It'll be a mistake. When red and black flags are out in the streets—*Le rouge pour naître à Barcelone, Le noir pour mourir à Paris* [a line from Ferré's "Thank You Satan"]—it's not enough to sing about them, you have to be with them."[64] A long history of support for the Fédération anarchiste did not shield Ferré from attack, nor did his celebration of anarchist principles in song. Rather, his lack of direct participation turned such gestures into broken promises, at least in the eyes of militants.

Such pressures compelled artists to undertake a broader reconsideration of their identity during the course of May. The aesthete, the bohemian, the alienated genius—these and other long-standing representations of artistic identity lost much of their attraction as pressure was exerted to intervene directly in political action. The Union des Arts plastiques, for example, contended that "buying into the cliché of the bohemian artist . . . can no longer continue. . . . Artists have the right to a place within society, they must participate by means of their works and their actions to elevating the cultural life of the people."[65] The expectation that a new society, a new culture, was in the process of taking shape also spurred the idea that a new kind of artist was needed. It was therefore essential that the social role accorded the artist be reconceptualized to allow for greater degree of political involvement. One solution to this problem was to be found in the legacy of artistic modernism. Many of the groups dedicated to cultural agitation hearkened back to the rhetoric, ideology, and imagery of the historic avant-gardes, namely the futurist, constructivist, Dadaist, and surrealist movements. This was the case with CRAC and, as we will see shortly, the Comité d'action révolutionnaire based in the Odéon theater. Even though the influence of these precedents could be manifest in a number of ways—ranging from the agitprop-style posters of the Atelier populaire to the (neo-) Dadaist interventions of CRAC—what tied virtually all of the cultural agitators together was a shared belief in the need to transform the art world, such that it would no longer constitute a specialized field of knowledge and practice. Another solution to the problem of fashioning an appropriate political identity was to be found in the heritage of working-class struggle. Efforts to organize artists by profession—seen in the Etats généraux du cinéma, or in the founding of both the Union des écrivains and the Union des compositeurs—drew from a different model, one furnished by the political culture of trade unionism (though some justifiably saw a more sinister, Soviet precedent for such enterprises).[66] The reimagination of the artist as worker also bore fruit in terms of the revitalization of existing artists' unions, such as the Syndicat des artistes-musiciens de Paris, groups whose influence had been on the wane in the years prior to 1968.

How, then, did the rhetoric of the avant-garde tradition inform the actions of CRAC? Perhaps the most pointed expression of the group's debt to the historical avant-gardes can be found in a document titled "Projet d'association internationale de dissolution culturelle." The short text, approximately two typewritten pages in length, takes as its target the ideology of artistic genius, echoing in many points Roland Barthes' roughly contemporaneous proclamation of the "death of the author."[67] But unlike Barthes' essay, the "Projet" outlined by CRAC is squarely activist in its orientation, detailing the measures necessary to dismantle the figure of the genius once and for all. According to the text's authors, deconstructing the myth of the artist-god would have implications beyond the cultural field, as this myth helps legitimize the ideal of personal authority in all walks of life. Undermining this particular excrescence of bourgeois individualism would thus undermine parallel figures in the political and economic domains: the boss, the manager, the entrepreneur, the president—in short, all persons and positions invested with charismatic authority. The document thus asserts that "to annul the artist as the central subject of art, as [a] 'creative authority,' not only comes to place the cultural system in peril, but also the ideological system still in place" since both rest on the principle of "pseudo-transcendental authority."[68] What CRAC envisions is the institution of a postindividualist society; and to hasten its arrival, they advocate flooding the cultural market with "inexpressive works, without quality, without rarity, without clarity, all identical, all of them irrecuperable in their anonymity and their radical simplicity."[69] The notion that mass production might prove a valuable tool in sabotaging the economic and ideological bases of the art world recalls Walter Benjamin's contention that mechanical reproduction posed a fundamental threat to art's auratic quality.[70] But the call to mass-produce nondescript art also looked back to the historical avant-garde's numerous attempts to deskill artistic labor, from Duchamp's readymades, through surrealist automatic writing, to the Fluxus event score. It would appear that CRAC's hope was that such undistinguished and undistinguishable artworks, if fabricated in large enough quantities, would prove so difficult to absorb that the entire cultural system would short-circuit.[71]

As intriguing as it may be, the "Projet" was exceptional in the output of CRAC. Generally speaking, the group expressed little interest in promoting a particular aesthetic or approach to cultural production, even one that promised to sabotage the workings of the art world. Judging from contemporary accounts, the group functioned more as an intermediary, facilitating both the organization of artists and the diffusion of "revolutionary" culture. The group is credited with staging *assemblées générales* for musicians and writers, arranging Jean-Paul Sartre's famed appearance in the Sorbonne in May, screening documentaries, and mounting musical performances.[72] Its intervention in the cultural sphere took place less at the level of production than that of diffusion. This makes sense given the group's ideological and rhetorical affiliations with the avant-gardiste tradition. Had CRAC acted as an atelier for politically engaged artists, it would have run counter to their stated goal of doing away with artistic specialization. In one of the group's later tracts, they characterize the "new culture" as one that is experienced not in the ossified forms of fixed works, but in the emancipation of creative impulses:

COMRADES, THE REVOLUTION TAKES PLACE EVERY DAY
IT IS A FESTIVITY, AN EXPLOSION WHICH LIBERATES PEOPLE'S ENERGIES
WE MUST ORGANIZE—WE MUST INVENT OUR MEANS OF ACTION
WE MUST COMBINE OUR ENERGIES!

For free exercise of the imagination in the streets. For transformation of the Sorbonne
   into an International Revolutionary Center for cultural agitation, open to all workers and self-managed by its participants.[73]

To be noted in this excerpt is how the ideal of permanent cultural revolution is likened to a festival, an occasion traditionally associated with the suspension of normative identities. This disruption of ascribed social roles, were it to be realized, would allow for the generalization of creative activity, the opening of artistic identity to all citizens. At least this is the utopian ideal to which CRAC aspired.

This aspiration becomes even more explicit later in the same document, when CRAC, responding to the decision made by certain actors' unions in early June to return to work, calls for the "occupation of all theaters in the Latin Quarter."[74] Their stated intention is to use these facilities as "operation bases for transforming outside space into a vast stage with infinite possibilities, on which each person becomes both *actor and author* of collective social-dramatic events" (italics added).[75] The ambivalence toward culture here reaches its acme, resurrecting the avant-gardiste call to sublate art into everyday life. Concomitant with this imagined liberation of creative energy is the simultaneous elimination and generalization of the figure of the artist. In the utopia envisaged by CRAC, artistic identity would be dispersed, with every person henceforth assuming the role of "actor and author." The role of the artist in the political movement is thus conceived in self-sacrificial terms. For CRAC, artists would fulfill their revolutionary potential only in yielding up that which identifies them as artists.

Still, CRAC's call for the elimination of a distinct artistic identity did not amount to a repudiation of culture per se, but only rejected the alienated form that it assumed in capitalist society. Other groups took a more stringent view of how to realize the utopian longings invested in art. Principal among these was the Comité d'action révolutionnaire (CAR), the driving force behind the most visible intervention into the cultural sphere, the occupation of the Odéon theater from mid-May to mid-June. The "conspirators" who planned the takeover of the Odéon had been inspired by the rapid escalation of the student protests after 3 May, which seemed to render older forms of artistic action obsolete. Jean-Louis Brau, erstwhile member of the lettrist movement, summarized the motivation behind CAR's actions: "The night of the barricades . . . confirmed the necessity of abandoning the freelance actions they had hitherto employed, of abandoning their place within the culture industry, to engage in an insurrectional act, in an act of war."[76] After considering a number of possible targets for their action—the Louvre, the Comédie Française, and the Académie Française—the group settled upon the Odéon, in part for tactical reasons (its location in the Latin Quarter, the heart of student unrest), in part for symbolic reasons, on account of its status as a state-operated theater.[77]

On the night of 15 May CAR, along with a contingent of students from the Sorbonne, descended upon the theater following a performance by the Paul Taylor Dance Troupe. The Odéon was immediately declared a "tribune libre," with a poster hung at the entrance announcing to passersby that "imagination takes power at the ex–Odéon theater. Entry is free."[78] The following morning those present in the hall voted on a motion declaring that the Odéon would henceforth cease operating as a theater and become instead "a meeting place for workers, students, and artists, a permanent assembly of revolutionary creativity, a site for uninterrupted political meetings."[79] The aim was to create an open forum where all were welcome to voice their ideas, hopes, and grievances. Realizing this goal required that the organization of the theater be subverted. Rather than segregating the assembly into two halves—one granted the privilege of speech, the other denied it— everybody present would be recognized as a potential actor. In this way the social relations inscribed in the layout of the auditorium would be dissolved. As one witness to the happenings at the Odéon would later put it, "No more barriers between actors and public, between authors and spectators, everyone will have the possibility of expressing their desires and of actively participating in the elaboration of a new culture."[80] To prevent the architecture of the hall from reinstating such barriers, a microphone was placed in the middle of an aisle, divesting the proscenium stage of its status as the focus of dramatic action.

Insofar as theatrical space provided both a metaphor and embodiment of the social hierarchies that CAR sought to overthrow, its inversion represented a potent act of political symbolism. But even as the figure of the theater became a way of framing, and thus comprehending, the social divisions contested by the May movement, the occupation of the Odéon further suggested that art's role in the movement did not reside in its subordination to utilitarian ends. Quite the opposite. Rather than looking to art as a vehicle for the transmission of revolutionary ideals, creative impulses were to be desublimated, lived and experienced directly. As was the case with CRAC, the legacy of the historic avant-garde informed the project adopted by CAR. The transcendence of art was cast as a necessary stage in overcoming alienation in society as a whole. According to Patrick Ravignant's "insider account" of the takeover of the Odéon, CAR's denunciation of art was predicated on a Marxist-humanist ideal of the "total person," "a vision of the integrated, reintegrated man, a man without specializations, without abstract specifications: no more intellectuals, no more artists, no more manual laborers, no more of the cultural or noncultural; simply man and life. . . . It is in this sense that they [members of CAR] cry 'Down with art! Down with culture!' That is to say: 'Down with art separated from life! Down with culture separated from life!'"[81] Even more so than CRAC, CAR advocated the dissolution of the artist as a specific social identity. But the utopian image of the total person that drove CAR's project went even farther, calling for the dissolution of any and every socioprofessional category into the ideal of the fully realized individual. With the attainment of "reintegrated man" (to use the masculinist language of Ravignant), identity itself would be transcended.

In abstract terms, the image of the reintegrated person was at best inspiring, at worst innocuous. After all, who could object to individuals realizing the multiple facets of their personality? Yet the actors employed at the Odéon did not look kindly upon CAR's occupation of the theater.[82] Their objections to the takeover were twofold. First, a number of actors contended that the Odéon was a "progressive" theater, with a deserved reputation for staging avant-garde or engaged plays, and as such should be respected, not denounced (let alone occupied). But from the perspective of CAR, such displays of political commitment, however sincere they may have been, still had to pass through a medium—that of theatrical representation—which froze "revolutionary impulses" and prevented them from "being expressed freely at the level of life, of quotidian reality."[83] Moreover, the fact that the Odéon was subsidized by the French state allowed the latter to present itself as a tolerant and benign regime: "People later reproached the occupiers for having struck at one of the most progressive theaters, run by a 'man of the left,' they pointed to the staging of Genet's *The Screens*, an anticolonialist play, etc. Yet it is precisely because of Barrault and *The Screens* that the Odéon was chosen, because—as the occupiers would say—[they] are the façade, the liberal mask of power."[84] While perfectly consistent with the logic of CAR's position, the polemic leveled against Barrault, Genet, and the Odéon can also be seen as an opportunistic maneuver, a way of discrediting competitors within the cultural field. In the context of the art world's intramural rivalries, the call to forsake art would constitute the ultimate move, the highest possible bid one could advance to demonstrate one's radicalism. Within a market of symbolic goods that rewarded both avowals of political commitment and the adoption of extreme ideological positions, the abandonment of art for sake of the revolution was a gesture that promised to accrue no small amount of symbolic capital.

The second objection to the occupation came from the unionized employees of the Odéon, a group comprising actors, stagehands, and support personnel. These professionals felt that it was they, and not some freelance cell of agitators, who possessed the right to occupy the premises. In making this argument, union members pointed to the fact that they themselves were workers, laborers within a branch of the culture industry. As such, they were engaged in the same struggle as the students and workers. This line of argument fell on deaf ears. CAR's stringent anti-aestheticism made them unsympathetic to such reconceptualizations of the artist along workerist lines. The rejection of art as a specialized field of activity trumped all other considerations, a point forcefully made by one of CAR's members in responding to the arguments of the Odéon's actors: "Isn't it monstrously unjust to expect some groups of the privileged few to blossom, leaving the masses passive, completely devoid of creation and expression? . . . If you want to perform, then go in the street or anywhere and improvise, help people to express themselves, to create, to cease being slaves of advertising and gadgetry! You have something very important to do; but it no longer involves performing on stages, in front of a docile and servile public."[85]

CAR's rejection of the actors' position was likely bolstered by the contempt that the extreme left held for the trade unions, which were deemed more interested in pursuing corporatist objectives than revolutionary ones. But the main problem, from CAR's perspective, lay in the fact that the professional status of actors was dependent upon the existence of a craft standard that set the "true artist" apart from amateurs and spectators. Artists' identity as cultural workers is, in this formulation, founded upon an illegitimate act of expropriation: having usurped the capacity for cultural production, they were able to profit—both materially and symbolically—from their exclusive claim to the honorific title of artist. Just as the students who sang "The Internationale" encountered resistance to their attempt to refashion themselves as political agents, artists who characterized themselves as workers saw their efforts to construct a more acceptable political identity for themselves rebuffed.

LA GRÈVE DU SILENCE

As a kind of protracted happening, the occupation of the Odéon may well have approximated the impossible goal that CAR was aiming for, the asymptote where art and life approach one another. Still, the establishment of the *tribune libre* ran into a number of practical impediments. The attempt to break down the barrier between actor and spectator did little to prevent the institution of a less visible split between the mass of people participating in the open forum in the main hall and the vanguard cell that seemed to be orchestrating affairs backstage.[86] Nor did such endeavors prevent a certain degree of factionalization from taking hold among militants as the weeks wore on. What is more, despite accounts attesting to the occupation's success in providing those whose voices were seldom heard the opportunity to speak their minds, such victories were overshadowed by the fact that the spot soon became something of a fashionable hangout for the Parisian beau monde. This led a number of observers to charge that the *tribune libre* was a failure, nothing more than "a circus for the middle classes."[87] But the widely held view that the Odéon was a sideshow, a bizarre parody of what was going on outside its walls, may just as well reflect the uncertain place that cultural affairs occupied within the May movement. While denunciations of the goings-on at the Odéon were often based on the very real deterioration of conditions there, they also reflected the widespread distrust of art as something frivolous, a distraction from political concerns.

Despite the criticisms leveled at the occupation of the Odéon, it soon spawned copycat actions at other cultural establishments. Indeed, this event, along with the first rumblings of unrest among the industrial working class—the Sud-Aviation factory in Nantes was occupied by its workers on the night of 14 May, the Renault factory at Boulogne-Billancourt the following day, succeeded by dozens of others in the days and weeks to come—indicated that the movement was expanding beyond the precincts of the university milieu. With the wave of occupations spreading, the government sought to protect certain key landmarks. Among these was the Palais Garnier, home of the Paris Opéra, which was circled by some four hundred CRS members in the days following the occupation of the Odéon to prevent a similar fate from befalling the high temple of bourgeois music culture.[88] Yet the security forces were deployed in vain. The police presence, intended to keep protestors from entering the building, was powerless to prevent the Opéra from being occupied from within—which is precisely what happened on Saturday, 18 May, when members of the Opéra's technical staff took control of the building (figure 3). The decision to strike was made at the end of a general assembly, during the course of which a list of demands was drawn up to be presented to the Ministry of Cultural Affairs.[89] Among other things, the employees of the Opéra called for an increase in wages and a greater say in the management of the institution. Upon learning that the ministry had rejected their ultimatum, the staff barred the doors to the Palais Garnier and unfurled banners from the second story announcing their strike.[90]

In the meantime, students at the Conservatoire national supérieur de musique had taken control of its buildings on the rue de Madrid, not far from the Opéra.[91] Although but a few days had passed since the

FIGURE 3. The Paris Opéra on strike, May–June 1968. Photograph by Michel Baron. Used by permission of Michel Baron.

"liberation" of the Sorbonne, the time lag was significant and did not go unnoticed by participants. In a statement published a few months after the end of the events, one young musician acknowledged that "our *prise de position* came late" and attributed this delay to the fact that "the majority of the students at the Conservatoire, who are recruited at a young age and are generally drawn from privileged social strata, were little prepared to question traditional structures."[92] Despite the lack of concrete data to back up such claims, the comments of other participants buttress the notion that the social composition of the student body of the Conservatoire hindered the implantation of the movement there, with the majority of pianists and string players coming from upper-middle-class backgrounds.[93] Probably a more significant factor was the highly specialized nature of the training offered by the Conservatoire, which meant that the students there had little formal exposure to political or social theory (unlike the militants at Nanterre, for instance, many of whom were sociology students). Nor should one discount the influence exerted by the ideology of absolute music, which would seem to rule out a priori the notion that matters such as politics should be a concern of the classical musician. Lastly there was the simple matter of the Conservatoire's physical distance from the Latin

Quarter, the center of the protests during the first two weeks of May. Sandwiched between the more bourgeois neighborhoods around the Parc Monceau on one side and the *grands boulevards* on the other, the Conservatoire's geographical isolation would be felt ever more acutely as the wildcat strikes spread, with gasoline hard to come by and public transportation idled.

Even so, the Conservatoire was not entirely untouched by the tumult in the days leading up to its occupation, nor did the student movement materialize there spontaneously. The first hints of disquiet among the student body came shortly after the Night of the Barricades, in the course of a meeting convened by the director of the Conservatoire, Raymond Gallois-Montbrun. Gallois-Montbrun called on the students to defend the institution in the event that it was attacked by the "red guards" of the Latin Quarter. Yet this plea to stand firm in the face of the rising tide of anarchy met with some resistance, as a number of those assembled took the opportunity to express their outrage at police brutality. Tapping into this growing discontent, the composition student Renaud Gagneux established a section of the national student union, the Union nationale des étudiants de France (UNEF) in the Conservatoire in the days after Gallois-Montbrun's assembly. Elected by his peers to head the newly formed UNEF section, Gagneux convened a general assembly of the Conservatoire's students. However, this initial attempt to give voice to the grievances of the student body proved unproductive; most of the complaints registered during the course of the assembly proved to be relatively petty, more concerned with issues like the cleanliness of the restrooms than with the reform of the Conservatoire's educational mission.[94]

Despite such inauspicious beginnings, Conservatoire students soon turned their attention to weightier concerns. A commission composed of both students and faculty set to work formulating demands to be presented to the Ministry of Cultural Affairs.[95] Many of the reforms the commission called for addressed material conditions at the Conservatoire. Among other things, the group urged the government to double the budget for fellowships, build a dormitory to house students from the provinces, increase the number of practice rooms, and improve the library facilities. Other reforms addressed the outmoded nature of the curriculum, especially with regard to composition. In particular, the commission pushed for electroacoustic music to be included in future course offerings to account for the significant technological changes taking place within the field of contemporary music.[96] Last but not least, the commission recommended broad changes be made to the place music occupied in the French educational system. The amount of time devoted to music instruction in primary and secondary education needed to be substantially increased, lest music be reduced to a luxury to which only the privileged had access. "It is necessary," one of the student leaders proclaimed, "to inundate primary schools, *lycées,* and colleges as soon as possible with the combined sonic power of five centuries [of music history]." Only then would "workers and laborers know what Music is."[97]

At the university level, the Conservatoire was to be transformed into a department of "sonic arts" within a broader, multidisciplinary Faculté des arts, itself folded into the university system as a whole.[98] The aim of this institutional reorganization was twofold. On the one hand, it would integrate music into the liberal arts, a change that, among other things, might help musicians overcome their social isolation. On the other hand, this change in musicians' training would provide students the kind of general education necessary to thrive in modern society. But beyond such practical considerations, there was a utopian aspect to the call to eliminate the boundaries separating music education from general education, one that was bound up with the broader critique of specialization voiced during May. The idealism driving the proposed educational reforms was perhaps best summarized by music critic Maurice Fleuret. This new institutional arrangement, Fleuret observed, would produce both "creators and teachers, the first having the possibility and right to teach, the second having the possibility and the right to produce creative work."[99]

The occupation of the Conservatoire had a galvanizing effect on other segments of the musical field. The day after the occupation began, singers and other "artistes de variétés" declared their intention to organize a number of galas, the proceeds of which would be directed to support striking workers.[100] The same day a meeting was organized at the Sorbonne that would bring together the entire musical community—performers, critics, composers, students, musicologists, amateur musicians, among others. Led by Fleuret and a young organist (unidentified in press accounts of the assembly), the event attracted many luminaries of the French musical world, including Henri Dutilleux, Paul Tortelier, Jacques Chailley, Claude Helffer, Gilbert Amy, François Bayle, Luc Ferrari, and François-Bernard Mâche. Notably, neither Pierre Boulez nor Olivier Messiaen attended: the former was not in Paris during the May uprising, while the latter was widely known to be a Gaullist and therefore unsympathetic to the student movement.[101] The debate lasted at least three hours, with much of the time spent discussing what musicians could do to advance the student-worker movement. By the end of the evening the assembly had issued a statement that expressed their solidarity with the protestors and striking workers, at the same time as they encouraged the students at the Conservatoire to continue the occupation.[102] Meetings were announced that would take place in the days that followed, where the issue of a musicians' strike would be decided.

The assembly at the Sorbonne triggered a flurry of activity in the music community. On 21 May approximately six hundred chanson artists decided to join the strike, with some going a step further and occupying concert halls.[103] The following day, instrumentalists gathered at the Institut d'art et archéologie on the rue Michelet to vote on a work stoppage. Given the general trend of events the outcome of the vote was scarcely in doubt, with nine hundred electing to go on strike and only forty voting against the action.[104] The same evening a group of composers met in order to chart their course of action. The immediate outcome of the meeting was the decision for composers to invoke their moral rights to prohibit the performance of their music indefinitely. In announcing the start of this "silent strike" *(grève du silence)*, the composers declared that there would be but one exception to this ban on the performance of their works; the strike, they declared, "does not concern artistic presentations organized for the support of the striking workers." In the longer term, the meeting led to the establishment of a new Union des compositeurs, which aimed at sustaining the political and social engagement generated in the preceding days and weeks. In its founding manifesto (dated 1 June), the union outlined a number of objectives. Two stand out. The first is explicitly political, expressing the composers' wish "to constitute a permanent force of contestation and movement at all levels and in all the domains of musical life." The other announces a more modest, corporatist function for the group, saying that it will "represent composers and . . . defend their moral and professional rights in the face of exploitative organisms."[105] The two objectives reflect the existence of competing priorities among composers. At the same time as they expressed their solidarity with a political movement that contested existing social arrangements, composers seized the opportunity to petition the government regarding a number of long-standing professional concerns, such as aid for new music and the regulation of the music market.

Just as the actions of CRAC and CAR put culture at the center of political struggle, so too did the musicians' strike. Yet this was about all the two modes of artistic engagement shared in common. Unlike the striking musicians, self-proclaimed "cultural agitators" were concerned above all with art's ideological effects. The argument that art divorced utopian aspirations from everyday life, cordoning them off in a specialized sphere of activity, rendered it a vehicle of false consciousness. By contrast, those involved in the musicians' strike focused their attentions on the other end of the commodity chain, on the production of art rather than its reception. To a certain extent, such differences in perspective ran along the fault lines of the old left/new left divide: whereas cultural agitation embodied the new left's rejection of vulgar materialism for a more generous evaluation of the social force exerted by "superstructural" phenomena such as art, the musicians' strike appealed to an older brand of workerist imagery, hearkening back to the labor movement's glory years in the first few decades of the twentieth century.[106]

That professional musicians found the economics of cultural production of greater concern than its ideological functions was hardly surprising given the steadily deteriorating employment prospects they faced. Since the 1930s the music profession in France as elsewhere had been subject to a variety of pressures that had severely reduced job opportunities. Chief among these was the displacement of the living labor of musicians by the dead labor of mechanical reproduction. This process played out in a number of settings, including the shift from silent to sound film; the increasing reliance on sound recordings to fill the programming schedule on radio stations; the use of canned music to accompany singers on televised variety shows; and the replacement of live music in nightclubs, bars, and cafés with jukeboxes and other sources of recorded music.[107]

In all of these instances, the incentive to reduce costs by using recordings rather than hiring musicians was reinforced by the peculiar economy of the performing arts. While all sectors of the labor market are subject to the pressures of technological displacement, they are particularly acute for music and other forms of live performance. This is due to what economists William Baumol and William Bowen have dubbed the "cost disease," which afflicts those sectors of the economy that are impervious to the sort of productivity gains that technological advancements bring to other sectors. As the economy as a whole produces more using less labor, professions that continue to require the same amount of time and effort to produce the same good (like a musical performance) become increasingly inefficient by comparison. Since the wages paid to musicians must rise roughly in step with those of other professions to keep up with the rise in the cost of living, the labor expenditures in the performing arts increase despite there being no change in terms of output: a string quartet requires the same amount of time and the same number of players to be performed today as it did when it was first composed. Hence, over the long run, labor costs consume a growing portion of the budget of an enterprise employing live music.[108] And if these expenses can be cut without discomfiting clients significantly (as when radio stations use recordings in place of live performances), then there is a strong incentive to use canned rather than live music.

Long preoccupied by the profession's bleak economic outlook, artists' unions like the Syndicat français des artistes-interprètes (representing singers) and the Syndicat national des artistes-musiciens, or SNAM (representing instrumentalists), used the strike to press their grievances with the Ministry of Cultural Affairs.[109] Particularly vocal in advocating an overhaul of the music sector was the Parisian branch of SNAM, the Syndicat des artistes-musiciens de Paris (SAMuP). Among the legal and fiscal changes SAMuP pushed for were an across-the-board wage hike, a tax increase on theaters using recorded music, a tax rebate for venues employing musicians, and—most importantly for the union—the institution of a professional license for performers.[110] One thing that stands out about this list is that it reiterated demands that SAMuP had already been making for some years, a fact decried by the union's critics, who saw this as evidence of SAMuP's desire to exploit the political situation to satisfy petty corporatist interests.[111] But the consistency of the union's demands was perhaps more a reflection of the fact that the conditions it sought to ameliorate were rooted in long-term trends. An open letter addressed to President de Gaulle from March 1965 enumerated a number of SAMuP's concerns. The letter began by noting that since 1939 the number of professional musicians in Paris had declined from seven thousand to two thousand, and of this latter figure eight hundred were chronically unemployed.[112] The main culprit for this decline was the use of recorded music to replace live performance, with little in way of royalties accruing to singers and instrumentalists.[113] A second concern was the unfair competition French musicians faced due to the influx of amateur and foreign musicians into the labor pool: "Whereas other countries defend their musicians by every means, and practically forbid the entry of foreign labor, France opens wide its arms even to countries that turn away French orchestras."[114] Like the demands made to the Ministry of Cultural Affairs in June 1968, the letter addressed to de Gaulle advocated that the tax code be adjusted to encourage businesses to feature more live music, and that a professional license be instituted to better regulate the labor market.

It is difficult to say what, if anything, a work stoppage would do to counter these trends. Indeed, at times the musicians' strike appeared to exacerbate the very problems they hoped to redress. This was particularly true with regard to the displacement of live performance by the "dead labor" of recording technology, as the shuttering of concert venues forced audiences to look to records and the radio to satisfy their musical needs during May and June. As was the case with the publishing industry, the record industry actually saw sales rise during the course of the general strike.[115] In addition, radio stations were compelled to increase the proportion of recorded music broadcast over the air, especially once employees at the Office de radiodiffusion-télévision française (ORTF) went on strike. Sometimes this situation led to striking juxtapositions; for instance, just below the article in the Communist daily *L'Humanité* announcing the occupation of the Opéra there is a small notice from the national radio network reassuring readers that there would be "uninterrupted recorded music on all the national airwaves and news updates each hour."[116] The challenges faced by composers in enforcing their strike action were perhaps even more daunting, since they had to deal not only with the obstacles thrown up by mechanical reproduction, but also with competition from canonic works. When the composer Henri Dutilleux refused to allow the Orchestre de Paris (which had returned to work in mid-June) to perform his composition *Métaboles* on a concert scheduled for 28 June 1968, the music director promptly replaced his composition with Debussy's *Prélude à l'après-midi d'un faune.*[117] One can hardly think of a more literal case of living labor being displaced by dead labor.

As straightforward as SAMuP's proposed solutions to the problems of technological displacement and foreign labor may have seemed, matters were complicated by questions of musical style. The call to reconfigure the tax regime to favor live music, to take one example, can be seen as an indirect subsidy that would grant preferential treatment to certain musical genres. Claims about the stagnant productivity of the performing arts must be qualified, since they do not take into account the capacity of technological fixes to help render live performance more productive.[118] It is here that the stylistic biases that underlay SAMuP's demands become more apparent. Amplification, for instance, may expand the audience size for a performance without requiring an appreciable increase in the labor involved. Likewise, the use of recordings in lieu of backing musicians can enable a vocalist, for instance, to avoid the costs of hiring an entire band.[119] What this suggests is that the cost disease affects different genres to varying degrees. For genres in which technical mediation is not just a means to an end but a crucial stylistic component (as with Anglo-American popular music and its Francophone adaptations), the cost disease poses far less of a problem than it does for those genres where tradition and aesthetic ideology make unamplified performance sacrosanct (as is the case with symphonic music, opera, and certain forms of jazz). In this light, SAMuP's attempts to intervene on behalf of live music appear aimed at shoring up musical genres placed at a competitive disadvantage. This implicit bias toward classical music and older styles of popular music was likely a function of SAMuP's membership, which, judging from the articles published in the union's bulletin during the 1960s, worked primarily in the classical and music hall traditions. But it was also institutional, as a branch devoted to rock music would only be established in the wake of May–June 1968. Even then, the "pop" section of SAMuP would possess a fairly weak profile within the union in subsequent years, the union's entreaties to rock musicians notwithstanding.[120] In short, SAMuP's efforts to protect live music were aimed not only at the threat posed by technological obsolescence, but at that posed by stylistic obsolescence as well.

More pronounced antagonisms emerged in response to the union's agitation for a professional identity card. The institution of a licensing system for musicians had long been on SAMuP's agenda, as it was seen as the only effective way to combat the steady encroachment of amateur and foreign performers. In 1965 one union official contended that, though hardly a panacea, a licensing system would nonetheless "bar the way to amateurism and foreign labor."[121] An anonymous article from a year later outlined the problem in a more forceful manner. Unlike other professions where education and credentials provided barriers to entry, music lacked such mechanisms: "Access to the profession of the musical artist no less than its exercise are entirely free. No legal clause, no certification of professional aptitude, no regulation of any kind provides the assurance of stability, of permanence for [the musician]."[122] This state of affairs meant that those for whom music was not the primary source of income could be hired in lieu of a professional at a severely discounted rate: "What is for him [i.e., the professional musician] a salary is a supplement for the amateur, whence the danger of underbidding."[123]

As was the case with the union's hostility toward mechanical reproduction, its call to banish amateur performers from the terrain reserved for professionals proves to be more complicated once the shifting stylistic landscape of French music during the 1950s and '60s is figured into the equation. Certain remarks made by union officials, for instance, suggest that the term *amateur* might have functioned less as an objectively measurable status than as a veiled reference to practitioners of musical genres that did not conform to established conventions of musicianship. Foremost among these were newer forms of Anglo-American popular music and their French cognates. While union officials seldom explicitly denounced rock and roll in the years leading up to 1968, insinuating remarks about "English" bands (or bands bearing English names) make it patently obvious that the fad for Anglo-American popular culture was being targeted by the union: "How to spot the teacher on holiday who is taking the place of a professional in a casino? . . . How to know if we are dealing with English musicians or a group of amateur French musicians bearing a fashionable name?"[124] In taking aim at contemporary youth culture, SAMuP failed to recognize that the traditional standards of musical skill (instrumental virtuosity, quality of tone production, the ability to read notated music) were not necessarily applicable to genres that valorized qualities like immediacy and authenticity.

A similar dynamic was present within the jazz section of SAMuP, for whom competition from foreign (particularly American) musicians was the point of contention. In an account of the founding of the jazz section of the union in October 1965, its principal organizers, Guy Lafitte and Michel Hausser, described how a sizable contingent of the French jazz community rallied behind the undertaking. They attributed the surprising level of solidarity in the jazz community to a growing awareness that the jazz musician in France was at risk of losing a principal freedom, "that of playing his music."[125] According to Lafitte and Hausser, this threat stemmed from the predilection of critics and concert promoters for foreign artists. And what lay behind this fascination with all things foreign? "Fashion, invented from scratch, following the dictates of an industry with precious little 'artistry.'" French jazz performers thus found themselves cast aside, replaced by "foreign 'tomfoolery,'" which the music industry was all too ready "to import by the truckload."[126] Though Lafitte and Hauser did not identify the object of their resentment, one likely candidate was free jazz, especially considering the massive influx of American avant-garde jazz musicians during the 1960s, many of whom came to France because of a lack of employment opportunities in their native country (see chapter 3).

Lafitte's comments indicate that criteria determining professional status were at times difficult to pin down. Standards were defined in terms of contingent musical styles, and as such were subject to the inertia of convention on the one hand and the vagaries of taste on the other. This uncertainty was not lost on radical elements within the musicians' strike, who formed a short-lived action committee to contest the position adopted by the union leadership.[127] This group, which adopted the name Action musique, argued that a professional card would lead to a "closed shop" system, with union bosses acting as its de facto gatekeepers: "The professional card . . . will be, as in the United States, a means of repression. How will it be granted, according to which criteria will skills be determined? Either it is the state that will distribute the card, which is unacceptable, or it's the musicians who do so, which is likewise unacceptable."[128] That the core membership of Action musique consisted of free jazz musicians explains in part their rejection of efforts to fix the boundaries of artistic identity, which is not surprising considering that the music they performed had often been characterized as "unmusical," a fad whose intellectual and political pretensions masked a lack of true artistry.[129] In one tract Action musique thus described the institution of the professional card as nothing more than "a musical POWER GRAB by a MAFIA that arrogates to itself the right to judge one's abilities without any legitimate justification."[130]

It was not just the union's insistence on regulating artistic identity that Action Musique found objectionable. The tactics employed by SAMuP also came under fire, especially its willingness to negotiate with the government even as the fate of the Fifth Republic hung in the balance. Particularly galling was the union's (unsuccessful) attempt to win an audience with André Malraux, the minister of cultural affairs, on 30 May, the same day that a general assembly had been convened to debate the next step in the musicians' strike. To Action Musique, entering into negotiations with government officials without first seeking the consent of the union rank and file was a consummate act of bad faith. It confirmed their suspicions about the undemocratic nature of the union and the opportunistic tendencies of its leadership. One member of the union hierarchy, cellist Manuel Recasens, was singled out for vilification. A member of the strike committee, Recasens had gone to meet with Malraux without consulting his confederates beforehand.[131] More troubling still was that such negotiations risked dismantling prematurely the one weapon that the musicians wielded: the work stoppage. This in turn cast doubt on whether the "strike was something that certain [union] leaders really wanted."[132] Whereas Action musique contended that the strike should take into account "the role of the musician in a capitalist society, where culture is an agent of the dominant class," the union leadership was, for their part, content to play "the game of Power." Instead of articulating links between the musicians' struggle and those of other workers, the SAMuP leadership was guilty of currying favor with the powers that be in the hope that they might benefit from the state's patronage: "Those who solicited audiences with de Gaulle's government, even while the regime was being cast into question, well understood how to recuperate the revolutionary situation to their advantage."[133] By entering into discussions with Malraux and his deputies, union leaders had revealed their willingness to trade broad social change for the short-term amelioration of the professional musician's material situation. In this respect, they were seen by *gauchisant* elements within the musicians' strike as being little better than the Parti communiste or the Confédération générale du travail, both of which had acted less as the motor of the revolution than as its "permanent brake."[134]

THE END OF MAY

An atmosphere of apprehension reigned on the 30th of May. Even as the leadership of the musicians' union met with representatives from the Ministry of Cultural Affairs, doubts abounded as to whether the government would survive. The preceding days had not been reassuring for de Gaulle's supporters. Over the weekend the government, industry leaders, and delegations from the two main union federations, the Confédération générale du travail (CGT) and the Confédération française démocratique du travail (CFDT), had met at the Hôtel du Chatelet on the rue de Grenelle. After two days of intense negotiation, a tentative agreement had been reached that would raise workers' salaries by at least 10 percent, reduce working hours, increase medical and social security benefits, and safeguard the right of unions to organize in the workplace.[135] All that remained was for the rank and file to vote on the proposed accord. On the morning of Monday, 27 May, the head of the CGT, Georges Séguy, went to the Renault factory in Boulogne-Billancourt— the same factory where the students had attempted to make contact with workers ten days earlier—to present the terms of the settlement. Initially attentive, the personnel assembled on the shop floor grew restive during Séguy's speech. By the end, his voice was drowned out by chants of "Workers' unity."[136] The response to the proposed contract was a resounding *non,* soon echoed in other factories across France. The strike would continue.

The spontaneous rejection of the Grenelle accords fired the hopes of the far left, who saw in this gesture a sign that the working class was in the process of constituting a political force independent of union and party bureaucracies. A situationist tract dated 30 May declared "All . . . will depend essentially on the workers' consciousness and capacity for autonomous organization: those who have already rejected the ridiculous agreement that so gratified the union leaders need only discover that they cannot 'win' much more within the framework of the existing economy, but that they can take everything by transforming all the bases of the economy on their own behalf."[137] Meanwhile, political parties on the left scrambled to respond to the unexpected turn of events. The non-Communist left rallied to the Parti socialiste unifié and former prime minister Pierre Mendès-France, regarded as the sole figure who could unify the different factions on the left.[138] François Mitterrand, head of the social-democratic party the Fédération de la gauche démocrate et socialiste (FGDS), also began to position himself for a leadership role in a new center-left regime, which now seemed all but inevitable. On 28 May he called for the formation of a transitional government comprised of Communists, socialists, and other left-wing parties.[139] As for the PCF, the rejection of the Grenelle accords threw the party into confusion. At first unsure how to act, by 29 May it too had begun to make noises about the need to institute a "popular government."[140]

By midweek the political crisis had reached its climax. On the morning of Wednesday, 29 May, de Gaulle failed to appear at the weekly cabinet meeting. Government spokespersons explained that the president had left the capital to go to his family home in Colombey-les-Deux-Églises. It was widely assumed that he had retreated to the countryside to compose a resignation speech, but by midafternoon news reports announced that de Gaulle had never arrived at his country home. That the president had disappeared in the midst of an acute political crisis, creating an apparent power vacuum, further fueled the sense of unease. The diary of a Canadian author living in Paris captured the mood of the moment: "We are quite literally waiting to see if there will be a civil war. De G. has vanished. . . . Rumor that he has been to see his son-in-law with the army in Mulhouse. Checking on what would happen if he quit? If he stayed? Rumor of troop movements and of tanks around Paris? Talk of a *gouvernement de transition.*"[141] Hearsay did little to calm frayed nerves. Reports that some members of the armed forces had gone over to the workers' side—including allegations that red flags were waving over naval ships—were contradicted by stories of troops being positioned around the capital in case the Communists tried to seize power. What would happen next was anybody's guess.

The decisive moment came at 4:30 P.M. on 30 May. Having returned from a meeting with military leaders stationed in Germany, where he tried to assess whether they would support him if he stayed on as president, de Gaulle made a brief but pointed radio address to the nation. As might be expected, he denounced the strike movement, characterizing the occupation of factories, universities, and cultural institutions as antidemocratic tactics meant to intimidate ordinary citizens. But the main target of his speech was neither student protestors nor striking workers but the Communist Party, which he cast as a sinister agent directing the crisis from the wings. De Gaulle suggested that demonstrators were not independent actors but were "organized in advance by a party that is a totalitarian enterprise."[142] This invocation of a Communist conspiracy opened the way for de Gaulle to identify the PCF as an entity that posed an existential threat to the future of the French nation: "Indeed, France is menaced by dictatorship. They wish to compel the country to surrender itself to a power imposed in a moment of national despair, a power that would in essence be that of . . . totalitarian Communism."[143] To ensure that the voice of every citizen might be heard, without fear of compulsion or intimidation, de Gaulle announced that he would dissolve the present government and call for new elections for the end of June. But if elections did not suffice in dispelling the totalitarian threat, de Gaulle let it be known that he would not hesitate to use every power available to him to "preserve the Republic." Presumably this would include the use of armed force, though de Gaulle did not come out and say so explicitly. Rather, he left it to his listeners to infer the veiled threat. But his allusions to the use of "other means than the ballot"[144] to safeguard the Republic were clear enough for most. "It is a declaration of war," one student observed, "of civil war."[145]

The impact of de Gaulle's speech might have been blunted were it not for the massive display of public support that immediately followed. Even before he had finished speaking, tens of thousands of supporters had gathered in the Jardin des Tuileries for a demonstration that sought to counter those staged by the left in recent weeks. By the time the march began, at around 7 P.M., the crowd numbered somewhere between 300,000 and 500,000. While not quite the million who marched through Paris on 13 May, the size of the demonstration attested to the substantial public support the government still enjoyed. But just as important as the sheer number of participants were their actions, which strove to undo the symbolic injuries the nation had suffered at the hands of the students and striking workers. As historian Frank Georgi has observed, the demonstration took on the appearance of a "rite of purification," by means of which events such as the march of the students down the Champs-Elysées on 7 May might be cleansed.[146] By brandishing the symbols of *la patrie,* the demonstrators sought to undo the damage done by their counterparts: a mass of *tricolores* would erase the image of red and black flags on the Champs-Elysées, just as the strains of "La Marseillaise" would drown out those of "The Internationale." The crowning moment of the procession came with the arrival of its head at the Tomb of the Unknown Soldier. An impromptu ceremony unfolded as the commemorative flame was rekindled, a moment of silence was observed, and the assembled dignitaries (which included André Malraux and Michel Debré) sang the national anthem.[147]

The intonation of "La Marseillaise" during the pro-Gaullist demonstration of 30 May reinforced perceptions of the song's increasingly partisan character. As a reporter for the weekly news magazine *L'Express* noted, the march capped a month during which the anthem had effectively "ceased to symbolize the unity of the French people."[148] At the same time, by claiming this emblem of patriotic sentiment as the exclusive property of the right, de Gaulle and his supporters cast themselves as the only true representatives of the nation. A dubious but nonetheless highly effective logic was established: if supporting de Gaulle's government was synonymous with being a patriot, then being a patriot was, according to this logic, synonymous with supporting de Gaulle's government.

In the context of the electoral campaign that had just begun, this symbolic conflation of patriotism and partisanship had the effect of placing the Gaullists' principal electoral opponents, the Parti communiste, on the defensive. The Communists had to work furiously not only to dissociate themselves from the perceived excesses of the previous month, but also to refigure the party as no less patriotic than its adversary on the right. To do so the PCF turned to none other than "La Marseillaise" as a way of burnishing its patriotic credentials. Although the demonstrations organized by the Communists in May had generally incorporated Republican symbols such as the *tricolore* and "La Marseillaise" to some extent, following de Gaulle's speech and the demonstration of 30 May, expressions of national pride increased substantially.

The Communists' lurch to the center was underlined on 10 June at a pre-election rally in Paris. The party's patriotic credentials were put on full display and reaffirmed in speeches given by party leaders. Louis Aragon, for one, contended that "the *tricolore* is [the flag] of the nation and not that of a single faction" and denounced those who wished to deform the meaning of "La Marseillaise" "to make it say the opposite of what it says."[149] Along similar lines the secretary-general of the Parti communiste, Waldeck Rochet, averred that "'The Marseillaise' isn't a Gaullist hymn, it is the national song of the French people, it is a song of struggle against oppression and for liberty."[150] Cutting a path between the Gaullists (whose repressive tactics, he argued, had stoked the previous month's unrest) and far-left *groupuscules* (whose "adventurism" had threatened to lead the movement down a blind alley of senseless violence), Rochet set up the PCF as the only responsible body in French politics. This rather tricky balancing act found its echo in his call to fuse the symbols of the Republican heritage and the workers' movement: "And so we unite indissolubly the accents of 'La Marseillaise' and those of 'The Internationale,' the French flag and the red flag of worker's struggle."[151]

As it turned out, the Communists' bid at repositioning themselves in advance of the legislative elections was undertaken in vain. When the votes for the second round were counted on 23 June, the PCF found itself with thirty-nine fewer seats in the Assemblée générale while the Gaullists had gained ninety-seven.[152] Just as the students' attempt to use "The Internationale" to identify with the working class had run up against ingrained preconceptions regarding their "real" or "proper" identity, the Communists' efforts to wrest "La Marseillaise" from the grip of the right did little to persuade others that they were the true "guardians of the national interest."[153] Indeed, the party's maneuvering backfired on all sides. Not only did the mingling of "La Marseillaise" and "The Internationale" fail to convince voters to the party's right that it was committed to upholding Republican institutions, but it also confirmed suspicions within the far left of the party's willingness to sacrifice its own ideals for the sake of political expediency. A column in the 17 June edition of the newspaper *L'Enragé* singled out the embrace of "La Marseillaise" and the *tricolore* as proof of this ideological backsliding, juxtaposing excerpts of speeches given at the 10 June rally with a poem written by Louis Aragon some thirty years beforehand:

> Je salue l'Internationale contre la Marseillaise.
> Cède le pas, ô Marseillaise,
> A l'Internationale, car voici
> L'automne de tes jours, voici
> L'octobre où sombrent tes derniers accents.

> *I salute "The Internationale" as opposed to "La Marseillaise."*
> *Give way, oh "Marseillaise"*
> *to the "Internationale," for here is*
> *the autumn of your days, here is*
> *the October when your last accents will fall.*[154]

By turning Aragon's own words against him, student radicals hoped to show how far the party had drifted from what should have been one of its primary missions, the dismantling of the bourgeois state. Instead, the PCF seemed to be falling over itself to embrace the sonic and visual tokens of this state, "La Marseillaise" and the French flag.

In the world of professional music, the conflict of competing identities took a somewhat different form, as music became not just a tool or weapon in a political contest but the object of the contest itself. Even so, the divisions that emerged in the ranks of musicians paralleled those that separated *gauchiste* militants from the Communists and their trade union allies. From the perspective of Action musique, CRAC, CAR, and other radical cultural groups, SAMuP and other artists' unions were guilty of the same kind of self-interested politicking as were the PCF and CGT. The parallels drawn between the musicians' union and the institutional left were reinforced by the concrete links binding the two together: as one member of SAMuP noted during the union's general assembly of 18 June, the reluctance of a sizable segment of the musical community to join the organization was mainly due to its affiliation with the CGT.[155] SAMuP, for its part, echoed the PCF and CGT in its dismissal of the more radical elements of the strike movement, casting them as naive idealists at best and dangerous provocateurs at worst. In an anonymous editorial in the union's newsletter, SAMuP's leadership argued that the strike presented a stark choice between false idealism and sober realism: "Do [musicians] wish to change everything, transform everything, bulldoze everything, with everybody hoping nevertheless to attach their name to the reform they advocate, have conceived of, and seek to realize? Or do they simply want a UNION, as men sensible to progress have always wanted?"[156] In case there was any doubt about where SAMuP fell on the matter, the author adds that while youth may be clamoring for "the transformation of society," it was imperative to have "men shorn of this sort of ambition" running things.[157] The leadership of SAMuP, it would appear, was more than happy to embrace their association with the institutional left.

The key site where such divisions played out was the struggle over the social definition of the artist. As we have seen, from SAMuP's perspective the main goal of the strike movement was to improve the material condition of working musicians, and to realize this goal the union sought to restrict who was to be recognized as a musician. For cultural agitators, it was precisely this corporatist mindset, which strove to safeguard professional advantages at the expense of cultural democracy, that had to be defeated. Rather than being closed, the doors to the artistic field needed to be thrown open. But even within the cultural left, antagonisms emerged that hindered efforts to form a single, unified front. Despite their denunciation of the union's attempts to legislate the social definition of the musician, Action musique did not go so far as to advocate a radical democratization of cultural production, as groups like CRAC did. In this regard it seems likely that Action musique was motivated, at least in part, by the desire to safeguard their own professional interests as purveyors of "unpopular" genres: namely, their right to push up against received stylistic norms without being barred from employment opportunities.

In contrast, CRAC's goal was more radical, involving the abolition of any distinction between cultural producers and consumers. Art would not only cease to be a commodity but would be enlisted in the struggle to overcome the specialization characteristic of advanced industrial societies. It comes as no surprise, then, that CRAC responded negatively to the decision of certain segments of the performing arts community to resume work in mid-June, having won what they felt were satisfactory concessions from the Ministry of Cultural Affairs. In a leaflet dated 8 June, CRAC urged students and "revolutionary artists" to "PREVENT the reopening of the theaters" to demonstrate their continuing solidarity with the strike movement.[158] At the Opéra, a handful of provocateurs took heed of CRAC's calls to impede the return to work. During the performance of Bizet's *Carmen*, which marked the reopening of the theater on 15 June, a group of militants threw stink bombs in the orchestra pit between the third and fourth acts. But they proved unable to bring the performance to a halt, as the musicians, "having stoically endured" the odors (according to *Le Figaro*), managed to see the work to its end.[159]

Acts of petty sabotage such as these give some sense of the frustration extremist groups like CRAC felt once the hopes stoked by the general strike were dashed by the return to work. Such frustration was only to be expected, given the all-or-nothing goals for social change that prevailed among *gauchistes*. When revolution is understood as involving a total transformation of society, anything falling short of this impossible standard is bound to disappoint. What the extreme left failed to recognize, however, was that even incremental gains do make a difference in the everyday lives of workers. For many musicians the strike action yielded marked improvements in their working conditions. At the Opéra, for instance, the Ministry of Cultural Affairs met many of the demands made by musicians and technicians. These included an across-the-board wage hike (16 percent on average), the restoration of the number of singers under contract to ninety after recent layoffs, and the creation of a consultative committee, comprising soloists, chorus members, pit musicians, choral directors, and dancers, to provide input on artistic and programming decisions.[160] At the Conservatoire, reforms were enacted to abolish a number of competitions (including the Prix de Rome), modernize the curriculum, add courses in electroacoustic music, and allow students some representation on various committees and juries.[161] SAMuP, for its part, proved less successful in winning concessions from its counterparts in the government. The professional license went unrealized, as did the changes to the tax code that the union had pressed for.[162]

Other, more far-reaching repercussions of May '68 on the musical field became visible in the months and years that followed. While it is important not to overstate the impact of *les événements*—not every transformation in French culture and society in ensuing decades can be laid at the feet of 1968—there is no denying that the protests and general strike served to enlarge "the field of the possible," to paraphrase Jean-Paul Sartre. Music was not exempt from such upheaval. Many of the changes in public life subsequently ascribed to the events of May (the liberalization of social norms, the democratization of creative expression, the *"prise de parole"* by various subaltern communities, and the reinvigoration of left-wing militancy during the late 1960s and early 1970s) had corollaries in the musical field (the transgression of generic norms, the promotion of amateur music making, the efflorescence of regional folk traditions, and a renewed interest in avant-garde and experimental musics). Of note is the sheer variety of musical actors, organizations, and communities affected by the events of May '68 and the variety of ways in which they were affected. This heterogeneity makes totalizing questions regarding the "success" or "failure" of the revolt beside the point. The impact that the events had on culture in general, and music in particular, cannot be gauged in terms of binary alternatives. Rather, this impact varied from one musical genre to another, and from one musical community to another. The more pressing task, then, is to trace the manifold paths that led out of May '68, as they passed through different genre cultures over the next decade and beyond. But in order to pursue the lingering impact of May '68 on musical life in France during the "long 1970s," it is necessary first to consider some of the ways in which genre, politics, and identity interact with one another. It is this set of questions that the next chapter addresses.

CHAPTER 2

Genre and Musical Representations of May

DOMINIQUE GRANGE AND THE *CHANSON RÉVOLUTIONNAIRE*

By the end of 1968 the mood in France was a far cry from the mix of euphoria and apprehension that had reigned that spring. After the legislative elections of June the rhythms of everyday life, suspended since the beginning of May, picked up where they had left off. For many, the return to the routine of work, vacation, and *la rentrée* was a relief. This was the case for pop idol France Gall, winner of the 1965 Eurovision song contest. "Goodness me," she exclaimed in an interview from late June 1968, "I was so scared! . . . But today, I'm completely reassured. Everything has gone back to normal."[1] For those who had placed their hopes on the success of the May movement, however, the return to normalcy was disheartening. Writing in September, Michel de Certeau captured this feeling of despondency, describing how "the rains of August seem to have changed the fires of May into ashes left behind for the street cleaners." But it was not just the passage of time that caused the memory of May to fade: "In an empty Paris, the streets and then the walls have been scrubbed. This cleanup operation also assails our memory."[2] Material conditions further contributed to the somber mood. By late autumn the economic outlook had grown bleak. Inflation nullified the salary gains workers had won a few months before and weakened the franc to such an extent that most observers assumed that the government would be forced to devalue the currency.[3] Meanwhile, an increased police presence in Paris and elsewhere fostered a stifling, oppressive atmosphere.[4] In this context, it was easy to understand Certeau's impression that May's impact had been negligible: "The *after* picks up where the *before* left off, we are back there once again."[5]

Still, disenchantment was but one element of the complex mood of *l'après-mai*. Concomitant with the belief that May's promise had gone unfulfilled was the sense that the uprising and general strike marked the first stage of a period of revolutionary crisis, which would give birth to a more decisive explosion of social unrest in the near future. The anticipation of a reprise of the May uprising was particularly acute among militants. The titles of books written by aspiring revolutionaries in the wake of May give some indication of their confidence in the imminence of revolution: *Vers la guerre civile* (Towards the civil war), *Une répétition générale* (A dress rehearsal), *Ce n'est qu'un début* (This is only a beginning). The hope that Marx's "old mole" would soon resurface and redeem the failure of May energized *gauchiste* groups. Late 1968 saw interest in Trotskyist, Maoist, and other revolutionary *groupuscules* increase markedly, particularly within the student milieu. Organizations like the Trotskyist Jeunesse communiste révolutionnaire and the Maoist Gauche prolétarienne swelled with students whose imagination had been fired by the experience of nearly toppling de Gaulle's government. If radicals found the return to daily life after the collapse of May dispiriting, for many this disappointment was channeled into an even greater commitment to the revolutionary cause.

Among those drawn into the newly revitalized world of left-wing agitation was the singer Dominique Grange. Born in Lyon in 1940, Grange had moved to Paris in the early 1960s to pursue a career in music. Grange met with modest success performing in Left Bank cabarets, and by 1963 she had released on the Bel Air label her first 45-rpm record, "Je ne suis plus ton copain." Her career took off in 1965 when she joined singer Guy Béart's televised variety show "Bienvenue à . . . ."[6] Her stint on the program brought greater public exposure, especially once she began singing duets with Béart. By April 1968 Grange had signed a seven-year recording contract with Béart's record label, Temporel, a sign that she was on her way to a successful career as a singer-songwriter.[7]

May '68 radically altered the direction of Grange's life and career. She plunged into *les événements,* participating in both CRAC (see chapter 1) and the strike committee at the Bobino music hall. Dissatisfied with the impact of the musicians' work stoppage, which she felt accomplished nothing apart from discomfiting bourgeois audiences, Grange joined the growing number of artists performing in occupied factories. Moved by the feeling of being "actively involved in the struggle that the workers were leading," she had little interest in returning to the well-worn routines of the music industry once the May events ended. In a later interview, she recalled that "the idea of a 'return to normal' was unbearable for us, and there were lots of people who felt that way, above all the workers who had gone back to work without having won anything."[8] Rather than returning to the stage or recording studio, Grange traveled to the countryside, where she and her fellow militants disseminated information about the May movement. Their main objective was to dispel misconceptions fostered by the state-controlled media, countering its one-sided reporting with first-hand accounts of what had transpired in May. To spread the word, Grange and her companions relied on a variety of media. They showed *ciné-tracts,* short films that directors like Jean-Luc Godard had made of demonstrations and factory occupations. And, not surprisingly, Grange used song to narrate *les événements.*[9]

Returning to Paris in fall 1968, Grange recorded a 45-rpm EP containing four of the songs she had written in response to the events of May: "A bas l'état policier" (Down with the police state), "La pègre" (The criminal element), "Chacun de vous est concerné" (You are all concerned), and "Grève illimitée" (All-out strike). Sold by militants in factories and universities, the record won Grange renown in *gauchiste* circles.[10] For the most part the music was simple and stripped down. Accompanying Grange's singing were strummed chords on the acoustic guitar, occasionally supplemented by a second guitar, overdubbed vocals, or backing singers (as in the chorus of "A bas l'état policier"). As for the lyrics, their most notable feature was the appropriation of slogans popularized during the May events, a verbal counterpart to the record's sleeve, which reproduced a poster created by the Atelier populaire (figure 4). The chorus to "La pègre," for instance, intones the phrase "Nous sommes tous les juifs allemands" (We are all German Jews), a slogan that protesters had chanted as a sign of their solidarity with Daniel Cohn-Bendit, who, because of his German parentage, had been dismissed as "un juif allemand" by the Communist-backed newspaper *L'Humanité.* This embrace of the opprobrium that establishment figures hurled at left-wing militants is central to the song's rhetorical strategy. Epithets like *la pègre* (the criminal element) and *la chienlit* (mess or disorder) are valorized as a source of shared identity.

FIGURE 4. Cover art for Dominique Grange, *Chansons de mai–juin 1968*.

La pègre on en est
La chienlit aussi
Des éléments parfaitement incontrôlés,
Des indésirables
Des autres enragés
Et quelques milliers de groupuscules isolés.

Criminals, that's us
Disorder as well
Completely uncontrollable elements
Undesirables
Still others enragés
And a few thousand isolated groupuscules

References to the slogans of May also helped sustain the movement's ideals within the collective memory. Indeed, the employment of slogans such as "down with the police state" in the choruses of songs had the effect of reactivating their meaning: to sing along with the chorus of "A bas l'état policier" was to enunciate—and revivify—the ideal that the slogan espoused.

Grange's political turn was affirmed in late 1968, when she happened upon a meeting in the Sorbonne on the subject of the Chinese Cultural

Revolution. Intrigued, Grange acquired copies of Mao's writings along with issues of *Pékin Information*, the French-language outlet of the Chinese news agency. One article in *Pékin Information* particularly struck her. It was the testimonial of a young Chinese actress who had forsaken her career to "serve the revolution." Grange later remarked that the actress was a role model for her: "She understood that so long as the revolution had not been completed, she could change nothing in the artistic domain, and that to continue [as before] could only serve the dominant ideology."[11] Inspired, Grange broke her recording contract and abandoned the commercial music circuit. She disregarded the entreaties of friends who contended that it was possible to satisfy the demands of both art and politics by singing songs with engaged lyrics. For Grange, this sort of compromise was unacceptable. The only honest path was to renounce her former life: "For a revolutionary artist, for an artist who has become a Maoist, and who is capable of putting [this belief] into practice, serving the people wholeheartedly means abandoning any idea of personal renown or material gain. It means going to fight in the ranks of the people: to share in the work at the factory, to find a collective outlet for revolt, to help in organizing, to live the same simple life."[12] Although such an understanding of political commitment seemed to preclude artistic activity altogether, for Grange this self-renunciation was what enabled an authentically popular music to blossom. Music, temporarily sacrificed, finds itself reborn: "When one fights, then, when one has made the cause of the people your own, the desire to sing comes back to you once again, but now they are songs of combat that rise up from the factories, the housing projects, the slums, the street, from the sweat and the blood of those who suffer."[13]

Grange joined the ranks of the Gauche prolétarienne (GP), one of the principal Maoist groups to emerge following the break-up of the Union des jeunesses communistes (marxistes-léninistes) after May.[14] A distinctive trait of the GP was the premium it placed on direct action. The GP held that militants could best learn how to conduct class struggle not by studying Leninist doctrine but by living among workers. This practice, known as *établissement,* led a number of students and middle-class youth to put down their books and go to work in the factories. By trading in one's middle-class identity for that of a worker, the militant was to gain practical knowledge of the struggles that took place in factories, working-class districts, and immigrant ghettos.[15] At the same time, the GP called for an intensification of the struggle against the capitalist state. The aim was twofold. On one hand, by provoking the authorities into cracking down on dissent, the GP aimed at revealing the repressive face of "capitalist despotism."[16] On the other hand, it hoped that exemplary acts of resistance might encourage a critical mass of workers to reject the electoral path of the Communist Party and instead embrace the idea of revolution. Historian Jean-Pierre Le Goff summarizes the GP's strategy: "The struggle against petty [union] chiefs in the factories, the sabotage of production, confrontation with the police, with the CGT and the PCF . . . all of these 'violent actions of a symbolic character' are supposed to 'make the ideology of revolt triumph over the ideology of submission.' . . . It is in the course of this kind of increasingly violent struggle that workers are supposed to become conscious of the fact that 'power is at the end of a gun' and to act accordingly."[17] The GP framed such attacks on the social order by likening their struggle to that of the much-mythologized French resistance to the Nazi occupation. "It's true," an article in the GP organ *La Cause du peuple* asserted, "this new resistance rekindles the armed resistance of the people against the invaders and their collaborators from 1940 to 1945."[18] The bourgeoisie, characterized as a parasite feeding off the labor of others, was identified as an alien occupying force. Unions and established left-wing parties played the part of "collaborators" *(collabos),* while the militants of the GP became the "partisans" of the "new popular resistance."[19]

In mid-1969 Grange left Paris for Nice, where she took a job in a paper factory on the city's outskirts.[20] Working during the day and organizing political meetings in the evening, Grange had little time for music. When, after a number of months, she finally did pick up her guitar again, the result was a song that crystallized many of the precepts of the Gauche prolétarienne. Released as a 45-rpm single in spring 1970, "Les Nouveaux partisans" thematized the idea of a "new popular resistance" to bourgeois exploitation. This was underlined by the title of the song, which alluded to Joseph Kessel and Anna Marly's "Le chant des partisans," a paean to the French resistance during the Second World War. The cover art of Grange's single gives some sense of how much her political beliefs had hardened since the release of her previous disc. In place of the arty primitivism of the poster that adorned the cover of her earlier EP, the sleeve of "Les Nouveaux partisans" is in a socialist realist style (figure 5). In the foreground, in front of a group of protesters, a clenched fist raises a wrench in the air, a blunt appeal to the iconography of working-class resistance. Of course, the poster that Grange had

FIGURE 5. Cover art for Dominique Grange, *Nous sommes les nouveaux partisans.*

used for her previous record also drew upon working-class iconography, but it had abstracted these symbols—the raised fist and the factory chimney—and juxtaposed them in a provocative manner. The cover for "Les Nouveaux partisans," by contrast, dispenses with any hint of playfulness. The image is deadly earnest, closer to the propaganda posters of the Chinese Cultural Revolution than the photomontages of the historical avant-garde.

The music is no less earnest. Each verse enumerates the abuses suffered by the working class and dares both the bosses *(les patrons)* and their trade-union flunkies *(les larbins)* in the unions to bear witness to the evils they have wrought. The second verse is typical of the song's rhetoric:

> Regardez l'exploité quand il rentre le soir
> Et regardez les femmes qui triment toute leur vie
> Vous qui bavez sur nous, qui dites qu'on s'embourgeoise
> Descendez dans la mine à 600 mètres de fonds
> C'est pas sur vos tapis qu'on meurt de silicose
> Vous comptez vos profits, on compte nos mutilés

Regardez nous vieillir au rythme des cadences
Patrons regardez nous, c'est la guerre qui commence!

Behold the exploited worker when he comes home at night
And behold the women who slave away all their lives
You, who mock us, who say that we've bourgeoisified
You should go down the mine that's 600 meters deep
It isn't on your carpet that we die of black lung
You count your profits, we count our maimed
Behold us aging to the rhythm of the assembly line
Look at us, bosses, the war is beginning!

Having ratcheted up the level of indignation in each verse, the chorus acts as a release valve that lets out some of the pent-up anger, an occasion to reaffirm one's commitment to the fight against capitalist exploitation:

Nous sommes les nouveaux partisans
Francs-tireurs de la guerre de classe
Le camp du peuple est notre camp
Nous sommes les nouveaux partisans

We are the new partisans
Guerrillas of the class war
The people's camp is our camp
We are the new partisans

Reinforcing the distinct rhetorical functions of verse and chorus are differences in musical setting. The vocal delivery in the verses is rapid, clipped, conveying a sense of urgency. This is due in part to the shorter note values that predominate (example 1). Moreover, virtually all of the rhythmic activity is compressed into the first three beats of each measure. Although each line of text requires two measures to complete, producing a kind of grammatical momentum leading from one measure to the next, this forward motion is undercut by the lack of rhythmic activity on beat four of each measure. These rests break up the song's flow, the text transmitted in a series of short bursts. As for the melodic line, it occupies a narrow ambitus. The first half of each verse moves within the space of a perfect fourth, between scale degrees 3 and 6 of A major ($C_{\sharp}4$ and $F_{\sharp}4$), with a few momentary dips down to the tonic, $A3$. In addition, the vocal part remains anchored on a single repeated pitch, $C_{\sharp}4$, during the first two lines of the first verse (mm. 5–8), shifting up to $D4$ in measures 9–10. As a result of this severe restriction in the range of melodic motion, the vocal part sounds less songlike and more declamatory. Grange does not sing so much as chant the lyrics. It is only in the fourth line that the melody breaks out of this narrow ambitus, leaping up to F$_\sharp$4, a gesture that tips the balance from speech toward song.

In the second half of the verses the progression from a declamatory to a more conventionally melodic style continues. While the first two measures return to the opening material, with its insistent repetition of C$_\sharp$4, by the end of the next line (m. 16) the melody has already attained the F$_\sharp$4 that occurred at the end of the first half of the verse. Over the

EXAMPLE 1. "Les Nouveaux partisans," first half of the verse. Used by permission of Dominique Grange.

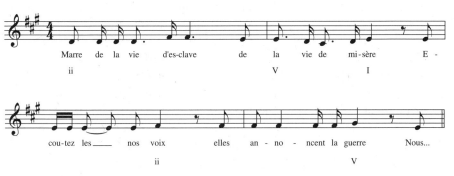

EXAMPLE 2. "Les Nouveaux partisans," second half of the verse. Used by permission of Dominique Grange.

EXAMPLE 3. "Les Nouveaux partisans," chorus. Used by permission of Dominique Grange.

next four measures the music climbs to the leading tone, $G_\sharp 4$ (example 2). The rising melodic line, along with the sense of tonal anticipation generated by the move to the dominant, reinforce the mounting frustrations described over the course of the verse—frustrations conveyed, in particular, by the repetition of the word *marre* (enough) during the second half of the verse. The accumulated textual and musical energy thus makes the arrival on the tonic A4 at the beginning of the chorus sound satisfying, even triumphant.

With the onset of the chorus, the transition from declamation to song is complete (example 3). The music no longer obsessively circles one or two pitches but now features "heroic" leaps and a more expansive rhythm. In place of the clipped phrases of the verse stands a greater sense of rhythmic flow: continuous melodic motion, uninterrupted by rests, conjoins each pair of measures to form a single phrase. But perhaps the most important change that takes place in the chorus is the addition of backing vocals, singing in unison with Grange. Dominated by male voices, the chorus acts as a not-very-subtle signifier of the masses; it is as if the (stereotypically masculine) working class raised its voice in song to express support for the revolutionary cause. The symbolic dimension of the backing singers—their role as a gendered signifier of *le peuple*—is reinforced by the use of reverb. Technology swells the ranks of the "new partisans."

The musical and rhetorical codes employed in "Les Nouveaux partisans" may have been straightforward, but they were effective. The song became the de facto anthem of the Gauche prolétarienne, its chorus "intoned at any opportunity, even the most trivial," by the group's members.[21] Outlets in the *gauchiste* press like *L'idiot international* and *La Cause du peuple* published the words of "Les Nouveaux partisans," no doubt to encourage its performance at meetings, rallies, and demonstrations.[22] A text published alongside the lyrics in *La Cause du peuple* situated it within a long transnational tradition:

> There is only one true song: it isn't that which one hears on the radio or on the television, but that which Gavroche sung before falling before the bullets fired by the policemen of capitalism, which murmured in the depths of the black ghetto in Harlem before bursting forth, which the Bolsheviks intoned in going forth to confront triumphantly the White Russian troops: the song of the people's soldiers.[23]

A little later, the author of the notice names the tradition to which "Les Nouveaux partisans" belongs: that of the *chanson révolutionnaire*. This designation is intriguing. Contemporaneous accounts of the *chanson révolutionnaire* held that it had experienced its golden age in the late nineteenth and early twentieth centuries. According to this narrative, the genre had reached a high point around the time of the Paris Commune (1871), a period that saw the composition of canonical songs like "Le temps des cerises," "La semaine sanglante" and, of course, "The Internationale." The genre went into decline with the onset of the First World War, when a wave of nationalist fervor swept away political dissent. For many authors, the trajectory of the *chanson révolutionnaire* was encapsulated in the career of the singer Montéhus (1872–1952).[24] Having composed such classic workers' songs as "La Butte rouge" and "Gloire au 17e" during the prewar period, with the declaration of war he embraced the Union sacrée. In his song "Lettre d'un socialo" (1914), he called on workers to put aside their grievances and support the war effort, proudly proclaiming that "We will sing 'The Marseillaise';/for during these terrible days/we will discard 'The Internationale.'"[25] While the revolutionary chanson would live on in performance, its repertoire replenished by the songs of the Spanish Civil War and other international struggles, by the post-war period most historians of the chanson regarded the genre as a thing of the past. Guy Erismann's remarks were characteristic: "One might justifiably think that the *chanson sociale*—or more precisely, the *chanson politique*—died with Montéhus. The French workers' movement would no longer give rise to revolutionary songs."[26]

In this context, the identification of "Les Nouveaux partisans" as a revolutionary chanson suggested that it might rejuvenate what was considered a defunct genre. Throughout the brief notice, the anonymous author characterizes the revolutionary chanson as collective, unmediated, and authentic, a form of musical expression diametrically opposed to the popular music peddled by the modern culture industry.[27] Attempts to "appropriate the bounty of the oppressed" were bound to fail, however, inasmuch as the social conditions that once gave rise to the revolutionary chanson remained intact. Within the GP's miserabilist interpretation of society—according to which the working class was trapped in a downward spiral of degradation and impoverishment—circumstances were now more than ever ripe for a rebirth of the *chanson révolutionnaire*: "Tomorrow hundreds of revolutionary songs will flower, written by calloused hands . . . in factories, in slums, in demonstrations. Tomorrow, in couplets made by the people and for the people, we will encounter sweat, the smothering presence of tear gas, the scent of spilled blood."[28] Here the eschatological imagination of *l'après-mai* merges with the language of folk authenticity: the coming revolution will not only liberate *le peuple* from the chains of oppression, but it will bring about the revival of a communal form of musical expression, where every man and woman is at once poet and worker, singer and revolutionary cadre.

GENRE, IDENTITY, AND POLITICS

The notice accompanying the text of "Les Nouveaux partisans" in *La Cause du peuple* indicates the central role that genre plays in mediating the political functions of music. By locating Grange's song within an established tradition, the author of the notice conveys a good deal of information to the reader in condensed form. This stands to reason: genre, as many authors have observed, serves as one of the major organizing principles of musical life, and generic classifications frame our expectations by situating musical works within a context of shared conventions, values, and practices.[29] In the case of "Les Nouveaux partisans," its identification as an exemplar of the *chanson révolutionnaire* conjures a host of assumptions regarding both its musical and extramusical attributes. These include its "proper" mode of transmission (oral), performance practices (amateur, collective), musical characteristics (tonal, metrically regular, easily singable), and subject matter (struggle, social antagonism). These attributes in turn define the range of potential political functions that the song affords. Amateur, collective performance, for instance, might prove useful in forging a sense of solidarity and common purpose, while the song's "engaged" text might rouse spirits and, it is hoped, translate into a desire to take action.

But the notice points to another, more significant way in which genre mediates the political uses of music. Its treatment of the *chanson révolutionnaire* as "the literature of the people," as the "bounty of the oppressed," underlines the way in which this and other genres identify— and are identified with—specific social formations. This identification can assume a number of different guises, as the notice attests. The description of the *chanson révolutionnaire* as the "bounty of the oppressed" characterizes the relationship between genre and social identity in proprietary terms, as the inalienable fruit of the masses' collective labor, while its description as "the literature of the people" highlights the genre's representational function. Here the link forged between genre and identity takes on a distinctly political flavor: the *chanson révolutionnaire* is envisaged as the medium by which the experience and aspirations of "the people" may be given voice.[30] But whether the relationship between genre and identity was conceived in proprietary, representational, or some other terms, what matters above all was the assertion of this relationship—that is, the assertion that this particular genre and particular identity were in some way inextricably intertwined. It was the correlation of the *chanson révolutionnaire* with the working class that enabled the genre to acquire, by a kind of contagious magic where like begets like, some measure of the political value ascribed to the group. This in turn indicates that the significance attached to the *chanson révolutionnaire* derived in large part from the significance attached to the working class within the political imagination of the Gauche prolétarienne. The genre, in other words, secured its claim to the honorific title "revolutionary" not simply because it was regarded as the expression of the masses. Rather, it was "revolutionary" to the extent that *le peuple* was construed as a revolutionary force within the GP's peculiar brand of Maoism, the agent whose millennial struggle against exploitation would usher in a socialist utopia. A transference of properties takes place such that the value assigned to a collectivity *(le peuple)* within a particular political ideology (Maoism) redounded upon the genre associated with this collectivity (the *chanson révolutionnaire*). That this particular brand of popular song received much of its political significance from its association with a privileged social group can be seen in the notice's declaration that "the *chanson révolutionnaire* is necessary, even if it is only a 'small cog and a small wheel in the general mechanism of revolution.'"[31] Chanson is acknowledged as possessing only limited political utility in itself, being but a "small wheel" in the revolutionary movement. But the fact that it is tied to the (putative) agent of social change lends it a value it would otherwise lack.

While revealing how ideology invests certain genres with political significance, the notice in *La Cause du peuple* at the same time illustrates the distortions and biases that such investments invariably entail. The identification of genre and social group is not an idle, impartial observation of some existing reality but a way of intervening in this reality. On one hand, such identifications fashion a highly selective image of the group that is aligned with a genre, emphasizing certain members and certain traits of a collectivity at the expense of others. On the other hand, it produces an equally selective image of the genre in question, emphasizing certain constituents of the genre community, certain musical attributes, and certain practices and institutions. Hence the argument that a genre like the *chanson révolutionnaire* represented the attitudes and aspirations of *le peuple* necessarily elided the manifold differences that existed both among the songs belonging to this genre and among the members of this expansive collectivity.

This last point was underlined by critic Louis-Jean Calvet in an article on the *chanson révolutionnaire* published in *Politique hebdo* a few years after the release of Grange's single. Calvet's article provides an interesting counterpart to the notice in *La Cause du peuple*. Singling out "Les Nouveaux partisans" for criticism, Calvet enumerated what he saw as the many failings afflicting recent attempts to revive the *chanson révolutionnaire*. In particular he underlined the reductive image of the proletariat that songs like Grange's traded in: "Working-class language as it is imagined by intellectuals is a curious thing. One finds a mélange of outdated slang, earthy language, and pitiful metaphors."[32] In Calvet's estimation, what songwriters like Grange had failed to recognize was "what the masses really expect, the language that they speak, the songs that they listen to."[33] Of course Calvet was in no better position than Grange or the author of the notice in *La Cause du peuple* to claim a special insight into what "the masses really expect." Nor was the connection that Calvet drew between genre and identity somehow immune to the pitfall of reductionism. In asserting that the contemporary *chanson révolutionnaire* was not so much the expression of the masses as the expression of intellectuals, Calvet evoked no less of an idealized construct than did the author of the notice in *La Cause du peuple*. Here, too, the identification of genre *(chanson révolutionnaire)* and social group (intellectuals) was not an innocent, impartial gesture. While perhaps not as evident as with the notice in *La Cause du peuple,* ideology and self-interest informed Calvet's conception of the *chanson révolutionnaire*'s true social identity.

Grange's song and the varied reactions that it prompted provide some sense of the complex interactions that bind together genre, identity, and politics. These interactions, sketched only roughly here, are developed further in the chapters that follow, in the course of charting how the free jazz, rock, and contemporary music scenes of the late 1960s and 1970s responded to the legacy of May '68. Of particular importance is understanding how the identification of genre and social formation shape the political uses of music. That each of these genres was linked with certain social identities in the collective imagination was key to the ideological investments (and disinvestments) that they elicited. Just as the appeal of the *chanson révolutionnaire* stemmed from its close affiliation with the mythic figure of the working class, so the fascination with free jazz and rock stemmed from their connection to privileged social groups (the black revolutionary and the transnational youth movement, respectively). By contrast, the demotion of contemporary music as a legitimate form of social and political expression during the same period was in large part due to its connection to a social group, the cultural elite, that was as vilified as it was nebulous. In all of these instances, the value that accrued to a social formation—and, by extension, to the genre with which it was identified—depended on how it was conceived within a specific ideology. Rock, for example, could be seen as either radical or reactionary depending on how youth's role in social change was construed. As we shall see in chapter 4, individuals and groups who viewed generational conflict as a principal motor of social change were more inclined to view rock favorably, regarding it as the musical expression of a new revolutionary class. The reverse was true of those who conceived generational conflict as a diversion from the real center of social antagonism, class conflict. The image of a formation as either revolutionary or reactionary, as dominant or subaltern, colored the image of the musical genre associated with that formation.

While a genre's identification with a privileged social group was often a major source of appeal, it was just as often a burden that weighed heavily upon musicians, listeners, and critics. This was particularly the case for those participants within a genre community whose identity did not coincide with the identity ascribed to a genre. This problem could be seen most readily with regard to rock and free jazz, genres that had arrived in France only in the late 1960s. As we shall see in chapters 3 and

4, musicians, critics, and fans of such genres had to contend with the disjunction between their French identity and the American (or African-American) identity of the genre's core practitioners, those who provided the benchmark according to which authenticity was judged.[34] But while most pronounced in the case of nonnative genres, similar disjunctions also played out in connection to indigenous musical traditions. The identification of the *chanson révolutionnaire* with the working class, for instance, posed problems for those who sought to make use of this repertoire for political purposes, as Calvet's critique of "Les Nouveaux partisans" makes clear. A similar dynamic was seen in chapter 1 with regard to the singing of "The Internationale" by student militants. Intended as a sign of solidarity, the rendition of the song by an "inappropriate" social group was construed as a form of playacting by those unsympathetic to the student's political claims.

As the foregoing indicates, the connections forged between genre and identity take shape within a broader field of relationships. To say that a genre like the *chanson révolutionnaire* "belonged to" or "represented" a certain social group was to say (if only by implication) that it did not belong to or represent other groups. This underlines the fact that musical genres, like the social categories with which they are affiliated, are relational terms. Whatever value or meaning individual genres acquire is a product of their relation to other genres and the position they occupy within the entire system of genres.[35] Furthermore, the fact that both musical and social fields are organized according to the same kind of differential logic reinforces the links that individuals and groups draw between the two. We will examine this issue in more detail below in connection with Bourdieu's notion of the homology. For now, what is important to note is the commonplace tendency to treat the relations between genres as reflecting or reproducing the relations that exist between the social groups with which they are affiliated.[36] If observers in the mid-1960s identified *yéyé* as "youth" music, for instance, it was only because other genres existed that could serve as their foil, that could be identified as the music of the adult world (which, depending on the circumstances, might be jazz, chanson, or classical music). A similar logic was apparent with regard to generic subdivisions. The arrival of Antoine on the musical scene in late 1965 (see below) was seen as articulating a split within French youth culture, one that set a resistant "beatnik" subculture against the *yéyé* mainstream. Such divisions became more pronounced once rock supplanted *yéyé* as the principal figure of youth music in the collective imagination. The tangled skein of subgenres and sub-subgenres within the French rock community functioned as a handy if not entirely reliable index of the class, geographic, and educational distinctions that transected youth as a social category.[37]

Taken as a whole, then, the system of musical genres provides a refracted image of the social world. Or, to be more exact, it corresponds to a particular ideologically inflected understanding of the social world. One implication that follows is that changes in how the social field is perceived have a corresponding impact on how the musical field is perceived. In this regard the radical remaking of French social space during the postwar period was a crucial factor in the post-'68 politicization of different musical genres, creating the conditions whereby certain social groups—and by extension certain genres—were assigned (or denied) a political import they hitherto lacked (or possessed). The rapid pace of economic modernization after World War II, the growth of the new working class of technicians and intellectuals, the steady decline of the agricultural sector, the integration of the working class and its representatives into Republican institutions, the influx of immigrant workers from former colonies, the postwar baby boom—all of these developments upset entrenched ways of imagining French society.

To be sure, the traditional opposition underpinning left-wing thought, which set industrial proletariat against capital, still exerted considerable sway (and not just among adherents of Marxist orthodoxy). But changing demographic realities challenged this simple model of social relations. Crucial in this regard was the perception that the economic boom of the postwar decades had absorbed the industrial working class into a smoothly functioning system of state-organized capitalism. The rise in standards of living, the increasing availability of mass-produced consumer goods, and the declining visibility of working-class struggle in the 1950s and 1960s fed a belief that the embourgeoisement of workers was underway. This led some figures within the intellectual left to search for alternative social groups that might act as a Marxian subject of history, the social formation charged with the task of overthrowing capitalism. For some, Jean-Paul Sartre most notably, the wrenching experience of decolonization suggested that it was the third-world revolutionary who best fit this vanguard role (this topic is explored further in chapter 3).[38] For others, it was the "new working class," a composite category of students, intellectuals, and technical workers, that was best positioned to take over the title of revolutionary subject.[39] Still others—particularly in the wake of '68—saw youth as constituting the cutting edge of social struggle, in large part because of the perceived generational alliance that was forged across class lines between students and young workers.[40] In the 1970s other groups would be identified as potential candidates for the role of historical subject: regional minorities, women, immigrant workers, homosexuals.

But if it was true that changes in the social field impinged on how the field of musical genres was imagined, the reverse was also true. Transformations taking place in the system of genres were often regarded as a reflection (or presentiment) of transformations taking place in the system of social relations. Jacques Attali's *Bruits* (1977) was perhaps the most thoroughgoing application of this kind of magical thinking to the musical domain, with its claim that changes in musical practice augur far-reaching changes in social structure. But the same kind of logic could already be witnessed in the remarkable cross-fertilization of genres after 1968—and more specifically in the optimistic social interpretations that this phenomenon generated. Examples of generic interpenetration were abundant in the post-May period. Fusions of chanson with avant-garde jazz could be heard in Brigitte Fontaine's collaboration with the Art Ensemble of Chicago in her 1970 album *Comme à la radio,* or in Colette Magny's work with François Tusques and other French free jazz performers on the 1972 album *Répression.* Rock and chanson merged in a number of Léo Ferré's post-1968 songs (as we shall see shortly). Rock also intermingled with free jazz: Barney Wilen's Free Rock Band of the late 1960s approached this intersection from the jazz side of the generic divide, while rock bands like Magma and Red Noise did so from the opposite direction. Parallel efforts at introducing free improvisation into contemporary music were undertaken by the New Phonic Art (one of whose members, Michel Portal, divided his time between this formation and his own free jazz group, the Michel Portal Unit). At the same time, a number of French free jazz players began to experiment with techniques drawn from the world of *musique concrète.* Examples include Wilen's *Auto Jazz: Le destin tragique de Lorenzo Bandini* (1968), Bernard Vitet's *La Guepe* (1971), and Jacques Thollot's *Quand le son devient aigu, jeter la girafe à la mer* (1971). Fusions of rock and contemporary classical music, while less numerous, generated considerable interest. Such was the case with *Ceremony,* Pierre Henry's heavily publicized "crossover" album with the British hard rock band Spooky Tooth, and composer Igor Wakhevitch's collaboration with the band Triangle on the album *Logos.*

What distinguished the period around May '68 was not so much the proliferation of generic hybrids like these but the utopian overtones

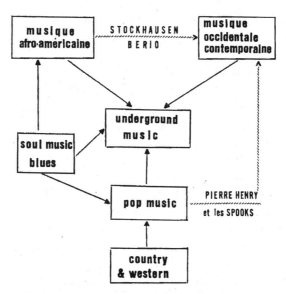

FIGURE 6. A map of the musical field ca. 1970. From
Gérard Noël, "Au confluent des musiques nouvelles,"
Jazz-Hot 261 (May 1970).

that they assumed. Much ink was spilled trying to make sense of the
changing musical landscape. (Figure 6 reproduces one such effort at
schematizing the interaction of new musical genres.) More often than
not the political aspirations stirred by May inflected how the interaction
of genres was understood. As record reviews, interviews with musicians,
and surveys of contemporary musical life make clear, the convergence of
different genres was rarely seen as a purely musical phenomenon. Rather,
it was almost always regarded as a symptom of some broader change
in social relations. This can be seen in an article critic Denys Lemery
penned for *Jazz Magazine* in which he described the numerous points of
contact that connected recent jazz and contemporary music. Lemery
identifies a number of aesthetic concerns common to both. These included an interest in expanding the timbral resources of traditional
instruments; an emphasis on spontaneity, seen in the privileged place
accorded free improvisation and/or indeterminacy; and a propensity for
addressing political or social issues through music. In addition to these
substantive similarities, Lemery takes note of a social basis linking the
two genres. Both, he contends, draw from the same pool of listeners:
"What is the audience [for these musics]? For new jazz as for new music,

it is young, desirous of finding in art the same preoccupations as its own."[41] For Lemery, what is distinctive about the youth audience was its disregard for generic boundaries. In imputing this ecumenical attitude to youth, Lemery casts age as the principal determinant of musical taste. The result was a "generation gap" within the metagenres of classical music, jazz, and popular music.[42] Neither free jazz nor avant-garde classical music has found an audience "among classically cultivated or experienced people."[43] It was youth alone who possessed the ability to look beyond superficial labels to appreciate the "music itself."

Lemery's optimistic reading of the trend lines of music history is not without its problems. His essay is less descriptive than aspirational: it does not depict the then-current state of the musical field so much as present an idealized image that accords with his own ideological preferences. Even so, Lemery's essay has the merit of showing how changes in the musical field around 1968 were invariably read as signs of social change. Pierre Bourdieu's concept of the "homologies" that link different fields of social activity provides a way of understanding the logic of such arguments. According to Bourdieu, what binds together the relatively autonomous fields that comprise the social world is the fact that all share the same basic organizing principle: competition, the motive force of the capitalist mode of production. Fields as diverse as the arts, politics, religion, economics, and the law all exhibit a similar dynamic, each governed by an opposition that sets competition over socioeconomic power against competition over alternative forms of symbolic power. As Bourdieu notes, "the field of cultural production produces its most important effects through the play of the *homologies* between the fundamental opposition which gives the field its structure [the opposition between economic and symbolic capital] and the oppositions structuring the field of power and the field of class relations."[44] The multidimensional social space thus described enables individuals not only to locate themselves within a given field, but also to identify parallels with similarly positioned groups (or objects) in other fields. It is by means of such structural affinities that connections may be posited between different genres occupying distinct regions of the musical field. The same principle also sheds light on how more distantly related fields can be mapped onto one another (as is the case when social relations are imposed on the musical field).

An example of this "play of homologies" can be seen in Lemery's identification of a "generation gap" within various music genres. It suggests that what united avant-garde jazz and contemporary music in the late 1960s were the structurally similar positions that they occupied within their respective metagenres. Free jazz stood in the same relationship to its parent culture, the metagenre of jazz, as the avant-garde stood with respect to its parent culture, classical music. A similar logic is at work in the linkage of genre and identity discussed above. It was by virtue of the homologies that could be drawn between social distinctions (youth versus adulthood) and musical distinctions (free jazz versus "traditional" jazz, contemporary versus classical music) that allowed these fields to be brought into alignment.

Similarities in structural position may facilitate connections between different genres (or between genre and identity), but the symbolic force that these connections acquire comes instead from the perceived social distance they traverse. It is in the seeming transcendence of difference that the "play of homologies" acquires its utopian charge. This was already apparent in Lemery's ruminations on the imminent fusion of jazz and new music communities. It was also apparent in Maurice Fleuret's roughly contemporaneous assertion that the blurring of the boundary between rock and avant-garde music presaged a synthesis of "high" and "low" taste cultures—and, by extension, elite and popular publics.[45] But perhaps the most revealing contribution to the post-'68 discourse on generic crossovers was to be found in the critical reaction to *Dear Prof Leary,* the first (and only) album by Wilen's Free Rock Band. Specifically, a pair of reviews by Philippe Constantin—one for *Jazz Hot,* the other for the Paris-based pan-Africanist journal *Jeune Afrique*—reveal the stakes involved in this discourse. In his piece on the album for *Jazz Hot,* Constantin argued that Wilen's blending of rock and free jazz proved effective inasmuch as both genres exhibited a tendency toward "regression."[46] That is, both sought to cast off the conventions that their parent genres had accumulated over the years in order to retrieve a more primal, immediate form of musical expression. In his review in *Jeune Afrique,* Constantin reinforced this aesthetic parallelism with a social one. It is not just the shared stylistic premises of rock and free jazz that ensure the success of *Dear Prof Leary;* it is the fact that both genres are the expression of dominated social groups: "There is a precise link between 'free jazz' and rock: they are both cultures of the oppressed (this is particularly clear for 'free jazz,' which has a close relationship with Black Power)."[47] Acknowledging that his description of youth as an oppressed group was something of a stretch, Constantin qualifies this remark by saying that youth is nonetheless in the process of becoming "politicized."[48] In other words, if the positions occupied by white youth and African-Americans on the one hand and rock and free jazz on the other were not perfectly homologous, it was just a matter of time before they came into alignment. In Constantin's reading, Wilen's album signaled that this process was already underway. As such, it offers a vehicle by means of which Constantin can imagine an emergent coalition joining white youth culture and black radicalism.[49] The fusion of genres thus becomes a way of imagining the fusion of different social groups.

Chapters 3 through 5 examine in more detail the interactions between genre, politics, and identity discussed here. The remainder of this chapter focuses instead on the broader question of how generic norms both enable and constrain the kinds of political expression to which music can give voice. To this end I examine compositions drawn from three distinct musical genres: in addition to Grange's "Les Nouveaux partisans," I discuss Léo Ferré's "L'Eté 68" and Evariste's "La révolution." What ties these songs together, despite their radical differences in style and idiom, is that they all were composed in response to the events of May '68. But *how* they responded to this event varied considerably based upon the genre within which they operated, be it the revolutionary chanson (Grange), the literary chanson (Ferré), or French pop-rock music (Evariste). In pursuing this line of inquiry, there is of course a risk of lapsing into reductionism. There is a reason for entertaining this risk, however. Whereas much of the musicological work that invokes the concept of genre does so to highlight the ways in which a particular work transgresses generic constraints (usually with an eye to demonstrating its distinctive genius), my purpose here is to show how individual works exemplify the genres to which they belong. In other words, I am interested not in identifying what individuates a work but in showing how the system of relations that constitute its generic context find expression through the work. This is not to deny that the works in question possess features that defy generic conventions. It would be hard to imagine otherwise. But for the sake of focusing attention on the way that genre shapes political expression, I will bracket questions of aesthetic value.

LÉO FERRÉ AND THE POETRY OF INSURRECTION

It is no exaggeration to say that records addressing the events of May '68 went on sale almost as soon as the last barricade had been dismantled. The bulk of these were produced by musicians situated squarely within the chanson tradition, itself a reflection of the genre's conventions. Whereas *yéyé* and *variétés* both tended toward light entertainment, rarely tackling political matters head-on, the chanson had a long tradition of chronicling and commenting upon current affairs, dating back to the *chansonniers* of the nineteenth century. As such, it is not surprising to find many of the major figures of the postwar French chanson responding, either directly or obliquely, to the events of May. These include Jean Ferrat ("Au printemps de quoi rêvais-tu?" and "Pauvres petits cons"), Claude Nougaro ("Paris mai"), Georges Moustaki ("Le temps de vivre"), and Colette Magny ("Nous sommes le pouvoir").[50]

Within this surge of *soixante-huitard* song, the work of Léo Ferré was at once exceptional and exemplary. One of the "big three" of postwar chanson along with Brassens and Jacques Brel, Ferré underwent a personal and artistic transformation after May. Long recognized as an engaged singer and an advocate of a libertarian brand of anarchism, he was well positioned to profit from the renewed interest in politically committed art that May had engendered. At the age of fifty-one Ferré saw his career revitalized. In the years after May he recorded some of his best-selling albums, including the hit singles "C'est extra" (1968) and "Avec le temps" (1970). His fan base also skewed younger during the post-May period, though this had its costs as well as its benefits. As noted in chapter 1, militants were quick to criticize Ferré, usually for having failed to adequately translate the principles espoused in his songs into action. A common complaint was that his self-proclaimed allegiance to anarchism—expressed in songs like "Graine d'un ananar" and "Les anarchistes"—was opportunistic. "Ferré, an old anarchist, a rebel . . . my ass!" read one article in *L'Idiot international*. "It's not enough to cry out against this rotten society, to grow your hair out, to wear black velvet jeans in order to stop being a bastard."[51] Such attacks on the sincerity of Ferré's political convictions continued through the early 1970s.

However fraught this newly minted relationship may have been at times, Ferré reciprocated his embrace by younger audiences. Or at least he did so on a musical level. Like Grange, he repositioned himself within the musical field in response to contemporary events. But rather than looking backward to the revolutionary chanson of yesteryear, he looked forward to what was then the cutting edge of popular music: rock. This shift manifested itself most clearly in his collaboration with the jazz-rock group Zoo from 1970 to 1973.[52] Prompting this move were the social and political implications Ferré read into *la pop*: "Pop music is the mirror of a liberation experienced by youth, in their manner of living, in the relationships between beings, finally rid of the old molds and taboos, ready to truly live together."[53] Concomitant with this turn to rock styles was a departure from the poetic conventions of the chanson tradition. In place of the customary alternation of verses and choruses, a number of Ferré's songs from the early 1970s featured the singer declaiming freely over a musical backdrop.[54] A case in point is the song "Le Chien" from his 1970 album *Amour Anarchie*. Against a largely improvised setting provided by the members of Zoo, Ferré recites a text whose obscure imagery is reminiscent of surrealist automatic poetry: "To the Spider the web in the wind / To Steak baron of lobster / and his technique of caviar / that looks like herring."[55] Cryptic language notwithstanding, the general drift of the poem is clear. "Le Chien" celebrates a regression to the state of animal nature, an abandonment of sedimented inhibitions. The structure of the poem mirrors this process, beginning with a series of octosyllabic strophes that give way to free verse in the second half of the song. This rejection of formal convention (and, concomitantly, societal constraint) culminates with the final lines of the song, in which Ferré proclaims: "I TALK and YELL like a dog. I AM A DOG."[56]

As fascinating as such transgressions of the chanson genre may be, I would prefer to focus upon Ferré's post-May work that fits squarely within its generic norms. While songs like "Le Chien" suggest that Ferré ultimately found rock to be a better fit with the libertarian ethos of the post-May period, this did not prevent him from composing a number of chansons that addressed *les événements* using the genre's established poetic and musical resources. The chansons collected on the album *L'été 68*—in particular the title track—provide a useful point of reference. The reading of the May events advanced by the song "L'été 68" sheds light on the norms of political expression governing the postwar chanson genre. But before undertaking a close examination of this song, a little background on both author and genre is in order.

Born in Monaco in 1916, Ferré began his musical career in the early 1940s. After a number of years of composing and performing intermittently in Monaco and southern France, in 1946 he moved to Paris, where he became part of the postwar cabaret scene then flourishing in Saint-Germain-des-Prés.[57] This period witnessed the ascendancy of both the Left Bank scene and the *auteur-compositeur-interprète,* a figure comparable to the Anglo-American singer-songwriter. The fusion of the roles of composer, lyricist, and performer in a single person distinguished this subgenre of the chanson from its Right Bank counterpart, which was more closely tied to the music hall tradition, with its emphasis on spectacle and a clear division of musical labor.[58] Another distinguishing feature of the Left Bank chanson was its modest performance style. Performances generally featured a solo singer with guitar or, in the case of Ferré, piano accompaniment. This stripped-down style made a virtue of necessity. Most Left Bank artists lacked the resources to employ backing bands, and the intimate venues where they performed could rarely accommodate large ensembles.[59] The most notable attribute of the Left Bank chanson was its emphasis on poetic craftsmanship. Although the textual element had long occupied a privileged position in French song, more so than in Anglo-American popular music, in Left Bank chanson the creation of a sophisticated poetic object became a paramount concern—if not *the* paramount concern—for artists after World War II.[60]

David Looseley's sketch of the paradigmatic Left Bank singer-songwriter synthesizes the various traits enumerated above. Such artists were typically "white, male, solo performers initially leading somewhat bohemian Parisian lives, accompanying themselves on guitar or piano as befitted the intimate Left Bank cabarets where they began, and writing songs whose lyrics were remarkable for their polish, complexity and wit, their dissidence and political incorrectness, their combination of personal emotion and social criticism."[61] Looseley's model has the merit of underlining the implicit gender and ethnic coding of the genre. It also points out how the figure of the Left Bank singer-songwriter has become (as Looseley puts it) the "Platonic ideal" for the chanson genre as a whole. If in the 1940s and 1950s "literary" Left Bank chanson was defined in opposition to the more lavish spectacles of the Right Bank music halls, with the decline of the latter beginning in the 1960s, "literary" chanson has since broadened to the point where it is now seen as virtually coterminous with the chanson as a genre. Meanwhile, the postwar growth of radio and television encouraged the development of newer, more thoroughly mediatized forms of *variétés*. These newer genres often bore the imprint of Anglo-American precedents (as was the case with *yéyé* in the 1960s or disco in the 1970s) and quickly assumed the role of the inauthentic, commercial other against which authentic, artistic chanson is defined.[62]

But if the Left Bank/Right Bank distinction has long ceased to possess the same power it once did, it is important to remember that not even during the postwar heyday of the *chanson rive gauche* was this division hard and fast. It was not uncommon for singer-songwriters who had originally made a name for themselves within the Left Bank cabaret scene to display traits more typically associated with Right Bank music hall once more prestigious performance and recording opportunities opened to them. Louis-Jean Calvet thus describes the Left Bank scene as a kind of proving ground for young artists, an artistic "purgatory" from which one could either advance to the "heaven" of headlining at one of the major music halls (like the Bobino or the Olympia) or to the "hell" of a failed career.[63] But as Calvet notes, even as certain artists made the symbolic journey from the Left Bank to the Right Bank, certain norms of the Left Bank subgenre remained intact. Principal among these was the premium put on the text: "The majority of the singers [who] issued forth from the 'Left Bank' will continue to consider the orchestra as having a sole function, that of accompaniment: it is still the text that occupies center stage."[64]

Ferré was among the fortunate few to make the journey described by Calvet and scale the heights of artistic celebrity. After he built a reputation in the Left Bank cabaret scene in the late 1940s and early 1950s, his career took off in 1955 when he first headlined at the Olympia.[65] His move from the bohemian margins of the chanson to its mainstream was reflected in his evolving musical style. While his music retained certain features of the Left Bank style—most notably its poetic ambitions— his mature chansons began to manifest musical traits associated with the Right Bank scene. After Ferré signed with the Odéon label in 1953, and especially after his move to the Barclay label in 1960, the influence of dance styles typical of the Right Bank music hall tradition (like the java and tango, or the more recently popularized rumba and cha-cha) became increasingly conspicuous in his work. At the same time his new collaborators at Barclay (in particular the conductor and arranger Jean-Michel Defaye) packaged Ferré's compositions in ever more elaborate big band and orchestral arrangements. The new sound of Ferré's recordings, which Peter Hawkins scathingly (but accurately) describes as "opulent but bland," clashed with the archetypal image of the solitary artist cultivated within the discourse of Left Bank chanson.[66] The shift in musical style signaled what one might generously call his arrival as a celebrated chanson artist, or might less generously be described as evidence of his social aging.

But even as his musical style evolved, Ferré's poetic aspirations went unchanged. If anything, they became even more pronounced as his career advanced. In 1956 he published his first volume of poetry, *Poète, vos papiers!*[67] Five years later, in 1961, he released his first album setting the poetry of an established literary figure, Louis Aragon. The key date in the ratification of Ferré's claim to poetic legitimacy—and, by extension, the chanson's bid for cultural recognition—came in 1962 with the publication of a selection of his chanson texts as part of Seghers's series Poètes d'aujourd'hui.[68] The assimilation of a "minor" form like the *chanson* into a prestigious art form like poetry was not unproblematic. In the introductory essay to the volume Charles Estienne preemptively voiced some of the objections that he imagined would greet the volume in an attempt to inoculate the endeavor against potential criticism. But in doing so he betrayed the anxieties that accompanied chanson's bid to artistic legitimacy: "You will rejoin that . . . one must not confuse genres; that '*chanson* is a *métier,* while poetry is a calling.' "[69] Such lingering insecurities aside, attempts to fold chanson into the more prestigious category of poetry were part of a broader postwar tendency, one that valorized cultural self-improvement and artistic attainment among groups traditionally excluded from the cultural sphere. Embodied by organizations like Peuple et culture and institutions such as the Théâtre nationale populaire, this tendency had two interrelated objectives: at the same time as it sought to elevate the cultural horizons of the working classes, it also sought to render art accessible through various outreach and educational programs.[70] In a sense, Ferré's poetic ambitions exemplified this dual objective. His settings of Aragon and other poets brought high culture to a mass audience even as he sought to win recognition for his own poetic endeavors.

By the time that Ferré recorded *L'été 68* in late 1968, the musical and poetic aspects of his mature style were firmly entrenched. Almost all of the tracks on the album feature lush orchestral accompaniments; the two exceptions are "C'est extra," which employs rock instrumentation supplemented by string orchestra and chorus, and "Comme une fille," which is given a big band setting. As for the texts, they adhere to the poetic style Ferré had cultivated over the past twenty-odd years of his career, a mix of "high" literary language, topical reference, and social critique. The two songs addressing May, "L'été 68" and "Comme une fille," are no different in this regard, indicating how the genre's overriding concern with poetic achievement colored Ferré's representation of the uprising. Unlike Grange's *chansons révolutionnaires,* which tended toward blunt social realism, the texts of "Comme une fille" and "L'été 68" treat the theme of social conflict through metaphor and poetic allusion. As its title suggests, "Comme une fille" romanticizes the act of insurrection by tying it to sexual desire: "Just like a girl/The street undresses/The paving stones pile up/And the cops that pass by/Take them on the face."[71] In eroticizing the uprising, Ferré's text forgoes reflection on its causes or aims. Rather, by drawing a parallel between the release of revolutionary and libidinal energies, Ferré casts insurrection as a quasi-natural urge. Instead of being tied to specific sociopolitical conditions, the uprising of May becomes the manifestation of a perennial desire for revolt.

The "poeticizing" of May is even more pronounced in "L'été 68." The song abjures a clear strophic layout and rhyme scheme, and it replaces the obvious sexual metaphor of "Comme une fille" with more obscure imagery. While the significance of certain images is clear enough, it is not immediately apparent how one should interpret the ensemble.

L'été comme un enfant s'est installé
Sur mon dos
Et c'est très lourd à porter
Un enfant tout un été
Sans cigales
Avec des hiboux ensoleillés
Comme les enfants du mois de mai
Qui reviendront cet automne
Après l'été de mil sept cent quatre-vingt-neuf
Ça ira ça ira ça ira

Summer, like a child, has settled down
on my back
And it is very heavy to bear
a child the entire summer
Without cicadas
With sunlit owls
Like the children of the month of May
Who will return this autumn
after the summer of 1789
Ça ira ça ira ça ira

Three important themes emerge over the course of the chanson. The first and most significant, given the song's relation to the May events, centers on the French Revolution. The twist that comes toward the end of the song, when the "summer of '68" of the song's title becomes the "summer of 1789," situates the May uprising within the broader arc of French revolutionary history. So too does the concluding intonation of the phrase "ça ira," an allusion to the revolutionary song of the same name. The second major subject that figures into the song is youth, incarnated in both the child of the opening line and the "children of the month of May" hailed at the song's climax. Last but not least are the recurrent allusions to the passing seasons: "summer, like a child," the "children of the month of May" who reappear "this autumn," after "the summer of 1789."

How, then, are we to assemble these elements to form a coherent interpretation of the song? A first clue is provided by the passing seasons alluded to in the song. The opening lines make it clear that the present of the chanson is the summer of 1968. Autumn, by contrast, is referred to in the future tense, while the spring, by implication, is in the past. This last point is significant: the title of the song, after all, is "L'été 68," which places the listener in the moment when the tumult of May has just passed into history. The song addresses not so much *les événements* as their memory. This moment of retrospection is painted in ambiguous terms. Its association with youth, in the guise of *les enfants,* instills the moment with a sense of hopefulness. Yet the promise of revitalization that youth incarnates is at the same time a burden weighing upon the narrator, although it is not clear in what sense it is a burden. Is it a question of the events' failure to "change life," as the socialist slogan goes? Is it the obligation to see the unfulfilled promise of May redeemed? Or is it a greater historical weight, as the references to 1789 suggest?

The musical setting of the poem goes some way in adjudicating the opposition that sets the burden of historical memory against the promise of youth. Like the poem, the music does not rely on a recognizable formal scheme; it is through-composed, to use the terminology of art song. Following a brief bombastic introduction, in which the tutti orchestra discharges with great fanfare three pairs of block chords, the musical atmosphere slackens. The texture thins to strings and harp and settles into a vamp around the tonic, C major. The vocal line in the first ten measures, up to the line "avec des hiboux ensoleillés," is equally relaxed, almost to the point of aimlessness. It has a quasi-improvised feel, circulating around a pentatonic subset (C, D, E, G, and A) of the diatonic scale. This, along with the harmonic stasis, empties the music of tension. Things change, however, with the arrival on the line "les enfants du mois de mai." The arrival on this line in measure 14 coincides with an ascent to the song's melodic highpoint (E4) and the first real harmonic motion (to IV), initiating a large-scale cadential progression (see example 4). The correlation of this reference to the "children of the month of May" with the music's first climax invests the words with an affective charge lacking in earlier passages. The music tips the balance. Where the text alone expressed a measure of ambivalence, the orches-

EXAMPLE 4. "L'été 68," first climax. © Editions La mémoire et la mer. Used by permission.

EXAMPLE 5. "L'été 68," final climax and close. © Editions La mémoire et la mer. Used by permission.

tral arrangement dispels all doubts, investing allusions to youth and the return of May with a high level of expressive intensity. This process continues in the final section. Following the climax of measure 14, the music begins to build toward a second, conclusive climax in measure 20 with the repeated phrase "ça ira." Over a dominant pedal the vocal line climbs the C-major scale, each utterance of "ça ira" echoed by horns in the distance (example 5). This culminates with the voice's attainment of C4 over tonic harmony in measure 25, which triggers a return to the block chords of the introduction. These chordal blasts, whose meaning remained uncertain at the opening, now assume a portentous air. In the wake of the repeated declaration of "ça ira," the orchestral tutti seems to anticipate the moment when the revolutionary embers of 1968 (and 1789) will be rekindled.

The triumphant close of "L'été 68" would seem to dispel any lingering ambiguities of the text. The exultant quality of the final measures is produced out of the convergence of a number of factors: text, melodic ascent, cadential closure, and, above all, the kind of orchestral grandiosity characteristic of Ferré's mature style. But for all the bombast of the close, the fact that triumph is signaled by the repeated intonation of a slogan dating from the French Revolution has the effect of blurring future and past. What is suggested here is less a progressive sense of history than a cyclical one, where future redemption is imagined as a return to the past (which has its musical corollary in the echo of the introduction's chordal blocks at the close). The youth of 1968 become the latest avatar of the revolutionary spirit of 1789 and other past insurrections. Bolstering the theme of cyclic return are the frequent allusions to the passage of the seasons, and more specifically the superimposition of spring and fall, birth and death, that takes place in the lines "les enfants du mois de mai / Qui reviendront cet automne." Collectively, these elements present May less as a singular event than as the latest manifestation of a persistent will to insurrection. As was the case with "Comme une fille," the "poeticizing" of May in "L'été 68" has the effect of lifting the event out of its historic context. This romanticization of the May events is due in part to the poetic imperatives of the postwar chanson. This is not to disregard the influence of other, equally important factors, nor is it to deny Ferré agency. His idiosyncratic brand of anarchism—which was less a political doctrine than an existential stance, an attitude of permanent revolt against society—played an equally important role in formulating the message of "L'été 68." But the fact remains that the generic norms of the postwar chanson, including the Left Bank subgenre's demand for poetic expression, furnished the matrix through which Ferré's aesthetic, stylistic, and ideological peculiarities could take form.

EVARISTE, PARODY, AND POP

Unlike chanson, surprisingly few youth-oriented pop songs explicitly broached the subject of May. The dearth of political pop in France in the immediate wake of May '68 is all the more striking when juxtaposed to the situation in the United States and Britain, where groups merging rock and left-wing politics were more commonplace. This absence is explained in part by the fact that the dominant form of youth music in France at the time, yéyé, conventionally skirted politically charged topics. The timorous remarks of France Gall, cited at the opening of this chapter, were representative of how yéyé stars reacted to May. But even ostensibly more rebellious forms of popular music, like the beatnik and folksong movements, were equally reticent in the face of the May events. One of the few exceptions was the singer Evariste, who in the summer of 1968 recording a single containing two songs, "La Révolution" and "La Faute à Nanterre," which he had first performed in the occupied Sorbonne. Like Grange, Evariste had participated in CRAC, which assisted in the production and distribution of the single (see chapter 1).

Indeed, the record appears to have been conceived as the first in a series of recordings released under the group's aegis. Taking advantage of the fact that recording studios were momentarily vacant, Evariste enlisted the support of studio musicians, recording engineers, and other personnel idled by the work stoppage, who agreed to forgo payment in return for a percentage of the single's sales. Once recorded, the single was sold for three francs, about half the price of commercial 45-rpm singles.[72] The low price propelled sales of the album; according to one source, forty thousand copies had been sold by 1971.[73] But the principal motivation for the low price was to rebuke the music industry's subservience to the profit motive: "This record was realized with the help of the movements and *groupuscules* that participated in the cultural revolution of May 1968. It is being sold at the price of 3F in order to unmask the extent to which capitalists feather their nests with the usual commercial recordings."[74]

Evariste was the pseudonym of Joël Sternheimer, a physicist turned singer-songwriter. Something of a prodigy, by the age of twenty-three Sternheimer had received a doctorate and had taken up a postdoctoral position at Princeton University. Dismayed by the university's complicity with the American military-industrial complex, he abandoned his post and returned to France, where, lacking a source of income, he decided on the advice of a former professor to try his hand at music.[75] After being turned down by a handful of record companies, he was signed in 1967 by Lucien Morisse, the artistic director of the Disc'AZ label.[76] Sternheimer adopted the pseudonym Evariste (after the nineteenth-century mathematician Evariste Galois) and recorded a handful of singles for Morisse's label, such as "Pommes de la lune" and "Connais-tu l'animal qui inventa le calcul intégral." These songs, which met with moderate success, mixed surreal, farcical lyrics with a musical style somewhere between garage rock and early psychedelia. These tendencies led him to be classed as part of the anachronistically titled "beatnik" movement in French pop music, which had gained prominence in the mid-1960s.

I will return to the place the "beatnik" movement occupied in French popular culture shortly. For the moment, it will suffice to say that "La Révolution" continued in the same vein as Evariste's earlier endeavors. The song has a fairly standard rock instrumentation and does not stray from tonic, subdominant, and dominant harmonies. The vocal line has a singsongy quality, a result of the triplet subdivisions of the $\frac{4}{4}$ meter and the constant oscillation between scale degrees 1 and 5. As for the lyrics, they dramatize the conflict of May '68 by means of an imaginary dialogue between father and son. The first verse and chorus are representative:

> Le père Legrand dit à son p'tit gars
> —Mais enfin bon sang qu'est-ce qu'y a
> Qu'est-ce que tu vas faire dans la rue fiston?
> —J'vais aller faire la révolution
>
> —Mais sapristi bon sang d'bon sang
> J'te donne pourtant ben assez d'argent
> —Contre la société d'consommation
> J'veux aller faire la révolution
>
> La Révolution! La Révolution!

> *Father Legrand says to his boy*
> *—For crying out loud what's going on*
> *What are you going to do in the street my son?*
> *—I'm going to start a revolution*
>
> *—But good heavens, goddamn goddamn*
> *I give you more than enough money*
> *—Against consumer society*
> *I want to start a revolution*
>
> *Revolution! Revolution!*

By personifying the social conflict in generational terms, Evariste's song already indicates one fairly basic way in which genre influences its representation of the May events. The fact that genres like *yéyé* and rock were commonly represented as "youth music" not only reflected the demographic makeup of the music's producers and consumers, but at the same time encouraged a certain way of imagining social space. Such representations, in other words, reinforced the notion that age rather than class, educational attainment, or status was the principal fault line of social division.

This goes some way toward explaining Evariste's depiction of the May through the lens of generational conflict. Still, at this level the shaping role of genre remains blunt and demands further refinement. Youth-oriented popular music, after all, encompassed a heterogeneous set of related but distinct styles, including early rock and roll, *yéyé*, and folksong, each of which had its own norms governing behavior, attitude, rhetoric, and degree of political engagement. To get at this finer level of differentiation, it is necessary to step back and examine in some detail the ways Anglo-American pop music had ramified since its introduction in France at the end of the 1950s.

Most accounts of French rock divide its development prior to 1968 into three main phases: the rock and roll phase, the *yéyé* phase, and the beatnik/folksong phase. The first of these was initiated in 1960. Although a few French artists had experimented with rock and roll in the late 1950s, such forays had little lasting impact. As early as 1956, essayist, composer, and jazz trumpeter Boris Vian had appropriated the music of Bill Haley and Elvis Presley in a handful of songs for music hall star Henri Salvador, who recorded them under the pseudonym Henry Cording. These, however, were broad parodies that mocked rather than embraced the latest American fad. Other, more sincere efforts to adapt the style soon followed, notably singer Danyel Gérard's 1958 hit "D'où viens-tu Billy Boy?" But it was the success of Johnny Hallyday's early singles "T'aimer follement" and "Souvenirs souvenirs" in 1960 that launched rock and roll as a cultural phenomenon in France. Hallyday's rapid rise to celebrity spawned other bands, including the Chausettes noires, the Chats sauvages, and the Vautours. For the most part, the material performed by Hallyday and his contemporaries consisted of adaptations of proven American hits. This heavy dependence on American models was not limited to the music alone but was manifest at all levels of the music's production and performance. Dress, hairstyle, comportment, on-stage theatrics, and even the anglicized pseudonyms that aspiring rock performers adopted (such as Eddy Mitchell, Dick Rivers, and, of course, Johnny Hallyday) all bore witness to the dependence of the nascent French rock and roll scene on its American forebear.[77]

The growing popularity of rock and roll in the early 1960s soon gave rise to a moral panic regarding its deleterious effect on French youth. This was motivated in part by the music's perceived association with juvenile delinquency, incarnated in the menacing figure of the *blouson noir*, the disaffected working-class youth who engaged in various acts of physical or symbolic aggression. Fears about the music's ability to incite violence came to a head with the riot that broke out at the Troisième festival de rock, which took place at the Palais des Sports in Paris in November 1961. This event marked the culmination of the first phase of rock's introduction into France. In response to such flare-ups of youth violence and the bad press they generated, record companies and radio stations began promoting a more clean-cut and respectable crop of performers in the hope of broadening the appeal of American-inspired popular music. By 1962 a bowdlerized style of pop music, *yéyé*, had supplanted rock and roll as the dominant form of youth music. Stylistically, *yéyé* moved away from the Afro-diasporic bases of early rock and roll and accommodated itself to both the sound and production regimes of traditional French *variétés*. While electric guitars and drums still figured prominently in *yéyé* records, distinguishing the music from older forms of French popular music, these instruments were generally integrated into a more polished orchestral setting than had been the case with earlier rock-and-roll recordings. No less important than changes in musical style were the changes in image that *yéyé* introduced. In place of the leather-clad *blouson noir, yéyé* ushered in a new kind of teen idol, one that was young, wholesome, and, more often than not, female. Teenage girls made up the bulk of the *yéyé* stars: Sylvie Vartan, Sheila, France Gall, Françoise Hardy, Chantal Goya. For their part, male *yéyé* singers like Claude François and Frank Alamo tended to have a boyish, unthreatening, almost asexual appearance. Whereas early rock and roll in France had been characterized by a sensationalized image of aggressive masculinity, *yéyé* offered a more comforting image of docile femininity.[78]

Almost from its advent *yéyé* was subject to withering critique. Defenders of traditional *chanson* were particularly hostile to the style, though in later years adherents of rock picked up this discursive thread, using *yéyé* as the inauthentic "other" against which they could valorize their own taste culture. Most detractors of *yéyé* deployed some variant of the standard mass culture critique against the movement. According to such readings, the *vague yéyé* represented an interregnum imposed on French youth by the music industry, which sought to make a quick franc by promoting a form of music that, by dint of its inoffensive banality, would have maximum public appeal. Artists, by this account, were fabrications of powerful commercial interests, and audiences were passive dupes. "Youth," critic and lyricist Georges Coulonges wrote, "don't listen to what they like: they like what they listen to, what they have been given to listen to."[79] Yet as is often the case with mass culture critiques, a mixture of prejudice and elitism informed discourse on *yéyé*. For defenders of "*chanson* de qualité," the principal complaint lodged against the movement was that it promoted sound over sense, rhythm over language, body over mind. In place of the literary values prized by chanson, *yéyé* served primarily as an inducement to dance. Elsewhere Coulonges remarked that "to judge *yéyé* on the basis of its texts would represent a kind of bad faith [as] it is an exclusively sonic phenomenon"; but this did not prevent him from going on to assert that these same texts were responsible for instilling "an emptiness in the spirit of youth."[80] Another line of criticism, one favored by later advocates of "authentic" rock genres, fell back on the gender coding that underpins most mass culture critiques.[81] *Yéyé* was cast as a lower, feminized form of expression, deficient compared to genres that supposedly resisted commercial pressures. The preponderance of female artists in the *yéyé* movement encouraged this line of argument. The remarks of Albert Raisner, longtime host of the television program "Age tendre et tête de bois," were symptomatic: "Records were produced on an assembly line, by copying copies of copies of real rock: imitations, emasculations."[82] *Yéyé*, by diluting rock and roll for purely mercenary reasons, was guilty of sapping its (masculine) vitality. The idea that *yéyé* might have its own virtues, or that it might supply listeners pleasures that had little to do with authenticity, was not entertained.[83]

The proliferation of such representations of *yéyé* had a number of lasting consequences. One was that the movement became a foil against which subsequent rock genres and subcultures defined themselves. Also, by portraying *yéyé* as a monolithic phenomenon, such representations obscured the diversity that characterized French youth culture of the early and mid-1960s. While there is no doubt that the styles grouped together under the umbrella heading of *yéyé* were ascendant during this period, a wide variety of offshoots and subcultures coexisted within the French pop scene. The dependence of French pop on American and British models meant that the diversity of the latter offered musicians a wide palette of stylistic options to choose from. On the one hand, *yéyé* adapted to changes in fashion by continually reinventing itself, as evinced by the series of short-lived dance crazes (the twist, the Madison, the jerk), adapted from U.S. and British models, that succeeded one another in the early 1960s.[84] On the other hand, French subcultures drew on the variety of Anglo-American popular music to forge distinctive musical identities. British invasion bands and garage rock, for instance, became countermodels that French groups like Les Gypsys and Les Bowlers mined in the hope of creating a sound that would set them apart from the *yéyé* mainstream.[85]

Most of these subcultures remained at the margins of French pop, eclipsed not just by *yéyé* stars like Sheila and Claude François but by the American and British originals that French bands had aped. By 1966, however, the emergence of a new movement brought these fissures into public view. Referred to as "protest song" or "beatnik music," the new style was heralded by the arrival of the singer Antoine in December 1965. With his long hair, flowered shirts, and provocative lyrics, Antoine was seen as embodying the new spirit of rebelliousness in French youth. His sudden and surprising success was contingent on at least two developments that had taken place over the course of 1965. One was the emergence of a new youth subculture, the oddly titled "beatnik" movement, which derived its name from the postwar American cultural movement. French "beatniks," like the *blousons noirs* earlier in the decade, elicited a new round of moral panic in France. The media stereotyped beatniks as disaffected youth who congregated in parks, played the guitar, and panhandled instead of engaging in productive work. Antoine, an erstwhile habitué of the Square Vert Galant, one of the principal beatnik haunts in Paris, incarnated the new subculture in the media.[86] The fact that he served as a useful figure for a broader social phenomenon fueled his notoriety.

The second development that explains Antoine's sudden celebrity was a growing interest in the American folk revival, and in the music of Bob Dylan in particular. The clearest expression of this interest was the success that greeted Hugues Aufray's 1965 album of Dylan covers. Seeking to tap into this shift in public taste, a talent scout for Vogue, Christiane Fechner, sought out a representative of the beatnik subculture who would do more than just sing Dylan covers but would occupy an analogous position in French pop.[87] Upon discovering Antoine, Fechner promoted him as the French Bob Dylan. Musically, there was some basis for the comparison. Antoine's backing band, Les Problèmes, bore an obvious debt to the sound of the mid-sixties electric Dylan. The same could be said for Antoine's crude harmonica playing and his nasal half-sung, half-spoken mode of vocal delivery. However, it was Antoine's lyrics as well as the controversy surrounding his music that generated the most comparisons with Dylan. A number of his songs addressed themes typical of the American folk revival, such as antimilitarism ("La Guerre" and "Pourquoi ces canons?") and the menace of nuclear warfare ("Juste quelques flocons qui tombent"). Yet songs broaching serious issues were overshadowed by Antoine's more irreverent lyrics, which appeared to have little purpose other than to provoke the ire of audiences. (The most famous of these was his hit single "Les Elucubrations," which, among other things, imagined putting Johnny Hallyday on display in a cage at the Medrano Circus.) The enormous amount of press coverage Antoine generated derived more from his transgression of accepted norms of behavior, appearance, and musical skill than from any social issues his songs explored.[88]

This points to a fundamental ambiguity of Antoine's music, and of the beatnik movement as a whole. In adopting an oppositional stance, beatnik music or protest song had to contend with the prevailing image of French pop as trivial and inauthentic, incapable of supporting serious social commentary. It is not surprising, then, that Antoine himself at times cast doubt on the import of his music: "I don't try to convey a message. . . . I sing what I want to. It can seem either serious or absurd, however you like it."[89] In this disavowal we can see another way in which negative representations of *yéyé* exercised their influence on subsequent movements in French pop. By reinforcing preexisting cultural biases against contemporary youth culture, such discourses called into question the possibility that pop music of any kind—even that, like Antoine's, which positioned itself in opposition to *yéyé*—could address serious social concerns. It would appear that members of the beatnik movement had internalized the pejorative image of French pop to such an extent that their own tentative efforts at creating an "anti-*yéyé*" alternative ran up against the belief that it would be no less frivolous than the *yéyé* mainstream it rejected. The negative reputation of contemporary French pop encouraged someone like Antoine to adopt a self-ironizing pose, to consciously distance himself from his role as a representative of French youth culture.[90] The effect of this was to blunt the critical edge of his music. One gets the sense that Antoine and his peers, unlike their American and British counterparts, did not take pop all that seriously.

Certain critics picked up on this hint of bad faith. Sylvie de Nussac, writing in *L'Express,* wondered if Antoine wasn't just "a hoax" *(un canular)* and doubted "at the very least his sincerity."[91] Such reactions became more commonplace as Antoine's example gave rise to successors and imitators. Some of these, like the young Michel Polnareff, succeeded in producing a less self-conscious and more persuasive form of French pop. More common were those who played up the satire and humor evident in Antoine's music. At one end of this spectrum were artists like Jacques Dutronc, who would meet initial popular success with "Et moi et moi et moi," a sly send-up of some of Antoine's more self-involved lyrics. At the other end of the spectrum were novelty acts like Benjamin and Edouard, the latter of whom donned a wig of knee-length hair as part of a not-terribly-subtle lampoon of the beatnik trend.[92]

It was in this fun house of parody and pastiche that Evariste's ephemeral music career took shape. Contemporary press accounts (as well as later histories of French rock) situated him squarely within the beatnik phenomenon, an affiliation that goes some way in explaining the depiction of May in "La Révolution."[93] Earlier I pointed out that Evariste's

FIGURE 7. Cover art for Evariste, "La Révolution/La Faute à Nanterre." Used by permission of Georges Wolinski.

song interpreted the conflict in generational terms, embodied in the opposition between father and son. I also pointed out that, in a crude way, this reflected the workings of genre, insofar as the imagined community constructed around pop music in France as elsewhere was defined above all by age. Pop was held to represent youth in a way that ostensibly cut across differences in class and ethnicity. However, if pop as an overarching metagenre was identified with youth as an undifferentiated social category, then the more refined picture of the 1960s French pop scene provided above sheds light on the various ways youth was represented in different pop subcultures. Notable in this regard is the strong comic streak that runs through "La Révolution." This is already evident in the cover art that the cartoonist Wolinski provided for the single, which presented the figures of adulthood and youth in caricatural form: the bald, heavyset father holds a racing form in his hand, while the skinny, shaggy-haired son hides a paving stone behind his back. It is also apparent in the kind of language Evariste provided the song's two protagonists (figure 7). Whereas the son's lines mix contemporary slang and political catchphrases, the father's lines are sprinkled

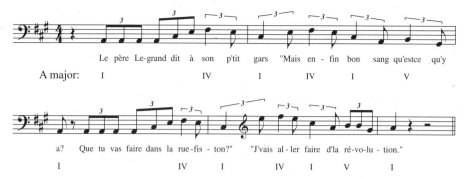

EXAMPLE 6. "La Révolution," opening verse. Used by permission of Joël Sternheimer.

with a somewhat old-fashioned vocabulary ("*sapristi*," "*bon sang*," and "*fiston*").

The song's farcical tone comes through most clearly in the vocal delivery Evariste uses to distinguish the two characters. Throughout the song Evariste shifts back and forth between registers; the father's lines occupy a lower ambitus, between A2 and F♯3, while the son's are sung in falsetto an octave higher, between A3 and F♯4 (example 6). Such changes in tessitura are, of course, an index of age, a sonic shorthand for generational difference. But it is not difficult to hear the registral difference as gendering the roles as well, masculinizing the father's persona and feminizing the son's. One way of understanding this gendering is to hear the feminization of the son's voice as a form of symbolic emasculation, deflating the figure of the son and, by extension, the figure of youth. This is reinforced by the strained quality of Evariste's falsetto, which makes the adopted persona sound somewhat ridiculous. But if Evariste's vocal delivery undercuts the figure of the son, it undercuts the figure of the father equally. The personification of paternal authority is rendered just as ridiculous, the register being clearly too low for Evariste. Taken together, the vocal personae cast both sides of the generational divide in an equally absurd light. Neither father nor son, neither the world of adults nor that of youth, escapes the song's deflationary rhetoric. Nor, for that matter, does Evariste himself, who comes off as more of a comic than a rebel.

What are we to make of this patent lack of seriousness? One could justifiably see it as reflecting Evariste's own peculiar aesthetic, professional, or ideological proclivities. One might well read it as representative of the *soixante-huitard* attitude of total contestation. But here as elsewhere genre plays a crucial role in shaping the characterization of May that emerges in the song. A disbelief in pop's significance betrays itself in Evariste's unserious treatment of May. But what is important to note is that genre shapes not only the content of the song—the depiction of May as a generational conflict—but also its rhetoric. It informs not only *what* could be expressed but *how* it could be expressed. Whereas Grange's post-'68 songs speak of class struggle in polemical terms, the better to stir the public to action, and whereas Ferré's song meditates on the eternal return of revolutionary esprit, Evariste's pokes fun at the generational divide that May disclosed. Each genre operated in its own characteristic mode: for the revolutionary chanson, it was the polemic; for the literary chanson, it was the lyric; and for the beatnik counter-genre of French pop, it was the satiric.

The present chapter considered the role that musical genre plays in mediating political expression. The three case studies focused on the level of the musical text, paying particular attention to how the representation of political themes varies from one genre to another. Differences in conventions governing musical style, rhetoric, and subject matter are, however, but one of the ways in which genres are distinguished from one another. Equally important are the norms and patterns of use that shape the various forms of collective activity that constitute a genre community (criticism, concert life, pedagogy, production regimes, distribution networks, pressure groups, cultural policy, and so forth). The chapters that follow will turn to such sites of musical activity—criticism in the case of jazz, festival culture in the case of rock, and cultural policy in the case of contemporary music—to chart how they responded to the upheavals of May.

CHAPTER 3

Free Jazz in France

The editorial committee of *Jazz-Hot,* taking into consideration the directives of Chairman Mao concerning the need for revolutionaries to partake in physical training, has formed a soccer team.

—"Flashes," *Jazz-Hot* (June 1969)

In France the fortunes of few genres were as closely linked to May '68 as free jazz. Contemporary accounts record its presence at key junctures during *les événements,* from the occupation of the Sorbonne and the Odéon to the funeral procession for Gilles Tautin, a student killed during a clash with police in Flins on 10 June.[1] That certain groups adopting the style (such as the Cohelmec Ensemble) or borrowing heavily from it (such as the rock group Red Noise) claimed to have formed during May further buttressed the perception that a subterranean connection existed between the spontaneous character of the protest movement and the improvisatory practices of avant-garde jazz.[2] And, as noted in chapter 1, free jazz musicians were among the most active members of the musicians' strike, forming the core of the group Action musique. Free jazz appeared to suffuse the May events from one end of the uprising to the other. Or at least this is the impression one gains in reading accounts recorded in subsequent years. Yet the veracity of these accounts is hard to gauge. "Various newspapers and commentators have talked of 'pianos on the barricades,' of jazz in May, etc.," wrote sociologist Alfred Willener, his skepticism barely disguised.[3] But even if the role of free jazz during May '68 was exaggerated, the fact that commentators saw fit to overstate its importance is revealing. It bespoke a belief that the genre somehow corresponded to the social movement, that the two were in some way connected.

Free jazz remained highly visible in subsequent years. This may appear surprising, given that the movement was both relatively new to France and widely perceived as inaccessible. Yet the assumption that free jazz would prove too rebarbative for audiences was refuted in the event. Concert reviews from the late 1960s make continual reference to auditoriums overflowing with a public that was young, enthusiastic, and demanding.[4] Equally notable was the attention the style attracted outside the cloistered world of specialist reviews. Whereas discussion of the jazz avant-garde prior to 1968 was the purview of magazines like *Jazz-Hot* and *Jazz Magazine,* after this watershed year the movement received significant coverage in mainstream publications, including *Le Monde* and *Le Nouvel Observateur.* During the peak years of public interest in free jazz, from 1968 to 1972, articles on the movement could be found in a bewildering variety of outlets, ranging from underground newspapers[5] to glossy art magazines,[6] from Communist-sponsored periodicals[7] to bulletins underwritten by the U.S. State Department.[8]

The heightened demand for free jazz was stimulated by increased supply. A sizable number of American jazz musicians decamped to France in the late 1960s and early 1970s, including Sunny Murray, Marion Brown, Anthony Braxton, Steve Lacy, Noah Howard, Frank Wright, Alan Silva, Steve Potts, and, most famously, the Art Ensemble of Chicago. The prospect of steady employment lured many across the Atlantic. The downturn in the jazz economy in the United States during the 1960s had made work hard to come by, and France's well-established reputation as a haven for African-American artists made it an attractive destination. Paris in particular had a long history of offering African-American musicians a warm welcome, from the jazz community that flourished in Montmartre during the interwar period to the postwar success of Sidney Bechet, Kenny Clarke, and Bill Coleman.[9] Tangible incentives also drove the transatlantic migration of musicians. Of signal importance was a series of recordings that the BYG/Actuel label undertook during the summer of 1969. Overseeing the series was drummer and record producer Claude Delcloo, who had contacted a number of musicians earlier in the year, promising them work should they come to France.[10] Delcloo also invited artists participating in the First Pan-African Cultural Festival in Algiers at the end of July to stop over in Paris on their way back to the United States and cut records for the label.[11]

The flurry of activity that began in July and August 1969 culminated in October at the Actuel festival, arguably the high-water mark for free jazz in France. Organized by BYG/Actuel to publicize Delcloo's record series, the event was billed as the first festival of its kind to be held in continental Europe, a francophone equivalent to the Monterey Pop and Woodstock festivals. The owners of the BYG label, Jean Georgakarakos and Jean-Luc Young, had wanted to hold the event in Paris but were forced to look elsewhere after French authorities, concerned about the threat to public order, refused to grant the necessary permits.[12] Failing to secure another location in France, the organizers ultimately settled on the town of Amougies, near the border in Belgium. Though modeled on Anglo-American rock festivals, the Actuel festival was distinguished from its predecessors by the quantity of jazz on the program. Between sets by Pink Floyd, the Soft Machine, and Yes were performances by Archie Shepp, Don Cherry, the Art Ensemble of Chicago, and Frank Wright, among others.[13]

The balance struck between rock and free jazz elicited considerable commentary in the press. Many journalists expressed hope that the event signaled a rapprochement between the two genres.[14] Others were more skeptical, considering the tensions that emerged between the jazz performers and the audience, which was composed primarily of rock fans. (These tensions were made abundantly clear when Malachi Favors, bassist for the Art Ensemble of Chicago, drew catcalls for lampooning the on-stage histrionics of rock guitarists.)[15] Still, the majority of commentators characterized the event as a breakthrough for avant-garde jazz. Writing in *Nouvelles littéraires*, Daniel Berger proclaimed that "the hits of the Actuel festival were as much Don Cherry or Sunny Murray as Pink Floyd or the Pretty Things."[16] To explain how such "difficult" music might win broad public support, critic Paul Alessandrini pointed to the alleged "immediacy" of free jazz. He lauded the performance of the Sunny Murray Quartet, which he described as "a long, furious, convulsive scream."[17] By his reckoning, the palpably physical exertions of Murray and his sidemen more than matched the sonic force that rock acts obtained through technological means.

Alessandrini's comments provide a window onto the beliefs that guided French discourse on free jazz. His emphasis on aggressivity, sonic impact, and the physicality of performance was typical, partaking of what had by the late 1960s become the standard lexicon for evaluating avant-garde jazz. In retrospect, it is clear that the prioritization of such traits reflected a blinkered view of free jazz, one that treated the rough, extroverted style cultivated by "second wave" artists like Shepp, Ayler, and Murray as representative of the movement as a whole. A particular kind of free jazz, one characterized by an absence of steady pulse, eschewal of tonality, high-energy solos, and an expanded repertoire of grunts, growls, bends, honks, and squeaks, thus became the benchmark against which all else was judged. Music that did not adhere to this narrow conception more often than not puzzled critics. Such was the case with the music produced by the Art Ensemble, Anthony Braxton, Leroy Jenkins, Wadada Leo Smith, and others affiliated with the Association for the Advancement of Creative Musicians, whose use of extended silence and textural disjunctions veered too closely to the cold abstraction of contemporary classical music in the eyes of many critics.[18]

Equally representative was the way in which Alessandrini accounted for the new thing's intensity. In describing the response free jazz acts received at Amougies, he remarked that listeners were "won over beyond all hope by the power and the cry of these spokesmen of black people in revolt."[19] His linking of the music's expressive power to political factors was typical. Indeed, by the time of the Actuel festival in 1969 the equation of avant-garde jazz with African-American protest movements had become commonplace in French critical discourse. Almost from the moment the music arrived on French shores, critics treated free jazz as a mirror image of the radicalization taking place within certain segments of the African-American community, especially as black power ideologies began to eclipse the integrationist ethos of the civil rights movement after 1966.[20] Claims that free jazz was the "concrete cry of the ghetto," "a political instrument," or the adaptation of "the principles of black power to the musical universe"[21] abounded in the French press from the mid-1960s to the mid-1970s, so much so that Philippe Koechlin, jazz critic for the *Nouvel Observateur*, could quip that French critics were content "to explain everything with [the phrases] 'black power' and 'peace in Vietnam.'"[22]

Given this political coding of free jazz, it is easy to understand why the movement attracted such attention in late 1960s France. May '68, Pascal Ory has observed, whetted the public appetite for both politically engaged and avant-garde art. This created an environment that was receptive to free jazz, since its practitioners were viewed as having struck a near-perfect balance between aesthetic transgression and political expression.[23] This distinguished the new thing from other genres, even those that enjoyed a comparable surge of popularity after 1968. The profile of Iannis Xenakis, Pierre Henry, and other composers of avant-garde classical music may also have risen during these years; but, as we shall see in chapter 5, contemporary classical music had difficulty shaking perceptions that it was a music by and for elites. As for Anglo-

American rock music, it assumed an increasingly central place in French youth culture from 1967 on, dislodging *yéyé* from its dominant position in French youth culture. However, the rejuvenation of left-wing militancy in the years following May fostered a certain suspicion, if not outright hostility, toward rock and other manifestations of the counterculture. To the extent that *la pop' music* held any appeal for *gauchistes,* it was in purely instrumental terms, as a way of mobilizing youth. By contrast, free jazz offered a form of cultural resistance that better accorded with the militancy of student radicals. Its presumed connection African-American protest and its relative freedom from the taint of commercialism made it a more ideologically attractive alternative to either rock or contemporary classical music.

That said, how and why free jazz came to be viewed as the quintessential form of engaged music still needs to be addressed. While the political dimension of this movement was taken to be self-evident, it is vital to recall that this character was both constructed and contested. It was constructed insofar as the association of the new thing with African-American social movements of the 1960s was not intrinsic to the music itself but was a quality ascribed to it through the work of a handful of key intermediaries. In the United States the dissemination of Amiri Baraka's and Frank Kofsky's writings on the jazz avant-garde was especially critical to forging his association of free jazz and black nationalism. Yet, as recent work on the jazz scene of the 1960s has indicated, the links between music and politics during this period were considerably more nuanced than such narratives admit. As Eric Porter has pointed out, the range of political opinion within the jazz avant-garde was remarkably varied. The universalism and spiritual consciousness invoked by figures like Coltrane or Ayler provided a counterweight to the anticolonialism of an Archie Shepp or the cultural nationalism of an Amiri Baraka.[24] Even individual musicians could maintain seemingly incompatible positions, depending on the circumstances. This point is driven home by Ingrid Monson in her study of jazz and the civil rights movement: "It was not uncommon for individuals, both black and white, in the early sixties to express support for aspects of both black nationalism and integration. Moreover, emphasis on one side or the other was often *situational,* with African Americans drawing lines of racial solidarity in response to white power plays or insensitivity and whites charging reverse racism in response to the racial boundaries erected in the interests of self-determination."[25] It is also critical to bear in mind another point made by Monson—that the avant-garde did not exercise a monopoly on political activism during the 1960s. While many adherents of the new thing participated in benefits to aid African-American political movements, so too did "mainstream" jazz artists, a fact that should dispel the simplistic homology that converts an artist's rupture with musical convention into an indexical sign of political commitment.[26]

One aim of this chapter is to examine how the reception of free jazz in France skewed such realities by coding the music as a transparent expression of a single, consistent political ideology. While the resulting image of the new thing may have been reductive, ironing out the movement's complexities, the pressures that encouraged such simplification were themselves anything but simple. To get at these issues it is necessary to consider the position that members of the free jazz community in France occupied, given that their identity as French citizens shaped the image they constructed of the new thing. But while the main focus will be on how this image came to be constructed, it is vital to bear in mind that it did not go uncontested. Many musicians found the reflexive equation of experimental jazz with African-American political radicalism to be limiting. Interviews in the French press of the period frequently evinced a push and pull between interlocutors, as interviewers sought to elicit statements of political commitment from performers, who in turn refused to be pigeonholed as "engaged" artists.[27] When critic Daniel Caux asked the members of the Art Ensemble of Chicago about the political attachments of the Association for the Advancement of Creative Musicians (AACM), Joseph Jarman responded bluntly, "We don't have any affiliation with political groups. . . . [A]ll we can say is that the only thing that interests us is: music, music, music."[28] A similar exchange took place during an interview with saxophonist Frank Wright: "We play the music we love, and we don't have anything to do with people who protest, we don't even read the newspapers. The only thing that interests us is music."[29] As Stephen Lehman has noted, the tendency of French critics to treat avant-garde musicians as the standard-bearers of black radicalism operated on the assumption that "the African American community [was] essentially monolithic."[30] Papered over in the process were social and artistic differences that existed among the style's practitioners.

That the majority of French critics failed to recognize such diversity may be attributed to the cultural and geographic distance that separated them from the subject of their discourse. In addition, the reception of the new thing was inflected by the position jazz had historically occupied within the French cultural field, acting as a powerful object of

desire for French audiences. As Jeffrey Jackson and others have observed, the source of this fascination—the perceived alterity of jazz—
had been construed in one of two ways: either in terms of a mythic
(African) primitivism or in terms of an equally mythic (American) modernity.[31] Although this dialectic continued to shape the reception of
jazz through the 1960s, with the advent of free jazz the musical other
assumed a new guise: that of a revolutionary subject, identified with
various anticolonial liberation movements.[32] The penchant for viewing
African-Americans (and, by extension, African-American musicians) as
the group that, by dint of its historic subjugation, was poised to act
as the motor of social change became all the more compelling given the
difficulties in locating an equivalent social force in France. Identifying a
group that could fulfill the role of Marxian revolutionary subject had
proven difficult in the years prior to May '68. The ostensible bourgeoi-
sification of the working class since the end of the Second World War,
encapsulated by the French Communist Party's disavowal of revolutionary action in favor of electoral politics, reinforced the sense that the
industrial proletariat had ceded its claim to the title of historical subject. The embrace of African-American political radicalism during the
late 1960s and early 1970s thus offered the French left one way of filling the void that troubled the revolutionary imagination. Yet the magical solution that the embrace of free jazz offered posed its own set of
problems. How was a music identified (rightly or wrongly) with African-
American political struggle to be adapted to French concerns? How
was its particularism to be reconciled with the importance attached
to universalism within the French cultural sphere? What was the status
of French musicians within this genre community, considering the music's moral and political legitimacy was bound so closely in the French
imagination to a specifically African-American context? And—most
importantly—how did the different solutions to these problems evolve in
response to the new political climate that May '68 created?

THE MUSIC OF DECOLONIZATION

The period from 1968 to 1972 marked the high point of the new thing's
popularity in France. In addition to the arrival of expatriate musicians
in Paris, these years witnessed the movement's spread into nontraditional performance venues (universities, art galleries, rock festivals, and
political meetings) and the proliferation of small independent record
labels devoted to avant-garde jazz (BYG, Futura, and Shandar). But if

these years represented the pinnacle of the new thing's popularity, its ascendance depended on a series of earlier developments that set the stage for the movement's later success. The year 1965 stands out as a turning point. Although the controversies generated by Ornette Coleman's early albums had reached French shores in the first half of decade, prior to mid-decade French jazz fans had few opportunities to hear American avant-garde jazz firsthand. Recordings of musicians working outside of the mainstream were also difficult to acquire, a source of frustration for jazz aficionados.[33] In 1965 the situation began to change. Tours brought a number of American musicians to France, including Don Cherry, who had an extended engagement at the Parisian nightclub Le chat qui pêche in June.[34] Others soon followed: Steve Lacy performed at La Bohème in July, while Ornette Coleman made a much-anticipated appearance at La Mutualité in November. The following year, 1966, witnessed Coleman's return in March; an extended visit by Cecil Taylor in November and December; and a controversial appearance by Albert Ayler at the Paris Jazz Festival in November. A lull in tours by American artists during 1967 and the early part of 1968 gave the indigenous free jazz scene space to flourish. At the core of this local movement were musicians who had backed Cherry during his stint in Paris: pianist François Tusques, trumpeter Bernard Vitet, bassist Beb Guérin, and drummer Jacques Thollot. As early as October 1965 this group had reassembled to record an album entitled *Free Jazz*, released early the following year on an independent label run by the Franco-Algerian actor and singer Marcel Mouloudji.[35] With its dodecaphonic themes and hushed, restrained tone, the music on the album perhaps bore a closer resemblance to Third Stream experiments in bridging jazz and modern European music than it did to Ornette Coleman's album of the same name. Still, the recording represented a landmark, as it brought together musicians who would form the nucleus of the native free jazz community during the late 1960s and 1970s.

The Parisian specialist press greeted the arrival of free jazz with much fanfare, devoting considerable space to the movement beginning in 1965. The oldest jazz review in France, *Jazz-Hot*, published an article on Cecil Taylor in February, the first in a series of profiles on avant-garde musicians that appeared over subsequent months.[36] The main rival to *Jazz-Hot*, *Jazz Magazine* responded by publishing two special issues devoted to the avant-garde.[37] This surge of critical interest reflected the renewed attention the new thing was receiving in the United States at the time. The emergence of "second wave" free musicians like Archie

Shepp, Albert Ayler, Marion Brown, and Pharoah Sanders in New York had garnered a fair amount of press, both positive and negative, in *Downbeat* and *Jazz*. It was perhaps inevitable that French jazz magazines would echo such coverage, given that they relied heavily on their American counterparts for firsthand accounts of the New York music scene.

But just as important as such external factors was the demographic remaking of the field of jazz criticism. Driving the newfound interest in free jazz was the emergence of a new cohort of critics—Yves Buin, Michel Le Bris, Guy Kopelowicz, Philippe Carles, and Jean-Louis Comolli—who took up the cause of experimental jazz.[38] No doubt their advocacy of free jazz was overdetermined, a function of professional and generational factors as well as aesthetic proclivities. By aligning themselves with the new wave of jazz musicians, younger critics carved out a distinct niche within a field dominated by established figures like Lucien Malson, André Hodeir, Michel-Claude Jalard, and Jean Wagner. Just as the promotion of bebop in the years following the Second World War had helped set this older generation of critics apart from their precursors (namely Hugues Panassié and other self-appointed guardians of "hot jazz"), so too did the advocacy of free jazz allow members of the younger generation to forge a distinct professional identity. The incomprehension that initially greeted the music allowed these critics to make the argument that new criteria were needed to address it adequately—a task for which they were ideally suited.

But what would these new criteria entail? And what was it about the aesthetic standards that had hitherto guided jazz criticism that made them inadequate to the task of appraising free jazz? To answer these questions, members of the rising contingent of jazz critics looked to the work of author, poet, and playwright Amiri Baraka (then LeRoi Jones), whose writings would play a key role in mediating the French encounter with avant-garde jazz. Baraka, as George Lewis notes, was the only American writer that "really mattered" to younger French critics.[39] By the mid-1960s, Baraka had already won recognition within intellectual and artistic circles. Antoine Bourseiller's productions of *Dutchman* and *The Slave* at the Théâtre de Poche in fall 1965 had brought Baraka's work to wider public attention, as had Jean-Luc Godard's inclusion of an excerpt from *Dutchman* in his 1966 film *Masculin/Féminin*. One sign of Baraka's prominence as an interpreter of African-American culture for French intellectuals could be seen in an article that Jean-Louis Comolli penned for the April 1966 issue of *Jazz Magazine*.[40] Entitled "Voyage au bout de la New Thing" (an allusion to Céline's 1934 novel

Voyage au bout de la nuit), Comolli's article sought to explain the displeasure that avant-garde jazz had aroused in listeners. The nub of the problem, as Comolli saw it, was not that avant-garde jazz had forsaken "timeless" musical values, but that it had repudiated those attributes that appealed to a particular listenership—namely, the (white) European jazz fan. But while the new thing might stand "at the opposite extreme of what we savor in jazz, that is to say, at the opposite extreme of our canons of taste and beauty," the significance of this rupture extended beyond the aesthetic domain, narrowly conceived.[41] It is at this point that the influence of Baraka becomes apparent. Comolli adopted the basic thesis Baraka had advanced three years earlier in *Blues People*: that black music acts as a mediated expression of African-American consciousness, and as this consciousness had changed in response to economic and political forces, so too had the music.[42] With this materialist reading of black music in place, Comolli argued that the break signaled by the new thing must therefore reflect the emergence of a new, oppositional attitude within the African-American community: "'Free music' is not a formal revolution, it is not the upsurge of a new style, but is the fire-sign of a radically different *[autre]* sensibility, recalcitrant, out of tune with us."[43]

Despite Comolli's evident debt to *Blues People*, his essay departs from its model at its crux. Whereas Baraka saw the dynamic that played out in jazz as stamped by American race relations, Comolli saw it as a symptom of the broader transnational process of decolonization. The "race problem" in the United States, he wrote, "has only recently (thanks to a certain Malcolm X) taken on its true proportions: at the exact moment when, curiously enough, black Americans have understood that they are not so much a racial minority victimized by a racist majority as one of the countless races, one of the civilizations throughout the world victimized by European colonization."[44] This recasting of Baraka's narrative reflected the vantage point Comolli occupied as a French citizen writing in the wake of France's collapse as a colonial power. Particularly traumatic was the Algerian War of Independence, which had laid bare deep-seated antagonisms within the French polity at the same time as it destroyed cherished myths regarding France's self-appointed role as a defender of humanist values. Even after the Evian Accords of 1962 officially ended French rule in Algeria, the legacy of decolonization continued to shape social relations in France. Over a million settlers—the so-called *pieds noirs*—repatriated to metropolitan France following Algerian independence. Though ethnically French, most of the *pieds noirs* had never set foot on the mainland prior to 1962, and their difficulties in adjusting to their new environs were amplified by the sense of resentment many felt at the ostensible abandonment of *l'Algérie française* by their fellow citizens.[45] At the same time, immigration from West and North Africa accelerated in the early 1960s, thanks to a strong economy and an open-door policy for former colonial subjects. After arriving in France, however, Arabs and black Africans faced persistent discrimination in terms of employment, housing, and opportunities for social advancement.[46] Despite the relative calm that settled in France in the years following decolonization, the patterns of immigration and social inequality that French colonialism had established set the stage for the breakout of racial tensions both during and after the economic downturn of the 1970s.

Given this context it is not surprising that revolutionary anticolonialism would occupy a more prominent place in Comolli's interpretation of free jazz than the distant struggles of the American civil rights movement. In his eyes the true meaning of the new thing was located in the synecdochal relation connecting the local struggles of African-Americans and the global struggles of anticolonial national liberation movements. However, the line of argument Comolli developed in "Voyage au bout de la new thing" not only responded to the general experience of decolonization, but it can also be seen as partaking of a specific ideological reaction to this experience—that of *tiers-mondisme*. The *tiers-mondiste* ideology had developed over the course of the 1950s, partly in response to the failure of left-wing parties to take a sufficiently forceful stand on the colonial question. The socialists had been complicit in sustaining the colonial system, having led the government under Prime Minster Guy Mollet during the height of the Algerian conflict. The Communists were little better, skirting the issue lest they alienate certain segments of the French electorate. Given the sins of omission and commission perpetrated by the established parties of the left during the early years of the Algerian conflict, a number of disillusioned intellectuals, led by Jean-Paul Sartre, began to look past the Western and Soviet blocs to the anticolonial movements of Africa, Asia, and Latin America for inspiration.[47] The Cuban revolution, the Sino-Soviet split, and, most significantly, the struggle of the North Vietnamese against the military might of the United States signified for a sizable portion of the French left that the subject of history had relocated beyond the ranks of the industrial proletariat of the "developed" world. The title of Frantz Fanon's *Les damnés de la terre*—the key text of *tiers-mondisme*—made this displacement abundantly clear: by appropriating the opening line of "The Internationale," Fanon proclaimed that the "wretched of the earth," the driving force behind revolutionary change, was henceforth to be found in Europe's former colonies. In the words of Kristin Ross, it was "the North Vietnamese peasant, and not the auto worker at Billancourt, who had become, for many French militants, the figure of the working class."[48] That anticolonial movements exerted a decisive influence on the nascent black power movement in the United States buttressed the interpretive leap Comolli had made in linking the new thing to decolonization.

"Voyage au bout de la New Thing" quickly became a touchstone for the French criticism of free jazz. This is not to say that it met with universal approbation. For all those who endorsed the contention that "the new thing is an instrument of decolonization,"[49] there were just as many who took issue with his treatment of free jazz as a transparent ideological vessel. Curiously, a fair amount of the criticism directed at Comolli's essay came from writers sympathetic to its basic premise, that free jazz was as much a political as a musical phenomenon.[50] For these critics, the problem lay in Comolli's methodology, which failed to adequately address how the relation between art and ideology is mediated. The article thus catalyzed a broader debate on music's ability to encode political ideologies. The years 1966 to 1968 witnessed an intense period of methodological self-examination as the new generation of jazz critics sought to clarify relationships binding together music, society, and politics.

Two changes in the French intellectual field encouraged this reflexive turn. First and foremost was the ferment taking place in *les sciences humaines* during this period. Pierre Bourdieu, Michel Foucault, Gilles Deleuze, Alain Badiou, Roland Barthes, and Louis Althusser all exerted a strong influence on the new generation of jazz critics, especially among the writers affiliated with *Jazz-Hot* (Michel Le Bris, Bruno Vincent, Yves Buin, and Philippe Constantin). In one essay, Le Bris and Buin adopted Bourdieu's notion of the intellectual field to make sense of how the dominant ideology found expression in traditional jazz criticism (albeit in sublimated form).[51] In another, Le Bris looked instead to Foucault's idea of the "episteme" in order to explore the themes of "otherness" and black cultural particularism.[52] Whatever their explanatory value may have been, such references to "high" theory served as a form of quasi-scholarly distinction, imbuing the new jazz criticism with a patina of intellectual respectability. By the late 1960s, such posturing had opened up a fissure between the two main specialist reviews: in heated polemics, writers for *Jazz Magazine* and *Jazz-Hot* attacked one another for their pretension (the main charge leveled at *Jazz-Hot*) or for their paternalism (the countercharge leveled at *Jazz Magazine*).[53] The use of academic jargon also alienated a wide swath of the *Jazz-Hot* readership, who felt that the "music itself" had been given short-shrift in favor of esoteric philosophical debate. Letters to the editor from 1968 and 1969 evince frustration with the new direction assumed by the magazine. One reader mocked the trend in a letter to the editor, asking if "Monsieur Le Bris, Vincent, or Buin would be willing to give me . . . two or three saxophone lessons in the structuralist style."[54]

The second major development that encouraged the politicization of jazz criticism involved the ongoing de-Stalinization of the Parti communiste français (PCF). The repercussions of this process were felt far and wide in French intellectual life. During the height of the cold war in the late 1940s and early 1950s, the party had adopted a stringently class-based approach to cultural matters. Following the lead furnished by Zhdanov's 1948 antiformalist campaign in the Soviet Union, French party leaders called on intellectuals to reject bourgeois thought in all its manifestations. Although the party's line regarding cultural production had relaxed in the years following Stalin's death in 1953, decisive affirmation of a "liberal" cultural policy only came at the 1966 meeting of the party's central committee in Argenteuil.[55] During the course of the meeting, the PCF affirmed a "humanist" position that saw all forms of artistic and intellectual production—irrespective of class origin—to be the collective property of humankind. Attention would henceforth turn to democratizing access to art, including works that just a few years earlier had been regarded as irredeemably bourgeois. The meeting at Argenteuil also marked the temporary downgrading of Louis Althusser's position in the ranks of the party's intelligentsia, as well as the demotion of his structuralist Marxism in favor of the Marxist humanism of Roger Garaudy. Yet these internal party struggles did little to diminish the increasing influence that Althusser's writings exerted, both within and outside party circles. And in a sense the growing prominence of Althusser's work was itself a symptom of the Communists' drift away from the ideological rigidity of the cold war period, given his belief in the autonomy of theory from the prerogatives of political strategy.

Althusser's growing influence within the French intellectual scene manifested itself in a response to Comolli's essay penned by the philosopher Eric Plaisance entitled "Ideology and Aesthetics in Free Jazz."

Published in the *Cahiers du jazz* just a few months after the appearance of "Voyage au bout de la New Thing," Plaisance's rejoinder drew heavily from the work of Althusser's circle (including Pierre Macherey) to correct what he deemed to be the simplifications of Comolli's "aesthetic leftism."[56] According to Plaisance, Comolli had disregarded the specificity of the various levels comprising the social world (e.g., the economic, legal, cultural, scientific, and political spheres). Rather than seeing these as marching in lockstep with one another, it was vital to recognize what Althusser had dubbed their "relative autonomy"—the fact that each field possesses its own unique set of structuring principles. It was necessary, in other words, to envisage "art as a relatively autonomous structure that has its own rhythm of development, its own history."[57] For this reason it would be a gross methodological error to conflate aesthetics and ideology, as Comolli had. By appropriating Althusser's notion of "relative autonomy," Plaisance was able to both affirm the determination of music by politics *and* safeguard a free space for artistic production.

Plaisance's rejection of Comolli's "aesthetic leftism" points to a broader context against which his remarks need to be read. For even as the Communists softened their line on artistic freedom, other parties on the far left did not follow suit. The PCF's renunciation of revolutionary action and its willingness to play the part of the loyal opposition within the Fifth Republic—not to mention its timidity in the face of the Algerian War—had led to the proliferation of *gauchiste* groups in the years prior to 1968, especially within the university milieu. In the mid-sixties a handful of extreme left splinter parties, most notably the "pro-Chinese" Union des jeunesses communistes (marxistes-léninistes) and the Trotskyist Jeunesse communiste révolutionnaire (JCR) (see chapter 1), broke away from the PCF's student organization, the Union des etudiants communistes.[58] While the doctrinal disputes among these *groupuscules* were often quite violent, a shared contempt for the PCF bound them together. Trotskyists and Maoists alike concurred that the party had grown quiescent, that it was blindly obedient to the dictates of the Soviet Union, that it had succumbed to "revisionism" and other theoretical lapses, and that—generally speaking—it had betrayed the workers' movement in favor of short-term political advantage. Unlike the post-Argenteuil PCF, such left-wing groups had fewer hesitations in viewing art as an instrument of class struggle.[59] This in turn became a flashpoint between the Communists and *gauchistes,* as the two sides attacked one another either for their reductionism or their revisionism. In this light

Plaisance's charge that Comolli partook of a vulgar "aesthetic leftism" assumed a particular resonance, rehearsing in the sphere of jazz criticism the kind of rhetorical put-down the PCF reserved for its rivals on the left. "Is it not an illusion, this purported transparency of musical forms by means of which one may read without ambiguity their social signification, *a leftist illusion,* this straight line from political action to artistic production?" (emphasis in original).[60] Plaisance, using Althusser as a theoretical stick to beat back Comolli's interpretive adventurism, sought to delegitimize the latter by relegating him to a fringe position in the political sphere.

A GREAT UNIVERSAL ART

It was not only adherents of the intellectual left who took issue with Comolli's arguments or who looked to the political sphere in order to frame their objections. For Lucien Malson, the resident jazz critic for *Le Monde,* Comolli's spirited defense of "engaged jazz" hearkened back to the bad old days of the cold war and smacked of Zhdanovism.[61] Malson's reaction to the politicization of discourse surrounding jazz criticism was not atypical. Whereas for the younger generation of jazz critics disputes revolved around issues of methodology—how the art/politics relation was to be articulated—for members of the generation of critics who had come of age toward the end of the Second World War, the problem was more substantive in nature. A common complaint was that partisans of the new thing, in emphasizing the music's political implications, had disregarded the "specificity of music."[62] Worse yet, many critics of Malson's generation feared that this political turn might function as a censoring mechanism, whereby doubts regarding a work's artistic quality could be effectively suppressed. Radio announcer and critic Carlos de Radzitsky would complain in a letter to *Jazz-Hot* that "jazz reviews are literally suffering from the gangrene of 'politics,'" adding that "it is no longer a secret for anyone that the motor driving the jazz dubbed 'free' ('free' from what I ask you?) is politics. Whence the entrenched habit of saying: 'If you don't like my music, you are against black people.' From now on, when one speaks of musicians of the 'new thing,' one will no longer judge them except in terms of their convictions."[63] For others the contention that the music gave voice to a specific ideology was accepted, only to invert the values ascribed to both. Hence the remark of one author who contended that "the intentional incoherence of saxophonist John Coltrane's final recordings correspond perfectly to the political confusion of a Rap Brown [sic]."[64] Aesthetics and ideology were linked, but only insofar as the shortcomings of the one mirrored the defects of the other.

Perhaps the most telling exchange between representatives of the two generations of jazz critics came in May 1966, during a broadcast of the weekly radio program *Knowing Jazz (Connaître le jazz)*. Malson, the moderator of the program, had invited Comolli to take part in an on-air debate on the significance of the "new jazz" with composer and critic André Hodeir.[65] Hodeir had been a key figure in the postwar rejuvenation of the jazz scene in France. As a composer, he had won plaudits in both the jazz and new music communities for his experiments in blending the rhythmic and harmonic language of bebop with modernist compositional techniques, most notably those of *musique concrète* in his 1952 tape piece *Jazz et jazz*.[66] In his work for *Jazz Hot*, first as a critic and then, from 1947 to 1952, as editor in chief, he had succeeded in elevating the intellectual profile of jazz, replacing the poetic rhapsodizing of his predecessor, Hugues Panassié, with a balance of rigorous analysis and philosophical reflection.[67] Given his penchant for dealing in musical specifics, it was not surprising that Hodeir was skeptical of claims made concerning the political import of the new thing. What mattered was whether such assertions were supported by the "music itself." Even if texts, titles, and other discursive accoutrements unambiguously testified to the political beliefs of musicians, in Hodeir's opinion such intentions remained "anecdotal" to the resulting work. They contributed nothing to the production of aesthetic value: "Anybody can take an instrument, anyone can attach the title 'Ode to Malcolm' to the sounds that he extracts from his instrument, to the music—good or bad—that he makes."[68] But Hodeir's main concern lay in the practical consequences that the political turn in jazz criticism might have for the genre. Were jazz to be valued henceforth according to its capacity to reveal something of the social conditions or political attitudes that prompted its creation, then its relevance for those outside the particular community from which it issued would be limited. To accept Comolli's argument that an unbridgeable ideological gulf separates European listeners from African-American artists meant that any possible fusion of their separate aesthetic horizons was precluded from the outset—a possibility that Hodeir despaired of: "Thanks to . . . free jazz you end up with a sort of condemnation of any sort of exchange between the white Westerner and the black Westerner. There can be no exchange since there exists no form of cultural osmosis. Jazz, therefore, has no chance of one day being a worldwide music."[69]

To fully understand the stakes involved in Hodeir's exchange with Comolli, as well as his defense of the idea of intercultural exchange, one must take into consideration the unusual position jazz had come to occupy in the French cultural landscape by the 1960s. Ever since its introduction in the final years of the First World War, jazz held an ambiguous place in French society, marked by a double alterity. Its otherness was defined in both national and racial terms, as simultaneously American and, more specifically, African-American, the two determinations performing a complex counterpoint with one another over the years. In the interwar period the music's perceived racial identity was a major source of attraction for French listeners, offering the latter a site where various primitivist and colonialist fantasies might be enacted.[70] In the decades following World War II, the relationship between these two terms shifted. In the context of the heightened anti-American sentiments triggered by the cold war, the music's identification with an oppressed minority group in the United States inoculated it against whatever negative connotations its national origins might have carried in tow. Indeed, this identification not only increased the esteem accorded jazz but also brought into focus the prejudices that pervaded mainstream American society. For French audiences, being a jazz fan assumed a moral dimension.[71] At the same time, by valorizing jazz French critics assumed for themselves the mantle of transnational cultural arbiters, invested with the power to decide which cultural products from across the Atlantic were worthy of bearing the honorific title of art.[72] Significantly, this bid for cultural authority coincided with (and may have compensated for) France's loss of stature in the face of America's rise as the dominant economic and cultural force in the West after World War II.

But to be valorized in this way, to win the recognition it was denied in its country of origin, jazz had to conform to certain precepts of legitimate culture. Above all, claimants to the title of high culture in France have long had to demonstrate the prized quality of universality, understood as an essential hallmark of civilization. Arguing the universal significance of jazz thus became crucial to French efforts to legitimize the genre during the 1950s. In a way, this paralleled trends in American jazz criticism of the same period. As John Gennari and others have pointed out, the adoption of the language of universalism by critics such as Marshall Stearns during the 1950s aimed at bringing jazz into the mainstream of American culture.[73] But whereas Stearns and others would contend that the ability of jazz to transcend racial and national boundaries was something that could only have occurred in the United States (an argument that appealed to the U.S. State Department, as it enlisted jazz for cultural diplomacy initiatives during the cold war),[74] for French critics the rhetoric of universalism served to dissociate jazz from its American identity. Representative of this tendency is the introduction to Michel Dorigné's book *Jazz*. Though published in 1968, the text adhered to the universalist consensus forged over the course of the 1940s and 1950s. Dorigné in particular marveled at how "a music of vulgar character, perfected by the black community in the United States," has today become "a quasi-universal form of musical expression."[75] According to this account, jazz was no longer tied to a specific ethnic community or national context, enabling it to rise above its "vulgar" origins.

The locus classicus of this universalist trope appeared in Hodeir's landmark study *Hommes et problèmes du jazz,* published in 1954.[76] The book opens by describing the music's global appeal, having successfully transcended national, racial, and geographic boundaries during its short lifetime: "What contemporary observer would have guessed that the folk music of a small group would become the language of an entire people fifteen or twenty years later and, in a few more years, a world-wide phenomenon, with jazz bands existing simultaneously in Melbourne, Tokyo, and Stockholm?"[77] But despite its global reach, jazz remained a subcultural phenomenon wherever it had sprouted up: "We must not delude ourselves. . . . Jazz has found followers everywhere, but these followers are always in the minority."[78] To explain this paradox, Hodeir acknowledged that prevailing cultural values in those societies where jazz had managed to take root presented barriers to its appreciation. In Europe the genre had to contend with a cultural elite for whom it seemed repetitive, anti-intellectual, and regressive. And yet the very fact that the music managed to find followers in diverse cultures demonstrated that it had the potential to be meaningful for listeners outside its immediate social milieu. For this reason Hodeir struck what he saw as a compromise, an "intermediate position" in which jazz acted as the complement to European high culture. Election to the ranks of the universal, in this reading, was not a zero-sum game: "I am convinced that we have the ability to adopt differing attitudes of receptivity and comprehension as the need arises. This does not necessarily force us to judge jazz in the perspective of European art; instead it invites us to broaden our view in order to make room for the only popularly inspired music of our time which is universal and has not become lost in vulgarity."[79] Hodeir's balancing act acknowledged the existence of cultural difference but sublated it by claiming for jazz the *potential* for universality. Jazz may not have appealed to all French listeners, but it had the capacity to do so, and this is what was important if it was to attain legitimacy.

Even if the arguments advanced by Hodeir and like-minded critics proved persuasive to French readers, they were but a first step in the process of legitimation, a precondition rather than a guarantee of its recognition. To be ratified, this discursive valorization needed institutional support. Lacking this, jazz remained trapped in what Bourdieu dubbed the status of the "legitimizable." By this he designated those forms possessing the potential for official recognition but whose potential remained unrealized (a category that, circa 1965, included jazz, photography, and cinema). Unlike the traditional high arts, these newer forms, marginalized within educational and cultural institutions, were unable to exert a claim upon cultivated individuals. As Bourdieu notes:

> Jazz, cinema and photography do not give rise—because they do not claim it with the same urgency—to the attitude of dedication. . . . Erudite knowledge of the history of these arts, and familiarity with the technical or theoretical rules that characterize them are only encountered in exceptional cases because people do not feel as forced as they do in other areas to make the effort to acquire, preserve and communicate this body of knowledge.[80]

Members of the jazz community concurred with Bourdieu's assessment. Malson remarked in an editorial published in *Les Cahiers du jazz* that jazz, like cinema, "has managed to overcome little by little the majority of obstacles that kept it in the realm of cultural illegitimacy. . . . It only remains for it to penetrate into the universities and the backrooms of 'research.'"[81] Despite the upbeat assessment concerning jazz's prospects for transcending its "intermediate" position in the cultural field, Malson's comment tacitly acknowledged that this status has not been completely overcome.[82] And since the sort of institutional support that would allow jazz to move beyond "the realm of cultural illegitimacy" was erratic up until the 1980s and '90s, it continued to occupy an uncertain position in the cultural field.

Pressure was also being exerted on jazz from "below," in the form of Anglo-American rock and roll and its various French imitations. Through the 1950s jazz had retained much of its interwar stature as a broadly popular genre. Or at least this was the case with certain subgenres of jazz: even as bebop, for instance, clearly staked out a position on the high modernist side of the divide between art and mass culture (expressed in the association of bebop with Left Bank existentialism prevalent in the 1940s and '50s), older prewar styles—in particular that of the New Orleans revival—remained central to postwar French youth culture. This subgenre remained at the center of moral panics that various acts of youthful rebellion provoked in the fifteen-odd years after the Second World War. When a Sidney Bechet concert at the Olympia in Paris in 1955 degenerated into a riot, as would-be attendees were turned away at the door, commentators blamed the unrest on a "jazz disease" that had stricken France.[83] However, rock and roll, once it arrived in France around 1960, dislodged the New Orleans style—or any kind of jazz for that matter—as the musical focus for French youth culture. The agitation that Sidney Bechet once occasioned now coalesced around the likes of Johnny Hallyday, Eddy Mitchell, and other pop idols. As Ludovic Tournès notes, "From now on it was rock and no longer jazz that symbolized the violence of a fraction of the adolescent population," with the actions of the latter "clearly surpassing those of the most excited jazz fans."[84] The confluence of these two factors—critics' efforts to raise the profile of jazz on the one hand, and the music's ouster from a central position within youth culture on the other—marked the beginning of its journey from popular entertainment to elite subculture.

At the turn of the 1960s, then, jazz in France thus found itself entering a strange no-man's-land, not quite popular music, but not quite recognized as high art. In this respect its situation in France was not dissimilar from that in the United States, where its commercial viability was ebbing away in the face of rock and roll, but musicians had not yet found alternative forms of institutional support.[85] A key difference, however, lay in the fact that jazz fell outside the purview of the national patrimony in France, which rendered its position all the more tenuous. This explains Hodeir's hostility both to free jazz and to the claims that left-leaning critics had made on its behalf. With French jazz's diminishing fan base, the continued viability of the community was increasingly dependent on the success of arguments that held jazz to be an art form that transcended both national and ethnic divisions. But insofar as partisans of the new thing presented jazz in general and free jazz in particular as expressions of a specifically African-American (or anticolonial) attitude, they threw into doubt the capacity of French listeners to comprehend the genre adequately. At the same time, they jeopardized jazz's bid for legitimation. The cultural particularism imputed to free jazz contradicted the universalist image that Hodeir had worked so hard to establish. There is thus an element of pathos, of youthful ambition thwarted, that haunts Hodeir's exchange with Comolli: "In our youth, you see, we thought that the value of jazz was precisely that it was not limited to being a manifestation of the ghetto, that it was on the way to becoming a great universal art. That even seemed to us its most distinguished characteristic."[86] Its progress toward the domain of legitimate culture temporarily impeded, the prospects that jazz might win recognition as high culture appeared to have been further endangered by the identity politics of the new thing.

FREE JAZZ BLACK POWER

As the foregoing indicates, the repudiation of universalist values that critics like Comolli read into free jazz explains in part the hostility it generated among older critics. Ironically, this particularism proved equally troublesome for advocates of the new thing. For younger jazz critics, the most fervent champions of the new thing, the identity politics of the movement presented a different set of challenges. In constructing an image of the African-American jazz musician that accorded with their political prerogatives, this younger cohort painted themselves into a corner. When Yves Buin contended that negative reactions to Ayler's performance at the Paris Jazz Festival in 1966 were a sign of critics' inability to recognize that the music "has been taken away from *us*" (emphasis in original), he peremptorily condemned the music's exponents as well as its antagonists to incomprehension.[87] Not only did such a stance call into question whether French critics and fans were capable of understanding the new thing, it suggested that attempts to do so might constitute an illegitimate act of cultural expropriation. To avoid this, it was incumbent upon advocates to downplay the music's perceived association with black cultural nationalism, disassociating it from forms of revolt that were tied to a specifically African-American subject position.

One solution to this problem had already been advanced, if only implicitly, in Comolli's "Voyage au bout de la New Thing." Recall that Comolli's essay read the political import of the movement through a double prism, as a revolt against American society as well as a moment in the broader transnational process of decolonization. This inflation of the ideological import of free jazz was further fleshed out in a book Comolli coauthored with Philippe Carles, whose title, *Free Jazz Black Power,* announced in no uncertain terms the homology their work explored.[88]

Much had changed in the five years between the appearance of Comolli's initial essay in 1966 and the book's publication in 1971. The events of 1968 had raised hopes that revolution was imminent in the capitalist West, which intensified efforts to identify a suitable "subject of history" who could bring the revolutionary moment to pass. In the United States, the proliferation of various black power organizations—most notably the Black Panther Party—in the intervening years provided Carles and Comolli with an alternative model of African-American political radicalism, one that fit better with their anticolonialist reading of the new thing. The growing split between "cultural nationalists" like Baraka and "revolutionary nationalists" like the Black Panthers offered Carles and Comolli a way of distinguishing their critique of the political economy of jazz from Baraka's. Although they credited Baraka for having pointed the way past the "aesthetic" approach that had hitherto dominated (white) American and European readings of jazz, they contended that his work failed to follow its implications to their logical conclusion: "For all that we owe to the theses of [Baraka], we are compelled to distance ourselves from him on an important point. The totality of the facts and the determinations that he has noted *introduces* the possibility of a *political reading* of jazz's evolution and its forms. [Baraka] refrains from undertaking such a reading."[89] The fact that Baraka was too caught up in the struggles on the ground in the United States meant that he was unable, in their opinion, to achieve the "objective" view available to outsiders (such as themselves). As a result, Baraka failed to connect the conflict to the transnational struggle against imperialism.[90]

In this reading, the valorization of black identity undertaken by cultural nationalists like Baraka was important only as a stage in a broader process of political awakening: "Black nationalism ('Black Beauty,' 'Black Power,' etc.) appears as a necessary moment in the development of the struggles of the black community in America."[91] For Carles and Comolli, the variety of political opinion within the African-American community was not a function of its immanent diversity; rather, they chalked this up to the fact that certain elements within the black community, in particular the black middle classes, were victims of false consciousness. In creating an evolutionary ladder of political awareness—with integrationism at the lowest rung, passing through cultural nationalism, all the way up to revolutionary nationalism—Carles and Comolli recast diversity of political opinion in quasi-teleological terms, as stages in a journey toward ideological self-realization. Unlike Baraka, whose conception of a collective African-American identity during the mid- and late 1960s was rooted in what Eric Porter has called "a biological and ontological conception of blackness,"[92] Carles and Comolli imagine the fusion of African-Americans into a single political bloc in Marxian terms: it is not to be achieved through the collective recognition of "blackness" but through the collective recognition of exploitation—exploitation that had been enabled and perpetuated by the American racial hierarchy. Carles and Comolli thus subsume race into class, which ultimately allows the monolithic black identity they constructed to be absorbed within an even broader identity, that of the colonized subject: "We consider that this contradiction between the value systems of whites and blacks, at work in the colonization of jazz and the resistance to this colonization, is but one moment in the *principal contradiction* between the colonizers and the colonized, exploiters and exploited: between capitalism and its victims."[93]

A parallel situation obtained in the jazz world. By aestheticizing jazz, stripping the music of its latent social content, European critics, along with their American counterparts, had long participated in the "colonization" of jazz by white middlebrow culture. To fight this cultural colonization it was vital that committed critics like Carles and Comolli promote a correct hearing of jazz, one that restored the music's "proper" function as a weapon of ideological struggle. But if *Free Jazz Black Power* can be seen as an attempt to expiate the sins of French jazz criticism, it may no less be seen as a sublimated response to the French experience of decolonization. As noted above, Comolli's substitution of colonialism for race as the optic through which free jazz was best understood was likely a function of his position as a French intellectual writing in the wake of the Algerian War. Jazz functioned as a surrogate by means of which the more immediate, local questions raised by decolonization could be negotiated. Authors who have written on jazz's reception in France (especially those authors focusing on the period following World War II) have made similar claims regarding the music's utility for addressing localized concerns, contending that jazz has often functioned as a space where issues of race and cultural difference could be broached. According to this interpretation, knowledge of American race relations, made possible through critics' contact with jazz musicians, afforded French listeners a venue where they could confront certain social dynamics that were perhaps less pronounced (but still present) in French society, and that would come to the fore in the wake of decolonization. "Enthusiasm for jazz," Tournès writes, "constituted for young readers a footbridge—certainly modest but nonetheless real—towards a recognition of this problem [i.e., racism], as much in the United States as in France."[94]

It is important, however, not to overstate the impact jazz had in alerting French fans to the growing problem of racism in their native country. One may just as easily read the fascination with racial politics of free jazz as a form of displacement, whereby critical reflection upon French race relations was deflected in favor of a more distant—and correspondingly less fraught—parallel. Indeed, considering the importance that Carles and Comolli attached to the colonizer/colonized dialectic as an organizing principle in their text, it is surprising that there are so few direct references in their text to recent French history, or to the situation of minority groups in France. While taking a stand against colonialism as a general phenomenon, they have little to say about French colonialism or neo-colonialism. The same evasiveness can be seen in the French reception of free jazz in general, where denunciations of American racism are seldom accompanied by critical reflection upon analogous conditions closer to home. But as the ranks of *travailleurs immigrés* from France's former colonies swelled during the 1960s, such parallels became increasingly apparent, at least to African-American expatriates. Frank Wright's memories of his time in France are peopled by images of "police patrolling the streets and asking for identification, stopping mostly Algerians and Africans," and "blacks sweeping the streets after the market at Belleville."[95] Although acutely sensitive to the social and economic marginalization of sub-Saharan Africans (as witnessed by Wright's allusion to the stereotyped figure of the African street sweeper), the violence to which Algerian immigrants in particular were subject both during and after the Algerian War of Independence called to mind the brutality that expatriate artists had left behind in the United States. "One afternoon I attended a demonstration for the Algerian people in the square in front of the Sorbonne," Angela Davis recalled, describing her year as an exchange student in Paris. "When the *flics* broke it up with their high-power hoses, they were as vicious as the redneck cops in Birmingham who met the Freedom Riders with their dogs and hoses."[96] The parallel that Davis and others drew between French and American racism toward minority groups found little echo in the jazz press from this period. Occasionally allusions to racial antagonisms in France did crop up, as when one author offhandedly described the African-American subject as being "as alienated as an Algerian in Paris,"[97] or when satirist Delfeil de Ton sardonically explained that the French welcomed African-American artists so warmly because they "already had Arabs to despise."[98] The effect of such remarks is a jolt of recognition, as the repressed subtext of the colonizer/colonized dialectic is disclosed.

FREE JAZZ À LA FRANÇAISE

Few were as sensitive to the problems posed by the cultural politics of free jazz as the musicians who took up the style, a group that included Tusques, Vitet, Jacques Thollot, Michel Portal, Beb Guérin, and Barney Wilen. While the widespread perception of the music's inextricable connection to black political radicalism (and thus to the specificity of the African-American experience) may have threatened to mark it as something irrelevant or incomprehensible to French audiences, for performers it presented a more pressing challenge. What was at stake was not just symbolic questions of identity and difference, however charged these may have been, but the legitimacy of musicians' professional activities. To ignore the new style was to court being labeled as passé. France's position on the periphery of an American-centered jazz world meant that local musicians had long been obliged to combat the perception that they were a step or two behind their American counterparts. In the face of audiences who tended to prefer the "authentic" jazz of African-American performers, there was a strong incentive to avoid being seen as provincial or dated. But adopting the style presented its own risks, leaving musicians open to the charge of being overly beholden to fashion. More significantly, the fraught political climate surrounding free jazz's reception exposed musicians to the accusation that they were perpetuating the white (European) colonization of African-American expressive culture. These issues were further complicated by the sizable number of American musicians entering France during the late 1960s. The presence of individuals like Alan Silva and Sunny Murray offered both artistic stimulation to their French colleagues and, at times, a potential source of employment, as headlining artists looked to local musicians to fill out ensembles. Yet expatriates could just as easily represent a source of competition for limited performance opportunities, even during the post-'68 boom years of free jazz.

It would take some time for these issues to come into focus for French practitioners of free jazz. Indeed, the most striking thing about their initial forays in the style—especially in light of the intense politicization of the discourse surrounding free jazz after 1966—was its "formalist" character. Prior to 1968 members of the emerging French free jazz scene played a double game. At the same time as they declared their allegiance to figures like Dolphy, Coleman, or Taylor, they expressed an unabashed enthusiasm for contemporary classical music. Composers such as Schoenberg, Varèse, Webern, Boulez, and Stockhausen were consistently identified as points of reference for the new jazz, just as representatives of the *nouveau roman* (e.g., Michel Butor and Alain Robbe-Grillet) and new wave cinema (e.g., Alain Resnais) were cited as a way of situating their work within the matrix of postwar French modernism.[99] In one interview Bernard Vitet remarked that were he to have more free time, he would listen to more modern music, "especially that which derives from serial music, that is Schoenberg; for instance, I very much enjoy composers like Ferrari or Varèse."[100] Such attestations of high modernist taste were the norm during the mid-1960s and point to an alternative strategy to legitimation than that pursued by postwar critics like Hodeir and Malson. Instead of asserting that they partook of a universal art form, French free jazz musicians staked their legitimacy on a claim to timeliness rather than timelessness. Just as importantly, the invocation of contemporary music indicated that, at least at this point, French practitioners of free jazz understood it to be a means by which they could call into question the genre's conventions. Its ruptures were still primarily located in the formal rather than the social field.

Yet allusions to serial and postserial music proved to be more than just a matter of dressing up jazz in more respectable clothing. They reflected a real engagement on the part of musicians like Tusques and Thollot with the techniques of contemporary classical music. A crucial factor in this engagement was the interpenetration of jazz and new music communities in France. A handful of performers (most notably Jean-François Jenny-Clark and Michel Portal) circulated between the two genres, successfully pursuing careers in both. A graduate of the Paris Conservatoire, Portal in particular became renowned for his "polyvalence," working as a studio musician for *variétés* artists like Claude Nougara and Sheila, performing as a soloist with the Orchestre de Paris, and playing contemporary music as part of Diego Masson's ensemble Musique vivante.[101] His movement across generic boundaries culminated in New Phonic Art, the free improvisation group he formed in 1969 with composer-instrumentalists Vinko Globokar, Carlos Roques-Alsina, and Jean-Pierre Drouet. Jenny-Clark also kept a foot in both musical universes, performing with the Musique vivante ensemble in addition to various jazz groups (he had been part of the rhythm section that backed Don Cherry during his 1965 visit to Paris).[102] The interest that a number of contemporary composers evinced toward avant-garde jazz provided another bridge between the two communities. On a few occasions this led to collaborations, as when *musique concrète* composer Bernard Parmegiani enlisted improvisers Bernard Vitet, Gilbert Rovere, Charles Saudrais, and Jean-Louis Chautemps for his 1966 tape piece *Jazzex*.

The influence that contemporary classical music exercised on French free jazz was apparent in the music Tusques composed for the October 1965 recording sessions for *Free Jazz*. As Vincent Cotro has shown, the introduction to "Souvenirs de l'oiseau" (Memories of Bird) is twelve-tone in design, while its phrasing and rhythm bears the imprint of Charlie Parker (as indicated by the song's title, an homage to Parker's nickname, Yardbird). Tusques' use of the twelve-tone technique was unorthodox. Instead of subjecting a single row to various transformations (inversion, retrograde, retrograde inversion), Tusques strings together five unrelated series in the theme of "Souvenirs." Clearly the aim is not to use the row to provide harmonic or motivic coherence. Rather, it performs the more basic task of suppressing a sense of tonality. But even this function is not always evident in Tusques' theme, whose first two phrases present short melodic figures, each containing seven discrete pitches that outline a fairly straightforward harmonic progression, with the remaining notes of the aggregate filled in afterward. Other tracks on the record betray a similar concern with the harmonic and technical means of European musical modernism. The second take of "Description automatique d'un paysage désolé," for instance, opens with a succession of harmonies (played on trumpet, saxophone, and bass clarinet) that also run through the chromatic aggregate, at the same time as they eschew the standard repertoire of jazz harmonies in favor of tonally indeterminate trichords.

The modernist influence is less apparent in the improvisations that follow the themes. In an effort to find a suitable frame for the improvisational aspect of the new jazz, Tusques looked to an altogether different kind of modernism. In an interview with Yves Buin published shortly after the release of *Free Jazz*, Tusques described free improvisation as being analogous to the surrealist practice of automatic writing. The titles of a number of Tusques' compositions underlined this connection, as was the case with "Description automatique d'un paysage désolé." For Tusques free improvisation, like automatic writing, allowed one to tap into the unconscious. Both practices brought out into the open repressed impulses and seemingly illogical associations. Free improvisation thus complemented the constructivism of Tusques' themes, providing an "irrational" counterweight to the "rationality" of the twelve-tone technique. More significantly, both automatic writing and improvisation provided access to an alterity that lies dormant within the self, an idea that Buin elaborates when he says that the unconscious is a way of seeing that which lies "beyond" *(au-delà)*.[103] Given that part of jazz's appeal to French audiences rested in its ability to embody otherness, the invocation of the unconscious by Tusques enabled the difference usually identified with African-American subjectivity to be relocated, such that it was now located within the psyche of French musicians.

As ingenious as it may have been, this rhetorical move could not fully dispel the belief that the music produced by Tusques and company was not adequate to the expressive or ideological demands of the new thing. As one reviewer noted, the performances captured on *Free Jazz* seemed "cold" compared to its American models: "The music of François Tusques is not particularly impassioned, or even jubilant. Our world isn't particularly jubilant, admittedly, but it is impassioned. One would like a bit more of the fervor of Jackie McLean, Booker Ervin, John Coltrane, a little more of the fury of Mingus."[104] Compounding the charge of intellectualism were doubts about the capacity of French musicians to tap into the sort of collective experience that African-American musicians purportedly drew upon in their performances. Free improvisation may have let one delve the recesses of the unconscious, but with the political turn of French jazz criticism, it was unclear whether the recesses opened up to French musicians contained the angst, alienation, or anger that was deemed essential to "authentic" free jazz. Such doubts were voiced by Buin himself a year after his interview with Tusques, in a polemic defending Ayler's music against his detractors. For Buin, "naked violence" lay at the emotional core of free jazz. The root cause of this violence was in Buin's opinion self-evident, a product of the racism African-American musicians endured at the hands of white America. But in an intriguing twist, he added that a similar experience of violence must likewise rest at the heart of French free jazz: "It is still the case that free jazz in France is born of violence as well: our violence, as unformulated and unformulatable as it may be."[105] If French musicians successfully perform free jazz, then there must exist *some* source of righteous anger that they are tapping into.

But what Buin offers with one hand he takes away with the other. Almost as soon as he proposes that French free jazz is founded upon its own unique experience of injustice, he puzzles over what precisely this might consist of: "What will this free jazz nourish itself on? I don't know. . . . I don't know of a disgrace as terrible as that of racism. What could it be? The crisis in the market for Frigidaires? Brigitte Bardot holding court at one of Tixier-Vignancour's meetings? The strike at Régie des tabacs? How should I know?"[106] Buin's inability to identify a social injustice that could adequately motivate the sort of rage that free jazz allegedly required cast doubt on whether the music might legitimately be played by French musicians. Working on the assumption that postwar prosperity had dissipated any justified sense of grievance among French citizens, practitioners of free jazz were condemned to emotional inauthenticity. Precisely the same conditions that made (American) free jazz so attractive to a certain segment of the French intellectual left—the perceived absence of a revolutionary subjectivity within French society—rebounded negatively on musicians like Tusques and Vitet.

With the politicization of jazz criticism, pressure was placed on French practitioners to justify their adoption of the style in social terms rather than according to the exigencies of musical modernism. Interviews with performers during these years bear witness to a sense of unease regarding their right to play the music. Portal articulated a number of these anxieties in an interview conducted just prior to May '68. A principle concern was whether European musicians such as himself, despite their solidarity with African-American struggles, were contributing to the sort of colonization of jazz that the new thing ostensibly opposed: "The trouble for us is that we are playing a stolen music. It's a black music, born in a specific context, in reaction against a specific political and ideological situation. A context and situation that isn't our own."[107] Exacerbating this problem was the fact that widespread social unrest had been largely absent in France ever since the end of the Algerian War. Portal was not persuaded that French musicians operated within a social milieu conducive to the sense of outrage the music required: "Black people have something that crystallizes everything that they rebel against: the white American and his culture. Oh, of course there are causes for revolt here, but everything is vague. . . . Of course you can be against Vietnam, but if you are against it then it's no good staying in France, you need to go there yourself."[108]

Portal's comments regarding opposition to the Vietnam War are telling, insofar as the conflict had served as the pretext for one of the few attempts by French free musicians to present their music in a political setting prior to 1968. On 29 March 1966 a concert was held at the Mutualité in Paris, organized by the Comité d'action du spectacle to rally opposition to the war in Vietnam. In addition to an ensemble led by Tusques, the concert featured celebrities such as the protest singer Colette Magny and *variétés* artist Claude Nougara. Notably absent from the event was a contingent of American musicians that were originally slated to participate. These musicians had decided against taking part at the last minute, out of fear that their visas would be revoked by American authorities for appearing in an event protesting (as one organizer explained) "the policy of American interference in the development of the countries of Latin America, Africa, and Southeast Asia." For certain commentators, the decision of American musicians to withdraw from the concert pointed to a principal flaw in the entire undertaking. Taking a stand against U.S. foreign policy had real repercussions for American musicians, whereas such a gesture remained purely symbolic for their French peers: "It's one thing to express solidarity with just causes . . . , another to translate this solidarity into a spectacle (especially a musical one), and another thing to want to join together, in an imaginary synthesis, a political and an aesthetic action."[109] The attempts of French free musicians to align themselves with American political movements only reinforced the perception that their appropriation of free jazz was illegitimate. Not only had the music been imported, but so too had been the injustice against which it protested.

Given this context, the dramatic revival of political dissent in the wake of May–June 1968 appeared to provide precisely the sort of social grounding that French free jazz had seemingly lacked. As the state clamped down on unrest in the post-May period, the notion that French free jazz musicians lacked a legitimate source of grievance lost some (though hardly all) of its rhetorical force. The government's refusal to allow Clifford Thornton entry into the country in 1971 brought the crackdown on dissent close to home for the jazz community.[110] So too did the arrest of Michel Le Bris, who had assumed the editorship of the banned Maoist newspaper *La Cause du peuple* after having been forced out of the same position at *Jazz Hot*. (His arrest led Tusques to title one of the compositions "Liberez Michel Le Bris.") Meanwhile, opportunities for engaged musicians to intervene in social struggles—by performing in factories, at benefit concerts, or at political rallies—became more frequent in the late 1960s and early 1970s.[111] In the charged political atmosphere of *l'après-mai,* a good deal of the anxiety that had accompanied French musicians' earlier forays into free jazz faded. The linkage of free jazz and politics could now be made in a more persuasive manner.

But even if the emergence of radical social movements after 1968 made such expressions of political solidarity more credible than had previously been the case, the problem of musicians' relation to the communities whose interests they sought to serve was scarcely resolved. African-American practitioners of avant-garde jazz musicians were, after all, members of the group whose oppression their music was seen as protesting against; rightly or wrongly, French observers believed they had an inalienable stake in the civil rights and black power movements. The same could not be said of French musicians. Their relationship to the French working class—whose grassroots militancy in 1968 had rekindled hopes that it might act as a homegrown revolutionary subject—was less straightforward. Were musicians themselves workers, the only difference being that they were employed in show business? Or were they entertainers, standing outside the labor-capital dynamic? The musicians' strike of May–June 68 had already shown how intractable such questions could be. As a result of the ambiguity surrounding the social status of the musician, a degree of overcompensation is evident in the political positions that musicians espoused after 1968. This is not to question the good faith that lay behind musicians' assertions of political commitment, but simply to point out that such pronouncements were often overdetermined, impelled by a need to demonstrate an engagement that could not be presumed on the basis of one's identity. A comment of Portal's gives some sense of the lingering doubts felt by French free musicians: "I don't circulate among the outsiders of 'free' without reservations. My grandfather was killed on a picket line by the fascists in Spain. When I climb on the stage in order to 'squawk,' I happen to think of him."[112] That Portal felt obliged to articulate both the injustice that gives his music its emotional intensity and its connection to his own life experience bespeaks the uncertain legitimacy of French free jazz. The political commitment that was automatically (indeed, stereotypically) assumed of African-American free jazz musicians had to be spelled out in no uncertain terms by their French peers.

INTERCOMMUNAL MUSIC

Undoubtedly the most politically outspoken member of the French free jazz community was François Tusques. Having participated in the Comité action musique during May '68, in subsequent years he espoused a political ideology heavily influenced by Maoism on the one hand and the Black Panther Party on the other. This sharpening of his political sensibilities was made clear in a series of recordings released in 1971–72. These included two albums of solo piano music, *Piano Dazibao*

(1970) and *Dazibao no. 2* (1971), and the record *Intercommunal Music* (1971), on which Tusques led a group featuring Alan Silva on cello, Beb Guérin and Bob Reid on bass, Steve Potts on alto saxophone, Sunny Murray on drums, Alan Shorter on trumpet, and Louis Armfield on percussion. The titles of these albums testified to Tusques' ideological evolution. *Dazibao* refers to a genre of political poster developed in China at the turn of the century and that had played a key role in the Chinese Cultural Revolution. As for *Intercommunal Music,* its title alludes to the principle of interethnic solidarity formulated by Huey P. Newton, a founder of the Black Panther Party. In an interview Tusques explained the notion: "The United States is composed of minorities that live side by side: blacks, Puerto Ricans, Chinese, Poles . . . and Huey says that it is necessary to unite these different communities. That's what intercommunalism is: that each and every community defends itself against the bourgeoisie."[113] But if references to Chinese political posters and the policies of the Black Panther Party risked being lost on the average listener, the titles of individual pieces clarified Tusques' politics. The track listings on *Piano Dazibao* are typically blunt. Titles like "Que 100 fleurs s'epanouissent" (Let a hundred flowers bloom), "La révolution est une transfusion sanguine" (The revolution is a transfusion of blood), and "La bourgeoisie périra noyée dans les eaux glacées du calcul égoiste" (The bourgeoisie will perish drowned in the icy waters of selfish calculation) indicate in no uncertain terms where Tusques' allegiances lay.

Far from being empty rhetoric, or something Tusques pasted onto his music after the fact, such textual cues presented a solution to a problem that his political turn had raised. Although critical discourse had solidified public perceptions that free jazz was broadly synonymous with protest, it was unclear how it might go beyond such generalized connotations to express more specific ideals. This problem was amplified by the modernist heritage with which Tusques and his cohort had affiliated their music in the mid-1960s. As was the case with contemporary music, the decision to abjure convention condemned the new jazz to a certain degree of semiotic indeterminacy. Yet the stance adopted by Tusques required precisely the opposite: that music convey a direct and unambiguous ideological message. (As he put it during the course of a roundtable discussion on Ayler's legacy, "Music is nothing other than an instrument! It is used to express something.")[114] Though he would acknowledge on other occasions that things were not so straightforward, that music may indeed possess "relative autonomy," Tusques regarded this as an impediment to be overcome: "It seems to me that musical discourse is not reducible to another form of discourse, which is not to say that it does not belong to a particular ideology; in his intervention in the discussions on literature and art at Yenan, Mao Tse-Tung shows that art belongs to a determinate class, and is dependent upon a distinct political line."[115] Music is no less implicated in politics than any other medium. Yet because it cannot be conflated with forms better equipped to express ideological aims, music proves inadequate as an arm of the class struggle. But rather than abandon his chosen métier, Tusques indicates one way that music's deficiencies as an ideological instrument might be remedied: "The fact that music is irreducible to other kinds of discourse has impelled me to mix it with other 'disciplines,' like theater or film, for instance."[116] Too vague on its own, music had to be wed with other media to guarantee that its message was conveyed.

Tusques' participation in mixed media projects dated as far back as 1967, when he first collaborated with actors in a theater piece based on Lewis Carroll's "The Hunting of the Snark."[117] By the early 1970s this tendency had been transformed from an essentially aesthetic endeavor into a way of specifying the latent political import of music.[118] It is in these terms, as a kind of mixing of media, that the titles to Tusques' pieces should be construed. No less than film or theatrical accompaniments, titles and other framing devices provided a means for honing the inchoate responses of listeners, of narrowing down the multiple and potentially contradictory meanings afforded by free jazz. This is evident on *Intercommunal Music*. Despite the makeshift nature of the recording session—some of the musicians showed up to the studio so late that there was no time for rehearsal, and all the pieces had to be recorded in just one take—a clear narrative arc is traced over the course of the album's two sides.[119] Like *Piano Dazibao*, the track listings for *Intercommunal Music* convey their ideological content unambiguously. The album is composed of three distinct parts (see table 1). Parts I and II are subdivided into a series of shorter sections, giving the whole a suitelike structure. The first side is taken up by a single track, which is divided roughly into two halves: the first section bears the title "Intercommunal music," while the second is titled "Les forces progressistes." Parts II and III fill the second side of the album. The first of these is split into smaller subsections: the track opens with "Les forces réactionnaires," which is followed by "La bourgeoisie périra noyée dans les eaux glacées du calcul égoiste," a reprise of the piece on *Piano Dazibao*. The second part of the triptych is rounded out by a return to the music of the opening, an event underlined by the title of the section: "Intercommunal music!

TABLE I.   TRACK LISTINGS AND TIMINGS FOR *INTERCOMMUNAL MUSIC*

	Track	Title	Timing
Part I	Side 1, Track 1	"Intercommunal music"	0′00″–8′26″
		"Les forces progressistes"	8′26″–18′18″
Part II	Side 2, Track 1	"Les forces réactionnaires"	0′00″–3′44″
		"La bourgeoisie périra …"	3′44″–6′44″
		"Intercommunal music!"	6′44″–12′36″
Part III	Side 2, Track 2	"Portrait d'Erika Huggins"	0′00″–8′32″

[The timings given here differ from those given on the album sleeve.]

L'impérialisme est un tigre en papier." The third and final track on the album, "Portrait d'Erika Huggins," refers to a member of the Black Panther Party who, along with Bobby Seale, was accused of murdering a suspected police informant in New Haven, Connecticut. (Her picture graces the record sleeve, along with a caption by Tusques that reads, "ERIKA, revolutionary, twenty-two years old when this album was re-corded, is the symbol of the forces who will overthrow the 'pigs' who govern the United States at the present moment.")

Already these titles give some sense of the album's "program." By sandwiching elements marked as negative or antagonistic (namely the "bourgeoisie" and "imperialism") between those identified as positive, the track listings create a straightforward narrative, one that stages a conflict that ends with the triumph of the progressive forces over their foes. Mapping the program intimated by the track listings onto the music poses little difficulty, as almost every entity named on the album sleeve finds a corresponding rhythmic, melodic, and/or harmonic figure. Thus the opening of the first side presents a repeated rhythmic motto, presumably the "intercommunal music" of the album's title (example 7). First introduced as a disembodied, metallic sound on one of the basses (probably obtained by bowing beneath the bridge), the motto is picked up by Steve Potts, who intones a repeated $A\flat 4$ to the pattern, above a nimbus of white noise created by the rhythm section. The textural accumulation continues with the entry of Alan Shorter around twenty-five seconds into the performance, playing muted trumpet at unison before taking off the mute to obtain a fuller sound just before the one-minute mark. The sonic and textural progression unfolded over the first minute of the piece contrasts with the lack of development within the motto itself. Despite slight inflections in timing, accent, and pitch, the motto remains essentially unchanged during this time span. While this absence

EXAMPLE 7. François Tusques, "Intercommunal Music," opening rhythmic motto.

of variation or development denies the motto much by way of intrinsic musical meaning, the title that is attached to it makes up for this lack. As the sonic figuration of the "progressive forces," the motto, in its unwavering repetitions, signifies a range of appropriate attributes: commitment, resolve, willfulness, or determination.

The "hermeneutic window" that the title opens for listeners also illuminates other dimensions of the music.[120] Deviations from the A_b4, which occur sparingly at the outset but become more frequent as the music continues (leading ultimately to the motto's dissolution two minutes into the work), assume a more precise meaning in this context. If the motto's incessant repetition is taken to embody determination, then such slips may signal—negatively—the effort required to maintain this resolve. The cacophonous halo emanating from Sunny Murray's cymbals likewise fit into this interpretive matrix, perhaps signifying the kind of resistance that "intercommunal music" must struggle against in order to make itself heard. The point here is not to ascribe a single meaning to the music; rather, it is to show how the correlation of rhythmic motto and verbal cue sets off a chain reaction of sorts, allowing other, unmarked elements to be brought into the widening gyre of signification. In addition, such correspondences change how particular figures are heard. For instance, the motto's rhythm, unremarkable at first blush, acquires greater significance within this programmatic context. The four-square quality of the first half of the pattern, which stresses the first two beats of the measure through a pair of sixteenth-note upbeats, sets in relief the syncopation of its second half. As a result, the attack that "should" fall on the fourth beat of the measure, but which enters a sixteenth too early, juts out from the rest of the motto. This gives the pattern a lunging or thrusting character, which accords well with the affective attributes implied by the title. This characteristic is reinforced when Potts, around 1′25″, begins inserting short rests just before the syncopated attack, setting it off in an exaggerated fashion.

The entry of the "antagonistic" figures in the second track follow the model established by the first. The first 3′45″ of the piece, titled "Les forces réactionnaires," is in some ways more unambiguous in its deployment of conventional markers. *Glissandi* played on cello and musical saw predominate, set against a "free" backdrop provided by the rhythm section. Although the sliding figures played by Tusques (saw) and Silva (cello) eschew tonal centricity or conventional melodic design, they nonetheless manage to evoke familiar referents. Silva's cello lines, for instance, have a strongly mimetic quality, resembling the sound of sobbing or wailing. Tusques' squibs on the musical saw evoke more culturally specific precedents. The combination of the saw's colorless, sine-wave-like timbre and its movement along a fluid pitch continuum makes it sound like a theremin. As such, it calls to mind the associations this instrument has been laden with since its first appearance in a Hollywood film soundtrack. The result of these quotidian and/or culturally bound allusions is to give the music an eerie quality. The import of this overall affect is clarified by the verbal cues provided by the track listing. The "horror movie" music fashioned at the outset of this track is assigned to the "reactionary forces," coloring our perception of the latter accordingly.

In the section that follows—"The bourgeoisie will perish drowned in the icy waters of selfish calculation"—the task of conjuring a similarly sinister atmosphere falls to the piano. Again, conventions associated with film music are marshaled for representational purposes: here it is left-hand octave tremolos, the melodramatic signature of the villainous, that produce a sense of apprehension. The intervallic profile traced by the tremolos also contributes to the uneasy ambiance. Initially the piano plays a pair of falling three-note figures, consisting of a minor second followed by a perfect fifth. The figures exude a minor-mode quality, each outlining ♭6–5–1, at first in an implied F♯ minor, then in C♯ (example 8a). As the music continues, this motif is distilled into a series of alternating minor seconds and tritones (example 8b). The preponderance of intervals traditionally marked as dissonant reinforces the affect evoked by the tremolos. As was the case with "Les forces réactionnaires," a handful of timeworn conventions prove adequate to the demands of signification pressed by the title. Despite the free improvisational context in which they are inserted, with its characteristic absence of harmonic or rhythmic frameworks, such clearly coded elements provide landmarks that assist the listener in navigating the musical program.

With the principal personae introduced by the midpoint of Part II, the stage is set for the dramatic centerpiece of the album, the confrontation of "progressive" and "reactionary" forces. This conflict is engaged at 6′44″, when the saxophone and trumpet (to this point absent from the second track) reenter playing the "Intercommunal" motto. In a way,

EXAMPLE 8A. François Tusques, "La bourgeoisie périra," opening.

EXAMPLE 8B. "La bourgeoisie périra . . . ," continuation.

the reintroduction of the figure reverses the process of dissolution that had taken place in Part I. At first the motto's return is hesitant. But gradually it regains its forcefulness, culminating in the half-tempo statements of the motto around 9′52″. Meanwhile the piano part undergoes its own transformation. While it maintains the tremolo figures of "La bourgeoisie périra" at first, the instrument eventually cedes to the persistent iterations of the "Intercommunal" motto. The turning point in this process comes around 7′45″, when the tremolos, having come to rest on a cluster in the middle range of the piano, gradually change into a series of repeated eighth notes, which in turn mutate into the "Intercommunal" motto (at 9′14″). The triumph of the "progressive" forces assured, the remaining three minutes of the track act as an extended denouement, with statements of the motto in the saxophone and trumpet alternating with spasmodic interjections by the cello and drums. The sense is one of the accumulated energies slowly dissipating, there being little dramatic tension left now that the "progressive" forces have subsumed the piano, the instrument primarily associated with the "reactionary" forces.

It is perhaps to be expected that the program of *Intercommunal Music* follows such a clear trajectory, given the political use value with which Tusques wished to invest his music. Indeed, it might not be too great a stretch to say that the album marries the ideological precepts of socialist realism with the sound world of experimental jazz. But as straightforward as the album's narrative may be, the bond between musical performance and verbal frame is weak, always at risk of coming undone. The album is vulnerable to the sort of criticism habitually leveled at program music: that there is nothing intrinsic to the music that obliges its ascription to the given narrative. One could just as easily switch the personae assigned to the various musical figures so that the piece would tell the story of the triumph of the virtuous bourgeois over the perfidious Bolshevik and the musical drama would still make perfect sense. But then again, it is doubtful that Tusques would have cared whether the program was grounded in the music or not. His embrace of multimedia was nothing if not a frank acknowledgment of music's semiotic limitations.

More problematic is that the program supplied by the track listings fails to account for the entire album. The final track, "Portrait d'Erika Huggins," presents the greatest interpretive stumbling block. The piece is constructed around a repeated riff that is redolent of R&B (example 9). Like the "Intercommunal" motto of Parts I and II, the riff is repeated with little variation, present through virtually all of Part III (a bridge that enters at the 2′15″ mark offers some respite). How should this final track be construed? What relation, if any, does it have to the narrative presented in Parts I and II? One answer to these questions lies in the sense of release the riff furnishes, especially after the discordant free playing of Part II. The buoyant, festive quality of Part III's music, which presents a stark contrast to the first two parts, suggests that the finale might be heard as the celebration that follows the struggle. It represents the joy that greets the final victory of the "progressive" forces over their adversaries. The use of material that so clearly evokes the communal traditions of African-American music making, associated with the collective activities of dance and/or religious celebration, may itself assume a programmatic significance. From this perspective what Tusques and his collaborators play is perhaps not an R&B riff so much as a representation of an R&B riff. The figure acts as the emblem of an entire musical tradition.

A second possibility is to see the final movement as essentially divorced from the program enacted in Parts I and II. From this perspective the resolution of the narrative conflict over the course of the preceding track clears a space for a music absolved of the obligation to signify.

EXAMPLE 9. François Tusques, "Portrait d'Erika Huggins," opening.

EXAMPLE 10. François Tusques, "Portrait d'Erika Huggins," failed trumpet entry.

Supporting the sense that the final track takes leave of the narrative established to this point is the intrusion of various ambient sounds before the music gets started: a drum roll, the sound of the double bass tuning up, and the voice of someone saying "Right on, right on." These sounds constitute an irruption of the real world into the closed, fictive space of the album. They mark a break between the "representational" music that has gone before and the "presentational" music that follows. Further bolstering this interpretation is the fact that we actually hear two takes of "Portrait d'Erika Huggins" over the course of the final track. The first run-through quickly breaks down. Once the riff has been introduced by Tusques on the piano, he is joined by Potts on the saxophone and then by Shorter on trumpet. However, Shorter enters two beats early, causing the ensemble to fall apart soon thereafter (example 10). This disruption proves to be brief: after a little banter, the group recommences, this time successfully. Along with the studio sounds at the overheard beginning of the track, the breakdown of the initial take has the effect of piercing the narrative veil drawn about the work.

That "Portrait d'Erika Huggins" can support both interpretations—that it may be heard as both representational and presentational, as both standing in and outside the musical narrative—has a significance that extends beyond this particular album. As it turns out, the music that formed the basis of "Portrait" acted as a pivot in Tusques' musical development. The year following the release of *Intercommunal Music,* Tusques (along with Vitet, Guérin, Juan Valoaz, and Noël McGhie) collaborated on an album by Colette Magny entitled *Répression* (1972). While the second side features two chansons sung by Magny, along with a composition by bassist Barre Phillips, the first side of the album is taken up by a nineteen-minute jazz "suite" entitled "Oink Oink." Reminiscent of precedents like Max Roach's *Freedom Now Suite*, "Oink Oink" consists of a series of short pieces composed by Tusques over which Magny recites fragmentary statements culled from the speeches and writings of various leaders of the Black Panther Party. Particularly notable is that the music that makes up the first of the four "movements" of the suite, "Babylone USA," essentially recycles "Portrait d'Erika Huggins." Like its precursor, the piece is based largely on the riff shown in example 10. But the manner in which this riff is presented is very different. The loose, chaotic feel of "Portrait" is gone. There is no improvisation, no halos of white noise emanating from the rhythm section, no studio banter, and nothing like the collapse that prompted the repeated takes heard in "Portrait." The riff may be the same, but it is stripped bare of the transgressive qualities of free jazz. Absent as well are the programmatic implications of *Intercommunal Music*. Although the employment of an R&B-influenced riff in "Oink Oink" is fitting given the subject matter of Magny's recitation, it does not serve the same kind of illustrative function as was the case in *Intercommunal Music*.

The shift in stylistic priorities that *Repression* marks—away from representational music on the one hand and free styles on the other—continued in Tusques' subsequent endeavors. Over the next few years he devoted most of his energies to an ensemble called the Intercommunal Free Dance Music Orchestra, made up of musicians from France's various regional, immigrant, and minority communities. Among the group's founding members were the Algerian-born drummer Guem, the Togan trombonist Adolf Winkler, the Occitan trumpeter Michel Marre, and the Guinean saxophonist Jo Maka. In terms of its makeup the ensemble realized the ideals glorified in *Intercommunal Music,* putting into practice that which was only represented (via musical programs, titles, and liner notes) in Tusques' earlier work. The same may be said of the group's music, an amalgam of the various traditions from which its members hailed. To be sure, the changing social context in France played a role in this aesthetic shift, from the embrace of intercommunalism at an ideological level to its realization at a practical, musical level. As ethnic diversity became an increasingly visible aspect of everyday life in France, reference to American racial dynamics was no longer de rigueur. The kind of interethnic problems that had once seemed distant from the French experience became less so as the country's demographic profile evolved. Telling in this regard is a 1974 interview in which Tusques once again defines the term *intercommunal,* but no longer with reference to the United States: "Intercommunal: bringing together all the communities. . . . For example, there are in France several communities of workers: North Africans, Portuguese, Pakistanis, etc."[121] Another factor in Tusques' turn away from free jazz was a desire to address audiences in a more direct fashion. One sign of this was the inclusion of the word *dance* in the name of his new ensemble. Tusques explained in this connection an epiphany he had while watching a rock concert some years before: "There was a pop group that made people dance, and the relations that existed between this group and the audience seemed to me much more important than what we were doing."[122] As free jazz's failure to mobilize a mass audience became apparent, the promise of popular music as a medium for political agitation became more difficult to resist.

Tusques' turn away from free jazz in the early 1970s was part of a broader evolution in the musical field. As early as 1971 certain critics were arguing that the genre's moment had passed. Writing in the underground magazine *Actuel* in September of that year, Paul Alessandrini observed that "free jazz has lost its power to provoke and as a result some of its interest. We have come to the hour of its ebbing, the hour of reassessment."[123] To this Gerard Terronès, writing in *Jazz-Hot,* added that "both young and old musicians seem to be moving toward a more structured music and a less seething language than in the past."[124] As Terronès's comment makes clear, this change in atmosphere was due in part to changes within the jazz community itself. The widening stylistic horizons of many practitioners eroded the distinctive profile that free jazz once possessed within the public imagination. The declining stature of free jazz in public discourse also owed something to the belated arrival of the counterculture in France, which, once it became established in the early seventies, ate into the fan base for avant-garde jazz. Viewed from this angle, the import of the Actuel festival in Amougies was equivocal. It may very well have marked the high point of the new thing's public exposure, as jazz musicians shared equal billing with rock groups. But it also marked the moment when the counterculture, for so long the object of rumors from abroad, finally arrived in francophone Europe. From this point on avant-garde jazz would have to vie with *la pop' music* as the primary vehicle for the expression of cultural resistance.

Concomitant with these changes in the musical landscape were changes in the critical reception of free jazz. Although macrosocial issues such as identity and ideology remained central to much writing on free jazz, microsocial questions of interpersonal interaction and group dynamics claimed an increasing share of critical attention. This tendency was most pronounced in the work of sociologist Alfred Willener, who in his 1970 book *L'Image-action de la société* would treat free jazz as a symptom of a broader transformation, one that signaled the transition from traditional, "established" societies (in which preexisting institutions and codes constrained social action) to "nonestablished" societies (in which codes are invented in a spontaneous or ad hoc fashion).[125] Within this schema, free jazz functioned as a forerunner to the "new culture" that was taking shape insofar as it represented the cultural form that had taken the practice of improvisation to its logical extreme. But given that improvisation could be found in other cultural practices, its growing prominence in critical discourse did not translate into lasting interest in free jazz. Indeed, the opposite appears to be the case. Significantly enough, in Willener's subsequent book, *Musique et vie quotidienne* (1973), free jazz figured alongside avant-garde classical music, rock, and live electronic music as but one setting in which the liberatory power of free improvisation might be experienced.[126] As counterintuitive as it may seem, the triumph of improvisation in both theory and practice went hand in hand with the decline of interest in free jazz.

Ultimately, it may have been the loss of another source of free jazz's singularity that contributed most to its decline in the public sphere. Though the radicalization of students and intellectuals brought about by the May '68 uprising may have sparked a temporary surge of interest in the style, in the long run the rebirth of social activism in France after 1968 meant that the void the African-American subject once occupied in the French imagination had, in a sense, ceased to exist. Intellectuals no longer had to look abroad to find symbolic forms adequate to their political commitments. Perhaps the most pronounced manifestation of this turn can be seen in the unusual career of critic Michel Le Bris. One of the most vocal partisans of free jazz in the late 1960s, in December 1969 he was forced out of his position as editor of *Jazz-Hot* on account of his role in politicizing the magazine's coverage of contemporary jazz.[127] However, his forced resignation from *Jazz-Hot* gave Le Bris the opportunity to make the transition from the realm of cultural politics to that of politics pure and simple. In spring 1970 he became editor of *La Cause du peuple* (see chapter 2), whose previous editor, Jean-Pierre Le Dantec, had been arrested by French authorities on charges of inciting violence. (Le Bris would be arrested on similar charges shortly after taking over the magazine's editorship, leading to his replacement by Jean-Paul Sartre.)[128] Although the trajectory pursued by Le Bris was extreme, it was nonetheless emblematic of the changing field of political possibility for members of the French intellectual left.

Le Bris was not alone in turning his attention away from African-American struggles to France's own internal political upheavals. With the advent of the new social movements of the 1970s—the feminist, regionalist, and immigrant rights movements—a variety of social groups imposed themselves on the political stage, groups that had hitherto been excluded or disregarded as agents of radical social change. Where candidates for the role of revolutionary subject had once been lacking in France, there was now a surfeit, obviating the need to look elsewhere for proxies. In particular, the advent of social movements seeking to protect the rights and interests of both regional minorities and immigrant workers in the post-'68 period led to a heightened interest in the cultural and musical traditions of these communities.[129] For French jazz musicians, this development translated into an alternative set of musical identities that they could reclaim and make their own. For some, it was regional folk traditions then in the process of being revived that became the new wellspring of musical inspiration; such was the case for Michel Portal and the groups comprising the Association à la recherche d'un folklore imaginaire (ARFI).[130] Others, like Tusques and his Intercommunal Free Dance Music Orchestra, turned to the musical traditions of France's various immigrant communities for inspiration. Neither of these tendencies—the embrace of regional folk traditions on the one hand, or what would later come to be known as "world music" on the other—may be separated from the growing force assumed by identity politics within French society itself. In this regard, the changing sociocultural context of the 1970s did not defuse the problematic that free jazz had brought into focus as much as displace it. As free jazz receded in the French cultural landscape, the dynamic governing its reception persisted—a dynamic that set republican ideals of universality and social integration against postcolonial realities of cultural difference. The threat and promise once identified in free jazz would henceforth be displaced onto other musical genres—rock, folk, rap, and raï—and onto other others.

CHAPTER 4

La Cause du Pop

In France, pop equals helmets, billy clubs, cops, iron bars,
riot, repression, free concerts. The music oftentimes disappears behind the social phenomenon. Nothing surprising
about that. Since May '68 the youth movement has been
severely repressed, militants jailed, political actions smashed
or by necessity cloaked in secrecy. Outside the factory or
workplace, youth has but one shared place of its own where
it can gather: the rock concert.

—*Actuel,* "Free, pop et politique"

In December 1969 a new publication, *L'Idiot international,* went on
sale across France. The journal had been conceived as a platform that
would speak to the entire ideological spectrum of the French far left, in
contrast to the factionalized readership of party organs like *La Cause
du peuple, Rouge,* and *L'Humanité rouge.*[1] In addition, the journal en-
deavored to attract readers outside the ranks of committed militants,
among those curious about the left-wing groups to which May '68 had
given birth. The contents of *L'Idiot* reflected its ambitions. Alongside
pieces addressing the standard concerns of the extreme left—class conflict, the role of youth in the revolution, the exploitation of immigrant
workers, American imperialism abroad—were those tackling issues that
to date had received scant attention in Maoist or Trotskyist discourse.
Religion, feminism, drugs, psychiatry, and other topics falling outside the
traditional confines of Marxist-Leninist thought were scrutinized, ap-
praised for any utility they might have for the revolutionary project.[2]
This widening of intellectual horizons was itself a symptom of changes
taking place in the outlook of militants. No longer was political conflict
exclusively, obsessively conceived as something that took place in street

demonstrations and factory occupations. Rather, it extended to include the spaces of everyday life.

Among the subjects addressed in the pages of *L'Idiot international* was rock music. The fascination inspired by rock (and by the American counterculture in general) was evident from the first issue, which contained a ten-page insert on the emerging French rock scene.[3] The author of the article, Bruno Queysanne, related how he had been commissioned to write on "pop music and politics" but had been at a loss as to how to proceed.[4] The two dominant interpretations of rock's political significance—as either an expression of youth revolt or a means of recuperating this revolt—were, in Queysanne's opinion, overly "simplistic," failing to account for how different social groups interacted with the music. The same band, even the same song, does not signify the same thing "for a group of young bourgeoisie attending a party, for students in their dorm rooms at the Cité Universitaire, or for workers after eight hours at the factory."[5] To correct the shortcomings that marred journalistic accounts of the counterculture, Queysanne decided to conduct an ethnographic study of the tastes and attitudes of French working-class adolescents. To that end he interviewed a group of four teenagers, just returned from the Amougies festival in Belgium, who discussed the appeal rock held for them.

The resulting dialogue was somewhat meandering, as Queysanne's efforts to nudge the conversation toward the question of rock's political significance encountered little success. On those occasions when he let slip his own opinion on the matter—as when he asked whether rock wasn't just a way of "shunting all the youth . . . off to the side, [in the hope] that they might keep quiet"—Queysanne was unable to elicit much indignation from his interlocutors, or even much of a response at all.[6] Far from expressing outrage, the teenagers he interviewed seemed unconcerned with the idea that rock might be a diversion from social protest. One of his informants, William, remarked that he and his friends would happily "keep quiet" if left alone to enjoy their music. The problem was that there were always people who were just out to "fuck things up" *(foutre la merde),* caring little for the music. Included in this category, in William's eyes, were militants seeking to politicize rock. Such agitators failed to recognize that youth culture and politics were domains that ought to be kept at arm's length from one another: "Everyone does politics, but when you are on a high like that, it's important not to talk about politics. Nothing but music. You came to listen to music, not to listen to politics." Seconding William's attitude was his friend Alain, who voiced relief that the efforts made by certain festival-goers at Amougies to mix music and politics had proven unsuccessful: "That would have ruined everything. Personally I'm not against politics, but I think it would have ruined everything. There would have been fights, the police would have been obliged to intervene."[7]

If politics, let alone the politics of rock music, were of little interest to Queysanne's informants, other problems confronting French youth culture preoccupied their thoughts. A recurring theme in their conversations with Queysanne was the sense of isolation they felt as part of what was then a miniscule counterculture in France. Throughout the interviews they wistfully imagined what it would be like to live somewhere like Britain, where hippies, they believed, found greater acceptance. William, for one, complained that "in France, people look at us. Because we have long hair."[8] But in Britain things were different: "In England . . . they have hair twice as long as ours, and over there it's fine because the young and the old, they don't look at you."[9] French youth were also to blame for the lack of an indigenous counterculture. According to Queysanne's interlocutors, most French teenagers were obsessed with fashion, image, and other superficialities, making them unreceptive to the antimaterialist ethos of the hippie lifestyle. To the extent that elements of the American counterculture had penetrated *l'Hexagone,* they had done so in a watered-down, commercialized form. But what France lacked in the way of "real" hippies, it made up for in poseurs. Describing the scene at Amougies, Alain remarked that "there were lots of young snobs who consciously dressed up as hippies, consciously because they were going there and you needed to dress like that."[10] Such youth may have appropriated the external signs of the counterculture—long hair, jeans, tattered clothes, beads—but they lacked a true understanding of its significance ("you aren't a hippie as soon as you dress like a hippie," he observed).[11] For the teenagers interviewed in *L'Idiot international,* what counted as a real counterculture was always to be found elsewhere, beyond France's borders.

Queysanne's own reflections on his interviews, appended at the end of the article, adumbrated themes developed in later research on youth subcultures. The conclusions he drew on the role played by style and taste preferences, for instance, calls to mind the work of the Birmingham Centre for Cultural Studies, particularly in his contention that these served as a means of self-recognition.[12] Rock music appealed to William, Alain, and their friends precisely because it gave material form to their subjective experience of alienation: "Why are they excited by pop music? It is, I think, because it is the first thing they have been able to appropriate for themselves. By listening to it, this music that did not at first fit in. Neither real jazz nor the good, traditional chanson of the people, what was this strange, bastard music? It was a bit like them."[13] Elsewhere Queysanne remarks upon the fact that rock offered his interlocutors a form of "subcultural capital" that they could use to distinguish themselves from an imagined mainstream: "Like everything else in bourgeois society, [rock] had itself become a commodity. It was therefore necessary that its adepts distinguish themselves from mere consumers."[14]

But, in the end, Queysanne was less interested in the rock counterculture as an object of impartial study than as a resource to be put to use for political ends. How, exactly, was a self-avowed "revolutionary militant" such as himself to appeal to the vague aspirations of working-class youth? How were forms of symbolic resistance like long hair and rock music to be converted into "real" political resistance? While Queysanne acknowledged that his informants had expressed little interest in politics per se, he refused to conclude from this that they were "depoliticized." Rather, their revolt was intuitive and immediate, taking place on the plane of quotidian experience. Within this context, the standard discourse of *gauchisme* appeared abstract, having little bearing on the concerns of working-class youth. Queysanne's advice for fellow militants was not to dismiss the counterculture, nor to treat it simply as a medium for political propaganda, but to offer youth the same kind of pleasures and satisfactions that rock promised: "To be masters of themselves, this is what [working-class youth] find in pop and what all of society refuse them. That revolutionaries may know how to offer them concretely, in deeds and not only in words, this same right to be oneself."[15] In order to win working-class youth over to the cause of revolution, militants had to transform political activism from something that required self-denial into something that enabled self-realization. Militancy needed to involve not just sacrifice, but gratification.[16]

The profile of the French rock subculture that appeared in the initial issue of *L'Idiot international* was significant less for the conclusions that it drew than for the questions it raised. Queysanne's ethnography offers a snapshot of the varied reactions the American counterculture provoked once hippies, psychedelia, and acid rock had begun to penetrate the French public consciousness at the end of the 1960s. While there was a consensus that the new styles of music coming from Britain and the United States in the latter half of the 1960s were qualitatively different, both aesthetically and sociologically, from the rock and roll that had stirred the passions of French youth earlier in the decade, how members of the nascent genre community conceived of rock diverged from the views articulated by political actors. The curiosity that Queysanne exhibited toward rock prefigured the subsequent evolution of *gauchiste* attitudes toward youth culture, as militants looked for some means to reignite the spark of May '68. For the extreme left, what was at issue was whether rock music and other elements of the counterculture—in particular, rock festivals—could be put to work for political purposes. While there was little doubt that rock's appeal was rooted in its putative opposition to mainstream French society, it remained unclear whether this cultural resistance represented a gateway to political radicalism or a fatal distraction from the cause of class struggle. Rock, in other words, was regarded as both an opportunity and a threat: it was a potential resource that *gauchistes* could utilize in mobilizing individuals, but it was also a potential competitor for the attentions of French youth.

Queysanne's ethnography is equally notable for the rare glimpse it provides into the attitudes of French rock fans of the period. The remarks made by William, Alain, and their peers reveal that the arrival of rock and the Anglo-American counterculture raised an entirely different set of issues for enthusiasts than it did for *gauchiste* militants. For Queysanne's informants, the idea that rock represented a form of symbolic revolt held little sway. Their hostility to those who sought to inject politics into the rock scene made that abundantly clear. Far more pressing in their eyes were questions of authenticity. In this regard, their utterances reveal an oscillation between desire and self-doubt: even as William, Jacques, and Alain expressed a longing to participate in the transnational youth culture that was then flourishing in the United States and Britain, they were plagued with insecurities as to whether they—or French youth in general—could accede to this imagined community. Rock may have been attractive to French youth in part because of its seeming distance from a monolithic parent culture, as sociologist Paul Yonnet has argued; but this very distance threatened to place membership in the transnational rock community just beyond the reach of French aspirants.

The encounter between Queysanne, a *gauchiste* militant, and a group of teenage rock fans provides an opening onto a broader encounter that forms the subject of this chapter: the meeting of the political culture of post-'68 *gauchisme* with the genre culture of French rock. A number of the issues raised in Queysanne's article recur in the course of tracing the evolution of this often fractious relationship. The emergence of an indigenous rock scene in the late 1960s and early 1970s, discussed in the first section of this chapter, both responded to and reinforced the insecurities of French rock fans. The far left's fascination with rock—and its (reputed) ability to mobilize youth—resurfaces in the examination of *gauchiste* interventions in rock festivals that follows. Finally, Queysanne's call for militants to take into account the pleasure afforded by rock presaged subsequent efforts to find common ground between the counterculture and *gauchisme,* efforts that sparked heated disagreements among Maoists, Trotskyists, and other far left groups. At stake in these debates was the question of how French youth culture was to be defined going forward. Was it to be primarily a political phenomenon or a cultural one? Or, to frame the question somewhat differently, which community represented the proper heir to the legacy of May '68, *gauchisme* or the counterculture?

The responses to these and other questions took on a heightened significance given that rock and the Anglo-American counterculture arrived in France at precisely the moment when the post-1968 rebirth of the far left was reaching its apogee. In a sense, the encounter between these two communities took place at the point where an ascendant counterculture intersected with a *gauchisme* that, if not yet in decline, had already attained its high-water mark. But if it seems evident in retrospect that the growth of the counterculture facilitated the transition from political to cultural leftism, it is vital to bear in mind that at the time this outcome was hardly clear. It was the sense of uncertainty surrounding the future of both communities—the uncertainty as to whether *gauchisme* would maintain its post-'68 stature or return to the marginal position it occupied before 1968, whether rock would find a home in France or remain stigmatized as an "imported" genre—that made debates concerning rock's relationship to revolutionary politics so contentious.

ROCK IN FRANCE

The counterculture was late to arrive in France. It is of course impossible to pinpoint a precise date when it ceased being the object of rumor and achieved a critical mass among French youth. Very little hard data exists on the changing complexion of youth culture in France in the late 1960s. Reliable statistics measuring participation in activities closely identified with the counterculture (for instance, consumption of *la pop' music*) only began to appear in 1973, when the research division of the Ministry of Cultural Affairs published its first survey of French cultural practices. Even then, the data gathered by official agencies often failed to register the subtle yet important distinctions that separated one style of popular music from another, or that differentiated the casual listener from the committed enthusiast. Nonetheless, anecdotal accounts provide some clues. Reports such as Queysanne's article in *L'Idiot international* suggest that the first glimmerings of a local, gallicized version of the counterculture could be seen in late 1969, with the phenomenon becoming an increasingly visible part of the cultural landscape after 1970. A number of roughly contemporaneous developments signaled its arrival. References to French bands emulating the sounds and styles of recent British and American rock music—groups like Martin Circus, Triangle, and Zoo—multiplied in the popular music press in the latter half of 1969 and the first half of 1970.[17] At roughly the same time the first rock festivals were held on French soil, though, as we shall see, these were afflicted by a number of financial, logistical, and legal difficulties. Another defining trait of the Anglo-American counterculture, the underground press, had been virtually nonexistent prior to 1970. While May '68 gave rise to an array of small self-produced broadsheets, publications such as *Action* and *La Cause du peuple* owed more to the rich literature of the socialist, Communist, and anarchist movements of late-nineteenth- and early twentieth-century France than they did to Anglo-American contemporaries such as the *Los Angeles Free Press,* the *East Village Other,* or the *International Times.*[18] It was not until the founding of magazines like *Actuel* (second series) or *Parapluie* in the fall of 1970 that the mixture of music, sex, radical politics, comic strips, and psychedelia characteristic of the British and American underground press found a parallel in France.

If a specifically French counterculture materialized only around 1970 or so, it was not because the public was unaware of the changes taking place in Anglo-American youth culture. Quite the contrary. The counterculture in general and the hippie movement in the United States in particular attracted a fair amount of attention in the media prior to 1970. Books, newspaper and magazine articles, television programs, and radio broadcasts all documented the new lifestyles of American youth.[19] For the most part, reports from abroad echoed existing American accounts of contemporary youth culture (such as Theodore Roszak's *The Making of a Counter Culture*).[20] But such surface similarities belied deeper differences. Anglo-American observers generally treated the counterculture as one pole within a binary opposition that set it against an "establish-ment" or mainstream American culture (an opposition implicit in the term *counterculture* itself). By contrast, French writers, by virtue of their position as outsiders scrutinizing American culture from afar, introduced a third term to this binary schema. French society, and more specifically French youth culture, formed the tacit backdrop against which the inter-pretation of the mainstream/counterculture dualism took place. One upshot of this was to highlight the attributes of French society that were presumably ill suited to the development of an indigenous countercul-ture. French writers seeking to explain what it was about the United States that enabled the hippie movement to emerge typically drew a contrast with their native country, showing what it was about France that *did not* allow for a comparable movement to come into existence. Another consequence was to elide what appeared to Anglophone writers as a stark gulf separating American youth from their parent culture. What was cast as a simple dichotomy in American accounts assumed the form of a dialectic in French writings. The hippie lifestyle, far from being a re-pudiation of the American value system, was instead seen as one of its purest embodiments.[21]

Observers advanced a number of reasons to explain why America had given birth to a counterculture and France had not. These included the changed balance of cultural power during the postwar period as the United States overtook Europe as the main incubator of new cultural movements;[22] the relative affluence of American society, which provided the material basis for the hippie movement's very rejection of material-ism;[23] and, most notably, the extreme politicization of French youth culture in the wake of May '68, which, as historian Chris Warne notes, "provided an important resistance to the importation of foreign popu-lar cultures into the milieu of young middle-class revolt."[24] Among the most frequently invoked explanations for the absence of a French coun-terculture prior to the early 1970s was the pernicious influence of the local culture industry. Something like the hippie phenomenon, it was argued, would have been strangled at birth in France by commercial interests. One author, describing the first tentative efforts at bringing the hippie movement to France, underlined the commercial pressures to which it had been subjected: "Like everything that comes from America, [the hippies'] universe has become the object of fashion, a dandyism adopted by the wealthy—in short, by an ironic reversal, an element in the game of social distinction and a product for consumption."[25] By this reading, the various accoutrements of the counterculture joined Coca-Cola, Frigidaires, and Chevrolets as emblems of a mythologized America, ready to be sold to a French public anxious not to fall behind the times. More problematic still was that such commodification threatened to crowd out more "authentic" grassroots efforts at developing an alternative youth culture in the country. "In France in particular," one author observed, "the hippie underground is more or less masked by the direct importation (by the mass media) of a hippyism of consumption."[26]

Gloomy forecasts for the counterculture's prospects in France were not without basis. The record industry did not take long to release albums that sought to capitalize on the latest trend to emanate from "Anglo-Saxon" countries. Pop idol Johnny Hallyday, always on the leading edge of the Americanization of French youth culture, was one of the first to adjust his image to accommodate changing musical fashion. A year after mocking the "beatnik" singer Antoine (see chapter 2) for his "long hair" and "small ideas," Hallyday, without the slightest hint of irony, traded in his rocker persona for that of a flower child. Publicity photographs used to promote his 1967 adaptation of Scott McKenzie's "San Francisco" showed him outfitted in full hippie regalia, sporting beads, a flower-print shirt, and ample sideburns. Newcomers and lesser-known acts were also eager to profit from the latest fad. Bands with names like Les Herbes Tendres (Tender Grass) and Les Fleurs de Pavot (The Poppy Flowers) appeared and disappeared overnight. Les Fleurs de Pavot exemplified the dubious nature of some of these undertakings. According to a press release, the group was formed when two musicians—Jesus and "Groovy" Pat (one allegedly from San Francisco, the other from London)—met at a rock concert in Paris.[27] As it turned out, the band had more prosaic origins. It was the creation of record producer Jean-Pierre Rawson, who had refashioned an early '60s rock-and-roll outfit, Les Bourgeois de Calais, into a psychedelic rock band.[28] It is telling that Rawson saw fit to identify the group's leaders as having come from San Francisco and London, the two epicenters of the transnational underground. The native origins of the band members had to be suppressed in order to maintain the illusion of authenticity.

These early efforts at exploiting the hippie fad suggested that psychedelia was on its way to becoming simply the latest in a succession of American popular styles bowdlerized by the French music industry. Still, it would be incorrect to infer from this that a taste for the American counterculture was being imposed on audiences from "above" by powerful commercial interests. Contemporary developments indicated the considerable fascination that Anglo-American rock held for a growing number of French youth. The emergence of a specialist press devoted principally to British and American rock—*Rock & Folk* was founded in November 1966, followed two years later by the rival publication *Best*—attested to the fact that a community of enthusiasts existed for the repertoire.[29] These publications further expanded the ranks of the emerging rock community by bringing new trends to the attention of French readers. The success of radio programs featuring Anglo-American rock on their playlists was another sign of this burgeoning popularity. Michel Lancelot's program *Campus,* for instance, with its eclectic mixture of jazz, experimental chanson, and Anglo-American pop, witnessed the fastest ratings growth of any program in the history of the radio station Europe 1 in its first year on the air.[30] Record sales charts also indicated that British and American rock acts were gaining traction with French audiences. Until the late 1960s, the French public had been comparatively slow to embrace foreign-language artists.[31] Unlike in Germany, Holland, and other Western European and Scandinavian countries, where the record charts had long been dominated by Anglo-American pop acts, the strength of the record industry in France had ensured that foreign records had little success in penetrating the market.[32] This is not to deny the considerable influence that British and American styles exerted on French popular music prior to the late sixties. It was rather that this influence manifested itself primarily through francophone adaptations of anglophone songs. Whereas rock and roll, folk, "beat" music, and their various offshoots had once passed through cultural brokers like Hallyday and Eddie Mitchell, after 1967 the role of such local mediators diminished. By the end of the decade it was not uncommon for as many as half of the top-ten bestsellers in major retail outlets to consist of recordings by British and American artists.[33]

One of the strongest indicators of the growing interest in British and American popular music was the proliferation of French rock bands after 1968. In contrast to the French music industry's attempts to retrofit older artists to meet the demands of the new pop style, groups like Martin Circus, Blues Convention, Devotion, Tac Poum Système, Alice, and Magma started out on the margins of the commercial music sector. This burst of grassroots musical activity in many ways paralleled what had transpired some ten years before, when the initial arrival of rock and roll in France had given rise to a flood of local bands. However, the French rock groups of the late 1960s interacted with Anglo-American models in an altogether different manner. Early performers of rock and roll drew their repertoire from English-language hit records, which were re-created with varying degrees of success (generally speaking, the different production standards of French *variétés* radically transformed the sound of these cover versions, placing greater emphasis on the vocals and on professional-quality orchestrations).[34] By contrast, the "second wave" of French rock bands typically performed original material, however indebted it may have been to Anglo-American models.[35] Two trends in particular exerted a decisive influence on the nascent French rock scene. One was the hard rock and British blues style popularized by bands like Cream, the Yardbirds, and Led Zeppelin. The heavy, riff-oriented sound of these bands was quickly taken up by French groups like Blues Convention, Dynastie Crisis, Alan Jack Civilization, Tac Poum Système, and the Variations. A second tendency within the French rock scene followed in the path of "progressive" rock and was exemplified by groups like Triangle, Zoo, Martin Circus, Magma, and Red Noise.[36] While modeled on British and American bands such as Pink Floyd, Soft Machine, and the Mothers of Invention, French progressive acts tended to be distinguished from their Anglo-American counterparts by the greater influence that jazz (and particularly free jazz) exercised on their music. In a number of instances musicians who had begun their careers playing jazz found themselves drawn to the new musical trend, either for professional or for aesthetic reasons. Such was the case with saxophonist François Jeanneau, who joined Triangle in 1969, or Henri Texier, bassist for the jazz-rock supergroup Total Issue. In other instances the connection between the worlds of jazz and rock was based on personal ties, including those of family: Christian Vander (drummer and leader of the band Magma) was the son of noted jazz arranger Maurice Vander, while Patrick Vian (guitarist for Red Noise) was the son of author and trumpeter Boris Vian.

French groups from across the entire spectrum of musical styles faced a host of challenges. Principal among these was the difficulty in winning over audiences weaned on the music of British and American rock bands. Radio and television offered few opportunities for French groups to bring their music to the attention of the wider public. Broadcasts devoting substantial airtime to rock were scarce on both public and private stations. By 1972 there were but a handful of rock-oriented radio programs (*Pop Club* on France Inter, *L'Émission Pop* on Radio-Télévision Luxembourg, and *Carré Bleu* and *Campus* on Europe 1). Even fewer platforms for rock existed on television (*Pop 2*, *Rockenstock*, and *Point Chaud*).[37] The paucity of media outlets was only part of the problem. The latest British and American rock consumed the bulk of the coverage on both radio and television. A similar situation existed within the French record industry. Many bands had trouble obtaining record contracts, and those that did faced difficulties in getting their albums promoted—or even released.[38] Bernard de Bosson, head of the artists and repertoire (A&R) department for the Barclay label, noted that the company's rock catalogue consisted almost entirely of American and British product (he estimated the figure to be around 95 percent). This was despite the fact that four out of every five imports in his opinion deserved to "be thrown into the trash." This persuaded him that in the rock world there was "a kind of racism directed toward the French."[39]

A more convincing explanation for the problems faced by French rock bands resided in the structure of the French music industry. By the early 1970s, most major labels operating in France were either subsidiaries of multinational record companies or had distribution deals with American and British firms. The result was a two-pronged business model. Major French labels (Barclay, Vogue) and the subsidiaries of multinational firms (Pathé-Marconi/EMI, Philips, CBS) continued to cultivate local French talent but tended to promote only those artists who fit into established native genres like chanson or *variétés*. These labels had little incentive to seek out French practitioners of foreign genres like rock, since it was cheaper and less risky simply to distribute records by proven Anglo-American artists. As Gérome Guibert observes, this strategy meant that labels "did not have to finance either the search for artists or the productions of discs, these costs [having been] already amortized in their own countries by foreign artists."[40] A handful of French bands did have the good fortune of signing with major labels, and some even produced hit records. Martin Circus, for instance, sold a respectable fifty-seven thousand albums for the Vogue label. But such success stories were infrequent, and they were overshadowed by the sales generated by popular British and American groups.[41]

The result of this business model was the division of the popular music market into two discrete sectors, with French-language chanson and *variétés* on one side and English-language rock on the other. This division was reinforced by the media, with magazine, radio, and television coverage likewise segmented along the anglophone rock/francophone *variétés* line. With the market partitioned in this fashion, there was little opportunity for French rock bands to attract a following. Such difficulties were evident in the limited coverage of French rock that the magazine *Rock & Folk* provided during its early years. From the beginning, the magazine's coverage was centered squarely on American and British music. To the extent that French popular music merited mention, it was existing genres like chanson or *yéyé* that figured into the magazine's reporting. The result was a disconnect between the different styles initially featured in the magazine. Articles on Left Bank singer-songwriters such as Ferré, Serge Gainsbourg, and Brigitte Fontaine were published alongside notices describing the latest albums by French teen idols like Hallyday, Jacques Dutronc, and Antoine. Meanwhile, feature articles in the magazine discussed the very different musical universe inhabited by British and American rock stars like Bob Dylan, Jimi Hendrix, and the Rolling Stones. By the summer of 1969, however, the gulf separating the anglophone and francophone popular musics featured in *Rock & Folk* began to close. Increasingly, the new wave of French rock bands dislodged chanson and *yéyé* from the place they had previously occupied in the magazine's pages. Yet the shift from older forms of youth-oriented popular music to rock did not translate into increased coverage of French bands. If anything, the reverse was true. The space given over to reporting on native rock groups remained limited. As one reader complained in a letter to the editor, four out of five articles published in *Rock & Folk* dealt with American or British groups. Of the remaining articles, about half addressed French groups, while the remaining half discussed bands from other countries.[42]

When the specialist press did report on the local rock scene, its coverage proved double-edged. Even as it gave French rock some degree of recognition, the discourse employed often served to reinforce entrenched prejudices about its inadequacies. Even the most laudatory remarks were qualified, and approbation was generally mixed with a dose of incredulity. It was as if critics were pleasantly surprised at the quality of the music they encountered in local venues. The reservations voiced in a review of the Alan Jack Civilization's debut album, *Bluesy Mind,* in *Rock & Folk* were typical. The author of the review, Philippe Paringaux, greeted the album with a palpable sense of relief, as though it signaled that the long drought in French rock had finally come to an end: "*Voilà,* the extraordinary has taken place, our wait has paid off. Not that this makes us want to hoist the *tricolore* . . . , but it is infinitely satisfying to say to yourself that finally you can set foot in a nightclub and hear some good 'live' music."[43] Paringaux went on to explain that the long gestation period for French rock was due to the fact that bands first had to pass through a period of apprenticeship, during which groups did little more than copy Anglo-American models. He singled out one band, the Variations, as exemplifying this kind of mimicry: "The success of the Variations, an extremely average group, has had the enormous merit of opening wide the door that had until then remained obstinately closed to a French pop music. . . . Groups like Alan Jack Civilization, Triangle, Martin Circus, [and] Zoo rushed through this breach and have offered us a music that is no longer inferior to its sources."[44] Even while praising the new wave of French bands, Paringaux's review and others like it pointed to the low expectations of most critics and fans. The default assumption was that French rock would inevitably reveal itself to be "inferior to its sources." Few anticipated that it could prove otherwise.

Paringaux's remarks reflected an emerging consensus among critics about how French rock was to be evaluated. A hierarchy was established that placed hard rock and blues bands below progressive groups, the latter being seen as less derivative, less dependent on Anglo-American prototypes. By and large this hierarchy was cast in diachronic terms, as an evolutionary process: French rock had to pass through a preliminary stage of crude, unthinking mimesis before it could develop a distinctive voice. Critic Paul Alessandrini, for one, characterized the maturation of French rock as a dialectical process in which the desire to assimilate foreign models inevitably gave rise to an opposing impulse, one that valorized sophistication and originality. In certain cases this antithetical movement misfired, as the search for originality devolved into cliché or artifice. Such was the case with Martin Circus, Zoo, and Triangle; in Alessandrini's opinion, their increasing sophistication had come at the price of dissipating the explosive energy of rock. These bands may have moved past the simple imitation that characterized the Variations or Tac Poum Système, but in doing so they had failed to retain the primal energy that was the saving grace of hard rock bands. In other cases, the development of a more distinctive French sound met with more satisfactory results. For Alessandrini, the bands that succeeded in this respect were "underground" or avant-garde groups like Red Noise and Moving Gelatine Plates, which fused rock with free jazz and/or contemporary music: "Open to everything that seems to 'move' or overturn intellectual comfort, passivity and disengagement, they want their action to provoke more than simple, momentary excitement."[45] To be sure, this way of ranking the subgenres of French was informed by a number of extramusical variables, including those of class, education, and geography. The elevation of avant-garde groups over those bands like the Variations, who contented themselves with "simple, momentary excitement," performed the work of social distinction that Bourdieu has identified as the principal function of assertions of artistic taste. In the context of French rock, however, subnational distinctions based on class and region were overlain by supranational distinctions based on whether a given group either slavishly adhered to or broke away from foreign models. The more vulgar the group, the more dependent it was on Anglo-American precedents; the more sophisticated the group, the less dependent.

Alessandrini was not alone in his belief that progressive bands represented the best hope for freeing French rock from its overreliance on foreign models. Like-minded observers argued that the musical innovations pioneered by French progressive bands pointed the way forward for the genre. As the rock scene atrophied in Britain and the United States, one critic remarked, "relief will come from Europe (and more precisely from Germany and France), who will be transformed from a spectator to an actor of the highest degree."[46] But in spite of such vocal support for more experimental forms of rock, there were tacit limits on how far French bands could go in deviating from Anglo-American antecedents. Originality may have been privileged, but only so long as it did not rob the music of the very qualities that made it identifiable as rock. One criticism habitually leveled at progressive bands was that they were guilty of overintellectualizing what was an essentially corporeal form of music. This line of argument was already present in Alessandrini's criticism of the polished sound of groups like Triangle and Zoo. Similar charges were, of course, laid at the feet of British and American progressive groups during the same period. The difference, however, was that critics characterized intellectualism not as an individual shortcoming but as the manifestation of a quintessentially French sensibility. Gallic rationality and self-control, by this logic, made it difficult for French bands to fully embrace rock's physicality. Describing a performance by Triangle, the critic Jacques Chabiron complained that the group was "too reserved." But he immediately tempered this criticism by acknowledging that this was a "complex" that afflicted virtually every French band.[47] Along similar lines, the band Red Noise was faulted by critic Thierry Lewin for not acting directly upon "the body of the listener."[48] What these and other critiques reveal is the double bind that confronted French groups. A failure to depart from the conventions of Anglo-American rock led to charges that bands were overly derivative, while too great a departure from these conventions led to charges that they were robbing the music of its spirit.

Ultimately, the competing pressures to which French rock bands were subject reflected broader uncertainties about the status of rock in France, uncertainties that affected the entire community of enthusiasts. Anxieties about the inferiority of the French rock scene may have most directly affected bands, but critics and fans were not exempt from self-doubt. What was in question was whether French enthusiasts really understood rock, whether they had really assimilated its sensibility, or if they were merely appropriating the more superficial aspects of fandom. Queysanne's conversations with French rock fans in the inaugural issue of *L'Idiot international* bore witness to the kind of doubts that plagued participants of the nascent rock community. While his informants had little trouble identifying poseurs, they seemed less sure if they themselves qualified as "real" hippies. The same difficulty in discriminating between the authentic and the inauthentic was a common feature of the rock community. In large part this was because rock's utility as a means of forging a collective oppositional identity was overdetermined, a product of both generational and national markers. This made rock both highly effective as a means of distinguishing its enthusiasts from the broader parent culture *and* highly unstable. As a form of youth culture, rock proved useful in establishing a symbolic distance from adult society, in drawing a bright line between a subcultural "in-group" and a mainstream "out-group." But as a markedly *Anglo-American* form of youth culture, rock's capacity for drawing social distinctions always threatened to boomerang on French enthusiasts. It threatened, that is, to identify them as perennial outsiders, unable to claim the same organic connection to the music that British and American fans possessed.

In this regard, the anxieties expressed by members of the emerging French rock scene were symptomatic of broader anxieties about France's widely perceived decline in cultural stature after World War II. Such concerns echoed those voiced in the 1960s and 1970s by advocates of serious music, who bemoaned their country's failure to keep pace with other, more musically "advanced" nations (more on this in the next chapter). For rock fans, however, the problem was less one of wounded national pride than a sense that history was passing them by, as if all the significant transformations in transnational youth culture were taking place elsewhere. France was regarded as being "in the rear," a "musically underdeveloped country."[49] The sense of inadequacy evident in such comments remained a perennial feature of the French rock scene for years to come and played a decisive role in its subsequent development. In particular, this attitude would shape the rock community's ambivalent response to the growing interest that various political and commercial actors began to exhibit toward rock music after 1970. At times, the attentions of entrepreneurs and militants were welcomed, as they promised to expand the audience for the genre and thereby secure its position in the French cultural landscape. But just as often the possibility that external actors might seek to "recuperate" the burgeoning interest in rock music made them suspect in the eyes of the French rock community. Nowhere were the insecurities and ambivalences of the French rock scene more in evidence than in the heated reactions provoked by the commercial festivals organized during the summer of 1970, what *Rock & Folk* dubbed "l'été pop" (the pop summer).[50]

L'ÉTÉ POP / L'ÉTÉ CHAUD

Despite the challenges it faced, rock had achieved a tenuous foothold in France by the first half of 1970. A small but growing network of musicians, critics, and fans had developed. The rock scene was also beginning to attract attention outside the core group of enthusiasts, especially within the music industry. Although rock still ranked below traditional French chanson and *variétés* in terms of record sales, it was taking an increasing share of the market.[51] The number of finished albums imported into France was on the rise, which provided record companies with an incentive to expand their distribution agreements with American and British labels.[52] In an effort to take advantage of changing consumer preferences, many of the major labels operating in France launched new product lines with names like "Pop music révolution" (CBS-France), "Underground" (Compagnie européenne du disque), and "Progressive évolution musicale" (Polydor). These same firms also began to show a greater interest in cultivating native talent, following their first ham-fisted efforts at exploiting the hippie fashion.[53] Advertisements in magazines like *Rock & Folk* solicited bands to audition for the chance at winning a recording contract.[54] Meanwhile, tours by foreign artists were increasingly frequent, offering French youth (or at least those that inhabited larger cities) the opportunity to hear British and American bands live. In January 1970, for instance, Parisian rock fans could take in shows by Pink Floyd and The Who at the Théâtre des Champs Elysées, attend a six-day concert series featuring Decca artists at the Olympia Music Hall, or hear performances by French underground bands at Les Halles.[55]

Perhaps the clearest indication that rock was on its way to becoming a significant presence in France was the number of festivals slated to take place across the country in the summer of 1970. There was a great deal of anticipation in advance of *l'été pop*. Part of this was due to the publicity that megaevents like Woodstock and the Isle of Wight festivals had generated in the preceding year. The release of Michael Wadleigh's documentary on Woodstock during the summer of 1970 fueled this fascination with rock festivals.[56] Indeed, it was not so much the music as the entire culture of rock festivals that garnered the most attention. For journalist François Jouffa the greatest change effected by rock festivals was to be found in the role of the audience. No longer passive listeners ancillary to the music performed onstage, the audience had become equally important to the festival experience: "The public has a need to feel submerged. It matters little if this involves trekking several kilometers. What matters is to meet up with one's own kind; the spectator is the spectacle. Permanent happening, the festival is no longer simply an excuse for hearing some group. What is just as important is the environment."[57] Woodstock served as the paradigm for this inversion of roles. As noteworthy as the music performed at Woodstock may have been, the festival's import lay in its sheer magnitude, and in the fact that so many youth could come together and coexist peacefully (the violence at Altamont was the obvious counterexample to this optimistic reading of the festival phenomenon). From this perspective, programming choices took on a different meaning within the context of the rock festival. Paul Alessandrini observed that festivals, in bringing together acts appealing to different audiences, was able to produce "a complete intermingling of the public."[58] Whereas concerts by individual artists preserved the division of the rock community into discrete, non-overlapping subcultures—with hard rock bands attracting a working-class audience, folk singers attracting a middle-class audience, and progressive groups attracting university students and intellectuals—festivals offered this community an opportunity to experience itself as a totality. This suggested that festivals had important political ramifications. They allowed the rock community, understood as a proxy for youth, to "take consciousness of its proper force."[59] The festival, in Marxian terms, became the occasion where youth would cease to be a class "in itself" and become a class "for itself."

The notion that rock festivals were uniquely suited for awakening a sense of shared identity among youth was widespread, though not all shared Alessandrini's enthusiasm at this prospect. Others took a more jaundiced view of the galvanizing potential of rock festivals. With May '68 still fresh in their memory, government officials at both local and national levels blanched at the idea of young people assembling in such large numbers. The fear was that events of such magnitude could prove combustible. In this context, the decision of various entrepreneurs to take advantage of the growing public appetite for rock music and rock festivals during the summer of 1970 could not have come at a less propitious time. The ongoing efforts of the extreme left—in particular, the Gauche prolétarienne (see chapter 2)—to incite a new wave of protests and strike actions in the preceding year had led to a hardening of the government's position vis-à-vis radical organizations. After an initial attempt to address the root causes of youth unrest through a program of economic and social liberalization—the plan for a "new society" promulgated by Prime Minister Jacques Chaban-Delmas in 1969—hardliners in the government successfully pushed for a crackdown on threats to the social order.[60] The effects of this changing policy were apparent by spring 1970. Police were given greater leeway to quell demonstrations and detain perceived troublemakers, leading to numerous cases of police brutality.[61] Revolutionary parties like the Gauche prolétarienne (GP) were outlawed, and in some cases their leaders were arrested. Such was the case with Alain Geismar, the titular head of the GP, who was taken into custody in June 1970 on charges of "direct incitation . . . to violence and assaults against the agents of public order."[62]

Militant journals were also pursued by the government. As noted in chapter 3, the party organ of the GP, *La Cause du peuple,* was subjected to intense pressure; copies of the newspaper were repeatedly seized and its editors (including Michel Le Bris) incarcerated. *L'Idiot international* also ran afoul of the law. In 1971 the journal's editor, Jean-Edern Hallier, was put on trial for having advocated the overthrow of the government, along with erstwhile contributor Dominique Grange (the offending article in Grange's case was a notice she had written to accompany the lyrics of "Les Nouveaux partisans").[63] In addition to these targeted efforts at eliminating the *gauchiste* threat, the government enacted more sweeping statutory changes to discourage public protest. The most notorious of these was the *anti-casseur* (antihooligan) law passed by the Assemblée nationale in June 1970. Under the new law, protestors could be held legally and financially liable for damages inflicted during the course of an unauthorized demonstration, even if they were not personally responsible.[64] Instead of relying on the anonymity of the crowd to skirt prosecution, demonstrators now faced the prospect of a prison term and heavy fines should an action they took part in turn unruly.

Although the aim of the *anti-casseur* law was to curb "new forms of delinquency,"[65] the breadth of the statute meant that all sorts of public assemblies, not just the spectacular actions of the far left, were caught in its crosshairs. Festival organizers faced a new set of logistical hurdles in staging large-scale gatherings as a result. A festival planned for Barcarès, near Perpignan in southwest France, had to be abandoned at the last minute when organizers were unable to obtain insurance to cover against potential damages. According to one account, backers were worried that they would be held responsible under the terms of the new law should a group of "*gauchiste* commandos" ransack the area.[66] In other cases, promoters had to contend with the resistance of municipal governments. Obtaining permission to use a selected site at times appeared an exercise in futility. Jean Georgakarakos, organizer of the Actuel festival in Amougies (see chapter 3), once again had to endure a series of rejected proposals before finding a location for his second attempt at mounting a "progressive music" festival. After having been denied by officials in Le Mans, Grenoble, and Castelet, he settled on Biot, near Antibes, for the event.[67]

But the greatest challenge to *l'été pop* by far came in the form of governmental injunctions. Citing concerns about public safety, local officials and regional police prefects issued edicts that prohibited a number of festivals from going forward, including those planned for Valbonne in July and Aix-en-Provence in August.[68] Many doubted that public safety issues (such as the risk of forest fires) were the real cause for the injunctions, the claims of municipal officials notwithstanding. Rather, skeptics viewed the ban on festivals as being of a piece with the government's nationwide crackdown on left-wing militants. Some even accused the minister of the interior, Raymond Marcellin, of having coordinated the interdictions on a nationwide level. In an article in *L'Express,* an anonymous ministry official denied these charges: "Don't believe," the official was quoted as saying, "that M. Raymond Marcellin is anti-pop."[69] But, as the article went on to note, one of the letters that regional authorities had sent to Georgakarakos explained that the decision to disallow his festival from taking place in the area was made "in accordance with the instructions of the minister of the interior."[70] Reports such as these only served to confirm suspicions that rock festivals were being targeted by the government out of a concern that they might act as hotbeds of political agitation.

As excessive as the actions of the authorities may have been, apprehensions about the possibility of left-wing agitation were not unfounded. Following the arrest of Geismar and the government's dissolution of the Gauche prolétarienne in May 1970, the group's militants decided against reconstituting as an organized political entity. Instead, they opted to disperse, forming a loose network of "detachments" spread across the country. Some of these were to insinuate themselves within the ranks of the working class, while others engaged in spectacular guerrilla-style operations in the hope of restoking the embers of May '68.[71] To underline the fact that, despite the government's best efforts, the Maoists of the "ex–Gauche prolétarienne" still had the capacity to act against the "ruling classes," the group announced a campaign of sensational actions to be undertaken during the summer of 1970. Dubbed *l'été chaud* (the hot summer), the campaign aimed at discomfiting the bourgeoisie, preventing them from enjoying the wealth they had won off the backs of workers.[72] *Pas de vacances pour les riches* (no vacation for the rich) was the slogan the group trumpeted in the course of vandalizing the resorts, private beaches, and villas of France's moneyed elite. As was the case with most of the ex–Gauche prolétarienne's activities, the violence of *l'été chaud* was more symbolic than real. Unlike the Italian Red Brigades or the German Rote Armee Fraktion, French Maoists never really succumbed to the temptation of terrorist violence. Rather, they relied on creating spectacular events that would convey the impression of popular resistance to the existing order. These included throwing dead rats through the windows of the Hotel Negresco in Nice and dumping manure on the floors of the Hotel Plaza-Athénée in Paris.[73] But in addition to disrupting the holidays of the wealthy, the ex–Gauche prolétarienne also sought to make leisure pursuits and luxury goods available to disadvantaged communities. "Workers," a manifesto in *La Cause du peuple* announced, "we will reclaim our vacations from the bourgeoisie."[74] Maoists in the south of France thus "liberated" such items as volleyball nets, lawn furniture, and sporting equipment from vacation homes, delivering them to local working-class neighborhoods.[75] The point was to demonstrate that "liberty and joy can be seized."[76] Music festivals were also targeted for liberation. Instead of allowing commercial interests to profit from the recreational activities of youth, these were to be torn from their clutches and given back to *le peuple*.

It was against this backdrop of left-wing provocation and governmental repression that *l'été pop* got underway. Despite the interdictions issued by local authorities, a number of festivals proceeded as planned. At Valbonne, a festival staged by the club Music Evolution went ahead in defiance of the municipality's ban. Although the police did not try to stop the event once it had started, they did set up barriers on the roads leading to the site in an effort to discourage fans from attending. This did not prevent the more intrepid festivalgoers from making their way to the event on foot. It did, however, have the effect of depressing turnout: only 1,800 people ended up making it to the festival.[77] A similar fate befell a more ambitious festival scheduled for the first weekend in August near Aix-en-Provence. The driving force behind the event was a curious figure by the name of Claude Clément, a former French army general who had been forced to retire from military service because of ties to the far-right nationalist group Organisation armée secrète.[78] Clément, who had always viewed himself as a man of the arts, saw the hippie movement as heralding a renewal of humanist values.[79] But despite the general's establishment credentials and connections (among other things, he had served on the board of the annual classical music festival held in Aix-en-Provence), his plans to mount a "French Woodstock" encountered resistance, particularly from the socialist mayor of Aix. Once again, the event's alleged threat to public safety was invoked to justify a ban.[80] But the fact that it coincided with the municipality's yearly classical music festival also appears to have motivated the mayor's hostility. The prospect of a horde of unkempt youth descending on Aix-en-Provence was something to be avoided at all costs, lest it drive away tourists.[81] However, the blanket characterization of rock fans as occupying a demographic niche somewhere between vagabonds and left-wing provocateurs only reinforced their shared sense of persecution. If a classical music festival could be held in Aix and a jazz festival in nearby Antibes, why, observers asked, could a rock festival not take place in the same region?[82]

In response to such double standards, General Clément decided to disregard the municipality's injunction, contesting its legality. But, like the Valbonne Festival a week earlier, Clément's Progressive music festival was a disappointment, with the number of festivalgoers estimated between seven and thirteen thousand.[83] This was more than the Valbonne festival had mustered, but it still fell far short of the general's goal of creating a French Woodstock. As before, a heavy police presence deterred many would-be attendees.[84] So too did the controversial figure of the general himself. For many rock fans, Clément embodied the efforts to smooth off the rougher, more radical edges of the French counterculture. Alessandrini, for one, described the festival as offering a "caricature of all that (and all those) which we refuse: recuperators who carry around with them the fetid odor of commerce, 'officials' who 'understand the problems of youth.' "[85] Much of the distrust directed toward Clément had to do with his military background and his connections to the extreme right. Nor did it help when he was reported to have enlisted a contingent of *harkis* (native Algerians who had served on the side of the French army during the country's war of independence) to provide security for the event.[86] The resulting atmosphere of suspicion, exploitation, and menace that hung over the festival no doubt contributed to the depressed turnout.

Due in part to the lower-than-expected attendance figures, the festival in Aix was a financial disaster. Contributing to the shortfall was rampant gate crashing.[87] While some instances involved fans who could not afford the high entrance fee (55 francs), others represented an organized effort to undermine the event. A band of Maoists participating in the *été chaud* campaign forced their way onto the site, whereupon they demanded that the event be opened to the public free of charge.[88] In the melee that ensued, festival organizers and Maoist agitators vied over who legitimately represented the interests of festivalgoers. For the Maoists, it was a matter of rendering unto the people what was rightfully theirs—*their* music, *their* right of assembly—which had been expropriated by commercial forces. For Clément, the point was to supply youth with what they wanted; and what they wanted was music, not politics. In his recounting of the incident, Clément recalled that he was greeted with a "long ovation" once he had stated his case before the crowd, which he took as evidence that "the real youth had made their judgment" in his favor.[89] But as his remark indicates, Clément was not simply giving voice to the desires of youth, but defining who—and who did not—count as youth in the first place. By designating those who agreed to his representation of the festival's purpose as "real youth," his account disclosed what was truly at stake in the conflict: the assertion of a particular definition of youth, a certain conception of its attitudes, needs, and desires. The same applied to the Maoists, with their repeated references to the "people" and the "popular." In both cases, rock music stood at the center of the competing visions of youth. For the general, youth was defined principally by its desire for music, a desire whose satisfaction was impeded by the actions of left-wing demagogues. Implicit in this was a stark division between pleasure and politics. "Real youth" simply wanted to enjoy themselves; *gauchistes,* with their political obsessions, were biologically young but psychologically senescent. For the Maoists, the opposite was true. Pleasure was not be cordoned off from politics. This was not because rock was inherently political, but because exploitation could be found just as readily in the world of leisure as in the world of work.

A more dramatic Maoist intervention took place during the course of the Popanalia festival held in Biot a few days later. In a sense, this last event was the most successful of the festivals mounted during *l'été pop,* with an estimated twenty-five thousand attending. The lineup likely played a large role in drawing festivalgoers. In addition to a number of high-profile acts (Pink Floyd, Joan Baez, Soft Machine, and Eric Clapton), the festival was to include a number of French underground bands (Ame Son and Gong) and free jazz performers (Don Cherry, Archie Shepp). But, as was the case at Aix, gate crashing (encouraged once again by Maoist agitators) prevented the high turnout from translating into financial success.[90] Journalist Jean-François Bizot, who helped organize the festival, recounted the arrival of the Maoist brigade: "On the road, the cloud of *gauchistes* grew. As the swirl of dust lifted, we now could make out a formidable group, a banner at its head. Karakos had seen the flag that had been raised by the troop marching toward us. It was a red flag. . . . We yelled to them: 'Guys, you know that we're militants too!' They responded: 'My ass! Pop to the people!' The column entered like a massive wave. Without paying, of course."[91] In the process of storming the festival, the gate-crashers damaged the fencing that surrounded the site, making any further effort to control who entered or left pointless. A collection was started to help offset the shortfall in ticket sales but only mustered 11,000 francs, a fraction of what was needed for the festival to continue.[92] Certain headlining acts (like the Soft Machine) refused to appear onstage until they were paid in full. And since organizers had counted on making up the balance of what was owed musicians out of box-office receipts, the festival was forced to end prematurely.[93]

The failure of the Valbonne, Aix, and Biot festivals marked a significant setback for *la cause du pop* in France. Both enthusiasts and outside observers concurred that a unique opportunity to place the local rock scene on a firmer footing had been missed. Claude Fléouter, a reporter for *Le Monde,* took the debacle at Biot as a portent for the future: "Thus died a festival of pop music, perhaps the last that will take place in

France."[94] Recriminations abounded as critics and fans tried to come to grips with the disappointments engendered by what in their eyes should have been rock's triumphant arrival in the country. Various actors were castigated for contributing to the failure of *l'été pop*: government officials for having banned events, the mainstream media for having fueled a moral panic, and organizers for having insufficiently prepared for various eventualities.[95] But more than any other group, Maoist agitators were singled out for having jeopardized the prospects of the French rock scene. Virtually all of the contributors to *Rock & Folk*'s special issue on *l'été pop* complained bitterly of the Maoists' actions. For François-René Cristiani the latter were "idiotic agitators" engaged in "adolescent games"; for Jacques Vassal, they represented an "agitated minority of little lazy bums" whose behavior ranged from "puerile" to "vulgar."[96] But if *gauchistes* were the obvious target of enthusiasts' ire, the rock community itself was not spared criticism. The Maoists may have instigated the gate crashing, but others had joined in without compunction. What such behavior revealed, in the words of Fléouter, was "the lack of solidarity and discipline" among French rock fans. The latter were taken more with "a desire to 'play at Woodstock'" than with the music itself.[97]

The notion that French rock fans had failed to meet certain standards of behavior—the "lack of solidarity and discipline" invoked by Fléouter—indicated that membership in the rock community was seen as involving more than the cultivation of musical taste. It was not just a matter of listening to the "right" bands or demonstrating familiarity with styles popularized in Britain and the United States. Rather, rock fandom required the assimilation of an entire ensemble of ideologies, attitudes, and practices. It was here that the anxieties of French enthusiasts, shaped by media representations of the Anglo-American counterculture, were most keenly expressed. The "misbehavior" of fans during *l'été pop* appeared to bear out the belief that the counterculture was in some way incompatible with French sensibilities and traditions, particularly those of the French left. This point was driven home at the 1970 Isle of Wight Festival, where a handful of French agitators clamored for the event to be turned into a free festival.[98] Their disruptive behavior drew near-universal condemnation within the French rock press.[99] What had previously been a national disappointment now risked becoming the source of international ignominy. A letter to the music weekly *Pop Music* articulated this sentiment, denouncing "the young 'French' imbeciles . . . who once again demeaned France at the Isle of Wight."[100] For all that, the self-conscious effort of certain French fans to emulate the behavior of hippies fared little better. Critic Jacques Vassal may have decried what he saw as the antisocial conduct of gauchistes during *l'été pop,* but this did not lead him to view self-styled French hippies sympathetically: "We will quickly pass over those who, wanting to 'play at Woodstock,' felt obliged to walk around naked and bathe in the mud. It is a form of alienation, but at least [it] doesn't impede the unfolding of the festival."[101] French rock enthusiasts, like French rock bands, thus found themselves caught in a contradiction. Failing to adhere to the model of the Anglo-American counterculture posed the danger of being symbolically excluded from the transnational rock community. But trying too hard to emulate this model posed the danger of exposing one's cultural "alienation." Rather than resolving this contradiction, *l'été pop* threw it into even sharper relief.

POLITICS INTO ROCK/ROCK INTO POLITICS

Although the reaction of the rock community to *gauchiste* interventions in the Aix and Biot festivals had been overwhelmingly negative, other dissenting voices could be heard in the aftermath of *l'été pop.* One letter to the editor of *Rock & Folk* chided the magazine's critics for misrepresenting the activists who had disrupted the festivals. Far from being the "agitated minority of little lazy bums" described by Vassal, the individuals who had interceded on behalf of *le peuple* were, in the opinion of the letter writer, better attuned to the unfulfilled desires of French youth than the critics for *Rock & Folk* cared to admit. What these authors failed to recognize was that the hopes aroused two years before, during May and June 1968, still animated French youth culture: "In France, there was May. Whether one likes it or not, consciously or not, the pop movement at its deepest level . . . is inextricably linked to the need for revolution."[102] The experience of communion that youth sought out in rock festivals was symptomatic of deeper political aspirations— aspirations that had been displaced but not wholly extinguished. Should pop festivals be banned in France going forward, this would only fuel the public's hunger to see realized the utopia for which festivals were but a faint presentiment: "What if next year we aren't offered any more lovely pop festivals? But we are waiting for another, much more fabulous and much more generous festival, that of the oppressed. Do you know what that is called?"[103]

Judging from the bulk of articles and published letters, such full-throated support for the actions of the ex–Gauche prolétarienne represented a minority position within the rock community. Nevertheless, advocates for a more thoroughgoing politicization of *la pop' music* became an increasingly vocal constituency in the latter months of 1970. While most fans worried that the infusion of politics into pop simply increased the likelihood of governmental crackdowns, others contended that this represented the best way to make the music speak directly to the hopes, desires, and frustrations of French youth. From this perspective, the continuing resilience of *gauchisme* within French youth culture, instead of representing an obstacle to the emerging rock community, was a resource that it could draw upon, especially in warding off the threat posed by commercial interests. As Chris Warne has pointed out, this marked something of a departure: "What was once derided as an outmoded and restrictive force in France, preventing the emergence of a local counterculture . . . now appears to be acting as a kind of protection, the ground from which the countercultural resistance to recuperation will be conducted."[104] The tenacious grip of *gauchisme,* once viewed as an impediment, was transformed into a means of guaranteeing the French counterculture's integrity.

The emergence of a faction of politically engaged rock enthusiasts was underlined by the formation in fall 1970 of the Force de libération et d'intervention pop (FLIP), an organization that explicitly sought to marry rock music and left-wing agitation. In a manifesto published in October 1970, the group proclaimed that the events of the summer, far from discrediting the conjunction of rock and politics, had instead demonstrated how closely connected the two were.[105] Above all, the festivals had revealed the power of rock to mobilize youth, a power that disquieted the political and commercial establishment in France: "We are a certain number . . . who wish to draw the lessons of *l'été pop.* . . . Banned or tolerated, sabotaged, 'cursed' in every possible way, such festivals have shown the force of the pop movement among youth."[106] The failure of the previous summer's "spectacular" and "commercial" ventures did not reflect poorly on the rock community in France. On the contrary, the troubles encountered by festival organizers paradoxically demonstrated the very strength of this community. The hostility of French youth to the co-optation of its music was to be lauded, not denounced: "For them, pop is something more than a merchandise, it is a new way of living that passes necessarily by way of a radical contestation of bourgeois society."[107] In terms of concrete actions, FLIP called for rock to be liberated from closed performance venues. Rather than allowing music to remain trapped within the spaces conventionally designated for concerts, cordoned off from the outside world, FLIP proposed bringing music to everyday settings in the hope of rousing individuals to action. The energies unleashed by rock would no longer be safely quarantined in auditoriums and festival sites but would spill out into public space.[108]

FLIP concluded the manifesto by announcing that "henceforth we will choose the moments and the terrain where we will intervene, we will create situations ourselves."[109] It did not take long for the organization to make good on this promise. By the time their manifesto was published in October 1970, FLIP had already engaged in their first public action. On 22 September a group of some five hundred individuals, with FLIP leading the way, forced their way into a Rolling Stones concert at the Palais des Sports in Paris.[110] Having made their way past the outnumbered security guards, the throng proceeded to claim for themselves the best seats in the house, those that had been reserved for record company executives and local celebrities. One member of FLIP managed to mount the stage in the ensuing chaos and make a declaration to the crowd: "We have had enough of paying to listen to rock, of paying to go to the cinema, of paying to screw. The world belongs to us. Let's seize it."[111] Similar incidents played out during the following two concerts given by the Stones in Paris. (Asked in an interview why he allowed *gauchistes* to commandeer the microphone, Mick Jagger struck an indulgent tone: "These crazy French people love to talk, they want to talk all the time. I don't mean it's a bad thing, in any case I can't do anything about it. French people want to talk.")[112] According to FLIP, the intervention at the Palais des Sports was exemplary. It reclaimed pop for the people, for all those who wished to attend the concerts but could not afford the ticket prices. But it also revealed the complicity of bands like the Rolling Stones in diverting youth revolt. According to FLIP, the Stones offered their listeners a fantasy of contestation, all the while enjoying the monetary rewards provided to them by the very system they made a show of rejecting: "The Stones are trapped in an insurmountable contradiction: they protect their music of revolt with cordons of C.R.S. agents."[113]

While FLIP's intervention at the Palais des Sports followed the pattern established by Maoist agitators at the Aix and Biot festivals, there were significant differences between the two in terms of their methods and objectives. For the members of the ex–Gauche prolétarienne, the interest of rock festivals had little to do with the music per se and more to do with the conditions surrounding its distribution and consumption. The overriding imperative was to capitalize on various sources of public discontent by framing these in terms of the Maoists' Manichean vision of class warfare. Restrictions on access to rock, whether a result of government intervention or the price-rationing mechanisms of the marketplace, furnished grievances that *gauchistes* could exploit. Besides, the sheer number of rock fans that festivals brought together in one place made them opportune targets for those wishing to ignite the cycle of provocation, repression, and revolt. By contrast, the music itself occupied a far more central place in the program of FLIP. While they also sought to stoke anger at the commercial exploitation of rock, this was framed in terms of the corrupting influence it exercised on the music itself. Their willingness to put music to use for political ends was counterbalanced by a desire to "liberate" rock from its subjugation to heteronomous demands, principally those of the market. Hence the call to arms that concluded one of their communiqués: "Refuse to pay! Don't be caught in the trap of recuperation! Liberate pop music!"[114] Rock would only realize its full potential as the "folk" expression of the emerging youth movement once the commercial intermediaries who stood between performer and audience had been removed. If the "condition of the spectacle" was to be avoided, if rock was to be the organic expression of youth, it was necessary for the rock community to take matters into their own hands and self-manage the music's production and distribution.[115]

The desire of FLIP to free rock from the external pressures of the marketplace derived in no small part from the fact that most of its members were themselves rock musicians and thus heavily invested in asserting control over the music they produced. The preponderance of FLIP's militants came from underground bands like Komintern, Maajun, Dagon, and Fille qui mousse, bands that had gained notoriety in the media by virtue of their overt political posture.[116] This suggests that there was some measure of self-interest at work in FLIP's stance, as their denunciation of the Rolling Stones indicated. The argument that there was "an insurmountable contradiction" between the antiestablishment image of the Stones and their reliance on commercial circuits of production and distribution served to discredit a group whose dominant position in the media had crowded out French rock acts. Viewed from this angle, the politicization of rock advocated by FLIP offered a different set of criteria for judging rock groups, one that placed indigenous underground bands in a more advantageous position, at least in symbolic terms. Groups that visibly eschewed material success out of a dedication to higher ideological principles received a measure of legitimacy in return. The attempt to politicize rock thus amounted to an attempt to institute within the French rock scene what Bourdieu has described as the "upside down" reward system of the art world. However, in adopting the art world principle of "loser wins," FLIP filtered it through the political culture of *gauchisme*. In particular, the far left's tendency to romanticize the most abject of social categories, viewing them as the force that would topple the existing social order, further reinforced the inverted hierarchy of art world values. Refusal of the market may have diminished the economic fortunes of the bands that participated in FLIP, but it paid dividends within the French counterculture's economy of prestige.

At the same time as *l'été pop* encouraged some members of the rock community to take a greater interest in politics, it also led certain currents of the extreme left to reassess its attitudes toward the counterculture. One factor driving the turn toward "cultural leftism" was the desire to appeal to constituencies hitherto disregarded in *gauchiste* discourse. In seeking to form a broad common front, organizations like the ex–Gauche prolétarienne had started to look beyond the industrial working class, making overtures to what had once been regarded as peripheral social groups: women, ethnic minorities, immigrants, and youth. Concomitant with this more expansive definition of the revolutionary subject was a more expansive conception of political struggle, now understood to involve more than just the fight against workplace exploitation. Influenced by the writings of Henri Lefebvre and the situationists as well as American countercultural figures like Abbie Hoffman and Jerry Rubin, certain segments of the *gauchiste* milieu acknowledged leisure, lifestyle, and sexuality as important sites of political contest. Where *gauchistes* had once viewed the Anglo-American counterculture as a form of escapism lacking political import, a growing number of militants were beginning to see in it a counterweight to the dominant ideology. The valorization of hedonism, for instance, undermined capitalism's "Protestant ethic" of deferred gratification. Youth, one militant declared, "are less and less willing to submit to this philosophy of slavery, according to which it is 'highly honorable' to lead a life with neither the slightest pleasure nor real freedom."[117] Likewise, the alternative lifestyles the counterculture promoted had the practical benefit of showing that another world was possible. After the taste of freedom experienced during the course of a rock festival, for example, it was unclear that individuals would "quietly go back to the job and work overtime day after day in order to buy a Frigidaire."[118]

The turn toward cultural leftism widened the doctrinal fissures that ran through *gauchisme*. On one side of the divide were those who continued to view the counterculture and its offspring as suspect, the latest form of false consciousness to afflict the masses. Among parties that hewed closely to Marxist orthodoxy—the Trotskyist Ligue communiste révolutionnaire being a case in point—interest in rock was tempered by the sense that its fans were either wholly depoliticized or unaware of the political implications inherent in their cultural practices. In the most explicit exposition of its cultural policy, the Ligue adopted an ostensibly tolerant position vis-à-vis the counterculture. Contrasting its openness in matters of art and culture with the more illiberal tendencies of Maoism or Soviet-style Communism, the Ligue argued that phenomena like rock and the hippie movement possessed a diagnostic value: "Lacking more detailed information, we prefer to consider the hippie subculture more in its social than its cultural aspect. This youth movement, which cannot recognize itself either in the declining bourgeoisie or in the bureaucratized workers' movement, expresses the deepening ideological crisis of capitalist society. But left adrift by dint of its weakness or the absence of revolutionary politics, it can very well slide into various forms of retrograde populism."[119] Lurking behind this apparent open-mindedness was a thinly veiled condescension: rock fans were not treated as fully conscious agents but as naïfs ignorant of the true meaning of their tastes. This tendency to reduce rock to the status of a sociological document was also apparent in a review of the film *Gimme Shelter*, the Maysles brothers' documentary on the Rolling Stones' ill-fated appearance at the 1969 Altamont Festival. The author of the review, Eugène Vincent, argued that the film's merit lay in its demonstration of the incoherence of the youth revolt expressed by rock music. This being the case, it was incumbent upon militants to assist youth in decoding rock's latent meaning. What was necessary was to disabuse rock fans of the notion that they could "create a countersociety" simply by possessing "a counterculture (pop music)." Rather, Trotskyists should endeavor to use films like *Gimme Shelter* to "help those who listen to this music—with all the ideology it carries in tow—to draw the conclusions that it imposes."[120]

On the other side of the growing divide within *gauchisme* were militants who contended that rock music and the counterculture were not just symptoms of social malaise, but possessed a positive political value. The emergence of this libertarian strain of *gauchisme* was most apparent in the pages of *Tout!*, a newspaper produced by a diverse group comprised of Maoist militants and members of the various feminist, homosexual, and youth movements that came into being in the years after 1968 (the Mouvement de libération des femmes, the Front homosexuel d'action révolutionnaire, and the Front de libération de la jeunesse). At the center of this eclectic coalition were members of the short-lived Maoist group Vive la révolution, which had been born out of the breakup of the pro-Chinese Union des jeunesses communistes (marxistes-léninistes) (UJCML) in the months following May '68.[121] Like other offshoots of the UJCML (such as the Gauche prolétarienne), Vive la révolution vaunted the ideal of spontaneous insurrection. The revolutionary wave that would overturn the existing social order would be initiated not by some organism that stood outside or above the masses but by the masses themselves. But unlike their *frères-ennemis* within the Maoist movement, Vive la révolution contended that the revolt of the people against the reigning social order could be found in a wide variety of social contexts. While wildcat strikes, factory occupations, and street fighting with police may have been the most profound expressions of popular discontent, other, less conventional forms of dissent were not to be dismissed. Rather than minimize struggles taking place in the domains of culture and lifestyle, it was necessary to fuse these new sites of contestation with traditional forms of political intervention. To treat the battle against the educational system, sexual mores, or normative modes of behavior as a "detour" from class struggle, as the Gauche prolétarienne did, was to misread the lessons of May '68; it was, in the words of Vive la révolution, to "empty the occupation of the Sorbonne or of the Odéon of all its content."[122] And while the working class continued to occupy a privileged position within the discourse of Vive la révolution, this did not lead to the extreme self-abnegation that was to be found within the Gauche prolétarienne. The status of militants as "petty bourgeois intellectuals" was not a source of shame or something to be renounced but was to be used as yet another front from which an attack on the capitalist edifice could be launched.

It was in the pages of *Tout!* that the implications of this strange merger of cultural libertarianism with Maoist populism were most fully developed. Over the course of its short life span (the publication ran from September 1970 to July 1971) *Tout!* examined the emancipatory potential of such phenomena as *fêtes sauvages*, communes, and homosexual desire. Included in the constellation of liberatory practices that *Tout!* promoted was rock music. The very first issue of the publication featured a section devoted to the recent spate of rock festivals in France. For the contributors to *Tout!*, the events of *l'été pop* aroused a mixture of curiosity and suspicion. Given the enduring commitment of the journal's collaborators to the cause of revolutionary politics, it was only natural that the commercial and ideological trappings of the counterculture would come in for criticism. Singled out for denunciation was the central place accorded to spirituality within the American hippie movement. What had been characterized in mainstream journalistic accounts of the American counterculture as a refreshing alternative to the stale rhetoric of French *gauchisme* appeared to the writers for *Tout!* as an ideological straitjacket imposed on youth by powerful commercial forces. Fortunately, they noted, French rock fans had thus far resisted efforts to "have them ingest Buddhism or Zen, as in California."[123] Yet such lingering suspicions of the counterculture, residues of the journal's Maoist roots, tended to give way in the end to an appreciation of rock's positive attributes. Particular importance was attached to the music's ability to transform an otherwise atomized collection of listeners into a fused group. One article cited the testimonials of a number of individuals who had attended the Aix festival, highlighting the sense of communion they experienced: "We're all part of a gang, before I was alone and then we all encountered one another. We're all together, we share everything."[124]

The tentative interest in rock evinced by the first issue of *Tout!* became more pronounced over the months that followed. While certain aspects of the counterculture continued to come under fire, the rapprochement of libertarian Maoists and engaged rock musicians grew. The second issue of *Tout!* featured FLIP's first communiqué, an account of the intervention at the Rolling Stones concert a month earlier, while the following month saw the publication of FLIP's founding manifesto.[125] What most interested the contributors to *Tout!* was rock's accessibility, the ease with which it could be enjoyed and produced. This last point was crucial. In various articles published in the journal, rock was cast as an especially potent vehicle for the democratization of creative expression, one of the central preoccupations of *Tout!* (An editorial in the magazine's inaugural issue had recalled that one of the main achievements of May '68 had been the triumph of "the creative initiative of people over organized boredom.")[126] To be sure, the egalitarianism inherent in rock was not a given but a potential that awaited realization. And for this latent promise to be fulfilled, French youth had to cease being passive consumers of the products churned out by the record industry. They had to produce their own music. Furthermore, youth needed to avoid the blind imitation of foreign models. One author thus argued that the problems faced by the French rock scene were not to be resolved by "the importation of the American movement."[127] Rather, French rock had to reinvent the genre to make it better suit domestic concerns: "What's pop over there becomes something for elites here. Let us not be afraid, then: the French cultural revolution, plugged into a different reality than that of the United States, that of a secondary imperial center where the mass of people are [politically] involved, is not to be *récopied.*"[128] Complementing such calls to develop a specifically French countercul- ture were accounts describing individual efforts at seizing the creative ini- tiative, at producing one's own music. In one testimonial a teenager re- counted how he had finally had enough of the "bludgeoning" *(matraquage)* he received at the hands of commercial radio stations. Whereas once he would have had no choice but to endure the music imposed on him from on high, in the new era of post-'68 cultural emancipation this was no longer the case: "Gone is the age when the proletariat didn't play music because it seemed petty bourgeois. . . . We no longer are ashamed to be ourselves; in short, we create."[129]

Tributes to rock's power to liberate the creative energies of the work- ing class reflected the peculiar blend of ideologies at work in the dis- course of *Tout!* The practices of the American counterculture were filtered through Lefebvrian critiques of everyday life and theories of working-class autonomy.[130] The *prise de parole* that rock facilitated was characterized as a way of transforming life "here and now,"[131] as well as a means of empowering those groups previously excluded from the cultural sphere. Yet this democratizing potential was not the only aspect of rock to garner the attention of cultural leftists. Equally impor- tant was the perceived physicality of the genre, its appeal to the body rather than the mind. This valorization of rock's apparent ability to bypass language and intellect and to affect individuals at a corporeal level was tied to a larger breach that was opening between cultural left- ists and their more orthodox peers within the extreme left, one that centered around the issues of pleasure, desire, and the body.

In the case of Vive la révolution, the notion that pleasure itself was a site of political struggle—the notion that the revolution should provide roses as well as bread—was one of the features the group had used to distinguish itself from its *gauchiste* rivals. One militant, Hélène, explained in a profile of Vive la révolution that "traditional political organizations have no relation to joy. They use the same repressive system of little bosses and duties to be fulfilled."[132] Another militant added that nowadays "bread, peace, and land no longer constitute the motor driving the initiative of the masses," but rather that "it is the search for happiness that moves them."[133] This engagement with the problematic of pleasure found its most pointed expression in the space that *Tout!* devoted to the issue of sexual liberation, culminating in the publication's twelfth issue, whose front page was adorned with a photograph of a bared ass and a headline that called for the "free disposition of our bodies." The accompanying article called for an end to the regulation of physical desire, a right to pursue different forms of sexuality without harassment (most notably homosexuality), legalization of abortion, and the free distribution of contraception.[134] The imposition of certain normative sexual identities by the *"hétéro-flics"* (hetero-cops) of society was cast as one of the principal ways that the bourgeois order was able to capture the destabilizing force of desire and channel it into activities that would reinforce, rather than jeopardize, existing power relations.

With *Tout!* focusing much of its attention on sexual politics—a source of dissension within Vive la révolution and a major factor in the organization's breakup in June 1971[135]—the task of exploring rock's relationship to the new politics of pleasure fell to other platforms. Key among these were journals like *L'Idiot international* and its spin-off, *L'Idiot liberté,* as well as the magazine *Actuel,* one of the main propagators of the counterculture in France. Founded in 1968 by Claude Delcloo, the magazine in its first incarnation served as a journalistic adjunct to the recently inaugurated BYG/Actuel record label (see chapter 3), and as such provided a venue for documenting developments in avant-garde jazz. By 1970 *Actuel* had run into financial difficulties and was sold off to a group of former *gauchistes.* With a new editorial committee led by Jean-François Bizot in place, *Actuel* was reborn in the fall of 1970.[136] From the outset, the new series of *Actuel* devoted substantial space to rock, with the physicality of the genre assuming a central place in readings of the music's political significance. Exemplary in this regard was an article by Paul Alessandrini that appeared in the March 1971 issue as part of a dossier on the subject of music and politics.[137] Alessandrini's article situates rock's physicality within a chain of opposed terms: mind/body, order/disorder, code/excess, politics/revolt, and word/sound. By superimposing these binary oppositions, Alessandrini relates sonic transgression to acts of political transgression. Rock, in short, comes to represent "the affirmation of a desire for excess, for the plenitude of experience. . . . Pop music is *gauchiste* in its lack of constraint, the affirmation of its nonculture and of its primal character."[138] Tangled up in the series of dualisms that underpins Alessandrini's account are passing references to other genres that embody precisely those traits that rock negates. For the most part the musical others Alessandrini invokes are left unnamed, heaped together under the catchall rubric of "official music."[139] In other instances, however, Alessandrini identified the genres that stood in opposition to the "primal character" of rock. One of these was folk music. In rock, Alessandrini argues, language is dissolved into sound; in folk, by contrast, "the music is only the support for the accompaniment of the word." Even if a folk song's lyrics should prove radical, this political content is contradicted by "the conformism, prettiness, or charm of the voice and the acoustic accompaniment. The word disappears behind the tenderness and the calm that cradles it."[140]

The stakes involved in Alessandrini's opposition of rock and folk— indeed, in the entire chain of dualisms that his essay puts into play— extended well beyond the parochial concerns of the musical field. For it was not just the clarity and comprehensibility of folk music that were at odds with the physicality of rock. Conventional modes of political activism were likewise seen as incompatible with the sort of immediate corporeal pleasures that rock afforded. Alessandrini makes this clear from the very first sentence of his essay: "Rather than politics, which presumes a *prise de conscience,* the first electric formulations [of rock] were synonymous with revolt, in the sonic violence and the return to the body that they presupposed."[141] Implied in this juxtaposition is the notion that politics and rock operate on distinct levels of experience, one cognitive, the other precognitive. Also implied is the notion that rock did not serve politics so much as displace it, offering youth an alternative vehicle for expressing their discontent. The same was true for the other countercultural practices that *Actuel* promoted. These were presented as the means by which the *marxisant* dreams of changing life could be realized immediately without having to await for a complete and utter transformation of social relations.

Advocacy on behalf of the "new culture" that *Actuel* and other cultural leftists undertook was not an entirely disinterested affair. Nor was the declaration that rock was opposed to traditional forms of political action, including *gauchisme.* Rather, both lines of argument partook of the heated intramural debates that animated the *gauchiste* milieu. Both, that is, sought to discredit the more orthodox rivals of the cultural left, the various Maoist and Trotskyist groups that had undergone a renaissance during the *après-mai* period. Furthermore, the introduction of the issues of pleasure and desire into these debates transformed the terms in which they were conducted. Whereas extreme left groups had previously sought to outbid one another by arguing over which was the most radical, the most committed, the most faithful to the Marxist-Leninist heritage, the valorization of pleasure among cultural leftists turned this inflationary logic on its head. The contest over which organization was the most *pur et dur* was disrupted by the contention that this way of defining the debate was itself a symptom of *gauchisme*'s continuing adherence to the very value system it sought to overthrow. Groups like the Ligue communiste révolutionnaire and the GP were thus accused of promising little more than the substitution of one repressive regime for another, what Peter Starr has dubbed "structural repetition"—the notion that even the "'revolutionary vanguard' . . . is seen to reproduce essentially capitalist forms of rationality."[142] This line of criticism had already been sketched out in the inaugural issue of *Tout!*, where *gauchisme*'s unacknowledged commitment to the "Protestant ethic" of capitalism—its valorization of hard work, self-restraint, and deferred gratification—was vehemently denounced:

> On the left, and even to the left of the left, among all those who still speak in the name of those who work, [in the name of the] 'dignity of workers,' we find the solid pillars of the ideology of work. The bourgeoisie say: you need to work to earn some cash, in order to live off of household appliances and the movies. Séguy [the head of the Confédération générale du travail] and a good deal of *gauchistes* respond: Ugh! It's disgusting, our dignity is work. . . . Alongside those who exploit work in order to win some money from it we find those who exploit it ideologically in order to win power.[143]

The same critique was picked up by *Actuel*, not in order to reform *gauchisme* but in order to bury it: "The critique of militancy, the final liquidation of *homo politicus*, he who has no wish of living in the present, is the last and most difficult bastion to be seized. Militants—even those [who agitate for] sexual revolution—aren't those who fuck the most. Sublimation is typically their practice."[144] The repressive ethos of *gauchisme* could even be detected in the musical preferences of militants. Set against the vitality of rock was the dated, dead tradition of the revolutionary chanson: "[Leftists] still prefer 'The Internationale' to the Rolling Stones, 'La Jeune Garde' to Albert Ayler."[145] *Actuel*, by contrast, championed a "revolution for pleasure," a revolution that would put an end to the self-abnegating rhetoric of the extreme left. A teleological argument further buttressed the opposition established between a (vibrant) cultural leftism and a (senescent) *gauchisme*. The counterculture was not just an alternative to leftism but fulfilled the utopian dreams that Marxist-Leninist doctrine only spoke of in the future tense: "Communes, the liberation of women, of homosexuals, explosions in the high schools, wildcat strikes: the utopia of the here-and-now realizes *gauchisme* in destroying it."[146] The libidinal energies of youth, for too long captured by *gauchisme* and its infinitely deferred project of revolution, were released by new cultural practices (including rock) and put to work in transforming everyday life.

The response that such critiques generated among doctrinaire Maoist and Trotskyist groups was predictable. The Ligue communiste révolutionnaire brushed away the claim that it remained trapped in the same sclerotic rationalism that governed capitalist society. Against charges of "structural repetition," the Ligue retorted that the (counter)cultural turn of groups such as Vive la révolution was a sign of the degeneration of French Maoism. Having put their faith in the prospect of a spontaneous uprising of the proletariat after 1968, Maoist *groupuscules* had grown disillusioned once the mass insurrection they had anticipated failed to transpire. For some the result was a retreat into culture, which provided an imaginary space where their frustrated aspirations could endure in sublimated form. Politics proper had slowly given way to a "hippie-style infrapolitical revolt."[147] Similarly, the shattering of the naive hope in working-class autonomy, in the ability of workers to rise up without the institutional support of a party or union structure, had led to a disenchantment with the working class tout court. This in turn had given rise to the misguided search for other revolutionary subjects who might take the place of the proletariat within the Marxist vision of historical change. Groups like Vive la révolution, argued the Ligue, were guilty of "privileging mass (?) movements [comprised] of marginal strata, and neglecting as a result the struggle for winning over the organized proletariat. Nowadays, in fact, the motor force of the revolution is no longer an 'abstract' proletariat but youth."[148] While there was nothing wrong with trying to woo youth to the cause of revolution, or using rock to do so, such efforts must not lose sight of the primacy of class struggle. Otherwise militants risked succumbing to "petty bourgeois illusions concerning the possibility of individual 'liberation.' "[149]

A more curious response to the changing tenor of *gauchiste* debate was to be found within the ranks of the ex–Gauche prolétarienne. Although the group remained committed to the task of fomenting resistance to Pompidou's regime, paying little attention to culture or lifestyle issues, beginning in 1971 there was a subtle yet significant shift in the group's rhetoric, especially concerning the role of pleasure in political struggle. This was clearest in the increasingly indulgent tone the group adopted with regard to festivals—or, more precisely, to the institution of the *fête*. Previously the ex–Gauche prolétarienne had viewed such gatherings in utilitarian terms, as their interventions during *l'été pop* had made clear. The pleasures offered by rock festivals were of little interest to the group. What *was* of interest was the sheer number of spectators that such events could command, and the opportunities they presented by way of provoking confrontations with the police. By spring 1971, however, this instrumental view of the *fête* was yielding to a recognition of the intrinsic value that such events might possess. For this value to be realized, certain conditions had to be met. First, the *fête* needed to be integrated into a broader struggle, as both a culmination of prior endeavors and as a point of departure for subsequent engagements: "It [the *fête*] is preceded by a struggle that leads to it and makes it possible; it prepares a new stage, new forms. To forget this is to reduce the *fête* to individual satisfaction, pure and simple."[150] As part of a broader political project, the momentary release afforded by the *fête* was something that had to be won, not just consumed. Pleasure must not be purchased, but wrenched from the clutches of contemporary society (the ex–Gauche prolétarienne had in this regard progressed little from the justifications used to explain their interventions during *l'été pop*).[151] Finally, the *fête* must embrace all strata of society if it is to avoid lapsing into a form of individual gratification ("One frees oneself only in freeing others").[152]

By way of illustration, the group pointed to a recent *fête* in Lyon marking the end of a series of protests there. High school students who had mobilized in response to the imprisonment of left-wing militants formed an alliance with farmers protesting the state's agricultural policies.[153] To help seal this fragile solidarity the students organized a *fête* at a local high school that brought together different parties: "young workers, immigrants, high school students, university students, 'vagabonds.'"[154] Workers and students proceeded to write their grievances on the walls of the hall where the *fête* took place, food and wine were distributed, individuals improvised music, impromptu skits were performed, and a handful of bands performed: "In the great hall, pop and free jazz groups went at it. Four groups performed. All the mates played for free. They played on a somewhat narrow stage, in the middle of boys and girls who danced at the same time as the walls were being lit up with a projector. Everyone was feeling good, everyone was listening. It was a *fête*. But not just any *fête*, not a *fête* that flees from reality, from the daily struggle, but on the contrary one that is intertwined with this struggle, that arises out of it and takes it into account."[155] The *fête* may only have been valued as a symbol of worker-student solidarity, and music may have been reduced to a purely accompanimental role, but the simple fact that such diversions were being countenanced at all reflected a loosening of the ex–Gauche prolétarienne's hitherto doctrinaire stance.

FROM ROCK FESTIVALS TO *FÊTES POLITIQUES*

By 1971 a number of connections had begun to bridge the gulf that previously separated the rock community and the *gauchiste* milieu. On one side stood a contingent of radicalized musicians, listeners, and critics, FLIP being the most visible manifestation of this newfound engagement. On the other side were libertarian Maoists and cultural leftists, the latter increasingly disenchanted with the *doxa* of the extreme left. Both sets of actors stood to gain from the convergence of genre culture and political culture: engaged musicians won a degree of legitimacy for their activities, while cultural leftists were able to gain a rhetorical advantage over rivals within the agonistic field of *gauchisme*. At the center of this intersection of political and musical communities was a cluster of overlapping interests: the revolution of everyday life, the democratization of cultural production, rock's ability to galvanize youth, and the liberatory powers of pleasure—including musical pleasure.

Within this collection of shared concerns the *fête*, as both concept and reality, occupied a privileged position. It represented a nodal point where ideals like the democratization of expression, the release from quotidian constraint, the *rassemblement* of youth, and the gratification of desire converged. The embrace of the *fête* by the ex–Gauche prolétarienne was representative of the fascination that this institution exercised on the French left in the early 1970s.[156] Part of this fascination stemmed from its historical legacy in France, from its roots in the feast-day and market fairs of the *ancien régime,* through the *fêtes révolutionnaires* of the 1790s, up to the civic celebrations instituted under the Third Republic. The capaciousness of the term also contributed to its attraction. The word *fête* encompasses a wide range of events, from relatively intimate affairs to massive communal gatherings. It was this latter understanding of the *fête*—as an event that implicated the totality of a community—that had long attracted the attention of sociologists, anthropologists, and historians, from Durkheim and Caillois to Duvignaud and Certeau, and that became something of an idée fixe among left-wing thinkers during the course of the 1970s. The appeal of the *fête* for the latter is easy to discern: regarded as a collective enterprise that involved the temporary suspension of social codes, the *fête* appeared to stand in a proleptic relationship to the revolutionary transformation of society.[157] It offered a glimpse of the transfigured world that the end of capitalist exploitation would instate. Given this way of framing the phenomenon, certain traits that previous generations of social scientists had identified in the *fête* were valorized and others marginalized. Spontaneity, conviviality, the disruption of roles, and the dissolution of the self into the collective became the markers of the authentic *fête*. Within this politicized conception of the *fête*, events like rock festivals occupied a curious position. Viewed from a certain angle, they represented nothing other than the modern form of this age-old tradition.[158] Rock festivals were a manifestation of a perennial desire for *rassemblement*. As such, they were themselves a kind of *fête*, or could be if they met certain conditions. But to the extent that festivals failed to display the traits privileged within left-wing discourse, they could just as easily represent a corruption of this popular tradition.[159] In such cases they became the deformed double of the true *fête*: in the place of spontaneity there was structure; in the place of commingling there was a separation of performer and audience; in the place of gift exchange there was commercial transaction.

Lurking behind this newfound fascination with the *fête* was the specter of May '68. The ludic aspects of the May events helped reinforce the belief that disturbances in the fabric of everyday life, even playful ones, could trigger political revolt. This both encouraged and was encouraged by the increasingly popular reimagination of May '68 as a carnivalesque event (indeed, it is here that first emerged the tendency, discussed in the introduction, of treating May as more of a cultural than a political event). A number of key elements of this trope were already present in the reactions elicited by *l'été pop*. Alessandrini's notion that festivals offered youth the opportunity to experience itself as a collective subject, or *Tout!*'s celebration of rock's ability to unite disparate individuals as part of a "fused group": such claims cast rock festivals as evincing the sort of conviviality that lay at the heart of the *fête*. Similar reactions were prompted by the so-called *fêtes sauvages* (unauthorized or illegal *fêtes*) organized by *gauchiste* groups. Events like the unofficial commemoration of the Paris Commune held at the Marché aux Puces in Paris in March 1971 or the *fête sauvage* convened by Vive la révolution on the beaches near Montpellier in August of the same year, among others, signaled the growing importance ascribed to *fêtes* within the far left's repertoire of political actions.[160]

One of the clearest signs of the increasingly prominent place that the *fête* was assuming within the discourse of the far left could be seen in the responses generated by a rock concert that took place at the Palais des Sports in January 1971. Organized by the Ecole supérieure des travaux publics, the show was to feature five groups: Gong, Kevin Ayers and The Whole World, the Soft Machine, Yes, and Iron Butterfly. As had been the case at Aix, Biot, and at the Rolling Stones concert a few months earlier, a band of agitators forced their way into the arena.[161] At first, events followed what had by then become a predictable pattern: upon gaining entry to the auditorium, *gauchistes* mounted the stage and made a series of declarations over the sound system. "Pop music belongs to youth, all youth," one person exclaimed, "not to capitalism and a privileged few."[162] Others exhorted the crowd to acts of vandalism: "Burn the cars of the rich! Popular resistance!"[163] Yet others used the platform to air the grievances of French rock bands: "If you pay 50F to get into a concert, it's because English musicians demand such fortunes. Enough of the exploitation by English musicians; long live French musicians!"[164] After a short delay the music got underway. Didier Malherbe and Lol Coxhill, the saxophonists for Gong and The Whole World, warmed up the crowd with an improvised duet. Following an announcement stating that the show would be opened to the public free of charge, Gong began its set.[165] Meanwhile, a small group of individuals broke into a concession stand and showered the audience members with beer, ice cream bars, and cigarettes. The music continued until midnight, at which point the police cut the power and evacuated the auditorium.

While the hooliganism at the Palais des Sports bore little relation to revolutionary politics, it did conform to the model established by the ex–Gauche prolétarienne during *l'été pop*. This suggests that the aim of the provocateurs was not so much to "liberate" the music but to take advantage of the occasion for launching a series of escalating confrontations with the police in the hope of reaching the tipping point where sporadic revolt turns into mass insurrection. Curiously enough, this was not how the event was interpreted after the fact. What intrigued cultural leftists were not the ritualized skirmishes between militants and police but the convivial atmosphere that reigned for a few hours once the organization in the auditorium had broken down. A report that appeared in *Tout!* was characteristic. While applauding the fact that the police had been "tripped up" *(butés)* by "those of us who cried 'free concert' [and] 'liberate pop music,'" the article claimed that the true significance of the event was to be found elsewhere, in the spirit of the *fête* that prevailed.[166] And what had allowed this feeling of communality to emerge in the first place was a shared affinity for rock music: "We don't commune because we come from the same milieu, because we have the same social standing, the same-sized wallet, but because we all like pop music, . . . because we all like to *faire la fête.*"[167]

Notably, this way of reading the incident at the Palais des Sports—as a revivification of the spirit of the *fête*—was also voiced by members of the rock community. Jean-Marc Pascal, writing in the fanzine *Pop Music,* remarked that "despite a muted sense of apprehension, a feeling of uncertainty and incoherence, the *fête* set in. All of a sudden, everything is abolished: Money, property, taboos; we are among ourselves, among youth, and the Palais des Sports belongs to us."[168] But even as certain elements in the rock community joined with the extreme left in celebrating the sense of communion that had materialized at the Palais des Sports, others feared that such fleeting moments of festivity were purchased at a steep price. Brawls with security agents, rampant gate crashing, the pillage of concession stands—such disturbances threatened to sully the image of the rock community. The extreme left was again singled out for blame. Instead of setting upon the culture of the bourgeoisie, *gauchistes* had instead undermined "the only musical expression that could have supported them."[169] As had been the case in the aftermath of *l'été pop,* the intervention at the Palais des Sports was seen as jeopardizing the French rock scene, calling into question its viability. Some went so far as to ring the death knell of the rock concert in France (figure 8).

Concerns regarding the future of rock concerts, while exaggerated, were not unfounded. In the weeks that followed the show at the Palais des Sports a number of events were canceled for fear of *gauchiste* interventions, including concerts by Led Zeppelin and Pink Floyd in Lyon.[170] Booking agents for major venues in Paris and other cities announced their reluctance to program rock acts; such was the case with both the Olympia and the Gaumont Palace in Paris, as well as the Palais des Sports, which had suffered approximately forty million francs in damage on 31 January.[171] Still, if the incidents at the Palais des Sports represented

Méchamment pop a la douleur de vous faire part
du décès des

CONCERTS POP FRANÇAIS

après une longue maladie.

Frappée en plein effort par des agents provocateurs,
la bête s'est écroulée sous les lazzi
au Palais des sports de Paris
ce 31 janvier 1971.

Les obsèques ont eu lieu dans l'indifférence générale.

Requiescat In Olympia !

FIGURE 8. A death notice for pop concerts in France, published in *Charlie Hebdo* 12 (8 February 1971). The caption reads: "Méchamment Pop [pseudonym of critic Pierre Lattès] is saddened to inform you of the demise of FRENCH POP CONCERTS after a long illness. Struck down in the middle of its efforts by agents provocateurs, the beast collapsed under the weight of derision at the Palais des Sports in Paris on 31 January 1971. The memorial services have taken place in an atmosphere of general indifference. Requiescat in Olympia!"

a blow to the music scene in France, reports of the rock concert's demise were premature. Concert life soon recovered, as larger venues resumed booking rock acts and alternative spaces (community centers, Maisons des jeunes et de la culture, university campuses) opened their doors to native French bands. The prognosis for rock festivals, however, was less optimistic. Renewed interest in the *fête* notwithstanding, there were few large-scale events in the years that followed, and those that did take place were rarely successful. A free festival staged by couturier Jean Bouquin in the town of Auvers-sur-Oise in June 1971 turned out to be a logistical disaster. None of the headlining acts that Bouquin claimed to have booked (the Grateful Dead, Jefferson Airplane, The Rolling Stones, Pink Floyd, and Led Zeppelin) made an appearance, and the event had to be cut short because of inclement weather. A series of rock festivals that took place the following summer also proved disappointing, the sole exception being one that took place in Bièvres in June 1972. Even though none of the events organized for the summer of 1972 faced the threat of governmental interdiction, they failed to generate the same kind of excitement as the initial wave of French rock festivals two years earlier. Recalling the Festival de Saint-Gratien in Nantes, Jean-Pierre Lentin, a member of the band Dagon and staff writer for *Actuel,* described the "dejected air" *(l'air abbatu)* that hung over the small crowd that had gathered on the first night of the event. The "second 'Summer of Festivals' in France, that of authorized festivals," he remarked, was also "that of sad caricatures, failures, and flops."[172]

That later festivals proved no more successful than their precursors, either aesthetically or socially, was not altogether surprising and may be attributed in part to the fragmentation the genre had undergone in the years since *l'été pop.* To a certain extent this was a reflection of the continuing sway that Anglo-American musical trends held over the French rock scene. With a few exceptions, the proliferating divisions and subdivisions of English-language rock (glam, hard rock, heavy metal, folk rock, prog) found not only audiences in France but also emulators among French rock bands. Concomitant with this splintering of the rock community was the emergence of hybrid forms as the sound of rock was incorporated into the stylistic repertoire of certain *variétés* and chanson artists. By the mid-1970s the blending of rock and chanson in the music of Jacques Higelin and Bernard Lavilliers, or of rock and mainstream *variétés* in that of Marc Charlan and Patrick Juvet, had eroded generic distinctions operative just a few years before.[173] Together, the dual forces of generic fragmentation and hybridization helped dispel the simplistic notion that rock was either a unified or monolithic entity, or that it represented youth as a no less unified or monolithic community. The belief in rock's capacity to mobilize French youth en masse could not be realistically sustained in face of these two countervailing tendencies. This, in turn, diminished the import that had previously been assigned to the rock festival. Paul Alessandrini, who in 1970 had argued that such events marked an occasion where youth from all social backgrounds could come together as a collective subject, had by 1976 abandoned this optimistic understanding of the rock festival: "Rock music has become an abstract term, empty of meaning. . . . Ever since this fragmentation *the*

very notion of the great unitary gathering is outdated, if not dangerous."[174] With the splintering of the rock scene, the festival's symbolic
function, as the moment when the rock community affirmed itself as a
coherent and cohesive entity, could no longer be sustained.

But even as the short-lived era of the rock festival in France was drawing to a close, other institutions emerged to fill the artistic and ideological vacuum. In particular, the yearly *fêtes* organized by various political
parties picked up where rock festivals and unauthorized *fêtes sauvages*
had left off. The largest and longest-running of these was the Fête de
l'Humanité, a yearly event that raised funds for L'Humanité, the party
organ of the Parti communiste français.[175] Popular music had been a
staple of the Fête de l'Humanité since its inception in 1930, with chanson artists long a major attraction. Beginning in the 1960s organizers
made a concerted effort to attract a younger demographic by supple-
menting the roster of established singer-songwriters (Léo Ferré, Jean
Ferrat, Jacques Brel, Catherine Sauvage) with younger rock-and-roll
and *yéyé* artists (Claude François, Eddy Mitchell, Johnny Hallyday).[176]
Efforts to reach out to youth continued into the 1970s, adjusted to take
into account changing tastes in popular music. Starting in 1970 Anglo-
American rock acts featured on the festival program, part of an eclectic
mix of musical genres selected to appeal to diverse constituencies. During the first half of the 1970s, major international acts like Pink Floyd,
Soft Machine, The Who, and The Kinks appeared on the main stage
alongside *variétés* artists, new music ensembles, jazz performers, and symphony orchestras.[177] Such heterogeneity led some to charge that the event
was engaged in an incoherent form of musical demagoguery.[178] Others
dismissed the event as the caricature of the true *fête;* instead of breaking
with quotidian routine, the Fête de l'Humanité, with its stalls vending
sausages, *frites,* and souvenirs, merely replicated it in a scarcely disguised form.[179] And yet there was a sense that an event like this succeeded where rock festivals had failed. Even critics of the event—like
Alain Dister, writing on the 1971 Fête de l'Humanité in *Rock & Folk*—
had to admit that "it was a little bit the big festival that we have been
waiting for during the past couple of years."[180] Others were less guarded
in their evaluation: "On leaving Courneuve [the site of the 1972 event]
I had the impression that I had at last experienced the first successful
pop festival in France."[181]

In addition to major international acts like The Who and Pink Floyd,
French bands were also programmed at the Fête de l'Humanité, though
they were typically relegated to side stages. French bands fared better

among the numerous imitators that the event spawned. Political organizations such as the Parti socialiste unifié and Lutte ouvrière began holding their own *fêtes* in the early 1970s, as did various left-wing publications: *Rouge,* the organ of the Ligue communiste révolutionnaire; the newspaper *Libération,* founded in 1973 by former Maoist militants; and *Politique hebdo,* an independent newsweekly of the left.[182] Lacking the resources that allowed the Fête de l'Humanité to engage international rock stars, these smaller-scale events looked to French musicians to fill their programs. A wide range of genres found a platform at such *fêtes,* from alternative chanson and free jazz to folk music and French rock. The lineup of the festival organized by the Parti socialiste unifié in May 1973 was typical. Singer-songwriters Léo Ferré and Marcel Mouloudji headlined the event, with lesser-known "alternative" performers such as Colette Magny, François Béranger, and Brigitte Fontaine filling out the complement of chanson artists. Alan Silva, Frank Wright, and the ensemble Perception represented the world of free jazz, while groups like Kandahar, Catherine Ribeiro and Alpes, and Mahjun represented French rock.[183] As Patrick Mignon has observed, political *fêtes* were crucial to the development of the French rock scene in the 1970s.[184] At a time when performance opportunities were scarce, *fêtes politiques,* along with the network of Maisons de jeunes et de la culture, provided precisely the kind of institutional infrastructure otherwise lacking for rock music in France.

The proliferation of *fêtes politiques* over the course of the 1970s was, like the short-lived fascination with rock festivals, a manifestation of the broader post-'68 revival of interest in the ideal of the *fête.* This was underscored by the rhetoric that surrounded such events. A notice publicizing the 1973 festival of the Parti socialiste unifié declared that "to have a *fête* is already to break with this oppressive system, it is to find a path to collective liberation that opens up on revolution. The *fête* is thus in itself a form of rupture with capitalism."[185] But there were other factors that played a role in encouraging the rise of *fêtes politiques.* One was the retreat of *gauchisme* as a political force during the 1970s—and, along with this, the revolutionary dreams May '68 had awakened. After the breakup of Vive la révolution in 1971, other far left groups also ran aground: the last remnants of the Gauche prolétarienne disbanded in November 1973, while the Ligue communiste révolutionnaire was outlawed by the government in June 1973 following violent altercations between its members and the extreme right-wing group Ordre Nouveau.[186] At the same time, the "union of the left" forged between the Parti communiste

202 | La Cause du Pop

and Parti socialiste in 1972 helped revitalize the "official" left, rehabilitating electoral politics in the eyes of many disillusioned *gauchistes*. In this shift away from the political extremism of post-'68 *gauchisme,* the *fête* provided an outlet, a form of compensation for the aspirations to radical social transformation frustrated after 1968. As historians Noëlle Gérôme and Danielle Tartakowsky have argued, the political failure of *gauchisme* led former militants to embrace of the ideal of the *fête,* which was seen as "a prolongation of [the extreme left's] past action and its purest expression."[187]

As a surrogate for the utopia that had failed to materialize, the role ascribed to the *fête* assumed a function different from the one it performed in the immediate aftermath of '68. Gone was the belief that the *fête* was something that had to be wrested away from those who sought to derive profit from its explosive potential; gone, in other words, was the mindset that had motivated the interventions at Aix, Biot, and the Palais des Sports. Concomitant with this was a transformation in the role assigned to music in such events, and to rock in particular. No longer was rock conceived as the means by which youth could come into consciousness of itself as a political agent and thereby be incited to action. Rather, within the *fêtes politiques* of the 1970s rock increasingly came to serve as a means of targeting one political constituency among others. While this may have robbed the genre of some of its mystique, it did have the advantage providing rock with some measure of official recognition. Taken together, these transformations in both the political function of the *fête,* and of rock's place within it, serve as a barometer of broader changes taking place within the political culture of the left during the 1970s, as the romance of revolution ceded to the realities of electoral politics. We shall return to this changing political culture in the conclusion, in connection to the socialists' electoral victory in 1981. But first it is necessary to pick out another thread from the tangle of *soixante-huitard* discourses, one that revolves around the ideal of cultural democratization. This ideal, and its impact on the contemporary music scene during the late 1960s and 1970s, is the subject of the next chapter.

CHAPTER 5

Contemporary Music, *Animation,* and Cultural Democratization

Animation musicale really developed in the wake of '68. In May '68, a concert grand was set up in the courtyard of the Sorbonne (the Université de Paris), and in the midst of grand discussions about refashioning society and the world, a pianist would from time to time come and play a Chopin Ballade or a Klavierstück by Stockhausen. . . .

[A goal of *animation*] was to imagine new *forms* of exchange between musicians and the public.

It was one of the slogans of May '68: "power to the imagination."

—François Delalande

THE CRISIS OF CONTEMPORARY MUSIC

A sense of malaise pervaded the world of contemporary classical music in the mid-1970s. One of the few beliefs uniting the otherwise fractious community of composers, critics, and audiences was that new music had entered a period of crisis. Signs of the genre's troubles abounded. Statistics published by the research division of the Ministry of Cultural Affairs revealed a significant decline in the production of "serious" music during the 1970s. The number of symphonic, chamber, and electroacoustic works registered with the Société des auteurs, compositeurs et editeurs de la musique (SACEM), the principal copyright protection agency in France, dropped from 1,581 in 1971 to a mere 825 in 1975.[1] By contrast, the total number of new compositions registered with SACEM during the same period—taking rock and chanson into account—actually increased, from 41,691 in 1971 to 56,498 in 1975, throwing into relief the drop-off in the production of serious music. Similar signs of decline were evident in the record industry. According to statistics gathered by Pierre-Michel Menger, even the most successful recordings of contemporary classical music, those featuring renowned figures like Henri Dutilleux, Olivier Messiaen, or Iannis Xenakis, only sold between one thousand and three thousand copies per year, a tiny fraction of total annual record sales. Such meager returns made larger record companies wary of investing in new music: "The drop in sales . . . has been enough of a constant and generalized phenomenon within every country that publishers now only venture into the contemporary repertoire on an extremely sporadic basis."[2]

Alongside quantitative signs of crisis were qualitative ones. Foremost was the fact that no new movement had emerged during the 1970s to assume the hegemonic position serialism once occupied. Compared to the heroic years of the avant-garde during the 1950s and 1960s, recent trends offered little excitement or controversy. The fact that seemingly few aesthetic barriers were left to transgress contributed to this predicament, removing one of the musical avant-garde's guiding prerogatives: that of breaking with convention.[3] For many critics, the inevitable outcome of this state of affairs was a retreat into routine or, worse yet, academicism. Reviewing the closing concert of the 1975 Festival d'automne, Gérard Mannoni despaired at the lack of originality within the contemporary avant-garde. In his eyes, young composers seemed all too content to tread along well-worn paths: "We were hoping for the revelation of some new tendency, or at least of some new talent capable of asserting itself with verve. Nothing of the sort occurred. The music that was heard [in the concert] never departed from a safe conformism."[4] Likewise, critic Jean-Michel Damian lamented that the "new French school" had abdicated any sense of aesthetic risk. He dismissed works by composers like Didier Denis and Tristan Murail (who later gained fame as a cofounder of the spectral movement) as a bland mixture of Ligeti and Fauré. The two composers, he wrote, "are twenty-five or thirty years old." But judging from their works, one would think "they are a hundred."[5]

If the production of new music seemed to be in poor shape, the outlook was just as bleak in terms of its reception. The preceding half-decade had witnessed a decline in attendance at concerts and festivals of new music, a development that disquieted the genre's advocates. The journal *Musique en jeu,* a staunch defender of the avant-garde, underlined the problem in 1976 in an editorial entitled "Contemporary Music in Question." The typical concert of new music in Paris, the editorial observed, drew somewhere around two to three hundred people. Higher-profile events—concerts of works by "stars" like Xenakis, Henry, Boulez, and Stockhausen—fared better, at times attracting upward of 1,500 people. Still, this was a meager number considering that Paris had a population of 1.5 million at the time.[6] That in the best of conditions the cultural capital of France could only muster one-tenth of one percent of its populace for a concert of avant-garde music did not speak highly of the genre's appeal. And this was not taking into account the situation outside Paris. There performances of avant-garde music were less frequent and could not count on comparable levels of support. Most of the new music performed in the provinces occurred in the context of periodic festivals, like those held each year in the cities of Royan and La Rochelle. While such festivals were often vaunted for democratizing access to new music, for bringing internationally renowned composers and performers to areas deprived of an active cultural life, geographic displacement did not necessarily translate into a change in audience demographics. Surveys indicated that local inhabitants generally took little interest in such events.[7] Rather, Parisian aficionados comprised the bulk of the audience, having traveled from the capital to hear concerts of works by Paris-based composers, performed by Paris-based ensembles. All that changed was the scenery. Instead of expanding its audience, festivals like those in Royan and La Rochelle reinforced the sense that new music was the rarefied pursuit of cultural elites.

Despair at the woeful state of contemporary music circa 1975 was heightened by the sense that things could have turned out differently. Damian spoke for many when he looked back fondly upon a moment when the future for new music seemed brighter: "We were lulled by illusions. We thought, after '68, that the success of contemporary music, the attraction that it had begun to exert on a broader audience, that all of that was going to give rise to young composers who were full of vitality, who would overturn barriers and taboos."[8] Damian's recollections were not entirely a matter of misty-eyed nostalgia. Indeed, for a few years in the late 1960s and early 1970s there were signs that the avant-garde was, against all expectations, on its way to becoming a popular form of cultural expression. As was the case with free jazz, renewed public interest in "contestatory" genres in the wake of May '68 benefited new music. Composers profited from the historic association of artistic and political avant-gardes, which dated back to the origins of the concept in the nineteenth century.[9] According to a logic as dubious as it was durable, the transgression of musical barriers—between consonance and dissonance, sound and noise, art and the everyday, artist and audience—served as figures of social transgression. Given this context, it is not surprising that the musical avant-garde saw its fortunes improve from 1968 to 1971. Turnout for concerts of new music increased markedly, as did attendance at new music festivals. Record sales also increased. Albums by Pierre Henry and the new music ensemble Les Percussions de Strasbourg managed to break into the popular music charts, which in turn encouraged record companies to expand their catalogues of new music.[10] Contemporary composers even began to generate interest among pop and jazz audiences, judging by the coverage they garnered in the underground press. For a few years one could read profiles of composers like Henry and Xenakis in the pages of *Rock & Folk,* or articles on John Cage, Terry Riley, La Monte Young, and Music Electronica Viva in alternative publications like *Actuel* and *Parapluie.*[11]

The clearest signal of growing public interest in avant-garde music was the success of the Journées de musique contemporaine, a series of concerts organized by the critic Maurice Fleuret in late October 1968. The Journées were the latest incarnation of the Semaines musicales de Paris (subsequently the Semaines musicales internationales de Paris, or SMIP), an annual music festival started in 1956. The change in the festival's name bespoke a fundamental transformation in its mission. Originally conceived as a month-long concert series mixing canonical and contemporary works, the rechristened Journées took place over a matter of days rather than weeks and focused exclusively on avant-garde music.[12] Four composers were featured in the 1968 festival: Edgard Varèse, Iannis Xenakis, Luciano Berio, and Pierre Henry. Each was the subject of a one-day retrospective, which included concerts, roundtable debates, "meet the artist" sessions, and live radio broadcasts of concert performances.[13] The culminating event of the Journées encapsulated the ambitious, perhaps immoderate tone of the festival's program: a twenty-six hour marathon of Henry's music, framed by two "performances" of his recently completed electroacoustic oratorio, *L'Apocalypse de Jean.*

By all accounts the festival was a tremendous success. Approximately 10,500 people attended the concerts and debates that comprised the Journées.[14] Concert halls were filled to capacity and then some: eight hundred people reportedly squeezed into the auditorium of the Musée d'art moderne for a concert of Varèse's electronic pieces, even though the hall only seated two hundred. For the Xenakis concert on 26 October, the auditorium of the Théâtre de la Musique (ex-Gaîté-Lyrique) proved inadequate in the face of intense public interest, with more than a thousand would-be concertgoers turned away at the door. Even the public debates managed to draw a substantial number of spectators.[15] One observer described the "veritable ruckus" he had to circumnavigate to get into a roundtable discussion on Xenakis's music: "Once again we piled ourselves up on the steps [of the auditorium], we grabbed a corner of a cushion, we contorted ourselves into uncomfortable positions. Clusters of malcontents clung to the gates. And all of this not for Rubinstein, nor for Menuhin, but for an austere debate on music and mathematics."[16]

In addition to noting the size and enthusiasm of the festival's audience, observers remarked on their youthfulness. Roughly two-thirds of those who attended the Journées were students, a fact not lost on critics.[17] Many saw the demographic makeup of the festival's public as portending the rejuvenation of the avant-garde. A profound affinity seemed to exist between music and audience, with many accounts of the Journées treating youth and new music as homologous. Within this discursive trope, the characteristics of one mirrored those of the other, both functioning as emblems of vitality, modernity, and the future. Further validating this connection was the assertion that both new music and youth shared the same contestatory attitude—an attitude, as critics were wont to point out, that had found its fullest expression during the months of May and June. This point was underlined in a sketch of the Journées published in *Le Nouvel Observateur*: "There was of course the overweight lady with her hat, warts, and umbrella, who didn't understand, who stormed about, who stepped on people's feet in order to leave the concert because she found it 'idiotic,' 'intolerable,' 'scandalous.' But there were also those that nobody expected: two thousand youth who, every evening, elbowed their way in to hear Xenakis or Varèse, Berio or Pierre Henry. Youth without pretensions, demanding, strangers to the Concerts Lamoureux, in possession of a healthy temperament that came straight from May."[18] Like other accounts, the one published in *Le Nouvel Observateur* linked youth, contestation, and avant-garde music into a metonymic chain. And the glue joining these disparate elements together was the memory of May '68.[19]

The triumph of the Journées de musique contemporaine was not an isolated event. The following spring attendance at the Festival de Royan skyrocketed, while the sequel to the Journées in October 1969 replicated the previous year's success.[20] A report in *Le Monde* used what was by then a common trope to describe the newfound fashionability of the avant-garde: "They were there, in the great hall on the second floor of the Maison de l'O.R.T.F, squatting, leaning against one another, elbow to elbow or back to back, just like a certain evening during the summer of 1968 at the Sorbonne."[21] Concomitant with this growth in the audience for contemporary music was a flourishing of new aesthetic tendencies. For much of the postwar period contemporary music in France had seemed divided into two antagonistic camps. On one side stood representatives of the traditional *école française* (Daniel-Lesur, Tony Aubin, Jean-Michel Damase, Jacques Chailley, and Marcel Landowski, among others), entrenched within the hoary institutions of French musical life, most notably the Conservatoire national supérieur de la musique. On the other side stood the avant-garde, spearheaded by Boulez, which had created its own alternative set of institutions (most notably the Domaine musical, the new music ensemble Boulez founded in 1953). Only a few exceptional figures, such as Messiaen and Dutilleux, managed to stand above the fray. But after 1968 new movements and trends proliferated, dismantling the neat partitioning of the musical field.[22] The interest generated by André Boucourechliev's music gave aleatoricism and "open" forms a new lease on life, at the same time as more radical strands of American experimental music gained a foothold in France, mainly through the performances organized by the Groupe d'étude et réalisation musicale (GERM). Largely absent in France prior to the late 1960s, graphic scores and text compositions became a staple of composers like Costin Miereanu, Jean-Yves Bosseur, Pierre Mariétan, Philippe Drogoz, and Michel Decoust. Free improvisation also began to make inroads in France. In addition to dedicated improvisation groups like New Phonic Art and Opus N, other, more conventional chamber ensembles (like the Ensemble Ars Nova) experimented with collective improvisation.[23] Another area of interest was the new genre of *théâtre musical*, whose proponents included Georges Aperghis, Michel Puig, and Claude Prey. Finally, *musique concrète* experienced something of a comeback in the latter half of the 1960s. The emergence of a new generation of composers (Luc Ferrari, François Bayle, Bernard Parmegiani, Guy Reibel, and Ivo Malec), along with the publication of Pierre Schaeffer's magnum opus *Traité des objets musicaux* in 1966, did much to repair the damage that Boulez's withering critiques had wrought on the reputation of *musique concrète* some ten years earlier.

Yet for all these signs of vitality, the conjuncture that brought youth, new music, and contestation into alignment after 1968 was fragile. By the early 1970s cracks were already appearing in the facade. Attendance at festivals of contemporary music fell back to pre-1968 levels, while record sales dropped for all save the most successful composers.[24] This led many record companies that had increased their catalogue of avant-garde works in the late 1960s to slowly disengage from the genre. Waning public interest in new music was further thrown into relief by the growing popularity of rock after 1970. Indeed, the absolute decline in the popularity of the avant-garde was perhaps less striking than its relative decline. While the ten thousand attendees of the 1968 Journées may have seemed an impressive tally by the standards of new music, they were dwarfed by the numbers that rock festivals were able to command. The Festival d'Amougies had managed to draw about twenty thousand spectators in spite of all the uncertainties that had surrounded its location and program. Likewise, the festivals held at Aix and Biot during *l'été pop* were able to draw roughly ten thousand and twenty-five thousand, respectively. What counted as a failure for rock represented a resounding success for contemporary music. Such discrepancies became increasingly apparent as the 1970s progressed. As the rock counterculture became more firmly established in France, the association that observers had made between youth and new music in the wake of '68 proved difficult to sustain.

If the connection between youth and the avant-garde was weakening as the events of May '68 receded into the past, so too was the homology equating aesthetic and social transgression, the basis of much of the avant-garde's appeal. Part of the problem was that symbolic attacks upon social convention remained precisely that: symbolic, and thus limited in their capacity to act directly upon social realities. Introducing indeterminacy, improvisation, and audience participation into the musical work may have undermined the divisions separating composer, performer, and public, but it was unclear what impact such transgressions had outside the concert hall. It is not surprising, then, to find a number of individuals questioning the "false audacity" and "false subversiveness" of contemporary composers by the early 1970s.[25] One of the most scathing critiques of contemporary music's political limitations came in the inaugural issue of *Musique en jeu*. In an article entitled "L'oreille froide" (The cold ear), Jean-François Hirsch argued that the many ruptures effected by new music in recent years, ruptures that called into question the concert rituals of classical music, had nevertheless left the social relations governing its production, distribution, and consumption intact: "Open, mobile, aleatoric forms, spatialized performances, works conceived directly for tape and loudspeakers, these are the meadowlarks that do not by themselves make it springtime. For the simple reason that revolution within culture *is not* (and cannot be) [the same as] cultural revolution, which presupposes the opening up within the cultural super-structure of breaches of an entirely different magnitude."[26] Failing a transformation in the social composition of the contemporary music community—a transformation in who produced and consumed avant-garde music—such transgressions remained empty gestures. All they accomplished was to create a false semblance of modernity, one that masked the real "decrepitude" of society.[27] To overcome this state of affairs, the musical innovations of the avant-garde had to be translated to the social level. One way of achieving this would be to develop new "pedagogies," methods that would give everybody, not just composers, the opportunity to exercise their creative faculties. "When," Hirsch wondered, "will sound wave generators be in the hands of schoolchildren, variable control amplifiers in those of metalworkers, and band-pass filters in those of supermarket checkout clerks?"[28]

Hirsch's call to provide individuals of all backgrounds with access to the means of musical production echoed the demands made during May '68 to prize open the artistic sphere. Recall in this regard the position espoused by groups like CRAC and CAR-Odéon during *les événements:* their hope of transforming art from a consumer object into something produced by one and all may have fallen somewhere between the utopian and the quixotic, but it gave voice to a sentiment that exercised both wide appeal and enduring influence. Even as the post-'68 fascination with artistic avant-gardes waned, key tenets of avant-gardist rhetoric continued to animate cultural debate within the French left. The conviction that art should be more than just a leisure-time pursuit or mark of social distinction, but should rather be transformed into a collective activity, gained considerable traction. Underpinning such discourses was the belief that the untapped creativity of the masses represented a potential wellspring of social and political energies. By nurturing this dormant creativity, the productive capacity hitherto repressed by the prevailing social order would be released, made available for the task of reforming (or revolutionizing) society. And it was not just radical or fringe groups that placed great store in the powers of amateur creativity. Even major parties like the Parti socialiste flirted with elements of this discourse in the cultural policies they elaborated during the course of the 1970s.

For composers of contemporary music, calls to democratize culture represented both a challenge and an opportunity. On the one hand, agitation on behalf of a more egalitarian culture made the gulf separating the specialist world of avant-garde music and the general public a liability. Composers were exposed to populist critiques that castigated the new music scene for its elitism and isolation, qualities that seemed to typify the "old culture" that May '68 had sought to overthrow. On the other hand, many composers were receptive to demands to generalize artistic activity, especially as these overlapped with the vanguardist ideal of merging art and everyday life. The 1970s thus witnessed a profusion of works and practices that experimented with novel ways of bridging the gap between contemporary music and the public. These included the creation of pieces using texts or graphic notation to facilitate amateur performance; the development of pedagogies that drew on the sound world of contemporary music to "awaken" the individual's creative faculties; the dislocation of music from the confines of traditional institutions into more quotidian spaces; and the collaboration of music ensembles (such as the Atelier lyrique du Rhin and the Atelier théâtre et musique) with community groups in the *banlieues* and peripheral regions of France. Such endeavors offered composers a number of rewards. At best, they might succeed in winning new audiences for new music. Failing that, the simple gesture of reaching out to audiences was itself beneficial, countering perceptions that composers of contemporary music were indifferent to or contemptuous of the general public.

But there was still another advantage to be drawn from such endeavors, one that derived from their convergence with the cultural policies promulgated by the state. From its inception at the dawn of the Fifth Republic, the Ministry of Cultural Affairs had pursued an ambitious agenda. In addition to safeguarding the national patrimony and providing financial aid to artists and arts institutions, a central plank of the ministry's program was to reduce the cultural inequalities that existed among different segments of the population.[29] This objective, which went by the name of *action culturelle,* remained at the center of the government's cultural policy throughout the 1970s and 1980s, even as it mutated in response to changing political pressures. At the same time, the state's efforts to guarantee a "right to culture" *(droit à la culture)* encouraged the creation of new forms of mediation—known as *animation culturelle*—charged with ensuring that cultural outreach efforts had the desired impact on target audiences. These developments in cultural policy created an opening certain composers exploited. By framing their works as advancing the goals of cultural democratization, composers stood to gain from governmental support. But this recasting of composers' activities as a kind of social work entailed a change in the kind of support they received and the professional identity they fashioned for themselves. As Piérre-Michel Menger has observed, the wedding of the discrete tasks of musical production and cultural mediation altered the logic of state aid. No longer did the government simply provide material support, in the form of commissions and grants, to assist in the production of works; henceforth, composers could also be remunerated for "the production of services . . . within a community."[30] This in turn encouraged the emergence of new professional positions within the field of avant-garde music, positions that fused the function of artistic creation with that of public service.

The present chapter examines efforts to bring contemporary music to the masses, paying particular attention to how they evolved in tandem with discourses and practices of *animation musicale.* The narrative traced here unfolds along two separate but crisscrossing paths, those of cultural policy and compositional practice. In both cases the actors involved, be they policy makers or composers, had to balance social demands with their own professional and political interests. For composers, it was necessary in the wake of May '68 to put an end to contemporary music's identification with social and cultural elites. It was this imperative that motivated a number of endeavors examined over the course of this chapter, including Luc Ferrari's efforts to propagate an amateur practice of *musique concrète,* the children's operas produced by the Atelier lyrique du Rhin, and Georges Aperghis's work in the *banlieues* of Paris. For policy makers within the center-right governments that governed France until 1981, it was necessary to demonstrate that the state's interventions on behalf of the arts were not simply a matter of shoring up "bourgeois culture" but acted in the interests of the entire French polity. For musical and political actors alike, consensus about the need for cultural democratization masked differences in what this phrase meant and how it was to be realized. Indeed, the project of making artistic practice more accessible raised as many questions as it answered. Was this simply a question of redistributing cultural goods, or did it involve democratizing the means of cultural production? How was the apparently altruistic act of bringing culture to underprivileged communities to be distinguished from proselytism? And how did the process of democratization respond to or reshape the conventional hierarchy of musical genres? These are but some of the questions to be addressed in mapping out the interactions between new music and cultural policy during the post-May period.

STATE MUSIC POLICY IN THE EARLY FIFTH REPUBLIC

On 27 November 1962 André Malraux, acclaimed author and head of the recently constituted Ministry of Cultural Affairs, convened a task force charged with assessing the state of musical life in France. Among its members were many of the éminences grises of the French musical establishment: composers Georges Auric and Henri Dutilleux; critics René Dumesnil, Robert Siohan, and Claude Rostand; the director of the Paris Conservatoire, Raymond Gallois-Montbrun; and the head of the Office de radiodiffusion-télévision française (and respected composer in his own right), Henry Barraud. The creation of this committee, the Commission nationale pour l'étude des problèmes de la musique, was a way of countering the widely held sentiment that the ministry had neglected music since its inception. This sentiment was not unfounded. In part because of his background as a writer, in part because of his tastes, Malraux had exhibited greater interest in literature, theater, and the visual arts, preferences that trickled down through the lower echelons of the ministry. In addition, the ministry had looked mainly to the world of theater to staff its nascent cultural outreach programs, theater having been central to postwar efforts at cultural decentralization. Taken together, these factors placed music at a significant institutional disadvantage, lacking the representation or prestige accorded to other art forms within the ministry.

The commission set out to rectify this situation. After two years of work it issued a report in late 1964 outlining the challenges facing the musical community. Foremost among these was the decline of live music throughout France. "Concert halls," the authors of the report observed, "only rarely enjoy the crowds of yesteryear,"[31] a fact underlined by the financial straits confronting the four principal symphonic associations of Paris (the Concerts Lamoureux, Pasdeloup, Colonne, and the Société des Concerts du Conservatoire).[32] The main culprit for this situation, according to the report, was the proliferation of mass media since the 1920s. Radio and recordings had "taken the place of the living presence of orchestras," condemning musicians to chronic unemployment.[33] Echoing the diagnosis advanced by the Syndicat des artistes-musiciens de Paris (SAMuP) and other musicians' unions, the report argued that without significant investment in both performance ensembles and music education, current trends might very well lead to "the disappearance of all human contact between listeners and performers."[34] Lest their

proposals for state intervention be perceived as special pleading on behalf of musicians' interests, the report framed the problem in terms of
cultural democracy on the one hand and national prestige on the other.
Music, the report contended, was a universal good to which all citizens
should have access. Playing upon the ministry's mission to satisfy the
public's "right to culture," the commission cast support not as a subsidy
to prop up a failing market but as a moral imperative. Yet the goal of
improving musical life also had international implications. Even though
France possessed a rich musical patrimony, one "marked by the seal of
universality," the report's authors warned that the country's musical infrastructure had fallen behind that of other nations. Continued neglect
of music would risk diminishing France's standing in the world. The
conclusion of the report ties together these various lines of argument,
imploring the government "to finally give to musical art the place that it
deserves in the country of a Jean-Philippe Rameau, a Hector Berlioz, a
Claude Debussy; to see to it that this eminent form of culture be dis-
pensed to all French citizens; and that it may be able to have the prestige
of our country radiate beyond our borders."[35] Increased state support for
music was, by this measure, a matter of national urgency.

   A number of tendentious notions guided the commission's report.
The most glaring of these concerned the definition of music, a delicate
issue given that how the boundaries of the field were drawn determined
who received state support. Sections of the report dealing with cultural
democratization revealed the narrow definition of music adopted by the
commission. Even though music is cast as something to which all should
have access, the authors of the report clearly did not feel that *all* genres
merited this designation. This resulted in the curious, but revealing,
remark that "all music is certainly not [to be] considered music *[la mu-
sique]*."[36] The problem, then, was not public disinterest in music per se;
it was public disinterest in the *right* kind of music—which is to say, classical music and its contemporary avatars. By contrast, jazz, chanson, folk,
and *variétés* were excluded from consideration. Indeed, these genres represented the forces whose pernicious influence state intervention needed
to counteract: "How to transform intermittent or inattentive listeners
into conscious practitioners, how to develop the taste, knowledge, and
curiosity of those for whom music has no profound reality? Is there a
way of reaching true music taking as the point of departure the thousands of vulgar solicitations that often take the place of music?"[37] A
crucial part of improving musical life in France thus involved improving

the public's tastes. A less obvious fault line in the document concerned the question of who, precisely, was to be the principal beneficiary of state intervention. Was it to be members of the music profession or the general public? Or, to put it in somewhat different terms, was the main objective of governmental aid to increase the supply of classical music, or to increase its demand? While the rhetoric of cultural democratization implied that the satisfaction of the public's musical "needs" should be an overarching principal of cultural policy, the mechanisms proposed to accomplish this task (the formation of new orchestras, increased funding for ensembles, and improved music education) suggested that the interests of professional musicians were paramount.

Such tensions were not restricted to the commission's report and would resurface in the government's music policies for decades to come. How these tensions were negotiated varied considerably from one administration to the next, and from one branch of the Ministry of Cultural Affairs to another. Initially the ministry's actions on behalf of music placed greater emphasis on guaranteeing the economic well-being of the music profession. In May 1966 Malraux reorganized the ministry, carving out a new administrative unit in charge of musical affairs. To head the newly established Service de la musique, Malraux appointed Marcel Landowski, a composer who had previously worked for the ministry overseeing music education. The selection of Landowski was a source of controversy within the world of French classical music. The other candidate for the position—Emile Biasini, the head of the theater and cultural action branches of the ministry—had been backed by Pierre Boulez. Landowski, by contrast, had enjoyed the support of the Comité national de musique, a group led by musicologist and composer Jacques Chailley. To the extent that both Chailley and Landowski were widely seen as traditionalists, the selection of the latter to head the Service de la musique was taken as a triumph of the "conservative" establishment over its "modernist" adversaries.[38] This, at least, was how Boulez perceived the decision. In a caustic open letter to Malraux published in *Le Nouvel Observateur* in May 1966, he attacked the new head of music and his supporters for their retrograde sensibilities: "Musicians like Chailley and Marcel Landowski have always been extremely reactionary, and I cannot for the life of me see what sudden inspiration from above will make them change their deep-seated conservatism the moment they attack the problem of organizing French music."[39] More problematic still, in Boulez's eyes, was that Landowski, a composer, lacked the managerial competence that a more experienced administrator (such as Biasini) possessed: "Nobody could be less suited to the work of general administration than a composer; he will always remain an amateur working half-time."[40]

As it turned out, Boulez's objections were misplaced. Landowski proved a capable administrator, and his alleged "conservatism" had little impact on how he allocated resources. This is not to say that the Landowski's appointment did not influence governmental music policy, but this had less to do with Landowski's aesthetic proclivities and more with the decision to assign a composer—a member of the music profession, and thus subject to its guild mentality—to the post in the first place. In doing so Malraux virtually guaranteed that the balance of governmental aid would go toward corporatist initiatives. This was evident in the first major initiative launched by Landowski, the ten-year plan for music, which was unveiled in 1969.[41] In many ways Landowski's plan adhered to the arguments advanced in the 1964 report on music. Like the commission, Landowski justified state intervention on the principle of national prestige, noting that musical life in France was characterized by a "considerable lag" compared to other industrialized nations.[42] Compounding this backwardness were technological upheavals that fundamentally transformed the economics of the music profession. Again, Landowski followed the commission's lead in blaming the economic hardships professional musicians faced on media and recording technologies. To mitigate the effects of the latter, the ten-year plan called for an expansion in the number of ensembles subsidized by the government. The plan divided France into ten "music regions," each of which would receive at least one symphony or chamber orchestra in addition to a lyric ensemble or opera troupe.[43] In all, fifty-seven instrumental and twenty-five lyric ensembles were either to be created from scratch or taken under the government's wing.[44] It is in this ambitious overhaul of musical life that the corporatist nature of Landowski's intervention becomes apparent. For while the geographic distribution of the ensembles across France made a nod toward the promotion of cultural decentralization, the main effect of the ten-year plan was to secure increased employment opportunities for musicians. The measures proposed for inciting public interest in classical and contemporary music remained modest by comparison. Each of the ten regions would be assigned an *animateur musical départmental* who would be in charge of creating "an action on behalf of musical diffusion or initiation" for the entire area.[45] But that was all.

ACTION CULTURELLE AND THE
MAISONS DE LA CULTURE

One reason for the limited attention paid to public outreach in Landowski's ten-year plan was that a good deal of the ministry's resources had already been dedicated to addressing cultural democratization. Indeed, since the ministry's inception in 1959 the preponderance of its energies had been devoted to *action culturelle,* often at the expense of other sectors, including music. Underpinning the ministry's policies was the notion that beyond material, economic, and social needs, individuals have cultural needs, and as such have a fundamental right to culture. Unobjectionable in the abstract, this principle raised a host of thorny questions when put into practice. How, exactly, was culture to be defined, and by whom? How was one to distinguish between providing access to a (purportedly) universal good and promoting a particular taste culture? These questions occasioned little reflection on the part of Malraux and policy makers in the Ministry of Cultural Affairs during the early years of its existence. What counted as culture was self-evident, as was the social function it fulfilled. According to Malraux, art provided a substitute for the functions that religion had discharged in preindustrial society. Masterworks offered a glimpse of eternity, a source of meaning in a world in which traditional institutions had lost much of their authority. Pointedly excluded from this understanding of art as secular religion was mass culture, which Malraux viewed as actively impeding the kind of spiritual fulfillment that high art provided.[46] Thus *action culturelle* was cast as a project of disseminating masterpieces to the culturally deprived masses to help save them from the spiritual abyss of modernity.

The centerpiece of the ministry's cultural democratization efforts was the creation of a series of Maisons de la Culture across France. These were multidisciplinary centers combining auditoriums, exposition halls, screening rooms, and libraries under one roof. Inspired in part by the short-lived Maisons de la Culture of the Popular Front era (themselves inspired by Soviet models), these institutions were the principal instrument for combating cultural inequalities.[47] The *maisons* were to act on two fronts simultaneously. Geographically, their insertion in regional cities would close the gap between Paris and the "cultural desert" of the provinces.[48] Socially, they would ensure that art was no longer inaccessible to large swaths of the populace but was henceforth available to all, regardless of social background. But apart from providing a subsidized space for exhibitions and performances, the practical question of how the Maisons de la Culture would succeed in reducing cultural inequalities was unclear. This was due in part to Malraux's conception of the aesthetic experience, which informed early ministry policy. For Malraux, individuals possessed the capacity to understand art in an immediate and intuitive fashion. Prior exposure to the arts was unnecessary. So too was education. On the contrary: verbal exegesis, in Malraux's view, was a barrier to true understanding. In his speech inaugurating the Maison de la Culture at Amiens in 1966, Malraux voiced this conviction in unequivocal terms: "It was not the case that anyone in the world has ever understood music because someone else has explained the Ninth Symphony to them. Or that anyone has ever loved poetry because someone explained Victor Hugo to them."[49] Explanations cannot spark a love of art, Malraux contended, since such love is born out of direct, unmediated contact with the work itself. This conception of a quasi-mystical meeting of perceiving subject and aesthetic object found echoes in early ministry pronouncements. A sketch of the centers' objectives, dating from 1961, denies them a pedagogical role and instead casts them as sites of transcendent experience. The Maison de la Culture, it reads, "has no desire to organize arts education, and always makes way for the work. The confrontation that it enables is direct, [and] it avoids the pitfall and the impoverishment of a simplifying vulgarization."[50]

As Malraux's invocation of figures like Beethoven and Hugo during his speech at Amiens made clear, the *maisons* were to be neither purveyors of middlebrow culture nor gathering places for local dilettantes. Cultural democratization was to be a one-way street, through which high culture, and nothing but high culture, was made available to the people. Neither popular culture nor amateur practices were to figure into the framework of *action culturelle.*[51] Nor would there be a "vulgarization" of the arts, as this would mark the failure of cultural enfranchisement. The work presented at the *maisons* had to rise to international standards, which more often than not meant Parisian standards. Malraux, speaking at the opening of the Grenoble *maison*, remarked that the new facility would ensure "that everything essential that transpires in Paris should also transpire in Grenoble."[52] Comments like these fueled suspicion that the *maisons* were instruments of cultural *dirigisme*, vehicles for diffusing an essentially Parisian notion of artistic excellence to the culturally "backward" provinces.[53] Such suspicions were not unjustified. At the time of its founding in 1959, there was a shortage of qualified personnel to staff the ministry. To make up for this deficit Mal-

raux looked to the ranks of former colonial administrators, then returning to the mainland in the wake of decolonization. While these individuals
brought with them valuable organizational expertise, they also brought
attitudes and prejudices acquired over years of service overseas. They
knew, as one administrator put it, how to "fight against complacency
become habit, ancestral rites, tribal structures, ignorance of modernity, or
the influence of powerful shamans, who still held sway in many towns
and whole provinces of France."[54] Deprived of extraterritorial holdings
in Africa and Southeast Asia, the *mission civilatrice* of colonialism turned
its attentions inward, toward the provinces.[55]

Within the *maisons,* it fell to the figure of the *animateur* to facilitate
the encounter between audience and work. What *animation* involved,
precisely, was open to debate and became the object of contention over
the years. The principal model for cultural *animation* originated in the
postwar "popular culture" and popular education movements, a loose
array of private nonprofit associations that agitated at a grass-roots level
for people's "right to culture." Although these groups demonstrated
some sensitivity to the value of existing working-class cultures, and had
striven to raise workers' consciousness of the aesthetic dimensions of
their everyday lives, they devoted most of their energy to bringing high
culture to the people. At the same time, *animation* was invested with a
sense of high-minded civic duty, since cultural militants saw their work
as necessary for the formation of a socially aware citizenry. Brian Rigby
thus describes their enterprise as one "dedicated to the promotion of a
new humanist culture that would train people to be active and useful citizens in the modern technological society."[56] In short, "popular culture"
movements saw culture as the means by which the individual's relation
to society might be ameliorated.

Many of these foundational beliefs continued to shape cultural *animation* throughout the 1960s. As a result, the *animateur* often acted
less as a neutral conduit through which cultural knowledge passed and
more as a missionary or militant engaged in the task of connecting art
with social concerns. It was precisely this social engagement that transformed both the practice of cultural *animation* and the institution of
the Maison de la Culture into sites of political dispute. Controversies
surrounding the Maisons de la Culture, which had been contentious from
their inception, culminated during and after the events of May 1968.
Although the tendency of some *animateurs* to push avant-garde works
on provincial audiences had been a longstanding source of resentment, it
was their alleged role in disseminating subversive ideas that generated

the greatest hostility. Gérard Marcus, a Gaullist deputy in the Assemblée nationale, singled out *animateurs* in a speech on the floor of the assembly in November 1968: "One can say, without exaggeration, that they have . . . carried their own stones to the barricades of May, as much during the events as beforehand. To agitate, over the years, before a public of young students, revolutionary myths ceaselessly glorifying the October Revolution, Castroism, or Lumumba, to praise antimilitarism, to idealize every kind of rebellion, doesn't this create little by little a psychological terrain favorable to the development of events similar to those that we experienced in the month of May?"[57]

The *maisons* were equally suspect on the left. Particularly problematic was their affiliation with the Gaullist state. *Gauchistes* and Communist party intellectuals alike were quick to label *maisons* as "ideological state apparatuses," part of the system of institutions Louis Althusser had identified as central to the reproduction of existing social relations.[58] The *maisons* and their personnel were—perhaps unwittingly—tools with which individuals were molded to fit the exigencies of the capitalist economy: "Cultural mediators, agents of change, agents of development, educators, leisure 'animateurs,' educational 'animateurs'—the designations leave no room for doubt. They are, every single one of them, given the task of encouraging adaptability, openness, and mobility, all of which are indispensable for the survival and development of the economic system."[59] Another line of critique held cultural democratization to be a diversion from more fundamental issues. This was the position held by the Parti communiste, which argued that *animation*—no matter how well intentioned—placed "superstructural" concerns above those of the "base." Instead of working to change economic relations, *animateurs* operated at the level of individual attitudes. In this way they fell victim to the idealist trap, according to which a transformation of psychological dispositions was deemed sufficient to bring about a transformation of society.[60]

More damning than such critiques were sociological studies that revealed the extent to which the *maisons* had failed in their mission of bringing art to the people. Surveys indicated that most visitors to the centers came from social groups with high levels of educational attainment (teachers, university students, and young professionals), while those seen as culturally deprived (the working class and farm workers)—the very groups that the *maisons* sought to serve—made up a minuscule fraction of users. Statistics indicated how poorly democratization was faring. During the 1969–70 season at Amiens, 33.8 percent of the attendees identified themselves as university students, 15 percent as white-collar employees, 12.8 percent as teachers, 10.3 percent as housewives, and 10 percent as high school students. Meanwhile, a scant 2 percent identified themselves as workers, 1 percent as shopkeepers, and 0.4 percent as farm workers.[61] Similar findings were reported at other *maisons.*

One explanation for this failure lay in the fact that Malraux and his ministry, in envisaging the *maisons,* had not accounted for the degree to which differences in social background both prepare and condition attitudes toward high culture. This point was made most strongly by Pierre Bourdieu in a series of articles and books published in the 1960s. He argued that the kind of "cultural needs" that the *maisons* sought to satisfy were not innate (as Malraux would contend), but something inculcated only in those for whom familiarity with elite culture has real benefits: namely, individuals with access to the educational opportunities, careers, and social networks where cultivation pays dividends in the long run. Those lacking such privileges had no use for the *maisons.* Not surprisingly, Bourdieu's assessment of Malraux's grand project was unflattering: "The *Maison de la Culture* has attracted and gathered together . . . those whose educational formation and social milieu have prepared them for cultural practice. . . . [T]he members of the cultivated class feel that it is their right and duty to frequent these lofty places of culture, from which others, lacking sufficient culture, feel excluded. Far from fulfilling the function that a certain mystique of 'popular culture' assigns to it, the Maison de la Culture remains the *maison* of cultivated men *[la Maison des hommes cultivés].*"[62] Malraux's refusal to acknowledge the role of education in generating interest in art exacerbated the problem outlined by Bourdieu. His belief in the quasi-mystical encounter between audience and art removed one of the few vehicles that could reasonably be expected to impart an appreciation for legitimate art.

Toward the end of May 1968, the directors of a number of the Maisons de la Culture, along with the heads of various *théâtres populaires,* gathered in Villeurbanne to address the questions raised by critics of cultural democratization. On 25 May they issued a statement that expressed their dismay with the direction the *maisons* had taken, and which called for a renewed effort to reach out to the vast "nonpublic" still excluded from cultural life. The declaration began by crediting the events of May with revealing the shortcomings of their efforts, which appeared to many as promoting "a hereditary, exclusionary culture, which is quite simply to say, a bourgeois culture."[63] To address the "nonpublic" for whom so-called bourgeois culture held little interest, it was necessary for *action culturelle* to furnish the individual with "a means of breaking out of his current isolation, of leaving the ghetto, of situating himself more and more consciously in a social and historic context."[64] Not only did this redouble the *animateurs'* concern with linking cultural production to social affairs, but it de-emphasized their role in proselytizing on behalf of high culture. Instead, culture needed to be active, a site of "permanent creation."[65] Culture, in other words, was no longer to be conceived as a static patrimony, a collection of objects to be enjoyed by as many people as possible, but as a collective activity. This entailed a profound shift in the priorities of *action culturelle,* which had hitherto focused on cultivating an appreciation for works drawn from a particular artistic tradition, that of "serious" culture. Rather than democratizing access to *Culture* with a capital *C,* the new ideal forged in the crucible of May '68 was one that sought to democratize the practice and production of culture.

"POOR MAN'S *MUSIQUE CONCRÈTE*"

Music played a limited role within the network of Maisons de la Culture, owing to the historic links tying *action culturelle* to the theater. This was reflected in both the offerings and the personnel of the new institutions.[66] Stage actors, dramaturges, and directors comprised the bulk of the staff at the *maisons,* while dramatic productions dominated the programming. November 1966, for instance, witnessed 101 theatrical performances, forty-four film screenings, thirty-nine concerts, and only three dance recitals at the eleven *maisons* and national theaters in operation.[67] Music's relatively low profile in the *maisons* was also a product of the lingering hostility that certain quarters of the musical profession harbored toward a program that had consumed the bulk of the ministry's attentions, apparently at the expense of other domains.[68] The few musicians who did find positions in the *maisons* during the 1960s tended to be composers and to come from the experimental side of the contemporary music world. A case in point was Camille Roy, who ran the music program at the *maison* in Chalon-sur-Saône in the 1960s and 1970s. Another was Luc Ferrari, employed as an *animateur* at the Maison de la Culture d'Amiens during the 1968–69 season. His work during this period reveals some of the ways that the ideals of cultural democratization converged with the interests of the musical avant-garde, as well as *soixante-huitard* ideals of cultural revolution.

By the late 1960s Ferrari had an established reputation as a composer of electroacoustic music, having joined Pierre Schaeffer's Groupe de recherches musicales (GRM) shortly after its founding in 1958. Yet beginning in the mid-1960s his creative horizons had widened to encompass the most recent (and radical) tendencies in new music, including text composition, graphic notation, sound installation, and indeterminacy. This artistic reorientation marked the onset of what Ferrari later designated as his "red" period, a phase characterized by "a certain convergence of the social and the political with musical intentions" and "the demystification of the work, of art and the artist."[69] Although the first glimmerings of Ferrari's political turn dated from 1965 (the year in which he wrote the text piece *Société I*), the events of 1968 were decisive in ratifying his new direction as a composer. At the beginning of the year Ferrari traveled to Havana at the behest of the Cuban cultural ministry, which had commissioned him to write an orchestral piece to celebrate the city's bicentennial. This sojourn to a socialist state left a strong impression: "The encounter with a country that had undergone a revolution, that was a shock. There was also a confrontation with musics that had come from Africa, of Spanish influence, popular musics." No less shocking was what Ferrari encountered upon returning to France: "We came back to Paris in April, and then there was May '68."[70]

The uprising of May '68 left a marked impression on Ferrari. He was present in the occupied Odéon and participated in the founding of the composer's union in late May (see chapter 1). In addition, he took his portable tape recorder into the streets of Paris during May to capture the sound of the protests.[71] But beyond his involvement in the events themselves, the social upheavals of the period altered his conception of the composer's role in society. Like so many other engaged artists of the late 1960s and 1970s, Ferrari voiced a fervent belief in the need to change the audience's relationship to art, to create a more participatory culture. This in turn entailed the destruction of certain cherished ideals, in particular what Ferrari dubbed "the bourgeois myth of the composer," the notion that creativity was the province of a gifted few.[72] In this light, his embrace of techniques that eschewed established norms of compositional craftsmanship represented more than a modernist predilection for breaking with received tradition. Rather, such techniques, by deskilling the creative act, pointed a way toward the deprofessionalization of musical production. If this spelled the end of what was conventionally considered to be music, so be it: "The concept of music will need to disappear in any case. It has a long past; as a consequence it has engendered conventions; that has imposed limitations on it; now it stands in our way. . . . It is too specialized, and I believe that our thinking is evolving away from specialization."[73] At the same time, Ferrari recognized that it was not just the ideals that underpinned "bourgeois art" that needed to change for a more egalitarian culture to come into being. Institutions charged with the task of dispensing art to the public also needed to open up. On this count the policies of the French state had failed miserably. "Power," Ferrari argued, "governs the places and races of culture just as it governs the places and races of society. With barbed wire. And what is more, by calling that Protection. Of sites, of masterpieces in peril, etc. It is necessary to banalize."[74]

Ferrari's engagement as an *animateur musicale* at the Maison de la Culture in Amiens offered him an ideal platform for putting his beliefs into practice. His efforts to "banalize" contemporary music took a number of forms. Some of these adhered to traditional patterns of arts outreach. He organized educational programs, preconcert talks, and public debates, inviting composers to discuss their works with local audiences. Among those who presented their music at Amiens were Maurice Ohana, Iannis Xenakis, François-Bernard Mâche, Betsy Jolas, and Claude Ballif.[75] Ferrari also pursued a number of novel initiatives to encourage hands-on engagement with artistic practice. Upon arriving in Amiens, Ferrari announced his intention to create a new Center for Action and Spontaneous Creation, which would complement the concerts and exhibitions staged at the *maison.*[76] In a series of interviews with the journalist Hansjörg Pauli, Ferrari described his activities in greater detail. These included encouraging local youth to experiment with new media:

> At first I worked together with a number of youth groups, who were mostly well equipped, possessing tape recorders and photo and film cameras, and who also had some understanding of how to handle these devices. It was merely that they didn't yet trust themselves to use them. . . . I encouraged the young people to come [to the Maison de la Culture] with their equipment to interview the public and performers in order that they might become active during the performances and might afterward assemble the recordings they had made.[77]

To a certain extent, the eclectic nature of Ferrari's work at Amiens reflected the uncertain state of *animation culturelle* in the aftermath of '68. Activities like preconcert talks were, for all purposes, geared toward fostering the "encounter" between audience and artwork, and thus accorded with Malraux's philosophy of *action culturelle.* Yet Ferrari's efforts to involve local youth in the production of tape and film pieces bespeak a decidedly un-Malraucian interest in promoting amateur creativity. Instead of simply facilitating the individual's communion with the masterworks of Western civilization, there was an equal emphasis placed on fostering more egalitarian forms of cultural practice.

A handful of works Ferrari composed around the time of his engagement at the Maison de la Culture bear the signs of his experience as an *animateur* as well as his exposure to debates concerning cultural democratization.[78] One such work was the text piece *Tautologos III,* composed in Amiens in 1969. As its title indicates, the work was part of a series of compositions exploring the idea of repetition in music. The score calls for a number of instrumentalists to each perform a single gesture at a fixed interval throughout the piece. If, during the performance, the gestures of two players happen to coincide, each should be modified as a result of this "collision." The result is a texture at once simple and complex, as different cycles of repetition are laid on top of one another to form a continuously shifting mosaic. Yet just as important as the sounding result was its relative ease of performance. Given how little skill it required of participants, *Tautologos III* was an ideal vehicle for involving individuals lacking musical training in the act of performance. Ferrari underlined this potential of the work in the introductory notes to the score. He expresses a hope that works like *Tautologos III* might usher in a situation where "artistic creation is not generated by mythic individuals anymore, representing an intellectual aristocracy, but is generated by the greatest number of people."[79] There was also a symbolic dimension to this valorization of cyclical repetition, as it provided a marked contrast to the emphasis on the singular (masterwork, genius, etc.) that has long dominated Western art. Repetition, by contrast, privileged the mundane, the unremarkable: "Tautology is a popular activity, being the reflection of gestures, noises, words, and facts of life."[80] Repetition here fulfills a role similar to those that Walter Benjamin famously ascribed to processes of mechanical reproduction: in both cases the auratic quality of the traditional work of art, the sense of awe generated by the unique object or event, disappears by virtue of its replication.

Tautologos III exemplifies how Ferrari sought to integrate the ideals of cultural democratization into his work as a composer. The result was a piece that offered individuals an occasion to participate in a collective musical action, and as such put into practice the idea that art need not be produced by "mythic individuals." In a subsequent piece, *Presque rien, ou le lever du jour au bord de la mer* (1967–70), Ferrari would go even further in his efforts to provide a model for the amateur practice of experimental music. *Presque rien* presents the listener with an apparently unretouched recording of the sounds of daybreak in a fishing village on the Black Sea. There are few traces of Ferrari's handiwork in the finished work, despite the fact that the piece was the product of careful editing, Ferrari having compressed the events of an entire morning into the space of a thirty-minute recording. Yet it was not the actual craftsmanship that went into the piece but its apparent artlessness, its semblance of simplicity, that Ferrari stressed. In his interviews with Pauli, Ferrari cast *Presque rien* less as a work of art and more as an exemplar of a new kind of artistic practice: "These things, which I call 'The Presque Riens' because they are lacking development and completely static, because really almost nothing happens musically, are more reproductions than productions: electroacoustic nature photographs—a beach landscape in the morning mists, a winter day in the mountaintops."[81] Not only could one play these recordings in the comfort of one's home ("just as one might hang photos or pictures on the wall"), but, like photographs, they were easy to produce.[82] Pressed by Pauli as to whether he really believed that people might go out and record their own pieces of "electroacoustic nature photography," Ferrari responded affirmatively: "Why not? After all, people take holiday photos and make vacation films; they could just as well record their impressions in sound-pictures [Hörbildern]. The electroacoustic music that I make nowadays may be produced without any equipment beyond that available to every amateur."[83]

In subsequent years Ferrari continued to express his interest in transforming tape music into an amateur practice. In the liner notes for a 1969 recording of his tape work *Hétérozygote,* he reiterated his hope that the rudimentary nature of the work—what Ferrari dubbed "poor man's *musique concrète*"—might inspire listeners to follow suit: "My intention was to pave the way for amateur concrete music much as people take snapshots during vacations."[84] Statements like these underlined Ferrari's belief that magnetic tape represented an ideal medium for stimulating a participatory form of mass culture. There was some basis for this belief. Portable tape recorders had appeared on the consumer market in France in the early 1960s, and their increasing affordability, coupled with rising incomes, put them within the reach of many households. Still, for the amateur practice of tape composition to become a reality, it was necessary to strip away the aura of technical complexity that surrounded *musique concrète*. In this regard, the minimal editing of *Presque rien* appears to have served as a way of demystifying the production of tape music. But the value of the piece was not limited to its exemplary quality. The use of easily identifiable sounds in *Presque rien* had the additional merit of making the piece comprehensible to a general audience. Whereas Schaefferian *musique concrète* had insisted that a sound's source be disguised to better focus the listener's attention on its morphological properties, Ferrari saw the use of recognizable, "anecdotal" sounds as a way of facilitating comprehension, offering audiences familiar reference points to orient their listening. Instead of severing tape music's connection to reality, Ferrari foregrounded this connection. *Presque rien* thus strove to render experimental music accessible in terms of both its production and reception.

While Ferrari's project of creating a *musique concrète* for the masses was undoubtedly well-intentioned, it was premised on questionable assumptions regarding the "culturally deprived" groups it purported to serve. Some insight into these suppositions may be gained by reading this project through the lens of Bourdieu's roughly contemporaneous essay, "Éléments d'une théorie sociologique de la perception artistique" (1968).[85] Bourdieu's essay distinguishes two basic forms of aesthetic pleasure, "the enjoyment which accompanies aesthetic perception reduced to simple aisthesis, and the delight procured by scholarly savouring, presupposing, as a necessary but insufficient condition, adequate deciphering."[86] Whereas the first of these ("simple aisthesis") designates a kind of perception that responds directly to the sensory stimulus provided by the artwork, the second ("scholarly savouring") designates a species of mediated perception in which the viewer situates the work within a stylistic and/or historic context. In other words, "simple aisthesis" locates art's meaning in the immanent properties of the work itself, while "scholarly savouring" locates its meaning in the relation that emerges when the work is set against the backdrop provided by some broader, transcendent frame (movement, style, genre, etc.). However, it is another, even more basic approach to the artwork that Bourdieu sees as the most common alternative to both "aisthesis" and "scholarly savouring": "Those for whom the works of scholarly culture speak a foreign language are condemned to take into their perception and their appreciation of the work of art some extrinsic categories and values—those which organize their day-to-day perception and guide their practical judgment."[87] Lacking the proper artistic code to make sense of the work, individuals will by necessity draw upon the knowledge afforded by everyday experience. Confronted with a representational painting, the "learned" viewer will attend to how the object is represented in order to locate the work stylistically (as in "scholarly savouring"), or in order to appreciate its formal or sensual properties (as in "aisthesis"). By contrast, the "naive" viewer, having recourse only to the codes that organize "day-to-day perception," will attend to what is represented, not how it is represented.

Bourdieu notes that aesthetic discourse does not accord these different modes of artistic perception equal value. Interpreting an artwork according to the schemata of everyday experience has been seen since Kant's time as a vulgar form of appreciation, one that supposes "that every image shall fulfill a function, if only that of a sign."[88] Recast in light of Bourdieu's observations, we might say that Ferrari's objective for *Presque rien* was to invert this hierarchy, to revalue "uncultivated" perception as a privileged mode of hearing precisely because of its vulgarity. Ferrari's aim, it would seem, was to create a kind of music where the identification of what was represented would suffice for an adequate perception of the work. Unlike music that derives its meaning from the play of abstract forms, works that make use of referential sounds have the advantage of not requiring any specialized knowledge of musical syntax or style to be deciphered. Insofar as such music fashioned messages out of the quasi-universal code of everyday experience, it was potentially within the grasp of any listener, from the most naive to the most educated.

While recourse to referential sounds may have lowered barriers to the comprehension of tape music, in doing so it perpetuated the notion that those excluded from the domain of high culture were bereft of cultural knowledge altogether. In this respect, Ferrari's enterprise betrayed the same blind spot that afflicted the ideal of cultural democratization promoted by the Ministry of Cultural Affairs. In both cases the lack of interest in a specific form of artistic practice—what goes by the name of "serious culture"—was equated with a lack of interest in all forms of artistic practice. On account of their presumed commercialism, forms of musical expression like rock, *variétés,* or *yéyé* were discounted as potential representatives of an authentic popular culture, regardless of whether large segments of the population derived meaning or pleasure from them. Having dispatched what was conventionally understood as being popular, and with no alternatives to fill the resulting void, the very idea of popular culture became an empty concept in the eyes of *animateurs,* left-wing intellectuals and policy makers alike (and this was equally true of Bourdieu). It was precisely this notion—that the working classes

inhabited a cultural vacuum—that fueled initiatives for cultural democratization. It was the same notion that motivated Ferrari's advocacy
of "poor man's *musique concrète.*" One consequence of this is that the
"popular" mode of listening that *Presque rien* calls for is defined in
strictly negative terms, not by its embrace of a particular code or style,
but by its refusal of any form of acculturation as a precondition for
aesthetic appreciation. Yet the audiences *Presque rien* would have encountered outside the rarefied sphere of new music aficionados were not
the blank slates imagined by the benefactors of cultural democratization,
but individuals in possession of their own, distinctive forms of cultural
knowledge. And judged according to the standards of then-contemporary
popular music, the piece would have undoubtedly proven unsatisfying.
Ferrari's works after 1970 fared better in this regard, as he moved progressively toward a more affirmative conception of the popular, one
that acknowledged and incorporated a wide range of vernacular styles.
In the late 1960s, however, embracing music identified as "commercial"
appears to have been largely unthinkable for an engaged composer in
France. Hence *Presque rien,* rather than striving to formulate a positive
notion of popular culture, instead chased after a chimerical degree zero
of culture.

DÉVELOPPEMENT CULTUREL

Beginning in the late 1960s, the field of *animation culturelle* underwent
a period of tremendous expansion, both qualitatively and quantitatively.
It grew qualitatively as the number of social activities that the practices
of *animation* addressed increased. A survey of the field published in
1970 identified eight distinct genres of *animation* (cultural, sociocultural, social, socioeconomic, political, educational, rural, and commercial) and seven different areas where *animateurs* were called on to intervene (workplaces, tourist sites, rural areas, urban areas, commercial
centers, youth centers, and public gatherings).[89] The influx of new re-
cruits into the profession caused the field to grow quantitatively. Encouraging this growth was the transformation of *animation* from what
had been a largely voluntary pursuit into an officially recognized occu-
pational category. From 1967 to 1973, the government opened thirty-
five centers for training would-be *animateurs,* attesting to the field's
expansion as well as its increasing institutionalization.[90]

One consequence of this mushrooming of *animation* was that it made
it increasingly difficult to specify what the term meant. As one observer

remarked, "The vogue that the word *animation* enjoys today . . . has practically emptied it of all content."[91] Most efforts to define the field fell back on vague generalities (which was perhaps to be expected, given that *animation* was treated as a magical cure-all for an assortment of societal ills). For the Institut national d'education populaire, the *animateur* was essentially an arbiter of interpersonal relations. *Animation* entailed "all action within or upon a group, a collective, a milieu, aiming to develop communication and to structure social life."[92] Henri Théry, author of the government's report on *animation* for the VIe Plan, instead characterized the *animateur* as a catalyst. Practitioners should help create "the conditions such that every group or every individual may be revealed to himself," in addition to bringing "social groups into relation with one another, or with artworks and their creators, or with the centers of [political] decision making."[93] Sociologist Michel Simonot likewise underlined *animation*'s obligation to spur social change. But unlike Théry, he emphasized the fact that *animateurs* sought to induce such transformations by acting on individuals rather than political or economic structures: "*Animation socio-culturelle* is a sector of social life whose agents dedicate themselves to the goal of bringing about a certain transformation in attitudes and in interpersonal and collective relationships, by means of a direct action upon individuals, their attitudes, and their interpersonal and social relations. This action is generally exercised through the mediation of diverse pedagogical activities making use of nondirected or active methods."[94] Differences in nuance or emphasis notwithstanding, what these definitions of *animation* all pointed to was a shift in the vocation's center of gravity. Where *animation* had once been defined as a form of alternative education, a way of disseminating knowledge and culture among underprivileged groups, it was now seen as a means of negotiating a range of disparities—social, cultural, and psychic—that afflicted French society. Insofar as *animation* continued to address artistic practices, these were no longer treated exclusively as a gift to be bestowed upon "deprived" communities. Rather, culture was recast as an instrument for achieving the self-realization of individuals and communities.

Changes in state cultural policy responded to changes in the practice of *animation culturelle*. The Ministry of Cultural Affairs entered a transitional period following Malraux's departure in 1969. Bereft of its charismatic leader, the ministry suffered from a certain amount of institutional drift in the years that followed. It was only with the nomination of Jacques Duhamel to head the ministry in 1971 that this uncertain interlude came to a close. Previously the leader of a centrist bloc in the Assemblée nationale, the Centre démocratie et progrès, Duhamel approached cultural affairs in a manner befitting his moderate, socially liberal temperament. In place of Malraux's grandiose vision of art as a secular religion for a disenchanted world, Duhamel advanced the more prosaic (though in many ways more innovative) policy of *développement culturel*. In the essay "The Age of Culture," published a year into his tenure, Duhamel outlined the premises and objectives of his program. Culture, he argued, has an important role to play in contemporary society, being an essential resource for palliating the disruptions caused by industrialization and rapid economic growth. The increasing affluence of the postwar years had come at a steep social cost: the erosion of workplace autonomy robbed individuals of a principal site of self-realization; the urban milieu atomized interpersonal relations and induced a sense of anomie; and the mass media had engendered a passive mindset among individuals. It was the role of culture to mitigate problems like these by fostering self-expression, social interaction, and the formation of a more active, engaged citizenry. But to assume the therapeutic function that Duhamel ascribed to it, culture needed to be construed in a more expansive way than hitherto had been the case. No longer was cultural practice to be equated exclusively with the fine arts. Rather, it was now to be understood as "a form of knowledge," a "way of life," and a "practice . . . of communication among men."[95] In short Duhamel's concept of *développement culturel* proposed an anthropological understanding of culture, one that encompassed the expressive, symbolic, and aesthetic dimensions of social life.

This broadening of the definition of culture did not mean, however, that tasks hitherto central to the ministry's mission (most notably the protection of France's artistic patrimony) were abandoned. It was rather that these objectives needed to be rethought in light of the new social demands to which culture responded. In order to transform art from an object of blind reverence into a means of addressing social ills, it was necessary to cultivate more active approaches to artistic practice. Whence the greater emphasis placed on pedagogy within Duhamel's program, particularly *animation culturelle*: "It isn't enough that a work of art is put on display that a true contact is established. There are as many different ways of looking at a statue or watching a play as there are viewers, but most of these are virtually blind. The need for mediation becomes pressing, and it is this that one describes as *animation*."[96] Yet *animation* involved more than facilitating a "correct" or adequate comprehension of artworks. Above all it should impart new dispositions in individuals. *Animation,* Duhamel explained, is "not only a new way of presenting works of art; its domain extends to cover the entire field of culture. *Animation* is certainly a pedagogy. But it is more than that: it seeks to create a spark [in individuals]."[97]

The priority Duhamel attached to *animation* was clearly informed by changes taking place in the field itself. Nonetheless, there were significant differences in how Duhamel's program of *développement culturel* treated *animation,* and how *animateurs* themselves conceived their activities. Whereas a significant fraction of *animateurs* saw their work as a way of disseminating a critical, contestatory attitude with respect to "bourgeois" culture, for Duhamel's ministry one of the main goals of *développement culturel* was to turn back the rising tide of post-'68 radicalism. Cultural action, within this conception, aimed at channeling subversive attitudes into the safer arena of artistic, as opposed to political, expression. The hope was that individuals would not fall victim to what Duhamel described as the "temptation of radical solutions." In this capacity *développement culturel* was emblematic of the broader package of social reforms that Prime Minister Jacques Chaban-Delmas had included in 1969 in his New Society program.[98] The greater sense of autonomy, self-expression, and interpersonal communication that participation in cultural practice would ensure functioned as a vaccine that would inoculate French society from the kind of social unrest witnessed during May '68.

The challenge posed by the extreme left was not the only factor shaping state cultural policies in the early 1970s. Other pressures were being applied on the Ministry of Cultural Affairs from within the government itself. Unlike his predecessor, the newly elected president, Georges Pompidou, took an active interest in cultural affairs and was the driving force behind a number of highly visible governmental interventions in the arts during his term. Showcase events that received his backing—such as the Festival d'automne (founded in 1971) and the Exposition 60/72, douze ans d'art contemporain en France (1972)—betrayed Pompidou's proclivity for modernist art, as well as his dedication to the Gaullist dream of restoring France's cultural preeminence. The most ambitious of the president's initiatives was the creation of a center dedicated to modern art in central Paris, the Centre national d'art et de culture (renamed the Centre Georges Pompidou after his death). Although plans to build a museum and public library on the plateau Beaubourg in Paris had been in the works for years, Pompidou used the weight of his office to push the project forward. He was also able to persuade a number of eminent figures to participate in the project. Notable among these was Pierre Boulez, who was enticed back from self-imposed exile to head IRCAM, the music research institute attached to the center. Such spectacular undertakings painted a very different picture of state cultural policy than did Duhamel's program of *développement culturel.* The result was a certain dissonance between the image of cultural affairs put forward at the presidential and ministerial levels. Whereas Duhamel's policies treated culture as a means for addressing social dysfunctions, the Festival d'automne, the Exposition 60/72, and the Centre du Plateau Beaubourg were generally regarded as prestige enterprises, extravagant undertakings that reinforced rather than minimized cultural inequalities.[99]

Institutional inertia within the Ministry of Cultural Affairs also hampered the implementation of Duhamel's program of *développement culturel.* There was a good deal of continuity within the ministry from earlier administrations in the form of initiatives already underway and personnel already in place, which meant that broad changes in policy were slow to take effect. The Direction de la musique was a case in point. Landowski had stayed on as the head of the division after the departure of Malraux and continued to execute his ten-year plan for music until his own departure from the ministry in 1974. While he made some adjustments to the plan as state cultural policy evolved, these tended to be more cosmetic than real. An interim report on the progress of the ten-year plan revealed the new rhetorical gloss given to Landowski's projects. Tellingly entitled *Musique pour tous* (Music for everybody), the report framed the government's action in the music sector quite differently than Landowski's original proposal had, even as its actual policies went more or less unchanged.[100] In lieu of the corporatist focus of earlier years was an emphasis on democratizing access to music. No longer was governmental policy a question of saving a profession threatened by the rise of the mass media. Instead, radio and sound recording were now credited with generating a desire among individuals "to produce their own music . . . , music being the quintessential art of participation."[101] But if the newfound rhetoric of public participation accorded better with the changing cultural policy environment of the 1970s, the substance of Landowski's ten-year plan remained essentially the same. The stress still lay upon the creation of performance ensembles, the shoring up of the conservatory system, and the dispensation of subsidies to composers and performers of contemporary music.

To the extent that the broader goals of the Landowski plan were re-vised in light of the new ministerial prerogatives, it was largely by recast-ing performance and educational institutions as instruments of *anima-tion musicale*. In a speech given to the Académie des Beaux-Arts in 1972, Landowski described regional orchestras as "the commandos of [musical] *animation*," having the function of "sensitizing all strata of so-ciety" to musical culture.[102] Elsewhere Landowski depicted government-sponsored music festivals as vehicles for reaching those publics who had the misfortune to inhabit areas "severed from live music."[103] But if Landowski sought to retrofit festivals, orchestras, and other institutions as the agents of *animation musicale,* the relationship was reciprocal, as he put *animation* to work to help ensure the long-term viability of these institutions. Following his departure from the Direction de la musique, Landowski assumed a new position within the government, this time as part of a commission within the Ministry of Education addressing the paucity of arts instruction in primary schools. At the time, the level of music education in French elementary schools varied widely, as did the quality of the instruction on offer. Lacking the resources to institute universal music education in primary schools, Landowski instead pro-posed that, at a minimum, all French schoolchildren should be familiar-ized with *"la musique"* (which is to say, classical music) by means of periodic *animations*. He initiated a pilot program in five regions, where over the course of three years *animateurs* would give presentations on different orchestral instruments, to be followed by a series of educa-tional concerts.[104] The program also called for the creation of five thou-sand choral groups and a thousand youth orchestras across France, though Landowski offered few details about how this goal would be accomplished. As had been the case with his ten-year plan seven years earlier, Landowski invoked the "backwardness" of the classical music infrastructure in France to win support for his new initiative: "If we want to close this gap, it is necessary to bring music to millions of French children."[105]

While Landowski's conception of *animation musicale* adhered to tra-ditional forms of music instruction, more experimental approaches gained favor under Jean Maheu, Landowski's successor as head of the Direc-tion de la musique. A graduate of the Ecole nationale d'administration, Maheu was a career public servant, and as such less beholden to the corporatist impulses that had driven Landowski's agenda. During a press conference held in December 1975, Maheu introduced a number of innovations to the government's music policy.[106] Among these was an increase in both symbolic and material support for *animation musicale*. In broaching the subject, Maheu took note of the term's fluidity:

> The missionary work of some is denounced by others as a form of class-driven proselytism.

> The desire to share a certain cultural patrimony is accused of being an authoritarian practice impeding the expression of peoples in search of their own cultural identity.

> For certain individuals it is a question of moving past simple musical consumption . . . ; they wish to permit each person, if not everybody, to become an *animateur musical* as much in everyday life (for example vis-à-vis their children) as in professional and social [settings]; this approach is considered by others as utopian in that it fails to recognize the mediations that music inevitably demands, particularly those of a technical nature.[107]

In Maheu's view, the Direction de la musique had to avoid taking sides in these debates. It was incumbent upon policy makers to adopt a catholic attitude with respect to *animation.*[108] Even so, the balance of the measures that Maheu proposed favored more experimental forms of *animation.* He called for increased aid for groups operating in nontraditional venues such as hospitals, prisons, and housing projects.[109] In addition, he advocated that experimental pedagogies, especially those drawing inspiration from contemporary music, feature more prominently in primary education. In contrast to the reforms Landowski was busy promoting within the Ministry of Education, which focused squarely on classical music, the initiatives backed by Maheu were to be open to the entire "world of sounds." Above all, they were to avoid the limitations imposed by adhering to a single "grammatical system of reference," Maheu's euphemism for common-practice tonality.[110]

However, the emphasis placed on *animation musicale* was not the only innovation in the music policy outlined by Maheu. Figuring prominently among the measures proposed by Maheu's administration were those supporting the new field of *recherche musicale.*[111] He justified assistance for research centers carrying out work in acoustics, music technology, sound synthesis, and auditory perception partly on socioeconomic grounds: such initiatives promised to advance scientific and musical knowledge, and as such accorded with the government's broader agenda of technological modernization.[112] But just as important, this field represented for Maheu an indispensable instrument for addressing the crisis afflicting contemporary music: "Fundamental research on sound, in its relationship to music and to musical experimentation, today constitutes one of the major stakes in the future of musical life."[113] But if investment in research was defended on the grounds that it might somehow resolve the problems facing contemporary music, there were other, political factors driving investment in *recherche musicale.* Particularly notable was the advent of IRCAM, the most spectacular development in state support for contemporary music since the establishment of the Direction de la musique some ten years earlier. The creation of this showcase for *recherche musicale* demanded some kind of response within music policy, especially since IRCAM fell outside the jurisdiction of the Direction de la musique, being subsidized directly by the Ministry of Cultural Affairs. In this light, Maheu's creation of an entirely new sector devoted to *recherche musicale* can be seen as a way of rationalizing the place of IRCAM in French musical life by situating it within a broader and more coherent framework.

Given that the Direction de la musique exercised no control over IRCAM, most of the aid Maheu funneled toward *recherche musicale* was concentrated on a handful of smaller regional institutions. Existing electroacoustic music studios (like the Groupe de musique expérimentale de Bourges, or GMEB, an offshoot of the Maison de la Culture in Bourges) received greater support from the ministry, as did new institutions (such as the Centre européen de recherche musicale). In developing a plan to guide the work undertaken in these various centers, Maheu instituted a clear division of artistic and intellectual labor between IRCAM, the flagship center for *recherche musicale,* and its smaller regional peers. Whereas IRCAM was to pursue "fundamental" research into physical, acoustic, and psychological aspects of sound, provincial centers like GMEB were to engage in "applied" projects involving education, *animation,* and diffusion. Maheu explained that "electroacoustic music has permitted the development of a radically new approach to sound. . . . By means of electroacoustics children [can] experiment with sound in a pragmatic and open manner, without recourse to an instrumental practice."[114] It is clear that Maheu's policies treated research and *animation* as complementary. Technological innovation reshaped arts outreach, creating new ways of facilitating musical practice, at the same time as *animation* brought audiences into contact with unfamiliar repertoires.

Another factor linking *animation* and *recherche* was that both established novel career paths for musicians. Composers were the main beneficiaries of these alternative "host" professions, as research and *animation* joined conducting, teaching, and performing as ways that composers could earn income to underwrite their creative activities. These new career paths offered symbolic and material advantages for the government and musicians alike. Instead of being seen giving handouts to composers in the form of commissions or *bourses,* state support for new music could now be portrayed as serving a broader social purpose. For composers, employment in these new fields legitimized their activities, recasting compositional work as a corollary to social work. In the case of *animation,* the nature of the public service provided was fairly transparent. As we have seen, the role accorded to *animateurs* had expanded in the early 1970s to the point where they were seen as all-purpose social mediators, individuals who stimulated cultural practice as part of the larger project of creating a healthy, happy, and productive citizenry. In the case of *recherche musicale,* the public good served by the quasi-scientific work of the composer/researcher was rather more elusive. Its claim to social utility rested largely on the symbolic legitimacy that accrued to science and technology as motors of human advancement over the *longue durée.*

While Maheu's public utterances suggested that *animation musicale* would enjoy strong institutional backing, in fact the discipline occupied a relatively minor place within the policies of the Direction de la musique. In 1976, aid to both creation and *animation* accounted for 5.5 percent of the total budget for music, a drop in the bucket compared to the outlays made for orchestras, opera companies, and conservatories. Five years on, in 1981, little had changed.[115] As Denis Muzet argued in his 1979 study of *animation musicale,* Maheu, for all his rhetoric, was no less consumed than Landowski with the task of "improving and extending the traditional mode of diffusion that is the concert."[116] In Muzet's estimation, the real catalyst behind developments in the domain of *animation musicale* during the 1970s came not from the state but from work taking place on the ground.[117] This was equally true for the kinds of *animations* Landowski encouraged. Most of the educational concerts and classroom presentations that he advocated were to be conducted by nonprofit associations such as the Jeunesses musicales de France or the Centre France lyrique.

Still, one should not underestimate the impact of changing governmental policies. By giving this new form of public outreach their imprimatur, both Maheu and Landowski tacitly encouraged the expansion of *animation* into new social milieus. Even if the Direction de la musique invested a relatively paltry sum in direct support for *animation,* activities bearing this title were quickly adopted by a variety of institutions receiving governmental subsidies. Demonstrating one's commitment to the cultivation of new audiences for music became a virtual prerequisite for groups receiving state subventions. This applied even to such well-funded entities as IRCAM and its affiliated performance group, the Ensemble Intercontemporain, which was established in 1976. During its 1977–78 season, for instance, the Ensemble Intercontemporain boasted that its members had participated in 106 *animations,* including 55 in Paris, 28 in the greater Paris metropolitan region, and 31 in the rest of France. Many of these presentations took place in traditional concert settings and educational establishments, but no small number were held in nontraditional venues such as hospitals and factories.[118] Such activities served as a not-too-subtle means of justifying the generous support the group received from the Ministry of Cultural Affairs. With the status of classical and modern music as social goods no longer taken as self-evident, governmental aid from this point forward obliged visible demonstrations of public service on the part of musicians.

PRACTICES OF *ANIMATION MUSICALE*

So what, then, were the "experimental pedagogies" being promoted under Maheu's directorship? What impact did the widening ambit of *animation culturelle* have on the musical domain? And how did these practices intersect with the interests of the contemporary music community? Before considering some examples of the practice of *animation,* it is first necessary to chart the broader contours of the field. The different approaches to *animation* backed by Landowski and Maheu point to the existence of two broad currents within the field.[119] The first—what I will refer to as "traditional" *animation*—evangelized on behalf of "serious" music. The aim was to spark an interest in classical music by familiarizing targeted publics (mainly children) with its materials, forms, and practices. In many respects, traditional *animation* continued along the path blazed by the cultural democratization efforts of the 1960s, save for the fact that they placed a higher premium on pedagogy. This is evident in Landowski's educational reforms, which stressed such didactic activities as in-class presentation of musical instruments and instructional concerts. The guiding principle was that knowledge of classical music, once acquired, would dissolve the barriers that impeded its widespread appreciation.

The second current of *animation musicale*—what I will refer to as "experimental" *animation*—prioritized active involvement in musical practice. Instead of seeking to impart a specific competence, this approach aimed at cultivating a general sensibility in the individual, a way of engaging both musical phenomena and the social interactions that underpinned them. Coupled with this was an emphasis on ludic activities, which were seen as fostering both inventiveness and sociability.[120] Hence the importance attached to group improvisations, musical games, and the construction of homemade instruments—activities that were open, unstructured, and unburdened by convention. Doing music, rather than knowing about it, was the key to changing cultural behaviors.

Another factor distinguishing traditional and experimental *animation* involved genre. For the most part, traditional *animation* concerned itself with the classic-romantic repertoire. Groups charged with presenting educational concerts, such as the Jeunesses musicales de France and the Centre France lyrique, programmed music that was predominantly derived from the standard repertory.[121] In-class presentations of musical instruments betrayed the same bias. With few exceptions the instruments *animateurs* presented students were drawn from the domains of chamber and symphonic music.[122] The resulting generic bias was not lost upon those targeted by arts outreach programs. During the course of a presentation at a local school in Amiens, Edmond Rosenfeld, the *animateur musical* at the Maison de la Culture d'Amiens in the early 1970s, introduced students to the piano, playing excerpts from the classical and modern repertoire for their benefit. He framed his presentation by informing the pupils that "the music played all day long on the radio accustoms you to a certain [musical] style, which is not necessarily the one you would choose [for yourself]," adding that "that's how they sell albums."[123] The students did not meekly accede to the idea that they were dupes of the mass media, however. They demanded to know why they should be reproached for having never attended a concert of classical music when so few adults frequented concerts of rock music. Rosenberg's response to this question was simply to note that exposure to "serious" music allowed the students to make an informed musical choice: "You can only like what you know, and it is in this sense that *animations* are necessary."[124]

Experimental *animateurs* for their part prioritized contemporary music.[125] This was not entirely surprising, given that many were either composers or affiliated with groups dedicated to the production and diffusion of new music (such as the GRM, GMEB, or the Percussions de Strasbourg). There were methodological reasons for this generic bias as well. The stress placed upon open-ended, gamelike activities in experimental *animations* went hand in hand with a rejection of established standards. To reproduce the patterns set forth within a particular style or genre was seen as placing an undue restriction on the individual's capacity for free expression. Experimental *animateurs* thus dismissed what they termed "directed" methods, approaches that aimed at imparting a particular musical competence. The main target of their hostility was *solfège,* castigated for its abstraction and narrowness. But even pedagogies like the Orff and Martenot methods, both of which encouraged a more active engagement with musical practice, were subject to sharp critique. Such "active methods" were seen by experimental *animateurs* as Trojan horses, a way of instilling a taste for tonal music on an unsuspecting public. Their goal, one *animateur* remarked, was "to make the pill of *solfège* go down easier."[126]

By contrast, experimental *animation* trumpeted the virtues of cultural relativism. Yet this valorization of diversity did not necessarily translate into efforts at exposing audiences to a wide range of music traditions. Experimental *animations* made only passing reference to folk, popular, or non-Western musics. Rather, the ability to appreciate the gamut of musical genres was typically conceived in negative terms, as a capacity to suspend conventionalized expectations. Thus one of the main objectives of experimental *animation* was to help individuals cast off the shackles of learned musical codes, which were seen as blocking an appreciation of other traditions. In practical terms, the "deconditioning" of individual taste fostered by experimental *animation* was tantamount to a reconditioning in the values and norms of contemporary classical music, a genre whose principal convention was the repudiation of convention. As one *animateur* observed, the purpose of their work was "desacralizing the object," a sentiment that accorded with the transgressive ethos of avant-garde music.[127] Here as elsewhere, the desire to maximize the individual's expressive and communicative possibilities led to a rupture with the conventions of tonal music. But in seeking to remove the constraints that existing musical systems imposed on creativity, experimental *animateurs* ended up imposing a different constraint. The disavowal of one genre (classical music) resulted in the surreptitious embrace of another (contemporary music).

A final point where traditional and experimental approaches to *animation musicale* diverged concerned the social import ascribed to their endeavors. Advocates of traditional *animation* tended to rely on humanistic arguments concerning the universal value of music. Landowski, for one, justified the initiatives undertaken by the Ministry of Education on the grounds that music was an "irreplaceable element" in the cultural formation of the individual.[128] Proponents of experimental *animation* tended instead to emphasize the extramusical benefits that cultivation of the individual's creative faculties generated. Madeleine Gagnard, one of the most vocal advocates of nontraditional approaches to music pedagogy, credited *animation* with improving one's ability to engage in collective work; correcting the unhealthy competition and individualism of the French educational system; striking a better balance between bodily and mental activity; and engendering a more egalitarian worldview by "demystifing the artist-god."[129] In short, the unblocking of creative activity effected by *animation musicale* was cast as key to the formation of the total person, the future citizen of a more just and equitable society.

To be sure, the two currents of *animation* sketched here were not so clearly delineated in practice. They are better understood as ideal types, poles within a fluid continuum of practices. In fact, on many points the two sides of the disciplinary divide were more or less indistinguishable. One of the most significant of these concerned how *animateurs* conceived of the constituencies they addressed. Without exception, *animateurs* focused their efforts on the vast "nonpublic" identified in the Villeurbanne declaration, an entity defined less by any positive attributes than by its abject relation to the cultural sphere. This indistinct group was understood as standing outside culture, frozen in what cultural policy theorists George Yúdice and Toby Miller have called a state of "ethical incompleteness."[130] Despite the vagueness of the designation "nonpublic," there were a handful of demographic groups that constituted the main focus of *animation*'s solicitations. The blue-collar worker—including its most recent incarnation, the *travailleur immigré*—occupied a central place in the discourse of *animation culturelle*. Long conceived by intellectuals as the living antithesis of the cultured subject, the worker embodied the condition of cultural deprivation that *animateurs* sought to ameliorate. Another target audience of *animation* was children. Unlike workers, children were not deemed to be excluded from culture so much as situated before it, not yet caught in its snares. Their exile from cultural practice was a matter of chronology rather than ontology.

While the presumed lack of culture among children and workers represented a misfortune that *animateurs* strove to remedy, it also presented an opportunity. To the extent that these groups had not been indoctrinated into a particular taste culture (or at least were seen to be so), they were deemed particularly ripe for recruitment into the cultural practices promoted by *animation musicale.* For contemporary music in particular, this was quite a boon. Its eschewal of convention made new music appear better equipped to address those groups that had yet to transcend the condition of "cultural virginity" (to borrow a phrase from Pierre-Michel Menger). This is a theme that recurs in the practices of *animation* examined in the following sections. The lack of convention *animateurs* imputed to avant-garde music seemed to match perfectly the lack of cultural knowledge ascribed to the targets of *animation musicale.*

ANIMATION, CHILDREN, AND THE ATELIER LYRIQUE DU RHIN

In fall 1972 an installation of African and Asian musical instruments was presented at the Grand Palais in Paris, part of the annual Semaines musicales internationales de Paris, discussed earlier in this chapter. The instruments housed in the Grand Palais were not mere objects of display but comprised the Galerie sonore, an interactive *animation* designed to afford elementary school students from the greater Paris region the opportunity to try their hand at making music. The objective of the Galerie sonore was to combat the "musical passivity" rampant among children.[131] The decision to use non-Western instruments was seen as advancing this end. According to Maurice Fleuret, who had taken the lead in organizing the *animation,* Western orchestral instruments lacked the immediate appeal of their non-Western counterparts. Violins, clarinets, bassoons, and the like were too forbidding, too rarefied to allow for "direct expression."[132] By contrast, the "rustic" nature of African and Asian instruments made them more accessible to children who lacked musical training. Fleuret's description of the epiphany that had led to the creation of the Galerie sonore is revealing: "I had noticed that certain of these instruments imperiously beckoned the hand or the mouth, which was compelled to make them sound. . . . Without even being aware of it, I found myself in the process of manipulating them, even learning to play them little by little, but without any method, guided only by the instrument itself and by its irrepressible need to speak."[133] Taking notice of the quasi-magical power of attraction that these instruments exercised over him, it occurred to Fleuret that they would provide the ideal vehicle for encouraging nonmusicians to partake in musical practice. Children in particular would thus be able to discover "the way of making use of the most simple of instruments spontaneously."[134]

The ethos that informed the creation of the Galerie sonore in 1972 was typical of how *animateurs* approached their work with children. The latter were imagined as endowed with an innate disposition toward creative activity, which had not yet been regimented, repressed, or otherwise corrupted. This creativity remained latent, however, and required an outlet to be realized. As Fleuret's account suggests, the instruments best suited to channel the expressive powers of children had to be commensurate with their lack of cultural attainment; the result was his supposition that non-Western instruments, being less "advanced" than their Western counterparts, would prove a better match to the natural expressive drives of children. The irony is that this belief in the virtue of the child's cultural innocence did not quite play out as Fleuret and his collaborators had envisaged. The success of the *animation* in purely quantitative terms (it attracted more than forty-five thousand children during the course of the festival) proved to be its downfall, as the small team of *animateurs* found themselves overwhelmed, unable to control the crowds of unruly children. Most of the instruments ended up being damaged, if not completely destroyed.[135]

If the Galerie sonore evinced a belief in the innate creativity of children, it also encapsulated the kind of permissive approach to pedagogy that was typical of experimental *animation*. To unlock the artistic potential of children it was necessary to avoid imposing on them models, values, or standards of comportment that derived from the alien world of adults. This principle—dubbed "nondirectivity" by its advocates—followed logically from the Rousseauian image of children that most experimental *animateurs* held.[136] Still, not all were persuaded that the free, unconstrained development of the child's creative faculties could be ensured so easily. What nondirected pedagogies failed to take into account was the ubiquity in the everyday milieu of tonal music(s), which shaped children's tastes from infancy onward. François Delalande, head of the music pedagogy division at the GRM, thus noted that children's exposure to the mass media "conditions them . . . to existing music. In doing nothing, we accept that a certain pedagogy will take place by means of albums and the radio."[137] By this reasoning, nondirectivity was insufficient by itself. It had to be complemented by positive measures that corrected for the biases that the everyday soundscape inculcated. Children's cultural innocence could not be taken for granted but had to be actively imparted.

This was the conclusion that one group, the Atelier lyrique du Rhin, arrived at after a preliminary attempt at getting children involved in the creative process. Founded in 1972, the atelier had originally been conceived as a platform that would allow young singers to develop their métier. However, the group soon found itself squeezed out of this particular niche by the creation in 1973 of the Opéra-Studio de Paris. The ensemble suspended its activities until 1974, when it was reconstituted under the leadership of Pierre Barrat. To distinguish itself from the Opéra-Studio, the Atelier lyrique du Rhin now took on the more specialized goal of training singers in the performance of contemporary music. In conjunction with this new orientation was a focus on *animation musicale*. The group thus defined itself less as a "training school for singers" and more as a "center of permanent formation," with children being a principal target of the group's attentions."[138]

In 1975, the atelier staged one of its first productions, a children's opera entitled *Un roi sans soleil* (A sunless king). Though the music was nominally by Chilean émigré composer Sergio Ortega, its material was produced in collaboration with children enrolled in the local elementary schools in Colmar (near Strasbourg), where the atelier was based. *Animateurs* affiliated with the group worked with teachers to organize workshops, during which students devised themes that Ortega then elaborated. In other workshops students dreamed up stories, which *animateurs* used as the basis for the libretto. Yet the schoolchildren were not as free from convention as the *animateurs* had hoped. "One of the biggest obstacles to this work," recounted one *animateur,* "is that the child, during this latency period, reproduces a language that is shared, familial, scholastic; [he] does not dare, or does not want, to say what he truly desires."[139] The possibility that this "shared, familial, scholastic" language might actually correspond to what the student did, in fact, desire does not appear to have occurred to the *animateurs*. In their eyes what this situation called for was a more intensive interrogation of the child's musical intuitions: "Confronted with this it is necessary to respond with the most attentive listening, the most demanding questioning."[140] The cultural innocence of children could not be presupposed. It was something that had to be teased out through the painstaking work of *animateurs*.

The next work produced by the group, a theater piece by composer Yves Prin and librettist Marie-Noël Rio entitled *L'Ile de la vieille musique* (The island of old music), attempted to overcome such problems.[141] In contrast to *Un roi sans soleil*, the new piece granted children a limited, more highly structured role in the production. In an interview, Barrat acknowledged that Prin and Rio were the "true authors" of the work. But even so, he contended, "something in the production belongs properly to [the children]."[142] If *Un roi sans soleil* had been marred by students' failure to "free themselves from their traditional cultural schemes," *L'Ile de la vieille musique* would ensure that such schemes were held in check.[143] The suspension of convention played out at both musical and allegorical levels. Plot no less than performance valorized nontraditional forms of musical expression.

The action of *L'Ile de la vieille musique* unfolds on three uncharted islands in the middle of an ocean. Two of the islands are inhabited, one by a tribe of shepherds, the other by a tribe of warriors. These are depicted by two groups of schoolchildren, distinguished musically by means of instrumentation: the warriors play percussion instruments, while the shepherds play winds and strings (a third group of children depict the "elements," imitating the sounds of wind, waves, and forest). A third island, situated between the other two, is uninhabited. Or at least this appears to be the case, until one day a strange music is heard emanating from the island. Intrigued, the chieftains of the two tribes (played by members of the atelier) each decide to discover the source of this music.

Having arrived on the island, the two chieftains, Boitempo (head of the warrior tribe) and Okarina (head of the shepherds) encounter each other. Both covet the land and wish to claim it for their respective peoples. To settle the dispute they agree upon a competition: each will try to outdo the other in a display of instrumental virtuosity. The duel, however, ends in a draw, and the two chieftains agree to a truce. At that very moment, a ship carrying four European explorers lands on the island. As had been the case with the chieftains before them, the explorers wish to claim the island for themselves. They thereupon challenge Boitempo and Okarina to a new contest. Instead of a simple duel of virtuosity, they propose a competition whose winner will be the individual who can best imitate the musical language of the others. What the explorers neglect to tell to their adversaries is that they have a secret weapon, a tape recorder concealed in a box. Whereas the chieftains can only muster a rough approximation of the music of the Western colonizers, their adversaries play back recordings they had surreptitiously made of Boitempo and Okarina and thereby win the competition.

The natives now vanquished, the explorers begin to appraise their newly acquired holdings. The two chieftains suspect foul play, however, and soon discover the tape recorder. A fight breaks out between the natives and explorers, but before long it is interrupted by a violent storm.

In the storm's wake, the natives come to the aid of the injured explorers, who, in gratitude, renounce their efforts to take possession of the island. As they agree to recognize "the language of the other," the sound of the strange music that had lured the chieftains to the island in the first place is heard once again. Now all of the visitors set out together to find the source. At last they come upon a lone man sitting at a grand piano. It turns out that the aged virtuoso had been in a shipwreck years earlier and had managed to make his way to the island by clinging to his grand piano as it bobbed its way across the ocean. Ever since, he had passed each evening by playing *"la vieille musique"* for the beasts of the jungle. At this point all of those present—explorers, natives, and even the elements themselves—join in with the pianist. Afterward they all depart from the island, leaving the old man to play his music in peace.

As allegory, *L'Ile de la vieille musique* could hardly be more transparent. The final chorus dispels any lingering doubts about its underlying message: "If your language is different from mine, you remain nonetheless my equal."[144] Still, if the story extolled the virtues of tolerance, the roles assigned different genres within the narrative suggest that certain languages were more equal than others. A series of oppositions governs the symbolic work that various genres perform. While the most obvious of these sets contemporary idioms (the bulk of the music in *L'Ile*) against the "old music" of the work's title, the image of new music painted by the piece is hardly univocal. First of all, *L'Ile* consistently differentiates what may be described as "noise-based" idioms of contemporary music (that is, music that abjures articulated pitch structures to focus more on timbre and gesture) from pitch-based, postserial idioms. Whereas the latter is associated with the four explorers, the former tends to be associated with nature (the elements) or the "noble savage" (the two tribes). The implication is clear: pitch, temperament, and the technologies of postserial composition (transposition, inversion, etc.) serve as tokens of modernity. This linkage is underlined almost immediately upon the arrival of the colonizers in scene 7; for the first time in the work the singers are accompanied by a piano—the symbol par excellence of Western music technology—playing in a quasi-Boulezian style (example 11). The lines intoned by Geneviève, one of the four explorers, only strengthen the chain of associations that links modernity, Western imperialism, and postserial music: "In my capacity as representative of the health and decency movement, I hold that it is (first of all) necessary to provide these people with decent clothing."

EXAMPLE 11. Yves Prin, *L'Ile de la vieille musique*, scene 7: Geneviève greeting the natives. Used by permission of Yves Prin.

The resulting asymmetry in the portrayal of these two styles—with noise music the emblem of cultural innocence and postserial music its (corrupted) antithesis—is bolstered by the performative dimensions of the work. For the most part children perform the noise-based music, notated in the score by means of rudimentary graphic symbols. (To represent the sound of waves, for instance, the score uses curved lines, which indicate the general contour of the sound the students should produce.) One effect of this is to encourage the children to identify with the work's protagonists, both cognitively and corporeally, and hence to identify with the musical genre associated with these protagonists. Performance reinforces allegory. Styles breaking with conventional notions of musical sound are cast as morally superior, and the act of performance ratifies this coding of styles by ensuring the children's physical and psychic investment in noise-based music.

Embedded within this opposition is another, pitting technical accomplishment (associated with the postserial idiom) against amateur practice (associated with noise music). This may simply have been a by-product of practical concerns, insofar as the music assigned to the children had to assume a relative low skill level on their part. Be that as it may, the interpretive implications remain unchanged. Noise music is cast as a node linking representatives of a precultural, premodern world to a more egalitarian model of cultural production. By contrast, the postserial idiom epitomizes the specialization of musical labor in the modern world. The negative coding of instrumental virtuosity is reaffirmed elsewhere in the drama, most notably in the contest between Boitempo and Okarina to determine ownership of the island. Here too virtuosity is portrayed as unhealthy, linked to competition and interpersonal aggression.

Complicating the dichotomy established between different subgenres of contemporary music is the role the narrative accords to sound recording, the technology generally credited with having permitted the aestheticization of noise in twentieth-century music. The explorers' use of tape to ensure their victory over the indigenous peoples of the islands figures technology as a means of dominating nature, including those groups who inhabit the mythic state of nature that is the stuff of imperial fantasy. But even so, technology has only limited efficacy in the drama. Nature, in the form of the ensuing storm, destroys the explorers' equipment. As a result, they are forced to rely on the practical knowledge of the two chieftains, inverting the power relation between the two groups. As was the case with the valorization of amateur practice in the piece, the negative representations of technology within *L'Ile de la vieille musique* (and recording technology in particular) reflect the ideological preferences of experimental *animation.* The stress *animateurs* placed on cultivating an active, ludic relation to music rendered sound recording suspect. Despite its role in opening music to the entire world of everyday sound, recording technology was at the same time responsible for instituting the kind of passive relation to music that *animateurs* decried.

Standing over and above these various oppositions (postserial versus noise, amateurism versus virtuosity, live performance versus mechanical reproduction) is the central opposition that structures the narrative of *L'Ile de la vieille musique,* the dichotomy that sets contemporary music against classic-romantic music. This latter genre is incarnated in the person of the stranded pianist, who occupies an ambiguous role in the work. On the one hand, the admittedly clichéd music of the pianist drives the dramatic action in *L'Ile,* acting as a powerful object of desire for explorers and natives alike (example 12). On the other hand, the pianist remains curiously passive, a mute figure lacking agency. He utters no words, and the music he produces remains static, undergoing no development. As elsewhere, the allegorical function performed by the virtuoso is apparent. A castaway, isolated and seemingly forgotten by the rest of the world, the pianist epitomizes the position classical music occupies in contemporary life: a curious relic that still exerts a certain fascination, but that stands apart from the surrounding social world.

In many ways *L'Ile de la vieille musique* betrayed the tacit biases that underpinned experimental *animation.* The positive characterization of live performance, amateur practice, and experimental music genres followed from the basic tenets of *animation musicale.* The same could be said for the glorification of cultural diversity in the work, affirmed in the final chorus (example 13). Advocacy on behalf of musical pluralism was a commonplace within the discourse of *animation,* as was the critique of pedagogies that adhered to a narrow conception of music. But in a strange way, the work's celebration of difference turns out to be self-serving, a camouflaged way of advancing the interests of contemporary music. The promotion of diversity in *L'Ile,* and within the public utterances of *animateurs,* had the ancillary effect of delegitimizing attacks on new music. By associating contemporary music with the language of the (colonized) other, the work establishes a tendentious moral equivalence: lack of respect for nontraditional musical idioms is cast as a manifestation of the sort of blinkered prejudice that underpins the subjugation of subaltern peoples. This is not to deny the positive aspects of the work's message. The mere presence of a subtext does not rob the text itself of value. It is simply to point out that self-interest and altruism are not mutually exclusive. It is by preaching respect for the other that *L'Ile de la vieille musique* makes an oblique case for granting respect to such unfamiliar (and unpopular) genres as contemporary music.

EXAMPLE 12. Yves Prin, *L'Ile de la vieille musique,* final scene: the "old music." Used by permission of Yves Prin.

Si mon lan - gage est dif - fé - rent du tien   Je de meure - pour-tant

ton é - gal   é   gal   quand tu au - ras   com - pris ce - la

ce - la   vou - dras - tu en - core ne   faire la   loi   loi.

EXAMPLE 13. Yves Prin, *L'Ile de la vieille musique,* final chorus. Used by permission of Yves Prin.

CONTEMPORARY MUSIC IN THE *BANLIEUE:*
THE ATELIER THÉÂTRE ET MUSIQUE

In outlining measures in support of *animation musicale,* Jean Maheu singled out one initiative as a model for future undertakings: "As concerns immigrant workers and their families, the experiment . . . in the domain of *théâtre musical* conducted by G. APERGHIS in Bagnolet will be followed by other actions."[145] The "experiment" Maheu referred to was a project that the Greek émigré composer Georges Aperghis had embarked upon in January 1976 in Bagnolet, one of the *banlieues* of Paris. Part of the "red belt"—the working-class communities that surrounded the capital and formed the electoral base of the Communist Party—Bagnolet had undergone significant changes in recent decades. In the 1960s the construction of large housing projects (*habitations à loyer modéré,* or HLMs) had transformed the urban landscape. At the same time, the postwar influx of immigrant workers reshaped the demographic makeup of Bagnolet. The Parisian *banlieues* had been the destination of successive waves of immigrants since their development into industrial centers at the beginning of the twentieth century. What changed in the 1950s and 1960s was the geographic and national origins of the new immigrant groups. Unlike their predecessors, who had migrated to the Paris area from rural France and other parts of Europe, more recent arrivals came mainly from France's former colonies in Northern and sub-Saharan Africa. The racial and ethnic stigmatization endured by the latest generation of immigrant workers altered how this and other *banlieues* were viewed, even as the socioeconomic complexion of Bagnolet, which was dominated by blue-collar workers, remained essentially the same. As historian Tyler Stovall has remarked, "the spatial margins of the French capital have thus successively come to represent marginalities based first on class, then on race."[146] Ethnicity edged out class as the distinguishing mark of the *banlieue,* a transformation that would accelerate after 1980.

It was this changing urban context that Aperghis and his ensemble, the Atelier théâtre et musique (ATEM), intended to address. Aperghis had originally approached the mayor's office in Bagnolet in January 1975 with a proposal to compose a piece (eventually titled *La bouteille à la mer*) that would depict the everyday lives of the inhabitants of a recently completed housing block, Bagnolet Centre Sud. As Aperghis later explained, his inspiration had come from seeing one of the block's high-rises at night: "The idea . . . came into being while contemplating an apartment tower in Bagnolet, where all the windows lit up and went dark as if according to a plan. One might say [as if according to] a score. I wanted to show by means of music that everyone was alone in his niche but that everybody had certain things in common."[147] The piece was to be realized in collaboration with various local arts groups and *animateurs,* and performed as part of the annual Fête de la ville. The municipal government was quick to support Aperghis's project. A raft of governmental agencies and organizations soon followed suit: the Direction de la musique, the Secrétariat à la jeunesse et aux sports, the Secrétariat aux travailleurs immigrés, the interministerial Fonds d'intervention culturelle, and—most significantly for the profile of Aperghis and ATEM—the Festival d'automne.[148]

The readiness of the city government of Bagnolet to provide assistance to ATEM reflected changes that had taken place in the cultural policy landscape in the first half of the 1970s. Foremost among these was what historian Philippe Urfalino has described as the progressive "municipalization" of cultural policy, a process initiated in the 1960s.[149] Paradoxically, the top-down approach to arts outreach instituted by the Ministry of Cultural Affairs under Malraux encouraged this process. In planting the Maisons de la Culture and other, more modest cultural centers in regional cities and towns, the Ministry of Cultural Affairs had stipulated that local governments contribute a fixed percentage to their operational budgets. This compelled local officials to grapple with questions of cultural policy and led many to fashion distinctive strategies for addressing the arts.[150] Meanwhile, local policy makers were beginning to recognize that a burgeoning arts scene could boost the visibility of a city as well as improve the quality of life for local constituents.[151] The result was that by the early 1980s roughly half of all funding for cultural programs in France came from city governments.[152]

Political considerations also spurred the development of municipal cultural policy. Shut out of the national government, both the Parti socialiste and the Parti communiste used their municipal strongholds to highlight the concrete benefits that flowed from left-wing governance. The PCF had long criticized the center-right governments of the Fifth Republic for their weak support for culture, as measured in budgetary terms. The generous subventions for arts programs in Communist-governed municipalities thus provided a cudgel that the PCF could use to bludgeon their electoral adversaries. The comments of an official in Ivry, another Communist-governed *banlieue* of Paris, were typical: "Contrary to the current government which thinks that culture is superfluous . . . , we insist on the social dimension of culture, on the fact that culture is indispensable to the full development of the human being. These different ways of viewing culture are reflected in budget choices: the government spends 0.5 per cent of its resources on culture, whereas the municipality of Ivry devotes 4 per cent of its annual budget to culture, that is to say eight times more."[153] For arts organizations, this transformation of cultural policy into a site of contention among opposing political camps presented an opportunity. ATEM, for one, benefited from the desire of different parties to outbid one another in demonstrating their support for culture. The group's success in extracting funding from both the local (communist) and national (center-right) governments attests to this fact, as did Maheu's citation of the group as a model for the state's outreach programs.

Work on *La bouteille à la mer* commenced in January 1976. The approach Aperghis adopted in writing the piece departed from his standard working method. Rather than preparing a fully notated score in advance, he furnished the members of the ensemble with simple propositions with the aim of spurring group improvisation. On the basis of the recurrent musical or physical gestures that emerged out of improvisation sessions, Aperghis and the members of ATEM built up a "vocabulary." This in turn formed the material for the score, which assembled these gestures (or "words") into "phrases" and "sentences." To ensure a minimum of syntagmatic coherence, Aperghis relied on repetition and simple additive processes to connect successive gestures.[154] Example 14, taken from a published series of "exercises" for *La bouteille,* gives some sense of the quasi-minimalist idiom Aperghis employed. The opening instrumental fanfare consists of a series of repeated gestures in each instrumental part, whose staggered entries gradually fill out the musical space. By means of this simple additive process, the sparse music of the opening grows progressively more complex, both rhythmically and texturally.

In conjunction with the slow work of improvisation and assemblage being conducted inside the ensemble, ATEM also sought to integrate itself into the local community. They collaborated with arts groups, led *animations* in elementary schools and cultural centers, and invited local residents to attend (and on occasion participate in) improvisation workshops.[155] These outreach efforts did not always proceed smoothly. While many community arts organizations were eager to work with the group, some of the resident *animateurs* in Bagnolet took a jaundiced view of the enterprise, seeing Aperghis and his colleagues as interlopers

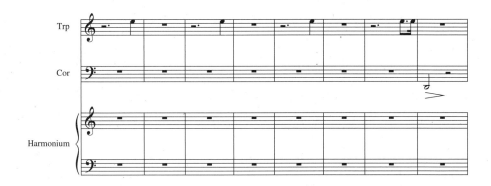

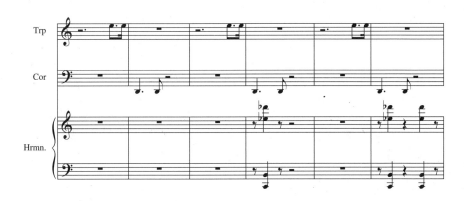

EXAMPLE 14. Georges Aperghis, *Exercices, variants, musiques de la Bouteille à la mer,*
"La fanfare des phrases," opening. © Editions Salabert. Used by kind permission of
Editions Salabert.

who had "parachuted" into an alien milieu.[156] More disquieting for the ensemble was the reaction of certain residents of Bagnolet Centre Sud to the group's open-door workshops. In one of the first, parents from the apartment complex that housed ATEM's rehearsal space came along with their children to learn more about the group's project. While the children were intrigued, the reactions of the adults ranged from luke-warm to hostile. Virtually all departed after only a few minutes. The same was true of a local folk group that had been invited to participate in the rehearsal; they came and left without saying a word.[157]

The group was taken aback by the response of the Bagnoletais. A radio program documenting ATEM's work in the *banlieue* recorded the self-doubt sown by this incident. While some members of the atelier argued that the lack of interest in their work was a sign that they needed to redouble their efforts at explaining their role in the community, others (including Aperghis) disagreed, suggesting that the only thing that could win over skeptics was the quality of the production itself.[158] Although he acknowledged the need to make some adjustments to the work, Aperghis held firm to the broader principle that contemporary music might benefit disadvantaged groups. Music, Aperghis explained, offered a species of social interaction that operates at a level that is at once more immediate and more profound than other forms of communication: "Music can easily convey things, more easily than theater. It helps con-vey things because it's something relatively common. To happen to play with somebody, with a musician for instance, to listen to him, to really listen to what he is doing and to play with him . . . there is a commu-nion that seems very difficult, very difficult to achieve with words in the same amount of time."[159] Yet the example Aperghis provided to illus-trate his argument—revolutionary song—contradicted his claim that music possesses a transcendent power of communication. As the host of the broadcast pointed out, such songs rely on texts to convey much of their meaning. Besides, revolutionary songs deploy precisely the sort of conventional harmonic and melodic language that contemporary music eschews. According to Aperghis, however, the theatrical dimension of *La bouteille à la mer* compensated for the music's failure to conform to listeners' expectations. The verbal and visual components of theatrical performance served as a supplement, one that ensured the transparency of the work's meaning and, in doing so, ensured its social utility.[160]

Nevertheless, Aperghis and his ensemble decided to narrow the focus of their "interventions" in the wake of this setback. The open workshops continued but were henceforth populated exclusively by children and teenagers. At the same time, the atelier, having settled on a narrative for the piece, began working in a more structured fashion with local performing arts groups. The culmination of this first phase of work came on 23 May 1976, when ATEM and their collaborators staged a preliminary version of the piece under a giant tent erected for the annual Fête du quartier.[161] By a curious coincidence, this early rendition of *La bouteille* made use of an allegorical conceit that was strikingly similar to that of *L'Ile de la vieille musique.* As with Prin's roughly contemporaneous work, *La bouteille* took place on an uncharted island and revolved around the exploits of a boat full of explorers who, shipwrecked, find themselves cast upon its shores. However, Aperghis's narrative was less linear than Prin's, featuring a series of digressions, interruptions, and inserts that disrupted its progress. But even so, the point of this narrative device was evident. The island depicted in *La bouteille* was nothing other than Bagnolet itself.[162] Far from being uninhabited, it turned out to be brimming with life. This vitality was conveyed by the inclusion of local community arts groups in the production, whose encounters with the shipwrecked explorers (the members of ATEM) were represented by performances interspersed throughout the body of the work: a song sung by a children's choir, a performance of North African music, a brief interlude by a local rock group, a piece of agitprop theater performed by local residents involved in a rent strike. This early version of *La bouteille,* in short, represented the journey of discovery that Aperghis and ATEM had undergone over the preceding months, a journey that ended with their recognition of the artistic agency of Bagnolet's inhabitants.[163] Even if the performance of ATEM and those of the local groups were not treated as equivalent within the representational space of *La bouteille*—with contemporary music acting as the unmarked context in which the tokens of local culture were embedded— the work nonetheless had the merit of treating the Bagnoletais not as the passive objects of *animation,* but as a vibrant community in possession of distinctive cultural practices.

Though *La bouteille* was widely regarded as a success, its performance at the Fête du quartier did not entirely satisfy Aperghis. The problem, in his opinion, lay in the work's failure to adequately integrate the performances of local arts groups into its musical frame. Shortly after a second performance of *La bouteille* a few weeks later, Aperghis and the members of ATEM thus set to revising the piece in preparation for performances at the Venice Biennial in September and the Festival d'automne in October.[164] The new version of *La bouteille* bore little resemblance to the piece performed under the same title in Bagnolet a few months earlier. The community arts groups had withdrawn from the work, a decision driven not only by aesthetic concerns but also by the logistical and financial difficulties posed by having these groups travel to different arts festivals. Added to this was Aperghis's worry that, in the very different contexts of the Venice Biennial and the Festival d'automne, the inclusion of these amateur groups might end up objectifying them: "The immigrants, the kids, if you put them on a stage in front of a bunch of people who aren't their neighbors, their friends, you turn them into circus animals."[165] Accompanying the departure of the Bagnoletais from *La bouteille* was a radical transformation in its narrative. The allegorical conceit of the earlier version—that of a shipwreck on an enchanted isle—was replaced by a more prosaic representation of life in Bagnolet Centre Sud, albeit one that abstracted the quotidian routines of inhabitants into series of empty, mechanized gestures. The additive processes and repetitive schemes that the group had developed earlier in the year assumed an altogether different meaning in this new context, now symbolizing the deadening repetition of everyday life in modern capitalist society.

Critical reception of the revised version of *La bouteille à la mer* was mixed. For some commentators the distillation of quotidian existence into a series of repeated gestures obscured the work's message. Writing in *Le Monde*, Jacques Longchampt complained that "the extreme concentration of gestures" had emptied them of significance for all save the members of ATEM. To the spectator, they seemed "totally absurd," cut off from the social context that gave them meaning.[166] Among left-leaning critics, the split between the work's supporters and its detractors was tied to broader attitudes about contemporary music. Fleuret, a fierce partisan of the avant-garde, lauded the attempt to address social concerns through the medium of contemporary music. His review in *Le Nouvel Observateur* characterized the work as a "harrowing parable" that presented, in distilled form, the "disorientation, mindlessness, slavery, oppression, and repression produced by capitalist societies."[167] Others were less sure that the marriage of new music and social engagement succeeded. A review in *Libération* criticized *La bouteille* for its miserabilism: "We understand completely. Aperghis and his actors reveal the absurdity of workers' everyday lives in the *banlieue*. It's critical, you could even say militant, sometimes you laugh, sometimes you think that the same evening, you could have gone to hear Patti Smith in Pantin. . . . All the same, life can't be reduced to the absurd, to the mechanical."[168] To counter the pessimistic image of working-class life projected by the revised version of *La bouteille*, the author of the review in *Libération* recalled the joyful, celebratory atmosphere that had greeted the version performed at the Fête du quartier in May. Surely this demonstrated that the Bagnoletais were not the poor wretches that peopled the spectacle put on during the Festival d'automne.[169] The problem was that the groups that had actively participated in the earlier version of *La bouteille* appeared in the revised work only as representations. No longer subjects, they became the objects of a theatrical spectacle.

The differences between the two versions of *La bouteille,* and between the different constituencies that they addressed, brought to the surface contradictions within ATEM's sociomusical project. Like other groups that sought to fuse the activities of artistic creation and social outreach, ATEM and Aperghis were subject to competing and at times incompatible imperatives. One of these was clearly social in orientation. According to Aperghis, the group was obliged "to open our work as much as possible to local residents, to make contact with them, to organize workshops for children, teenagers and others . . . , to have them participate in the spectacle and integrate them directly in our work."[170] A second objective responded to the professional demands of contemporary music: "to conduct research into the different forms that might issue forth from *théâtre musical.*"[171] The coexistence of these objectives meant that ATEM was forced to navigate a middle course between vanguardism and accessibility. In practice, this involved tacking back and forth between aesthetic and social considerations. The negative reaction of the Bagnoletais to the group's open workshop, for example, compelled the group to pull back from its "research" into new forms of music theater; by contrast, the atelier's appearance in the Festival d'automne pushed it in the opposite direction, toward an emphasis on aesthetic rather than social concerns.

These competing priorities within the group's mission mirrored ambiguities in the cultural policies adopted at both the local and national levels. Communist-governed municipalities like Bagnolet invested in avant-garde ensembles like ATEM not solely to provide a service to local residents. Rather, such support was undertaken as much for the benefit of middle-class professionals living beyond the city limits of Bagnolet, as a way of demonstrating to this growing slice of the electorate the party's commitment to artistic freedom. The function of cultural policy as a form of "display" is readily apparent here, part of a strategy to persuade professionals to back the Communist Party.[172] Similar calculations no doubt motivated the state's support for the atelier. Given the leftward tilt of French artists and intellectuals, it behooved the center-right government to demonstrate a liberal attitude in social and cultural matters. It was in the government's interest to fund avant-garde ensembles, even those that staged "contestatory" works, inasmuch as this support signaled a tolerance for artistic and ideological diversity. In this context, it is not surprising that a group like ATEM found itself pulled in opposing directions, forced to address different constituencies for different purposes at the same time.

THE DECLINE AND AFTERLIFE OF *ANIMATION MUSICALE*

"In the cultural domain, the word 'animation' is hardly used at all anymore, and is even forcefully denounced."[173] So begins the entry for *animation culturelle* in the *Dictionnaire des politiques culturelles* (Dictionary of cultural policies), published in 2001. The statement bears witness to the steep decline *animation* underwent following the field's rapid expansion in the 1960s and 1970s. It was not so much that the practices of *animation* per se had subsided. Rather, it was the term, along with its ideological trappings, that had fallen out of favor. Even though the ranks of cultural intermediaries continued to swell throughout the 1980s and 1990s, the utopian hopes once placed in the democratization of creative activity receded. Henceforth a more modest, technocratic view of cultural outreach would be the norm.

A key factor in the changing fortunes of *animation culturelle* was the mounting criticism it faced beginning in the late 1970s. The most pronounced critiques came from other actors within the cultural field, for whom *animation* represented a source of unwanted competition. Music educators were particularly vocal in denouncing *animation*. In the wake of Landowski's proposed educational reforms and Maheu's pronouncements in favor of *animation musicale*, interest groups like the Association des professeurs d'éducation musicale (Association of music teachers) and the Fédération nationale des associations de parents d'élèves des conservatoires et écoles de musique (National federation of associations of parents of conservatory and music school students) mobilized to stem the waxing influence of *animation*. The principal argument made by such groups was that investment in *animation musicale* diverted resources from proven pedagogical methods. In place of a real commitment to arts education (which would require greater outlays), the state contented itself with cheap alternatives that generated more publicity than results. In a letter that the Association des professeurs d'éducation musicale sent to *Le Monde*, the group denounced the erosion of funding for music education in elementary schools, replaced by periodic *animations* of dubious quality: "If much ado is often made about sessions of *animation musicale* in schools, [which are] sometimes brilliant but generally without lasting impact, nothing is ever said of the patient, daily, and reliable work that music teachers accomplish in educational establishments."[174] Although their letter went unpublished, proponents of traditional music education managed to air these grievances during the course of a national meeting, the Assises nationales de la musique, convened in February 1978. The conference, along with the preparatory sessions that led up to it, served as a platform to press the government to change its budgetary priorities. A preliminary report noted that in 1976, 55 percent of the budget devoted to music education went to *animation*, while only 35 percent went to "teaching properly speaking."[175] While the final report issued by the Assises nationales tempered its polemical tone, it nonetheless contended that the field of *animation musical* ought to be better regulated given the "notorious incompetence" of many of its practitioners.[176] To this end, the organizers of the meeting argued that *animation* should be taken over by trained professionals (presumably credentialed music educators). But even then *animation* ought to be relegated to a secondary position behind traditional music instruction in the government's budget.[177]

Another group that took aim at *animation* was professional artists. The rift between creators and cultural intermediaries was particularly pronounced in the world of theater, though the conflict reverberated throughout the entire field of *animation culturelle*. By the late 1970s, a number of stage directors were chafing at the outsized role *animateurs* had assumed within state cultural policy. In their view, the priorities of policy makers were backward, the government having placed a subordinate concern (cultural mediation) in front of the very creative work that *animation* was supposed to mediate. Echoing the complaints of music educators, these artists charged that the state's support for *animation culturelle* was a way of masking insufficiencies in other, more important areas. As a columnist for *Le Monde* put it, *animation* had become "the alibi that the government uses to justify its retreat from creation."[178] While such critiques of state culture policy suggested that the conflict between creators and *animateurs* aligned with left-right antagonisms, the reality was rather more complicated. Both sides of the debate positioned themselves as the victims of the state's unjust neglect. If, for theater directors, *animation* was responsible for declining state support for artistic creation, *animateurs* countered that such critiques provided cover for the government's disengagement from the cause of cultural democratization. Attacks on *animation culturelle,* the argument went, furnished the center-right government with a pretext to shift resources from outreach efforts toward flashier and more prestigious projects. The inevitable outcome of this process would be the sacrifice of egalitarian ideals at the altar of elite culture. The general public, left without the succor of cultural mediators, would find itself "ravaged by the mass media." Meanwhile the privileged few, "barricaded in its ghetto," would continue to enjoy the finest artistic offerings.[179]

Perhaps the most significant factor contributing to the diminishing stature of *animation* was to be found not in the cultural but in the political sphere, in the evolving positions of the Parti communiste and the Parti socialiste. For its part, the Parti communiste had long viewed the practices of *animation* as ideologically suspect. While the party was firmly committed to the ideal of democratizing access to culture, it viewed the problem as fundamentally economic in nature. Inequalities in access to the arts were to be corrected by increasing outlays for arts organizations, improving the social safety net for artists, and nationalizing certain cultural enterprises.[180] Within this ideological framework there was little room for *animation,* which uncomfortably blurred the lines between cultural and social concerns. *Animation,* as one critic wrote in the party publication *France Nouvelle,* represented a modern-day form of false consciousness, one that deceived individuals into thinking that they could change social relations simply by acting upon individual or collective attitudes. This "psychologization of social life" threatened to mask "real social mechanisms," inverting the proper relationship between base and superstructure.[181] To change culture one had to change the underlying economic conditions.

Meanwhile, the Parti socialiste was slowly elaborating a coherent cultural policy of its own, a process that would take much of the 1970s to bear fruit. The challenge facing the PS was how to thread the needle between the government to its right and the PCF to its left. The socialists' initial solution involved appropriating ideas from post-'68 *gauchiste* thought. Central among these was the notion of self-management *(autogestion),* which featured prominently in the platform devised by the party's Secrétariat nationale des affaires culturelles (SNAC) in 1974.

Capitalism, according to SNAC, was guilty of inducing in individuals a passive relationship with culture, a tendency that the specialized division of labor in modern societies reinforced. Socialism, by contrast, would engender a more active engagement with both the consumption and the production of the arts. The result would be a collapse of the distinction between creator and consumer: "It will be necessary to take leave of . . . cultural institutions such as they exist, always bearing in mind that our objective is to enlarge them, to deprofessionalize them little by little, in order to reconcile aspects of social activity that are currently isolated from one another."[182] Practically speaking, this emphasis on nurturing amateur creative activity brought the policies advocated by SNAC into close alignment with more radical forms of experimental *animation*. The rhetoric was virtually indistinguishable from the more extravagant statements of cultural militants: "The global culture that we wish to develop must be a culture for all, in the service of all. But it is also necessary that it be a culture made by all."[183]

The policy prescriptions issued by SNAC were stamped by a markedly utopian rhetoric. Divorced from the realities of governing, the Parti socialiste could content itself with pronouncements that were, in the words of David Looseley, "woolly, earnest and verbose."[184] (The same could be said of the discourse of intellectuals affiliated with the PS, most notably Jacques Attali, whose evocation of an impending age of composition in *Bruits* echoed the party's promise to institute a "culture made by all." Not surprisingly, some dismissed Attali's book as little more than "an electoral calling card" for the party.)[185] More pragmatic cultural policies materialized following the party's success in the 1977 municipal elections. Once in power, socialist mayors and city councils moved away from the *autogestionnaire* dreams of SNAC to invest in areas that had a more tangible impact on the urban environment. The main beneficiaries of this change were professional artists and arts organizations, emblems of the sort of innovation and creativity that socialist-governed municipalities wanted to project. Also at play in the socialists' political calculations was a recognition of the economic benefits that a lively local arts scene could produce. This shift in policy orientation—from an emphasis on cultural outreach to strengthened support for artistic creation—was echoed at the national level, as the Parti socialiste sought to reposition itself in advance of the 1981 presidential elections. The perceived weaknesses in Giscard's aid to artistic creation provided an opening that the PS exploited. The appointment of Jack Lang, founder of the Festival de Nancy and former director of the Théâtre de Chaillot, to lead the party's Délégation nationale à l'action culturelle in 1979 further cemented the new direction in socialist culture policy. As a result of his background in the world of theater, Lang was a strong advocate for increased governmental intervention on behalf of professional artists. While he continued to acknowledge the need for *animation,* it was subordinated to the exigencies of promoting artistic work.

By the time of the presidential elections of 1981, *création* had become a catchword for the Parti socialiste. In a sense, it occupied the same sort of position that *animation* had filled a decade earlier, cast as a panacea that would magically resolve a variety of social problems. The socialists, as Jean Caune has observed, replaced "*action culturelle,* considered as superfluous and ineffective, with a notion, creation, charged with every virtue."[186] Against the charge that this shift represented a retreat into clientelism as the PS strove to curry favor with artists, intellectuals, and other opinion makers, party officials insisted on the immanently "subversive" quality of artistic creation. A chain of associations, linking creation to innovation to the disruption of norms and thus to the subversion of power, shored up the oppositional credentials of the Parti socialiste's new cultural policy. The public utterances of Fleuret, designated in 1981 to head the Direction de la musique in the new socialist government, were characteristic. He echoed the socialist platform in an article published in *Le Matin* during the run-up to the election, arguing that the capacity of artistic creation to disrupt received notions made it a valuable resource in the struggle against entrenched economic and political powers. Fleuret pointed to contemporary music in particular as a model for the kind of insurgent, iconoclastic creativity the Parti socialiste was now valorizing. According to Fleuret, what defined this genre above all was the premium it placed on individualism: "Each musical creator finds it necessary to first of all distinguish himself from others and to address the world using words that belong only to himself."[187] To nurture this force for innovation it was necessary to support as wide an array of composers as possible. Fleuret here drew a contrast with the situation under Giscard, which, in his estimation, funneled the majority of resources to a handful of luminaries. He pointed to *recherche musicale* as exemplifying this tendency: "Today the encounter and the collaboration between scientists and musicians takes place only in discrete, isolated, subterranean places, submitted to the arbitrary authority of a single person with whom the state has entrusted the task of embodying in himself the whole of contemporary *recherche musicale.*"[188] Under a socialist government, presumably, the concentration of funds in the hands of a few celebrated figures (such as Boulez, the obvious target of Fleuret's broadside) would no longer be the norm.

The privileging of creation within the discourse of Lang, Fleuret, and other figures within the Parti socialiste resonated with changes taking place within the art world itself. The latter half of the 1970s had witnessed a revalorization of the status of the professional artist, as *soixante-huitard* critiques of specialization and the division of artistic labor gradually lost much of their suasive power. Coupled with this was a turn away from the experimentalism that had seemed to augur a deprofessionalization of artistic production and that had fueled the work of experimental *animateurs*. In the world of contemporary music, signs of the changing aesthetic landscape abounded. One by one, groups closely identified with free improvisation, text composition, and other experimental practices disbanded. This was the case with New Phonic Art and the Groupe d'Etude et Réalisation Musicale, both of which were essentially defunct by the beginning of the 1980s. Composers who had once worked to destroy the "bourgeois myth of the composer" returned to more conventional forms of composition. Ferrari, for instance, went back to writing notated scores after having largely abandoned the medium during the 1970s. Meanwhile, younger composers—most notably spectral composers like Gérard Grisey, Tristan Murail, and Hugues Dufourt— declared their independence not only from the serial legacy but from the experimentalism of the late 1960s and early 1970s. Despite the influence of electroacoustic music and live electronics on their music, the spectralists extolled the virtues of *écriture* as a way of realizing the new vistas opened by music technology. Taken as a whole, these developments signaled a significant recalibration of aesthetic priorities. Techniques that had once promised a radical deskilling of composition receded from view, displaced by a newfound appreciation for the virtues of compositional craftsmanship.

The election of Mitterrand in May 1981, along with the appointment of Lang to head the Ministry of Cultural Affairs and Fleuret to head the Direction de la musique, afforded the socialists the opportunity to usher in the "society of creation" they had envisaged. Fleuret's arrival at the organization led to a reorientation of its mission, as diffusion and outreach took a backseat to support for new work.[189] This marked a significant departure from precedent. Landowski's ten-year plan had stressed the formation of regional ensembles to win new audiences for art music, while Maheu's program of *animation musicale* had focused on the cultivation of new practices and publics. Under Fleuret's leadership, the emphasis would instead be placed upon nurturing diversity. This had a number of positive consequences, not the least of which was the support given genres hitherto excluded from the remit of state music policy (including jazz, chanson, and rock).[190] By and large, however, aid continued to be concentrated in the sphere of art music, with contemporary music and *recherche musicale* profiting in particular from the new dispensation. To avoid the kind of inequities in funding that Fleuret had denounced in the previous government, he sought to spread resources across a wide range of actors. "The revolution," he explained, "is no longer in quality but in quantity."[191] One manifestation of this new policy orientation could be seen in the number of research centers established during Fleuret's tenure. Whereas only six establishments devoted to *recherche musicale* existed prior to 1981, this number roughly quadrupled, with twenty-three in operation by 1986.[192] A special effort was made to ensure that this expansion of the research sector reflected the multiplicity of aesthetic tendencies within the contemporary music scene. As a result, figures hitherto denied significant government support (Ferrari, Pierre Henry, Jean-Claude Eloy) now found themselves furnished with the resources to start their own electronic music studios.

The changes Lang and Fleuret instituted to state cultural policy proved detrimental to *animation musicale.* New opportunities for composers opened up as the budget devoted to *recherche musicale* ballooned and the number of commissions and grants they could avail themselves of increased. Developments such as these lessened *animation*'s appeal as a host profession. Instead of having to engage in the little-publicized and often thankless task of community outreach to win funding, composers could now find more abundant—and more prestigious—alternatives to support their creative work. More importantly, the growing recognition of popular culture within state cultural policy undercut one of the key premises of *animation,* namely the idea that a sizable portion of the French populace subsisted in a state of cultural deprivation. Arts outreach, no less than nature, abhors a vacuum. But once this vacuum was revealed to be an ideological construct, the moral calculus of bringing music to the masses changed. The result was that departments within the Direction de la musique that had been charged with overseeing *animation musicale* were either dismantled or restructured to support popular music.[193]

But if the 1980s witnessed a steady disengagement of French cultural policy from the domain of *animation,* the idea that art might be put to work to attain certain social objectives has lived on. On the one hand, many of the private associations at the forefront of *animation musicale* in the 1970s have carried on their work, even as state cultural policy has moved in other directions. Groups like the Musicoliers, the Jeunesses musicales de France, and the Fédération nationale des centres musicaux ruraux have survived the vicissitudes of changing cultural policy, now securing their funding from a combination of public and private sources. The Musicoliers, for instance, receives aid from the Ministry of Culture and Communication, local governments in the Ile-de-France region, and corporate sponsors like Carrefour, J.P. Morgan, and Novartis.[194] This mix of public and private support has allowed these organizations (as the website of one group puts it) to continue "making music accessible to the greatest number possible, regardless of the social, geographic, and cultural situation of its beneficiaries."[195] On the other hand, there recently has been a return within French cultural policy to the idea of using art as a means of social intervention. The principal target of these new initiatives is postmigrant communities, especially the marginalized residents of the *banlieues.* Yet, as culture policy analyst Nadia Kiwan has pointed out, this rehabilitation of the "sociocultural" as a legitimate site of state intervention has involved a tacit stratification of cultural practices, most often along ethnic and class lines.[196] Whereas support for "serious culture" remains the core mission of the Ministry of Culture, support for "urban culture" is typically administered by an entirely different set of agencies, usually for the purpose of addressing extra-artistic issues such as urban regeneration or social exclusion. This institutional distinction is echoed in a tacit hierarchization of the musical genres involved: "art" music wins support on the basis of its presumed aesthetic qualities, while popular musics like rock and rap are valued not on artistic but on social grounds. One upshot of this partitioning is that it unduly limits both "serious" and "popular" cultures. Postmigrant artists, as Kiwan notes, often "find themselves subject to certain expectations on the part of cultural policy actors, namely, that art produced by [them] is somehow an expression of identity or citizenship, integration, etc."[197] Conversely, the cordoning off of contemporary music and other forms of experimental art into the domain governed by cultural policy proper means that it is peremptorily denied any social utility whatsoever. If experimental *animateurs* were guilty of giving too much credit to the liberatory power of cultural practices, their successors are perhaps guilty of giving it too little.

The historian Philippe Urfalino has described the trajectory of French cultural policy as a progression from the ideals of cultural democratization to the realities of cultural democracy. According to this narrative, the paradigm guiding state intervention in culture has evolved from the Malraucian view of art as a transcendent good, to be bestowed upon the benighted masses, to a relativistic view that acknowledges the value of cultural diversity. Within this shifting horizon of cultural policy, stretching from the 1950s to the 1980s, the short-lived ascendancy of *animation culturelle* from 1968 to 1981 represented a transitional moment. It marked an unsettled parenthesis, when the universal value of high culture was no longer taken for granted but the legitimacy of popular and vernacular cultures had yet to be recognized. Into this breach flowed experimental forms of *animation culturelle.* Under the influence of *soixante-huitard* ideals, these practices extolled the power of participation, the liberatory potential of amateur creativity. But with the accession of the Parti socialiste to power in 1981, this interregnum came to an end. The injection of funds into the new music sector made the rhetoric of "crisis" that had dominated public discourse a few years earlier seem irrelevant, as a massive increase in the supply of avant-garde music masked continuing weakness in its demand. At the same time, pluralism supplanted participation as the vehicle for realizing the ideal of cultural democracy. What was valorized was no longer the creative capacities of the individual but the diversity of practices across a range of communities. What was valorized, in other words, was no longer the *droit à la culture* but the *droit à la différence.* And with this turn away from a politics of redistribution toward a politics of recognition, the ethical claims made on behalf of cultural democratization efforts lost much of their force.

Conclusion

On 10 May 1981 François Mitterrand was elected president of France, ending twenty-three years of electoral futility for the French left. Mitterrand's victory over Valery Giscard d'Estaing was a surprise to many. Despite public dissatisfaction with Giscard's performance as president, Mitterrand had trailed in the polls until the day of the election. Just six months earlier, only 6 percent of the public believed that Mitterrand was capable of defeating Giscard, and even after the first round of voting in April, only 22 percent predicted victory for the socialist candidate.[1] It came as something of a shock, then, when at 8 P.M. on 10 May French television announced that Mitterrand had won the election with 51.7 percent of the votes cast. This unexpected outcome was the cause of ebullience for the left. Shortly after the election results were announced, thousands thronged to the Place de la Bastille in Paris to take part in an impromptu *fête*. The crowds gathering in this landmark of French revolutionary history could be heard chanting slogans both new and old: "On a gagné" (We won), "Giscard au chômage" (Giscard to the unemployment line), and, a refrain of May '68, "Ce n'est qu'un début, continuons le combat" (This is only a beginning, continue the struggle).[2]

Parliamentary elections held a few weeks later ratified the left's triumph. The Parti socialiste and its allies trounced their rivals on the right, winning a clear majority in the Assemblée nationale. The unprecedented nature of the left's electoral success, along with the public celebrations they sparked, led a number of observers to draw parallels to May '68, the last time such sweeping political change loomed on the horizon. Indeed, a number of observers saw the victory of the Parti socialiste as fulfilling the broken promise of May after a gap of thirteen years. As Alsatian singer-songwriter Roger Siffer remarked shortly after the election, May '81 felt "like a successful May '68."[3] But in a strange way, electoral success also threatened to dissipate the ideological ardor that had sustained the left during its years in the political wilderness. Deprived of real political power in the years after 1968, militants had found solace in various utopian projects. But such utopianism was hard to maintain once Mitterrand and the socialists confronted the realities of governance. Signs of ideological disenchantment were quick to manifest themselves. A case in point was the well-publicized failure of left intellectuals to rally behind the new government.[4] Another was the rapid deterioration of support for the socialists' partners-cum-rivals, the Parti communiste.[5] Another still was the growth of Jean-Marie Le Pen's Front nationale, with its appeals to nativist sentiment and promise to return "France to the French."[6] But discordant tones could already be discerned during the inauguration of the new president. It was telling that the tentative efforts to start a chorus of "The Internationale" during Mitterrand's procession to the Panthéon found little traction. Nor were there many red flags to be seen among the crowds, the traditional standard of the left having been replaced by the *tricolore*. Optimism at the prospect of a new, more progressive government went hand in hand with an apparent fatigue with the traditional political culture of the left. May '81 may have redeemed the unfulfilled promise of May '68, but in doing so it seemed to bring the historical parenthesis that had been opened thirteen years earlier to a close. One observer succinctly summed up the ambivalent mood by quipping, "May is finally dead . . . Long live May!"[7]

The mixture of euphoria and exhaustion that greeted the election of Mitterrand was the latest manifestation of a dialectic that had animated the French left since May '68, one that swung like a pendulum between anticipation and frustration. The conviction that sweeping social change was imminent made disappointment at once inevitable and easy to discount. That the May events had failed to topple de Gaulle's government, that a period of revolutionary crisis did not succeed the protests and general strike, that the union of *gauchiste* intellectuals and workers never quite came off: each of these defeats could be rationalized by looking to the *longue durée* and reading every setback as just another step in the long march toward revolution. Yet the cumulative effect of these dis-appointments was to chip away at the belief in the Marxist vision of his-tory that May had reinvigorated. The confidence of the left was further shaken during the course of the 1970s, as the harsh realities hidden be-hind the facade of "really existing socialism" were publicly aired. The publication of Alexander Solzhenitsyn's *Gulag Archipelago* in 1974, fol-lowed by revelations about the true nature of Mao's China a few years later, led no small number of *gauchistes* to loudly—and opportunistically—repudiate their Marxist-Leninist past.[8] Even so, the election of Mitter-rand and a socialist majority to the parliament in 1981 roused hope that it was indeed possible to "change life," as the electoral slogan of the Parti socialiste had put it. Yet this hope soon foundered, as Mitterrand's government, faced with capital flight, high unemployment, and a global economic downturn, was forced to abandon its ambitious plans for re-structuring the French economy.[9] Within a few years' time the poetry of socialism had given way to the prose of social democracy. And as the revolutionary dream subsided the symbolic value invested in various cultural practices examined throughout this book diminished in turn. Amateur creativity, once seen as a force for personal and social libera-tion, was now treated as little more than a form of self-improvement. The *fête*, once seen as a vehicle of collective release, containing within itself the seeds of revolt, now served as a substitute for this very revolt. And the convergence of genres, once seen as a way of imaginatively surmounting social difference, gave way to the celebration of difference as an end unto itself. The routes that once promised to lead from musical practice to some future utopia were, by all appearances, now blocked off.

These changes in the cultural politics of music went hand in hand with the ongoing revision of May's legacy. As noted in the introduction, an increasingly popular way of reading this legacy during the past quar-ter century has been to treat the May events as an essentially cultural phenomenon. According to this line of interpretation, the uprising was significant insofar as it challenged the prevailing values, attitudes, and cultural practices of French society. The political demands of the move-ment were cast, conversely, as little more than a rhetorical screen: what animated the movement was less an interest in social justice than an unspoken desire for personal liberation. It is no coincidence that this way of reading May '68, popularized by writers like Lipovetsky, Ferry, and Renaut, only came to prominence once Mitterrand's socialist ex-periment had been abandoned. Such interpretations, it would appear, were the corollary of the loss of faith in the socialist project. As the field of political possibility opened by May '68 contracted, as Marx's old mole returned underground, there appeared little choice but to look to the domain of culture to find sign of May's impact.

Nowhere was the changing cultural politics of the period more apparent than in the changing relation between music, politics, and identity. Among the many uses that rock, free jazz, *musique contemporaine,* and revolutionary chanson had afforded in the wake of 1968, one of the most important was the articulation of identity. By adopting genres associated with national, ethnic, generational, or social others, individuals were able to identify with a larger social formation, at the same time as they marked their distance from mainstream French society. This was seen most clearly in Bruno Queysanne's ethnography of the nascent French counterculture, discussed at the beginning of chapter 4. His informants openly acknowledged how identification with Anglo-American youth culture opened a space where their lived experience of difference could take shape. The same utility was derived by other groups in adopting other musical traditions. Such was the case with the advocacy of free jazz by a younger generation of enthusiasts in the years around 1968; in the short-lived infatuation with contemporary classical music during the same period; and in the appropriation of "The Internationale" by youthful protesters during May '68.

If such examples point to the boundary-work that genre performs, it is crucial to bear in mind that the appeal to the musical other involved not just the articulation but the imagined transcendence of difference. A perennial problem for those championing rock, jazz, or the revolutionary chanson was the perceived distance that existed between their identity and those associated with the genre in question. For French rock enthusiasts, the gap was that which separated them from their counterparts in Britain and the United States. For the practitioners of *animation musicale,* it was that which separated them from the vast "nonpublic" they imagined to subsist in a state of precultural grace. Various strategies were devised to bridge such divides, to find a point of contact that would allow difference to be surmounted without being effaced altogether. These strategies ranged from the discursive (as when jazz critics recast the new thing as the expression of the anticolonial, rather than the African-American, subject) to the practical (as was the case with the activities undertaken under the aegis of *animation musicale*). In all of these cases, however, the very difference that made a given musical genre the object of such intense attraction for musicians, fans, and political groups had to be moderated if its social and political use value was to be realized.

But what was truly distinctive in this interplay of identity and difference in the years after 1968 was the way in which it was structured by the left's eschatological vision of history. At the same time as genres, as bearers of musical identity, allowed individuals and groups to draw a certain symbolic distance from the existing social order, this difference was projected into the future, acting as the sonic figuration of some postrevolutionary utopia. This was most obvious with various self-styled vanguard movements, such as free jazz and contemporary music. Proponents of both genres cast the break with musical convention not as an act of artistic distinction, having tangible benefit in the here and now, but as a portent of an as-yet-unrealized musical—and social—order. Yet even in less self-consciously forward-looking genres, the same projection of the musical other into the future could be discerned. Recall, in this regard, the explanatory note that accompanied the text to Dominque Grange's "Les Nouveaux partisans" in *La Cause du peuple*, with its confident assertion that "tomorrow hundreds of revolutionary songs will flower, written by calloused hands . . . in factories, in slums, in demonstrations."[10] In this reading, Grange's song offered a glimpse of a future in which mass culture had been replaced by a culture of the masses. More importantly, the utopian charge her song acquired stemmed from its identification with a genre (the revolutionary chanson), as well with as a social group (the working class) regarded as the agent that would make this utopia a reality. It was through genre that a sense of contact with the other, and with an other social order, was established.

By 1981 such utopian reveries were on the wane. This was due in large part to the very different political climate of the times. But not exclusively so. Many genres that had once seemed alien to French audiences had, over time, become thoroughly assimilated into the nation's cultural life. Such was the case with French rock. The advent of punk in the late 1970s and the *alternatif* movement a few years later was crucial to this process of integration. The DIY aesthetic these movements espoused liberated rock musicians and fans from the inferiority complex that had haunted them just a few years before. Likewise, as the free jazz of the late 1960s developed into the more nebulous genre of free improvisation during the 1970s, the alterity that had once been imputed to the genre (and that had seemingly placed it beyond the ken of French audiences) subsided. To be sure, new genres such as rap, raï, techno, and world music rose up to take the place that their older counterparts had once occupied in the collective imagination. Such genres furnished new sites of identification around which various hopes and anxieties could coalesce. But with the prospect of radical social change now held in abeyance, it was increasingly rare for music of any kind to be invoked as an emblem of an alternative political order. As the *telos* of history disappeared into the horizon of a future perpetually deferred, the idea that a privileged group might act as the agent of radical social change—or that a privileged genre might act as the musical signifier of this change—became increasingly difficult to entertain.

Still, if May '81 marked the moment when the narrative of revolution that May '68 helped revive was interred, the withdrawal of this legacy permitted other legacies, other narratives of the uprising's effects, to come clearly into view. If nothing else, the end of what Gil Delannoi dubbed *les années utopiques* allowed for a more dispassionate assessment of what May did and did not accomplish.[11] Indeed, it is only when one has gotten past understanding social change in the sort of stark binary terms that belief in total revolution demands—the belief that change must be absolute or else regarded as a dismal failure—that the concrete achievements of May and the *après-mai* period can be perceived. And these achievements were not insignificant. For all their shortcomings, the gains that striking workers were able to exact from both industry and government were substantial, and set the stage for subsequent improvements to the French social model. Moreover, it was the spirit of contestation that infused the post-May era that propelled the nascent feminist, gay rights, and environmental movements to prominence in France. Indeed, the inspiration provided by May's *prise de parole* led a number of minority groups to assert themselves as actors on the political stage during the course of the 1970s. An example of this could be seen in the resurgent regionalist movements of the 1970s. Inspired by the national liberation movements in Algeria and other former colonies, activists in the 1950s and 1960s reconceived regional minorities as populations subject to a system of internal colonialism, subordinated politically, economically, and culturally to the Parisian metropole.[12] But it was only after May '68, with its proclamation that individuals possessed a right to seize speech, that the regionalist movement was able to gain much traction. A poster printed by Occitan militants in fall 1968 embodied the new sense of empowerment that May had inspired: "Man of Oc," it read in the Occitan tongue, "you have the right to speak: speak!"

The struggle for recognition also played out in the musical sphere. The belief that regional minorities possessed a "right to speak" was answered by the emergence of movements like the *nòva cançon occitana* and the Breton folk revival in the late 1960s and 1970s. But it was not just regional minority groups that rushed into the clearing that May had opened in the French cultural sphere. The different genre communities examined over the course of this book also responded May's call to "seize speech." What was the embrace of the Anglo-American counterculture among French youth if not an attempt to find a voice with which individuals could articulate their aspirations? What was the advocacy of free jazz by critics like Le Bris, Carles, and Comolli if not a way of asserting a certain form of resistant identity? In all of these instances, music served as a vehicle for the self-representation of communities hitherto marginalized within French culture. Viewed from this angle, the most significant response to *soixante-huitard* calls to democratize cultural expression was not to be found in the evolving policies of the Ministry of Cultural Affairs, or in the practices of experimental *animation* examined in chapter 5, but in the proliferation of rock bands, singer-songwriters, folk ensembles, and other forms of grassroots musical activity during the 1970s. It was also to be seen in the bid that proponents of rock, jazz, folk, chanson, and other genres made for a greater degree of cultural legitimacy as the decade progressed—a bid that would only be answered after 1981 in the new, more democratic cultural policies instituted under Jack Lang. It may well be true, as writers like Lipovetsky have argued, that a straight line may be drawn from May's *tribunes libres* and injunctions to speak out to the increased cultural permissiveness of recent decades. It may even be true that for some this "seizure of speech" amounted to little more than a form of narcissistic self-regard. But this should not blind us to the more important consequence of this *prise de parole:* that of opening up a space where other voices, other subjectivities, other communities could henceforth make their claims be heard.

Notes

INTRODUCTION

1. Fleuret in Patrick Loriot, "Dissonances à Saint-Etienne," *Nouvel Observateur* 182 (8 May 1968): 48.

2. Pierre Boulez, "Où en est-on?" in *Points de repère* (Paris: Christian Bourgois, 1985); translated as "Where are we now?" in *Orientations*, ed. Jean-Jacques Nattiez, trans. Martin Cooper (Cambridge, MA: Harvard University Press, 1986), 445–63.

3. Boulez, "Where are we now?" 452.

4. Ibid., 453.

5. Marc Kravetz, ed., *L'Insurrection étudiante: 2–13 Mai 1968* (Paris: Union Générale d'Éditions, 1968), 439.

6. Mavis Gallant, "The Events in May: A Paris Notebook—I," in *Paris Notebooks: Essays and Reviews* (Toronto: Macmillan, 1986), 21.

7. A recording of this broadcast is reproduced in Jean-Pierre Farkas et al., *Les journées de mai 68 par les journalistes de R.T.L.*, Philips 77.757.

8. Robert Lachene, "Renault: Les travailleurs administrent la ville des machines silencieuses," *Humanité Dimanche* 169 (26 May 1968): 11, 14–15.

9. Francesca Solleville, in *Mai 68 par eux-mêmes: Le mouvement de Floréal, An 176* (Paris: Editions du Monde Libertaire, 1989), 175–77; on Travail et Culture, see Evelyne Ritaine, *Les stratégies de la culture* (Paris: Presses de la Fondation Nationale des Sciences Politiques, 1983), 59.

10. Solleville, *Mai 68 par eux-mêmes*, 175.

11. Ibid.

12. Ibid., 176.

13. On the mobilization of political rhetoric in composers' position taking, see Eric Drott, "Spectralism, Politics, and the Post-Industrial Imagination," in *The Modernist Legacy: Essays on New Music*, ed. Björn Heile (Aldershot: Ashgate, 2009), 39–60.

14. There are few studies on the impact of May '68 on musical life in France. The only serious effort has been that of musicologist Pierre-Albert Castanet. See Castanet, "Les années 1968: les mouvances d'une révolution socio-culturelle populaire," in *1789–1989: musique, histoire, démocratie,* ed. Antoine Hennion (Paris: Editions de la Maison des sciences de l'homme, 1992), 145–52; "1968: A Cultural and Social Survey of Its Influences on French Music," *Contemporary Music Review* 8, no. 1 (1993): 19–43; *Tout est bruit pour qui a peur: Pour une histoire sociale du son sale* (Paris: Editions Michel de Maule, 1999); and "Rêver la révolution: Musique et politique autour de Mai 1968," in *Résistance et utopies sonores,* ed. Laurent Feneyrou (Paris: CDMC, 2005), 131–48. Other authors have published useful studies of May's influence on individual genres. On jazz, see Ludovic Tournès, "Amateurs de jazz français et mouvement noir américain," *Les années 68: événements, cultures politiques et modes de vie,* Lettre d'information no. 22 (February 1997); Tournès, *New Orleans sur Seine: Histoire du Jazz en France* (Paris: Fayard, 1999); and Jedediah Sklower, *Free jazz, la catastrophe feconde: une histoire du monde éclaté du jazz en France (1960–1982)* (Paris: L'Harmattan, 2006). On rock, see Sylvie Coulomb and Didier Varrod, *Histoire de chansons, 1968–1988: de Julien Clerc à Etienne Daho* (Paris: Balland, 1987), chapter 1. On chanson, see Jacques Vassal, *Français, si vous chantiez* (Paris: Albin Michel, 1976), chapter 1; and Louis-Jean Calvet, *La production révolutionnaire: Slogans, affiches, chansons* (Paris: Payot, 1976), 171–88.

15. Keith Negus, *Music Genres and Corporate Cultures* (London: Routledge, 1999), 28.

16. Howard Becker, *Art Worlds* (Berkeley: University of California Press, 1984).

17. First developed by Gabriel Almond and Sidney Verba in *The Civic Culture: Political Attitudes and Democracy in Five Nations* (Princeton, NJ: Princeton University Press, 1963), the concept of political culture has been adopted in recent years by a number of French historians, who have applied it to the study of the country's political traditions. See Serge Berstein, "L'historien et la culture politique," *Vingtième Siècle* 35 (July–September 1992): 67–77; Jean-François Sirinelli, "Preface," in *L'Histoire des droites en France,* vol. 2 (Paris: Gallimard, 1992); *Vingtième Siècle* 44, Numéro spécial: "La culture politique en France depuis de Gaulle" (October–December 1994); and Serge Berstein, ed., *Les cultures politiques en France* (Paris: Seuil, 1999). For an application of the concept to the musical domain, see Jann Pasler, *Composing the Citizen: Music as Public Utility in Third Republic France* (Berkeley: University of California Press, 2009), 159ff.

18. Boris Groys, *Art Power* (Cambridge: MIT Press, 2008), 13.

19. Dominique Grange, "Chacun de vous est concerné," *Chansons de mai 68,* Expression spontanée ES 68 DM 130.

20. Cited in Dominique Dhombres, "Une victime cachée de Mai-68," *Le Monde,* 2 May 2007.

21. Henri Weber, "Le Mai 68 imaginaire de Nicolas Sarkozy," *Le Figaro,* 4 May 2007.

22. Daniel Cohn-Bendit in "Par rapport à Mai 68, Nicolas Sarkozy se comporte en pur stalinien" *Le Temps,* 2 May 2007.

23. Peter Starr, *Logics of Failed Revolt: French Theory After May '68* (Stanford, CA: Stanford University Press, 1995), 2–3 and 16–17.

24. This point is underlined by Kristin Ross. See Ross, *May '68 and Its Afterlives* (Chicago: University of Chicago Press, 2002), 65 ff.

25. Raymond Aron, *The Elusive Revolution: Anatomy of a Student Revolt*, trans. Gordon Clough (New York: Praeger, 1969), 21.

26. Goldman, cited in Ross, *May '68 and Its Afterlives*, 66.

27. Ibid., 67.

28. This conceit can be found in Christian Victor and Julien Regoli, *Vingt ans de rock français* (Paris: Albin Michel, 1978); Coulomb and Varrod, *Histoires de chansons;* and Éric Deshayes and Dominique Grimaud, *L'Underground musical en France* (Paris: Le mot et le reste, 2008).

29. Starr, *Logics of Failed Revolt*, 114.

30. Luc Ferry and Alain Renaut, *La pensée 68: Essai sur l'anti-humanisme contemporain* (Paris: Gallimard, 1985); translated as *French Philosophy of the Sixties: An Essay on Antihumanism*, trans. Mary H.S. Cattani (Amherst: University of Massachusetts Press, 1990), 64.

31. Gilles Lipovetsky, *L'ère du vide: Essais sur l'individualisme contemporain* (Paris: Gallimard, 1983), 245.

32. Ross, *May '68 and Its Afterlives*, 8–9.

33. Ibid., 9.

34. Ibid., 99.

35. Ibid., 102.

36. Ibid., 15.

37. Ibid., 13.

38. An account of the "alternative" *chanson* of the 1970s can be found in Vassal, *Français, si vous chantiez.*

39. Michel de Certeau, *La prise de parole et autres écrits politiques*, ed. Luce Giard (Paris: Seuil, 1994), 78–79.

40. Ross, *May '68 and Its Afterlives*, 150.

CHAPTER I

The first chapter epigraph is an anonymous song composed during May–June 1968. A copy of the song's text is located at the Centre d'histoire sociale (hereafter CHS), fonds I, carton 17, dossier no. 1 ("Organisations culturelles"). The second epigraph is quoted in Philippe Labro et al., *This Is Only a Beginning*, trans. Charles Lam Markmann (New York: Funk and Wagnalls, 1969), 233.

1. Marc Kravetz, ed., *L'Insurrection étudiante: 2–13 Mai 1968* (Paris: Union Générale d'Éditions, 1968), 67; Daniel Singer, *Prelude to Revolution: France in May 1968* (New York: Hill and Wang, 1970), 118.

2. Michael Seidman, *The Imaginary Revolution: Parisian Students and Workers in 1968* (New York: Berghahn Books, 2004), 92; Kravetz, *L'Insurrection étudiante*, 70.

3. Labro et al., *This Is Only a Beginning*, 24–25; Kravetz, *L'Insurrection étudiante*, 70–71.

4. Kravetz, *L'Insurrection étudiante*, 71.

5. Daniel Cohn-Bendit, "Notre Commune de 10 mai," *Nouvel Observateur* 183 (15 May 1968): 32–36; Edgar Morin, "La Commune Etudiante," in *Mai 1968: La Brèche*, ed. Edgar Morin, Claude Lefort, and Jean-Marc Coudray (Paris: Fayard, 1968), 9–33; "La Commune Etudiante," *L'Evénement* 29 (June 1968): 36–45.

6. Jean Fourastié, *Les trente glorieuses* (Paris: Fayard, 1979), 165–68.

7. Ibid., 124–26; Nicholas Atkin, *The Fifth French Republic* (New York: Palgrave, 2005), 79.

8. On the lack of public commemoration of the Algerian War, see Frank Renken, "De Gaulle et l'effacement de la question coloniale," in *68: Une histoire collective (1962–1981)*, ed. Philippe Artières and Michelle Zancarini-Fournel (Paris: La Découverte, 2008), 177.

9. Pierre Viansson-Ponté, "Quand la France s'ennuie," *Le Monde*, 15 March 1968.

10. Kristin Ross, *May '68 and Its Afterlives* (Chicago: University of Chicago Press, 2002), 26.

11. Seidman, *Imaginary Revolution*, 53–55.

12. Singer, *Prelude to Revolution*, 84.

13. On *bidonvilles*, see Bernard Granotier, *Les travailleurs immigrés en France*, 2d ed. (Paris: Maspero, 1976), 110–13; on sleep merchants, see Alec G. Hargreaves, *Immigration, "Race" and Ethnicity in Contemporary France* (London: Taylor & Francis, 1995), 69.

14. Julien Besançon, ed., *Les murs ont la parole: Journal mural mai 68* (Paris: Tchou, 1968), pp. 154, 174, and 113, respectively.

15. Jacques Vassal, *Français, si vous chantiez* (Paris: Albin Michel, 1976), 13–14.

16. Ron Eyerman and Andrew Jamison, *Music and Social Movements* (Cambridge: Cambridge University Press, 1998), 2.

17. The few political songs composed during May '68 largely adopted the musical rhetoric of the *chanson révolutionnaire* of the late nineteenth century. These include the songs by Alice Becker-Ho that later appeared on the album *Pour en finir avec le travail*, or those by Aline Montels and Jean-Pierre Ronfard on the EP *Descendre dans la rue*. On the "dated" quality of the songs written during May, see Serge Dillaz, *La Chanson française de la contestation: Des barricades de la commune à mai 68* (Paris: Seghers, 1973), 165.

18. See the listings under "Les Concerts" and "Spectacles" in *Le Monde*, 10 May 1968, I and II.

19. "Spectacles annulés," *Combat*, 13 May 1968, 12.

20. Fleuret, "La culture passe aux actes," *Nouvel Observateur* 183 bis (20 May 1968): 8.

21. Jean Chesneaux, "Vivre en mai . . . ," *Lettres nouvelles* (September–October 1968): 142.

22. Michel Vovelle, "La Marseillaise: War or Peace," in *Realms of Memory: The Construction of the French Past*, vol. 3, ed Pierre Nora, trans. Arthur Goldhammer (New York: Columbia University Press, 1998), 34.

23. Laura Mason, *Singing the French Revolution* (Ithaca, NY: Cornell University Press, 1996), 97–99.

24. Georges Coulonges, *La Commune en chantant* (Paris: Les Editeurs français réunis, 1970), 95.

25. Maurice Dommanget, *Eugène Pottier, membre de la Commune et chantre de l'Internationale* (Paris: Editions EDI, 1971), 122–23; and C. Alexander McKinley, "Anarchists and the Music of the French Revolution," *Journal for the Study of Radicalism* 1, no. 2 (2007): 9–10.

26. For a discussion of the destiny of "La Marseillaise" in the nineteenth century, see Vovelle, "La Marseillaise," 46–61; Coulonges, *La Commune en chantant,* 63–64 and 95 ff.; and Regina Sweeney, *Singing Our Way to Victory* (Middletown, CT: Wesleyan University Press, 2001), 32–33. On the song's rejection by utopian socialists like the Saint-Simonians, see Ralph Locke, *Music, Musicians and the Saint-Simonians* (Chicago: University of Chicago Press, 1986), 158–61.

27. Dommanget, *Eugène Pottier,* 111 ff.; Marc Ferro, *L'Internationale d'Eugène Pottier et Pierre Degeyter* (Paris: Editions Noêsis, 1996); and Dillaz, *La Chanson française,* 37–41.

28. Sweeney, *Singing Our Way to Victory,* 33 and 39.

29. Vovelle, "La Marseillaise," 68.

30. Ferro, *L'Internationale d'Eugène Pottier,* 67 ff.

31. Vovelle, "La Marseillaise," 70.

32. *L'Enragé* 1 (May 1968): 4. A notice on the back cover urges readers to "apprenez à chanter *l'Internationale!*"

33. "La Marseillaise" featured prominently in the pro-Gaullist counter-demonstration of 30 May, discussed later in this chapter. Right-wing *groupuscules* (like Occident) also sang the anthem, particularly during confrontations with left-wing students. See, for instance, "Un commando d''Occident' tente de pénétrer dans le lycée Condorcet," *France-Soir,* 22 May 1968, 5.

34. C.T., "Une journée ordinaire (recit du 6 mai)," *Lettres françaises* 1234 (15 May 1968): 6.

35. Daniel Bensaïd and Henri Weber, *Mai 1968: Une répétition générale* (Paris: Maspero, 1968), 123 ff.

36. Ibid., 124.

37. Ibid.

38. Ibid.

39. See, for instance, the accounts in Alain Schnapp and Pierre Vidal-Naquet, *The French Student Uprising, November 1967–June 1968: An Analytical Record,* trans. Maria Jolas (Boston: Beacon Press, 1971), 175; Maurice Brinton, "Paris: May 1968," in *For Workers' Power: The Selected Writings of Maurice Brinton,* ed. David Goodway (Oakland, CA: AK Press, 2004), 240; and Pierre Peuchmaurd, *Plus vivant que jamais* (Paris: Robert Laffont, 1968), 40.

40. Siné, "Lettre de Siné à la redaction du Point," *Le Point,* supplement to no. 16 (May 1968): 2.

41. Claude Chisserey, in *Révoltes* 19 (15 May 1968); reprinted in Schnapp and Vidal-Naquet, *French Student Uprising,* 257.

42. Ross, *May '68 and Its Afterlives,* 25.

43. Patrick Seale and Maureen McConville, *Drapeaux rouges sur la France* (Paris: Mercure, 1968), 156.

44. Cited in Jean-Claude Kerbourc'h, *Le piéton de mai* (Paris: Juillard, 1968), 32.

45. Quoted in Brinton, "Paris: May 1968," 244.

46. Ibid., 245.

47. Ibid., 246. For a virtually identical account of the event, see Angelo Quattrocchi, "What Happened," in Quattrocchi and Tom Nairn, *The Beginning of the End: France, May 1968* (London: Verso, 1998), 47.

48. Brinton, "Paris: May 1968," 246.

49. Jean Ferniot, *Mort d'une révolution: la gauche de mai* (Paris: Denoël, 1968), 82.

50. Ibid.

51. This exchange is recorded in Kerbourc'h, *Le piéton de mai,* 101.

52. Ibid.

53. Ibid.

54. Georges Marchais, *L'Humanité,* 3 May 1968.

55. Quoted in Schnapp and Vidal-Naquet, *French Student Uprising,* 282.

56. Seidman, *Imaginary Revolution,* 118.

57. "Proposition d'Organisation Interne de la Sorbonne," CHS, fonds II, vol. 5, dossier no. 10 ("Censier, Sorbonne, CLIF"), document no. 1702. Portions of this document are reprinted in Sylvain Zegel, *Les idées de mai* (Paris: Gallimard, 1968), 64–66.

58. Permutations of the group's name included the Bureau d'agitation culturelle and the Comité d'agitation culturelle révolutionnaire.

59. Laurent Gervereau, "Les chansons de mai–juin 1968," *Matériaux pour l'histoire de notre temps* 11, no. 11 (1988): 198–99.

60. CRAC, "AGITATION CULTURELLE," *Tracts de mai 1968* (Zug, Switzerland: Inter-Documentation Company, 1986), microfiche no. 58, document no. 1419.

61. See, for instance, CRAC's call for artists to cease "clowning around in fashionable salons" and refuse "the sweets of the bourgeoisie." CRAC, "Ici on spontane," CHS, fonds I, carton 17, dossier no. 1 ("Mouvements et organisations culturelles").

62. On the paradigmatic forms of intellectual engagement, see Pascal Ory and Jean-François Sirinelli, *Les intellectuels en France: De l'affaire Dreyfus à nos jours,* 2d ed. (Paris: Armand Colin, 1992), 20–27. On repertoires of political contention more broadly, see Charles Tilly, *Contentious Performances* (Cambridge: Cambridge University Press, 2008).

63. "Union des écrivains: Documents," *Action poétique* 37 (1968): 6.

64. Peuchmaurd, *Plus vivant que jamais,* 44–45.

65. Union des Arts plastiques (20 May 1968), in *Quelle université, quelle société?* (Paris: Seuil, 1968), 132–33.

66. Mavis Gallant, "The Events in May: A Paris Notebook—I," in *Paris Notebooks: Essays and Reviews* (Toronto: Macmillan, 1986), 55.

67. Roland Barthes, "The Death of the Author," in *Image—Music—Text,* trans. Stephen Heath (New York: Hill and Wang, 1977), 142–48.

68. CRAC, "Projet d'association internationale de dissolution culturelle," CHS, fonds II, vol. 11, folder no. 26, document no. 4038.

69. Ibid.

70. Walter Benjamin, "The Work of Art in the Age of Mechanical Reproduction," in *Illuminations,* ed. Hannah Arendt (New York: Harcourt Brace Jovanich, 1968), 217–52.

71. Precedents for the idea of flooding the art market with mass-produced commodities include Giuseppe Pinot-Gallizio's proto-situationist "industrial painting" and George Maciunas's Fluxus multiples. See Michèle Bernstein, "In Praise of Pinot-Gallizio," in *Guy Debord and the Situationist International,* ed, Tom McDonough (Cambridge, MA: MIT Press, 2002), 69–72; and Owen Smith, "Fluxus: A Brief History and Other Fictions," in *In the Spirit of Fluxus,* ed. Elizabeth Armstrong and Joan Rothfuss (Minneapolis, MN: Walker Arts Center, 1993), 31–34.

72. "Rapport du C.R.A.C.," CHS, fonds I, carton 7, dossier no. 2 ("CRAC").

73. CRAC, "Join the Revolutionary Commune of the Imagination," in Schnapp and Vidal-Naquet, *The French Student Uprising,* 444.

74. Ibid.

75. Ibid.

76. Jean-Louis Brau, *Cours, camarade, le vieux monde est derrière toi: Histoire du mouvement révolutionnaire étudiant en Europe* (Paris: Albin Michel, 1968), 103.

77. Details on the occupation's planning can be found in Patrick Ravignant, *L'Odéon est ouvert* (Paris: Stock, 1968), 30ff.; and Brau, *Cours, camarade,* 103–5.

78. Zegel, *Les idées de mai,* 218.

79. Ibid.

80. Christian Bouyer, *Odéon est ouvert: Tribune libre* (Paris: Nouvelles Editions Debresse, 1968), 13.

81. Ravignant, *L'Odéon est ouvert,* 37.

82. The national actors' union expressed its dismay with the occupation in a communiqué issued 16 May. See Fédération Nationale du Spectacle, "Communiqué," 16 May 1968, Archives Départementales Seine–Saint Denis, Archives Syndicat Français des Artistes-Interprètes, 175 J 230.

83. Ravignant, *L'Odéon est ouvert,* 42.

84. Brau, *Cours, camarade,* 104.

85. Ravignant, *L'Odéon est ouvert,* 43.

86. Bouyer, *Odéon est ouvert,* 14.

87. Singer, *Prelude to Revolution,* 166.

88. "Barrault à Cohn-Bendit: 'Barrault est mort,'" *France-Soir,* 18 May 1968, 1.

89. Stagehands and other technical staff instigated the occupation, with musicians and singers initially hesitant to join. See "Il s'est créé à l'Opéra une situation particulière," *Le Figaro,* 22 May 1968, 22; "Grève illimitée à l'Opéra et à l'Opéra-Comique," *Combat,* 20 May 1968, 7.

90. "L'Opéra affiche: 'Grève illimitée,'" *Journal du dimanche-soir,* 19 May 1968, 1.

91. The exact date the occupation began is uncertain. According to Jacques Longchampt, it began 18 May, while according to *Combat* it began 16 May. Jacques Longchampt, "MUSICIENS: Grève provisoire reconductible au Conservatoire," *Le Monde,* 22 May 1968; and "Conservatoire: grève," *Combat,* 16 May 1968, 5.

92. L.D., "Le sens d'une grève," *Journal musical français* 170/171 (July–August 1968): 20. Jean-Noël Crocq, then an assistant in the clarinet studio of Pascal Moragues, seconded this observation: "The Conservatoire was one of the last educational institutions to react. There was no trade union tradition [there], no organization." Jean-Noël Crocq in "Mai 68, rue de Madrid," *Journal du Conservatoire* 30 (May 1998). Available online at http://mediatheque.ircam .fr/HOTES/CNSMDP/journal-30/note.html.

93. Renaud Gagneux, interview with author, 3 July 2006.

94. Ibid.

95. Jacques Longchampt, "'Révolution' au Conservatoire?" *Le Monde.* 7 June 1968.

96. "Le Conservatoire National Supérieur de Musique demande . . . ," *Tracts de mai 1968,* fiche no. 123, document no. 2829.

97. Alain Louvier, "La musique, reviendra-t-elle?" *Journal musical français* 170/171 (July–August 1968): 19.

98. These proposals are detailed on an undated typesheet held at the Centre d'histoire sociale. "La commission paritaire pour la réforme de l'enseignement de la musique . . . ," CHS, fonds I, carton 7, dossier "CAR-Odéon." They are summarized in Longchampt, "'Révolution' au Conservatoire?"; Maurice Fleuret, "L'éducation permanente," *Nouvel Observateur* 188 (19 June 1968): 47–49; and L.D., "Le sens d'une grève," 20.

99. Fleuret, "L'éducation permanente," 49.

100. CHS, fonds I, carton 7, dossier "CAR-Odéon."

101. Renaud Gagneux, interview with author, 3 July 2006. According to two of Messiaen's students of the time, Michäel Lévinas and Alain Savouret, Messiaen was "totalement perdu" during the events. Savouret, quoted in Jean Boivin, *La classe de Messiaen* (Paris: Christian Bourgois, 1995), 159. As for Boulez, an interview published in July 1968 revealed that he had followed the May events from abroad after his appearance at the Semaine de la musique contemporaine in Saint Etienne, though he felt that the musicians' strike had accomplished little. See Martine Cadieu, "Avec Pierre Boulez à Scheveningen," *Lettres françaises* 1240 (10 July 1968) : 16.

102. Quoted in Jacques Longchampt, "Débat à la Sorbonne," *Le Monde,* 21 May 1968.

103. Sylvie Coulomb and Didier Varrod, *Histoire de chansons, 1968–1988: de Julien Clerc à Etienne Daho* (Paris: Balland, 1987), 16.

104. "Chez les musiciens," *Le Figaro,* 22 May 1968, 18; "Les musiciens qui ont décrété la grève . . . ," *Le Figaro,* 24 May 1968, 12; Jacques Longchampt, "MUSICIENS: la grève des orchestres et de l'Opéra," *Le Monde,* 24 May 1968. The tally of the vote is given in "Les musiciens et la révolution de mai," *Jazz-Hot* 242 (August–September 1968): 14.

105. "Union des compositeurs," *Tracts de mai 1968,* fiche no. 309, document no. 7807.

106. See, for instance, the editorial that appeared in the first newsletter of the *Syndicat des Artistes-musiciens de Paris,* the principal musicians' union in Paris, to be published after May: "Éditorial," *L'Artiste musicien de Paris* 67, no. 22 (September–October 1968): 2.

107. Commission nationale pour l'étude des problèmes de la musique, *Rapport générale 1963–4* (Paris: Ministère d'État des Affaires Culturelles, 1964), 43 ff. See also Pierre-Michel Menger, *Le paradoxe du musicien: Le compositeur, le mélomane et l'état dans la société contemporaine* (Paris: Flammarion, 1983), 83.

108. William Baumol and William Bowen, *Performing Arts—the Economic Dilemma: A Study of Problems Common to Theater, Opera, Music, and Dance* (New York: Twentieth Century Fund, 1966), 161–76.

109. For SNAM's demands to the ministry, see Syndicat National des Artistes-Musiciens, "Communiqué," 21 May 1968, Archives Départementales Seine–Saint Denis, Archives Syndicat Français des Artistes-Interprètes, 175 J 230. For SFAI's demands, see Syndicat Français des Artistes-Interprètes, "Plateforme Revendicative du S.F.A.," Archives Départementales Seine–Saint Denis, Archives Syndicat Français des Artistes-Interprètes, 175 J 230.

110. Jacques Longchampt, "Les syndicats demandent une revalorisation de la profession," *Le Monde,* 18 June 1968; "Assemblée Générale Extraordinaire du 18 Juin 1968," *L'Artiste musicien de Paris* 67, no. 22 (September–October 1968): 11.

111. "Les musiciens et la révolution de mai," 15.

112. Arthur Haneuse and Fernand Franck, letter to Charles de Gaulle, in *L'Artiste-musicien de Paris* 64, no. 10 (April 1965): 14–15.

113. Ibid., 14. Performers received few royalties from radio broadcasts of recordings at the time. France, despite being a signatory to the 1961 Rome Convention, failed to ratify the treaty until 1985. See André Bertrand, *Le droit d'auteurs et les droits voisins,* 2d ed. (Paris: Dalloz, 1999), 891.

114. Haneuse and Franck, letter to Charles de Gaulle, in *L'Artiste-musicien de Paris,* 14.

115. Record sales for the second quarter of 1968 were up 6 percent compared to the second quarter of 1967. However, the work stoppage disrupted the pressing of records, which hurt sales during the second half of the year. Michael Way, "France Back on Production Track After June Setback," *Billboard* 80, no. 41 (12 October 1968): 69 and 71.

116. *L'Humanité,* 21 May 1968, 7.

117. "L'Orchestre de Paris jouera Beethoven le 28 juin," *France-Soir,* 15 June 1968, 13.

118. Dave Laing, "Music and the Market," in *The Cultural Study of Music: A Critical Introduction,* ed. Martin Clayton, Trevor Herbert, and Richard Middleton (New York: Routledge, 2003), 315.

119. This is not mere speculation. Léo Ferré incurred the wrath of SAMuP by using prerecorded accompaniments for his 1969 Bobino recital. See "Affaire

Bobino (Léo Ferré)," *L'Artiste-musicien de Paris* 68, no. 24 (March–April 1969): 6–11.

120. The first efforts at organizing a branch of the union dedicated to *la pop' music* reportedly occurred during May–June '68 but failed to win much support among rock musicians. "Section des Groupes (Pop' Music)," *L'Artiste-musicien de Paris* 69, no. 28 (Summer 1970): 19.

121. Rieux, "A propos de la Carte professionnelle," *L'Artiste-musicien de Paris* 64, no. 10 (April 1965): 21–22.

122. "Mémoire établi par le S.A.Mu.P. sur la situation économique et sociale de l'Artiste Musicien en France," *L'Artiste-musicien de Paris* 64, no. 14 (Winter–Spring 1966): 109.

123. Ibid., 110.

124. "Carte professionnelle des musiciens de variétés," *L'Artiste-musicien de Paris* 65, no. 19 (Summer 1967): 18. See also the letter addressed to the head of the British musicians' union complaining of the influx of English groups in *L'Artiste-musicien de Paris* 64, no. 13 (January–February 1966): 86–87.

125. Guy Lafitte and Michel Hausser, "Les musiciens de jazz s'unissent," *L'Artiste-musicien de Paris* 64, no. 12 (Summer–Fall 1965): 63.

126. Ibid.

127. An account of this group's role in the strike is given in "Les musiciens et la révolution de mai," 14–16.

128. Ibid., 16.

129. On the composition of the group, see ibid., 15.

130. Ibid., 16.

131. Ibid., 14–15.

132. Ibid., 15.

133. Ibid.

134. Singer, *Prelude to Revolution,* 10.

135. Ibid., 182.

136. Quattrocchi, "What Happened," 70.

137. "Address to All Workers," reprinted in René Vienet, *Situationists and Enragés in the Occupation Movement, France, May '68* (New York: Autonomedia, 1992), 138.

138. Singer, *Prelude to Revolution,* 188.

139. Ibid., 190.

140. Ibid., 191–92.

141. Gallant, "The Events in May," 73.

142. Charles de Gaulle, "La Déclaration du Présidente," *Le Monde,* 1 June 1968, 2.

143. Ibid.

144. Ibid.

145. Peuchmaurd, *Plus vivant que jamais,* 132.

146. Frank Georgi, "'Le pouvoir est dans la rue'. La 'Manifestation gaulliste' des Champs-Élysées (30 mai 1968)," *Vingtième Siècle* 48 (October–December 1995): 51.

147. Ibid.

148. Jacques Derogy, "Les trois drapeaux," *L'Express,* special issue, June 1968, 11.

149. Cited in Michel Legris, "Premier meeting parisien du P.C.F.," *Le Monde,* 12 June 1968, 4.

150. "Le discours de Waldeck Rochet," *L'Humanité,* 11 June 1968, 4.

151. Ibid.

152. Adrien Dansette, *Mai 1968* (Paris: Plon, 1971), 344; Singer, *Prelude to Revolution,* 216.

153. "Le discours de Waldeck Rochet," 4.

154. *L'Enragé* 4, 17 June 1968, 7.

155. "Assemblée Générale Extraordinaire du 18 Juin 1968," 11.

156. "Editorial," in ibid., 2.

157. Ibid.

158. "LES CRS FRAPPENT . . . ," in *Tracts de mai 1968,* fiche no. 101, document no. 2337.

159. "Leger Incident à l'Opéra," *Le Figaro,* 17 June 1968, 20.

160. "Chanteurs et danseurs participent à l'administration de l'Opéra qui rouvre ce soir," *France-Soir,* 16–17 June 1968, 11. See also Fleuret, "Les derniers feux," *Nouvel observateur* 190, 3 July 1968: 38

161. On the reforms enacted after May '68, see Boivin, *La classe de Messiaen,* 159–60; and Alain Louvier, "L'évolution des classes de composition et d'analyse depuis 1968," in *Le Conservatoire de Paris: Des menus-plaisirs à la Cité de la Musique, 1795–1995,* ed. Anne Bongrain and Yves Gérard (Paris: Buchet-Castel, 1999), 361–64.

162. The archives of the Syndicat français des artistes-interprètes hold a copy of the demands that representatives of the Fédération nationale du spectacle presented to Malraux on 30 May, with Malraux's reactions jotted in the margins. Apparently Malraux expressed his sympathy for demands to increase the budget for cultural affairs, but he claimed that his entreaties to the finance minister had been refused. He punted on the question of the professional license, though he assured union representatives that a commission would undertake a study of the problem. As for banning the playback of recorded music on the radio, Malraux noted that while this was feasible for the ORTF, he was unable to impose restrictions upon private stations. "Note remise à Monsieur André Malraux, Ministre d'Etat chargé des Affaires Culterelles, par la Fédération Nationale du Spectacle-CGT," in Archives Départementales Seine–Saint Denis, Archives Syndicat Français des Artistes-Interprètes, 175 J 230.

CHAPTER 2

1. France Gall, quoted in David Looseley, *Popular Music in Contemporary France: Authenticity, Politics, Debate* (Oxford: Berg, 2003), 32. The original interview appeared in "Ce qu'ils pensent de la 'révolution,' " *Noir et blanc* 1213 (27 June 1968).

2. Michel de Certeau, *La prise de parole et autres écrits politiques,* ed. Luce Giard (Paris: Seuil, 1994), 29.

3. Hervé Hamon and Patrick Rotman, *Génération* (Paris: Seuil, 1987), 2: 19.

4. Ibid.

5. Certeau, *La prise de parole,* 29.

6. Chantal Brunschwig, Jean-Louis Calvet, and Jean-Claude Klein, *Cent ans de chanson française* (Paris: Seuil, 1972), 179.

7. Dominique Grange in "Dominique Grange vs Jacques Tardi," *Barricata* 10 (June 2003). Available online at http://contre.propagande.org/pravda/ modules/news/article.php?storyid=140 (accessed 16 May 2008).

8. Ibid.

9. Ibid.

10. Serge Dillaz, *La Chanson française de la contestation: Des barricades de la commune à mai 68* (Paris: Seghers, 1973), 176.

11. Dominique Grange, "Nous sommes des nouveaux partisans," *L'Idiot international* 7 (June 1970): 19.

12. Ibid.

13. Ibid.

14. Overviews of the Gauche prolétarienne can be found in Christophe Bourseiller, *Les maoistes: La folle histoire des gardes rouges français* (Paris: Plon, 2006), 150–86 and 274–334; A. Belden Fields, *Trotskyism and Maoism: Theory and Practice in France and the United States* (New York: Praeger, 1988), 99–128; and Rotman and Hamon, *Génération,* vol. 2, chapters 1, 2, and 6.

15. Jean-Pierre Le Goff, *Mai 68, l'héritage impossible* (Paris: La Découverte, 2002), 152.

16. Ibid.

17. Ibid., 153.

18. "Construire le parti de la nouvelle résistance," *La Cause du peuple* 19 (14 April 1970): 2.

19. Ibid.

20. Grange, in "Dominique Grange vs Jacques Tardi."

21. Hamon and Rotman, *Génération,* 2: 147.

22. "Les Nouveaux partisans," *La Cause du peuple* 21 (8 May 1970): 2.

23. Ibid., 2.

24. See, for instance, France Vernillat and Jacques Charpentreau, *La Chanson française* (Paris: Presses universitaires de France, 1971), 108; and Guy Erismann, *Histoire de la Chanson* (Paris: Hermes, 1967), 196.

25. Brunschwig, Calvet, and Klein, *Cent ans de chanson française,* 256. See also Regina Sweeney, *Singing Our Way to Victory* (Middletown, CT: Wesleyan University Press, 2001), 57–58.

26. Erismann, *Histoire de la Chanson,* 196.

27. "Les Nouveaux partisans," 2.

28. Ibid.

29. Franco Fabbri, "A Theory of Musical Genres: Two Applications," in *Popular Music Perspectives,* ed. David Horn and Philip Tagg (Gothenburg and Exeter: IASPM, 1982), 52–81; Jeffrey Kallberg, "The Rhetoric of Genre: Chopin's Nocturne in G Minor," *19th-Century Music* 11, no. 3 (Spring 1988): 238–61; Simon Frith, *Performing Rites* (Oxford: Oxford University Press, 1996); Keith Negus, *Music Genres and Corporate Culture* (London: Routledge, 1999); Jason Toynbee, *Making Popular Music: Musicians, Creativity and Institutions* (Lon-

don: Arnold, 2000), esp. chapter 4; David Hesmondhalgh, "Subcultures, Scenes or Tribes? None of the Above," *Journal of Youth Studies* 8, no. 1 (March 2005): 21–40; and Fabian Holt, *Genre in Popular Music* (Chicago: University of Chicago Press, 2007).

30. This point is made by Toynbee. See Toynbee, *Making Popular Music,* 110.

31. "Les Nouveaux partisans," 2.

32. Louis-Jean Calvet, "La chanson révolutionnaire," *Politique hebdo* 13 (27 January 1972): 20.

33. Ibid.

34. Holt dubs these the "center collectivities" of a genre. Holt, *Genre in Popular Music,* 21.

35. Kallberg, "The Rhetoric of Genre," 244.

36. Adam Krims makes a similar point with regard to rap. See Krims, *Rap Music and the Poetics of Identity* (Cambridge: Cambridge University Press, 2000), 81.

37. This correlation can be seen in chapter 4, in the opposition between hard rock (identified with working-class provincial audiences) and progressive rock (identified with middle-class Parisian audiences). Hence the Variations, one of the principal hard rock bands active in France in the late 1960s and early 1970s, defended their musical style against detractors by arguing that it was tailored to satisfy the tastes of provincial rather than Parisian youth. Philippe Paringaux, "Variations mal jugés," *Rock & Folk* 38 (March 1970): 17.

38. On the role of *tiers-mondisme* in the far left movements of the 1960s, see Kristin Ross, *May '68 and its Afterlives* (Chicago: University of Chicago Press, 2002), 80–84.

39. See Serge Mallet, *La nouvelle classe ouvrière* (Paris: Seuil, 1963); André Gorz, *Stratégie ouvrière et néocapitalisme* (Paris: Seuil, 1964); and Frédéric Bon and Michel-Antoine Burnier, *Classe ouvrière et révolution* (Paris: Seuil, 1971).

40. The idea that youth constituted a "nouvelle classe d'âge" was popularized by sociologist Edgar Morin; see Morin, "Culture adolescente et révolte étudiante," *Annales ESC* 24, no. 3 (1969): 765–76. Political applications of this idea soon followed suit; see François Duprat, *L'Internationale étudiante révolutionnaire* (Paris: Nouvelles Editions Latines, 1968); Maurice Joyeux, *L'anarchie et la révolte de la jeunesse* (Paris: Casterman, 1970); and A. Lazar, "Les classes d'âge: Une lutte des classes d'âge?" *L'Idiot international* 5 (April 1970).

41. Denys Lemery, "Les présents conjugués," *Jazz Magazine* 165 (April 1969): 34.

42. Ibid.

43. Ibid.

44. Pierre Bourdieu, *The Field of Cultural Production,* ed. Randal Johnson (New York: Columbia University Press, 1993), 44.

45. Maurice Fleuret, "Le concert sera partout et le concert nulle part," *Nouvel Observateur* no. 210 bis, "Spécial littéraire" (20 November 1968): 25.

46. Philippe Constantin, "Disques du mois," *Jazz Hot* 246 (January 1969): 41.

47. Philippe Constantin, "Dear Prof Leary," *Jeune Afrique* 420 (20 January 1969): 11.

48. Ibid.

49. Not all were persuaded by Constantin's arguments or by the utopian image of social reconciliation they intimated. For critic Gérard Noël, the connections that Lemery, Constantin, and others identified between different genres were more apparent than real. While avant-garde jazz and contemporary music may exhibit superficial similarities, they emerged out of different social and institutional contexts. According to Noël, the true fusion of genres can only take place once social antagonisms have been resolved. See Gérard Noël, "Au confluent des musiques nouvelles," *Jazz-Hot* 261 (May 1970): 9.

50. A list of songs inspired by May '68 can be found in Louis-Jean Calvet, *La Production révolutionnaire: Slogans, affiches, chansons* (Paris: Payot, 1976), 171–88.

51. "Léo Ferré à Lille, *L'Idiot Internationale* 15 (March/April 1971): 19.

52. Jacques Vassal, *Léo Ferré: L'enfant millénaire* (Paris: Hors Collection, 2003), 122; Robert Belleret, *Léo Ferré: une vie d'artiste* (Arles: Actes Sud, 1996), 489.

53. Ferré, quoted in Belleret, *Léo Ferré*, 490.

54. For a discussion of "modernist" elements in Ferré's work of this period, see Peter Hawkins, "Léo Ferré: Modernism, Postmodernism and the Avant-garde in Popular Chanson," *French Cultural Studies* 16, no. 2 (June 2005): 169–78.

55. "A l'Araignée la toile au vent/A Biftec baron du homard/Et sa technique du caviar/Qui ressemblait à du hareng."

56. "Je CAUSE et je GUEULE comme un chien. JE SUIS UN CHIEN."

57. Belleret, *Léo Ferré*, 127 ff.

58. Marc Robine, *Il était une fois la chanson française: des origines à nos jours* (Paris: Fayard, 2004), 84–85. For an evocative description of the Left Bank scene in the 1940s, see Serge Dillaz, *Vivre et chanter en France*, vol. 1: 1945–1980 (Paris: Fayard, 2005), 34–43. Also useful is Gilles Schlesser's encyclopedic overview of the Left Bank cabaret scene, *Le cabaret 'rive gauche': De la Rose rouge au Bateau ivre (1946–1974)* (Paris: L'Archipel, 2006).

59. Looseley, *Popular Music*, 18; Louis-Jean Calvet, *Chanson et Société* (Paris: Payot, 1981), 72.

60. Calvet, *Chanson et Société*, 72; Hawkins, *Chanson: The French Singer-songwriter from Aristide Bruant to the Present Day* (Aldershot: Ashgate, 2000), 23–27.

61. Looseley, *Popular Music*, 68.

62. Barbara Lebrun, *Protest Music in France: Production, Identity and Audiences* (Farnham: Ashgate, 2009), 8.

63. See Calvet, *Chanson et Société*, 71; and Calvet, "Changing Places of the French Song from 1945 to the Present Day," in *France and the Mass Media*, ed. Brian Rigby and Nicholas Hewitt (London: Macmillan, 1991), 195–96.

64. Calvet, *Chanson et Société*, 72.

65. Vassal, *Léo Ferré*, 66.

66. Hawkins, *Chanson*, 112.

67. Ibid., 109.

68. Charles Estienne, *Léo Ferré* (Paris: Seghers, 1962).

69. Ibid., 23.

70. Paul Yonnet, *Jeux, modes et masses: la société française et le moderne 1945–1985* (Paris: Gallimard, 1985), 197.

71. "Comme une fille/La rue s'déshabille/Les pavés s'entassent/Et les flics qui passent/Les prennent sur la gueule."

72. Chantal Le Bidois, "Le Réseau parallèle," *Hermes* 4 (1968).

73. Yves Simon, "Evariste," *Actuel* 7 (April 1971).

74. Evariste, "La Révolution/La Faute à Nanterre" CRAC 001.

75. Gérald Asaria, "Evariste, le *yéyé* prof à Princeton," *Paris Match* 934 (4 March 1967): 86.

76. Philippe Bouvard, "La première trouvaille du MIDEM: un chercheur de Princeton," *Le Figaro,* 31 January 1967.

77. For accounts of the arrival of rock and roll in France, see Christian Victor and Julien Regoli, *Vingt ans de rock français* (Paris: Albin Michel, 1978); Jacques Barsamian and François Jouffa, *Vinyl fraise* (Paris: Laffon, 1993); Gilles Verlant, ed., *L'Encyclopédie du rock français* (Paris: Hors Collection, 2000); David Looseley, *Popular Music,* chapter 2; and Gérome Guibert, *La production de la culture: Le cas des musiques amplifiées en France* (Paris: IRMA, 2006), 109–27.

78. Chris Warne, "Music, Youth and Moral Panics," *Historia Actual Online* 11 (Fall 2006): 54.

79. Georges Coulonges, "Considérations sur la politique de messieurs les notables de la halle aux chansons," *Nouvelle Critique* 183 (March 1967): 57.

80. Georges Coulonges, *La chanson en son temps: De Béranger au juke-box* (Paris: Les Editeurs Français Réunis, 1969), 201 and 207.

81. On the gender coding of mass culture critiques, see Andreas Huyssen, *After the Great Divide* (Bloomington: Indiana University Press, 1986), esp. chapter 3; and Sarah Thornton, *Club Cultures: Music, Media and Subcultural Capital* (Hanover, NH: Wesleyan University Press, 1995), 99–105.

82. Albert Raisner, *L'Aventure pop* (Paris: Robert Laffont, 1973), 54.

83. For a useful corrective to dismissive accounts of *yéyé,* one that underlines the movement's role in giving young women a public voice they previously lacked, see Susan Weiner, *Enfants Terribles: Youth and Femininity in the Mass Media in France, 1945–1968* (Baltimore, MD: Johns Hopkins University Press, 2001). Weiner's observations are borne out by the remarks of *yéyé* fans in the 1965 book *La chanson et ses vedettes,* which indicates the liberating effects that *yéyé* had for its fans. See Jacques Marny, *La chanson et ses vedettes* (Paris: Centurion, 1965), 131–35 and 140–43.

84. Victor and Regoli, *Vingt ans de rock français,* 61.

85. On the "alternative" pop scene, see Christian Eudeline, *Anti-yéyé: Une autre histoire des sixties* (Paris: Denoël, 2006).

86. See, for instance Gilles Lapouge, "Antoine s'explique sur les beatniks," *Le Figaro Littéraire* 1058 (28 July 1966): 1 and 8. Such representations have been faithfully reproduced in histories of French popular music. See Jocelyne de Noblet and Franc Lipsic, eds., *Spécial-Pop* (Paris: Albin Michel, 1967), 112; Raisner, *L'Aventure pop,* 194; Victor and Regoli, *Vingt ans de rock français,* 81; Verlant, ed., *L'Encyclopédie du rock français,* 48.

87. Eudeline, *Anti-yéyé*, 207.

88. Jean-François Sirinelli, "La norme et la transgression. Remarques sur la notion de provocation en histoire culturelle," *Vingtième siècle* 93 (2007): 10.

89. Antoine, cited in Christophe Quillien, *Génération Rock & Folk: 40 ans de culture rock* (Paris: Flammarion, 2006), 42.

90. On the concept of "role distance," see Erving Goffman, *Encounters: Two Studies in the Sociology of Interaction* (New York: Bobbs-Merrill, 1961), 105 ff.

91. Sylvie de Nussac, "Antoine fait des malheurs," *L'Express* 773 (11 April 1966): 59.

92. Victor and Regoli, *Vingt ans de rock français*, 86.

93. Ibid. See also Brunschwig, Calvet, and Klein, *Cent ans de chanson française*, 22.

CHAPTER 3

The chapter epigraph appears as a short announcement in "Flashes," *Jazz-Hot* 251 (June 1969): 13.

1. For reports of jazz at the Sorbonne, see Alfred Willener, *The Action-Image of Society: On Cultural Politicization,* trans. A.M. Sheridan Smith (New York: Pantheon, 1970), 232; for the Odéon, see Patrick Ravignant, *L'Odéon est ouvert* (Paris: Stock, 1968), 57; for the funeral march of Gilles Tautin, see "Chroniques: L'art en mai–juin 1968," *Revue d'esthétique* 22, no. 1 (1969): 77.

2. On the Cohelmec Ensemble, see Alain Gerber, "L'improvisation instrumentale," in *Musique et vie quotidienne,* ed. Alfred Willener and Paul Beaud (Paris: Maison Mame, 1973), 189. On Red Noise, see Paul Alessandrini, "Pop aux Halles," *Rock & Folk* 37 (February 1970): 13.

3. Willener, *Action-Image of Society,* 232.

4. Daniel Berger, "Une chaude semaine," *Nouvelles littéraires* 2174 (22 May 1969): 12; Pierre Cressant, "Free à l'O.R.T.F.," *Jazz-Hot* 261 (May 1970): 7 and 26; Patrick Callagham, "Free Jazz dans les facs: De l'institut d'art à la Sorbonne," *Jazz-Hot* 259 (March 1970): 9; T. Trombert, "Soirée de soutien au Black Panthers Party, Mutualité le 2–11–70," *Jazz-Hot* 267 (December 1970): 9; and Laurent Goddet, "Alan Silva à l'O.R.T.F.," *Jazz-Hot* 269 (February 1971): 27.

5. See, for instance, the articles on free jazz published in *Actuel* 6 (March 1971); and *Parapluie* 2 (January–February 1971).

6. Pierre Lere, "Free jazz: évolution ou révolution," *Revue d'esthétique* 23, nos. 3–4 (1970): 313–25; "Free jazz," *Chroniques de l'art vivant* 12 (July 1970): 30.

7. Eric Plaisance, "Jazz: Champ esthétique et idéologique," *Nouvelle Critique* 26 (September 1969): 23–27; see also Pierre Lasnier, "L'esthétique du 'Black Power,'" *Droit et liberté* 277 (December 1968): 26–27.

8. Guy Kopelowicz, "La New Thing," *Informations & Documents* 230 (August 1966): 10–15.

9. William A. Shack, *Harlem in Montmartre: A Paris Jazz Story between the Great Wars* (Berkeley: University of California Press, 2001); Tyler Stovall, *Paris*

Noir: African Americans in the City of Light (New York: Houghton Mifflin, 1996), esp. 163–81.

10. George Lewis, "The AACM in Paris," *Black Renaissance/Renaissance Noire* 5, no. 3 (Spring/Summer 2004): 106.

11. These included Archie Shepp, Alan Silva, Clifford Thornton, Grachan Moncur III, Dave Burrell, and Sunny Murray. "Free Jazz sur Seine," *Jazz Magazine* 169–70 (September 1969): 18–22; and Jacques Renaud, "BYG à l'avant garde," *Jazz-Hot* 253 (September 1969): 16–18. On the pan-African festival, see Daniel Sauvaget, "Le festival culturel panafricain," *Jazz-Hot* 253 (September 1969): 30–33; and Paul Alessandrini, "L'Amérique noire au festival d'Alger," *Jazz Magazine* 169–70 (September 1969): 16–17.

12. Philippe Adler, "Les préfets n'aiment pas le pop," *L'Express* 954 (20 October 1969): 105.

13. Paul Alessandrini, "Freepop," *Jazz Magazine* 173 (December 1969): 26–31; Alessandrini "Les folles nuits d'Amougies," *Rock & Folk* 35 (December 1969); Daniel Berger, "Les inusables," *Nouvelles littéraires* 2200 (20 November 1969): 12; Philippe Koechlin, "Pas de ça chez nous!" *Nouvel Observateur* 258 (20 October 1969): 36–37; Claude Fléouter, "Près de vingt mille jeunes au festival de 'Pop' Music,'" *Le Monde*, 28 October 1969, 23; Eric Vincent et al., "Amougies, le festival maudit," *Salut les copains* 89 (January 1970): 38–45; and Daniel Caux, "Amougies: L'Europe, le 'free jazz' et la 'pop music,'" *Chroniques de l'art vivant* 6 (December 1969): 2–7.

14. Alessandrini, "Freepop," 27.

15. Caux, "Amougies," 3; Alessandrini, "Freepop," 29–30.

16. Berger, "Les inusables," 12.

17. Alessandrini, "Freepop," 28.

18. Stephen Lehman, "I Love You with an Asterisk: African-American Experimental Music and the French Jazz Press, 1970–1980," *Critical Studies in Improvisation* 2 (May 2005), esp. 39–41; George E. Lewis, *A Power Stronger Than Itself: The AACM and American Experimental Music* (Chicago: University of Chicago Press, 2008), 242; and Ronald Radano, *New Musical Figurations: Anthony Braxton's Cultural Critique* (Chicago: University of Chicago Press, 1993), 146.

19. Alessandrini, "Freepop," 28.

20. On this score, the present chapter is indebted to prior work on the reception of free jazz in France, in particular Ludovic Tournès, *New Orleans sur Seine: Histoire du Jazz en France* (Paris: Fayard, 1999), 387–412; Tournès, "Amateurs de jazz français et mouvement noir américain," *Les années 68: événements, cultures politiques et modes de vie*, Lettre d'information 22 (February 1997); Vincent Cotro, *Chants libres: Le free jazz en France, 1960–1975* (Paris: Outre Mesure, 1999); and Sklower, *Free jazz: la catastrophe féconde: une histoire du monde éclaté du jazz en France (1960–1982)* (Paris: L'Harmattan, 2006). In addition, there is a rich literature on the experience of AACM artists in Paris. See Lewis, "The AACM in Paris" and *A Power Stronger Than Itself*, chapter 7; Lehman, "I Love You with an Asterisk"; and Radano, *New Musical Figurations*, 142 ff.

21. Guy Kopelowicz, "Le nouveau jazz et la réalité américaine," *Jazz-Hot* 231 (May 1967): 23; Daniel Berger, "Archie Shepp," *Nouvelles littéraires* 2104 (28 December 1967): 12; Pierre Lasnier, "L'été torride du Lucernaire," *L'Express* 944 (11 August 1969): 49.

22. Philippe Koechlin, "Le continent perdu," *Nouvel Observateur* 168 (31 January 1968): 35.

23. Pascal Ory describes this superimposition of political and aesthetic radicalism in "Une 'Révolution culturelle'?" in *Les Années 68: Le temps de la contestation,* ed. Geneviève Dreyfus-Armand, Robert Frank, Marie-Françoise Lévy, and Michelle Zancarini-Fournel (Paris: Complexe, 2000), 221.

24. Eric Porter, *What Is This Thing Called Jazz? African-American Musicians as Artists, Critics and Activists* (Berkeley: University of California Press, 2002), 197–205.

25. Ingrid Monson, *Freedom Sounds: Civil Rights Call Out to Jazz and Africa* (Oxford: Oxford University Press, 2007), 171. See also pp. 266–82.

26. Ibid., 160.

27. Lewis, *A Power Stronger Than Itself,* 240.

28. Daniel Caux, "A.A.C.M. Chicago," *Jazz-Hot* 254 (October 1969): 17 and 19.

29. François Postif, "The Noah Howard-Frank Wright Quartet: une interview de François Postif," *Jazz-Hot* 257 (January 1970): 18–19.

30. Lehman, "I Love You with an Asterisk," 42.

31. Jeffrey H. Jackson, *Making Jazz French* (Durham, NC: Duke University Press, 2003), 72.

32. Lewis, for instance, cites a program note for an Art Ensemble performance in 1969 that "could not resist framing the AEC in terms of an updated version of the 'jungle' trope." Lewis, *A Power Stronger Than Itself,* 222–23.

33. The difficulties of keeping up with developments in New York are described in a letter to the editor of *Jazz-Hot* from March 1965. See Alain Lejeune, "Courrier," *Jazz-Hot* 207 (March 1965): 15–16.

34. Jacques Creuzevault, "Don Cherry en Europe," *Jazz-Hot* 205 (January 1965): 11.

35. Paul-Louis Rossi, "Silence on enregistre," *Jazz Magazine* 124 (November 1965): 20–21.

36. Francis Paudras, "Cecil Taylor," *Jazz-Hot* 206 (February 1965): 24–26; Gerald Merceron, "Face à la new thing," *Jazz-Hot* 209 (May 1965): 22–24; François Postif and Guy Kopelowicz, "Archie Shepp ou la marée qui monte," *Jazz-Hot* 210 (June 1965): 22–26; François Postif and Guy Kopelowicz, "Archie Shepp ou la marée qui monte (II)," *Jazz-Hot* 211 (July–August 1965): 38–41; and François Postif, "Albert Ayler le magicien," *Jazz-Hot* 213 (October 1965): 20–22.

37. *Jazz Magazine* 119 (June 1965) and 125 (December 1965).

38. Tournès provides a useful sketch of the new generation of critics in *New Orleans sur Seine,* 387–88.

39. Lewis, *A Power Stronger Than Itself,* 235.

40. Jean-Louis Comolli, "Voyage au bout de la New Thing," *Jazz Magazine* 129 (April 1966): 24–29.

41. Ibid., 25.

42. LeRoi Jones [Amiri Baraka], *Blues People: Negro Music in White America* (New York: William Morrow, 1963).

43. Comolli, "Voyage," 27.

44. Ibid.

45. Alastair Horne, *A Savage War of Peace: Algeria 1954–1962* (London: Macmillan, 1977), 533; Robert Aldrich, *Greater France: A History of French Overseas Expansion* (London: Macmillan, 1996), 311 ff.

46. Mar Fall, *Le destin des Africains noirs en France* (Paris: L'Harmattan, 2005), 83 ff.; Marc Tardieu, *Les africains en France: de 1914 à nos jours* (Monaco: Rocher, 2006), 99–116; and Jacques Simon et al., *L'Immigration algérienne en France: De 1962 à nos jours* (Paris: L'Harmattan, 2002). For a more general overview, see Alec G. Hargreaves, *Immigration, Race and Ethnicity in Contemporary France* (London: Routledge, 1995), chapter 2.

47. Paul Clay Sorum, *Intellectuals and Decolonization in France* (Chapel Hill, NC: University of North Carolina Press, 1977), 160–61; Claude Liauzu, "Le tiersmondisme des intellectuels en accusation: Le sens d'une trajectoire," *Vingtième Siècle* 12 (October–December 1986): 74.

48. Ross, *May '68 and Its Afterlives,* 81.

49. Jacques Laurans, in "Courrier des lecteurs" *Jazz-Hot* 222 (July–August 1966): 15.

50. For critiques of Comolli's essay, see Eric Plaisance, "Idéologie et esthétique à propos du free jazz," *Cahiers du jazz* 15 (1967): 6–23 (discussed below); Yves Buin, "La nuit noire (1)," *Jazz-Hot* 236 (November 1967): 20–24; and "La nuit noire (2)," *Jazz-Hot* 237 (December 1967): 51–55.

51. Michel Le Bris and Bruno Vincent, "La tête, le cœur et le pied (III)," *Jazz-Hot* 234 (August–September 1967): 23–25, 31.

52. Le Bris, "Le peuple du blues' par LeRoi Jones," *Jazz-Hot* 241 (May–July 1968): 9–13.

53. The most violent polemic took place between Jacques Hess (of *Jazz Magazine*) and Michel Le Bris (editor of *Jazz-Hot* at the time). Jacques Hess, "Hess-o-Hess," *Jazz Magazine* 167 (June 1969): 5; and Michel Le Bris, "A propos d'un certain S.O.S," *Jazz-Hot* 252 (July–August 1969): 7 and 48–49.

54. Cited in Philippe Constantin, "Courrier des lecteurs," *Jazz-Hot* 241 (May–July 1968): 4.

55. Speeches given at the Argenteuil meeting are reprinted in the *Cahiers du Communisme* 42, nos. 5–6 (May–June 1966). For discussions of the event, see Sunil Khilnani, *Arguing Revolution: The Intellectual Left in Postwar France* (New Haven, CT: Yale University Press, 1993), 108 ff; and Michael Kelly, *Modern French Marxism* (Baltimore, MD: Johns Hopkins University Press, 1982), 141–42.

56. Plaisance, "Idéologie et esthétique," 7.

57. Ibid., 12.

58. A. Belden Fields, *Trotskyism and Maoism: Theory and Practice in France and the United States* (New York: Praeger, 1988), 50 ff. and 88 ff.

59. Critiques of the PCF's post-Argenteuil cultural policy may be found in Patrick Kessel, ed., *Le mouvement 'maoïste' en France: Textes et documents* (Paris: Union générale d'éditions, 1972), 149–64.

60. Plaisance, "Idéologie et esthétique," 18.

61. Lucien Malson, "De LeRoi Jones à Gunther Schuller," *Le Monde,* 3 January 1969, 1. Malson's charge of Zhdanovism sparked a number of angry responses. See Jean-Louis Comolli, "Loin de Gunther Schuller, près de LeRoi Jones," *Jazz Magazine* 163 (February 1969): 47–49; and Bruno Vincent, " 'De' Gunther Schuller 'à' Lucien Malson," *Jazz-Hot* 247 (February 1969): 5, 48–49.

62. Malson, "De LeRoi Jones," 1. For other expressions of displeasure in the politicization of jazz criticism, see the letters published in "Courrier des lecteurs," *Jazz-Hot* 257 (January 1970): 6; and "Courrier des lecteurs," *Jazz-Hot* 247 (February 1969): 48.

63. Carlos de Radzitsky, in "Courrier des lecteurs," *Jazz-Hot* 240 (April 1968): 5.

64. Lasnier, "L'esthétique du 'Black Power,' " 27.

65. In Malson et al., "Neuf entretiens sur le jazz neuf," *Les Cahiers du jazz* 16–17 (1968): 8–60, esp. 22–37.

66. Jean-Louis Pautrot, "Introduction," in André Hodeir, *The André Hodeir Jazz Reader* (Ann Arbor: University of Michigan Press, 2006), 4.

67. Ibid., 11–12.

68. Hodeir in Malson et al., "Neuf entretiens sur le jazz neuf," 24.

69. Ibid., 26.

70. On French negrophilia of the 1920s and 1930s, see Petrine Archer-Straw, *Negrophilia: Avant-Garde Paris and Black Culture in the 1920s* (London: Thames and Hudson, 2000); and Brett Berliner, *Ambivalent Desire: The Exotic Black Other in Jazz-Age France* (Amherst: University of Massachusetts Press, 2002). For discussions of this dialectic with reference to the reception of jazz in interwar France, see Jackson, *Making Jazz French,* esp. chapter 4; and Andy Fry, "Beyond le Bœuf: Interdisciplinary Rereadings of Jazz in France," *Journal of the Royal Musical Association* 128 (2003): 137–53, esp. 142–43.

71. Ludovic Tournès, "La réinterpretation du jazz: un phénomène de contre-américanisation dans la France d'après-guerre (1945–1960)," in *Play it again Sim . . . : Hommages à Sim Copans,* special issue of *Revue française d'études américaines* (December 2001): 72–83; Matthew Jordan, "Jazz Changes: A History of French Discourse on Jazz from Ragtime to Be-Bop," Ph.D. diss., Claremont Graduate School, 1998, esp. 395–97.

72. Tournès, "La réinterpretation du jazz," 75.

73. John Gennari, *Blowing Hot and Cool: Jazz and Its Critics* (Chicago: University of Chicago Press, 2007), 152–53.

74. Penny von Eschen, *Satchmo Blows Up the World* (Cambridge, MA: Harvard University Press, 2004). See also Iain Anderson, *This Is Our Music: Free Jazz, the Sixties and American Culture* (Philadelphia: University of Pennsylvania Press, 2007), chapter 1.

75. Michel Dorigné, *Jazz,* vol. 1 (Paris: L'Ecole des loisirs, 1968), 4.

76. André Hodeir, *Jazz: Its Evolution and Essence,* trans. David Noakes (New York: Grove Press, 1956).

77. Ibid., 8.

78. Ibid., 8.

79. Ibid., 11.
80. Pierre Bourdieu et al., *Photography: A Middle-brow Art,* trans. Shaun Whiteside (Stanford, CA: Stanford University Press, 1990), 95–96.
81. Malson, "Editorial," *Les Cahiers du jazz* 16–17 (1968): 5.
82. See also Malson's overview of jazz's position in mid-sixties France in Malson, "Courrier des lecteurs," *Jazz-Hot* 209 (May 1965): 13.
83. Tournès, *New Orleans sur Seine,* 365.
84. Ibid., 368.
85. Anderson, *This Is Our Music,* 80 ff.
86. Hodeir in Malson et al., "Neuf entretiens sur le jazz neuf," 26.
87. Yves Buin, "La musique contre nous," *Jazz-Hot* 228 (February 1967): 26.
88. Philippe Carles and Jean-Louis Comolli, *Free Jazz Black Power* (Paris: Champs libres, 1971; reprint Paris: Gallimard, 2000).
89. Ibid., 39.
90. Ibid.
91. Ibid., 58.
92. Porter, *What Is This Thing Called Jazz?* 193.
93. Carles and Comolli, *Free Jazz Black Power,* 39.
94. Tournès, "La réinterpretation du jazz," 80. A similar argument is made by Elizabeth Vihlen, who writes that jazz offered "fans the chance to address the increasing problem of racism in their own country, helping them come to terms with the reality of French prejudices against minority populations." Elizabeth Vihlen, "Sounding French: Jazz in Postwar France," Ph.D. diss., SUNY Stonybrook, 2000, 3.
95. Frank Wright, cited in Michel Fabre, *From Harlem to Paris: Black American Writers in France, 1840–1980* (Urbana: University of Illinois Press, 1991), 260.
96. Angela Davis, *An Autobiography* (New York: Random House, 1974), 122.
97. Pierre Lasnier, "1910–1925: une diaspora musicale," *Droit et liberté* 279 (February 1969): 20.
98. Delfeil de Ton, liner notes to Archie Shepp and the Full Moon Ensemble, *Live in Antibes* vol. 1, Actuel/BYG 529338.
99. See, for instance, Denys Lemery, "7 noms, 7 têtes: Voici les nouveau-nés du Jazz français!!!!" *Jazz Magazine* 117 (April 1965): 39.
100. Bernard Vitet, in Paul Louis Rossi, "Un homme libre," *Jazz Magazine* 114 (January 1965): 40.
101. Paul Louis Rossi, "Polyvalent Portal," *Jazz Magazine* 142 (May 1967): 24–25.
102. Leméry, "7 noms, 7 têtes," 30.
103. Yves Buin, "La rêve et la liberté," *Jazz-Hot* 216 (January 1966): 17.
104. Michel Delorme, "Disques," *Jazz-Hot* 217 (February 1966): 30.
105. Yves Buin, "La musique contre nous," 27.
106. Ibid. Tixier-Vignancour was a far-right politician who ran for the presidency in 1965 and who counted Jean-Marie Le Pen among his advisers; Régie des tabacs was a cigarette manufacturer.
107. Portal, in Philippe Constantin, "Entretien: Michel Portal," *Jazz-Hot* 241 (May–July 1968): 15.

108. Portal in Constantin, "Entretien," 16. Similar comments can be found in interviews with Barney Wilen and Jean-Louis Chautemps. Wilen remarked that while French artists did have legitimate reasons for discontentment, they were "pas aussi grave que la situation de Monsieur Archie Shepp ou Monsieur Ayler." Wilen, in Cotro, *Chants libres,* 62. For Chautemps, the "weakness" of white jazz players can be attributed in the fact that their cause for revolt was "sinon absente, du moins dégradée." Chautemps, in Jean-Louis Ginibre, "Le libertaire controversé," *Jazz Magazine* 119 (June 1965): 61.

109. Jean-Robert Masson, "Jazz Meeting à la Mutualité," *Jazz Magazine* 130 (May 1966): 16.

110. See Pierre Cressant, "Qui a expulsé Clifford Thornton?" *Jazz-Hot* 271 (April 1971): 26.

111. Of particular note are the numerous benefit concerts held for the Black Panther Party during the late 1960s and early 1970s, such as the one that took place on 19 January 1969. Entitled "Jazz, Poésie et Pouvoir Noir," the evening featured films about the party, poetry recitals, and a performance of an ensemble led by Sunny Murray, featuring Vitet, Tusques, Guerin, Alan Silva, Ronnie Beer, and Kenneth Terroade. See Philippe Dubois, "Sunny Murray," *Jazz-Hot* 248 (March 1969): 8.

112. Michel Portal, in Lucien Malson, "Michel Portal, le musicien et la crise de la musique," *Le Monde,* 6 July 1972.

113. Tusques, in Philippe Carles, "Tusques: D'où viennent les sons justes?" *Jazz Magazine* 202 (July 1972): 22.

114. Tusques in "Un soir autour d'Ayler," *Jazz-Hot* 193 (October 1971): 5.

115. "Tusques parle," *Jazz Magazine* 185 (January 1971): 19.

116. Ibid.

117. For more on "La chasse au snark," see Michel Le Bris, "Briser la cercle magique des conventions," *Jazz-Hot* 247 (February 1969): 32–33.

118. A case in point was his multimedia piece "Qui a tué Albert Ayler?"

119. Clifford Allen, "François Tusques and the Nouveau Jazz Français," *All About Jazz,* available online at http://www.allaboutjazz.com/php/article.php?id =20242 (accessed 27 June 2007).

120. On "hermeneutic windows," see Lawrence Kramer, *Music as Cultural Practice, 1800–1900* (Berkeley: University of California Press, 1990), chapter 1.

121. Tusques in "Free', 'Jazz' et Tusques," *Jazz Magazine* 222 (May 1974): 6.

122. Tusques, in Carles, "Tusques: D'où viennent les sons justes?" 22.

123. Paul Alessandrini, "Free Jazz," *Actuel* 12 (September 1971): 72.

124. Gerard Terronès, "Cohelmec Quintet/François Tusques Quintet," *Jazz-Hot* 270 (March 1971): 25.

125. Willener, *Action-Image of Society.*

126. Beaud and Willener, *Musique et vie quotidienne.* Other texts privileging improvisation as a vehicle for individual liberation included Jacques Attali, *Noise: The Political Economy of Music,* trans. Brian Massumi (Minneapolis: University of Minnesota Press, 1985), esp. 138–40; and Denis Levaillant, *L'Improvisation musicale: Essai sur la puissance du Jeu* (Paris: Lattès, 1981).

127. Tournès, *New Orleans sur Seine,* 397.

128. Hamon and Rotman, *Génération,* 2: 160–62. See also Tournès, *New Orleans sur Seine,* 397.

129. Particularly important in this regard was the recasting of regions as "internal colonies" of France. On the connections between the regionalist movements of the 1970s and anticolonial discourse, see Herman Lebovics, *Bringing the Empire Back Home: France in the Global Age* (Durham, NC: Duke University Press, 2004), esp. chapter 1; and Eric Drott, "The *Nòva Cançon Occitana* and the Internal Colonial Thesis," *French Politics, Culture & Society* (forthcoming). For an overview of immigrant rights movements of this period, see Catherine Lloyd, *Discourses of Antiracism in France* (Aldershot: Ashgate, 1998).

130. Cotro, *Chants libres,* 131, 194, and 231–32.

CHAPTER 4

The chapter epigraph is from *Actuel 6* (March 1971): 6.

1. On *L'Idiot international,* see André Bercoff, *L'autre France: L'Underpresse* (Paris: Stock, 1975), 53–61; and Hervé Hamon and Patrick Rotman, *Génération* (Paris: Seuil, 1987), 2: 108–9.

2. Bercoff, *L'autre France,* 55.

3. Bruno Queysanne, "Liberté! Liberté!" *L'Idiot international* 1 (December 1969): 15–25.

4. Ibid., 16.

5. Ibid.

6. Ibid., 17.

7. Ibid.

8. Ibid., 19.

9. Ibid., 20.

10. Ibid., 17.

11. Ibid., 22.

12. See, in particular, Stuart Hall and Tony Jefferson, eds., *Resistance through Rituals: Youth Subcultures in Post-war Britain* (London: Routledge, 1993).

13. Queysanne, "Liberté! Liberté!" 25.

14. Ibid. The term "subcultural capital" is Sarah Thornton's. See Thornton, *Club Cultures: Music, Media and Subcultural Capital* (Hanover, NH: Wesleyan University Press, 1995), 11–14.

15. Ibid.

16. Ibid.

17. See, for example, the August 1969 issue of *Rock & Folk,* esp. Philippe Paringaux, "Soft Machine à Paris," *Rock & Folk* 31 (August 1969): 6; and Jacques Barsamian, "Le Triangle," *Rock & Folk* 31 (August 1969): 5–6.

18. On the contrast between American and French underground presses, see Edgar Morin, *Journal de Californie* (Paris: Seuil, 1970), 23.

19. Michel Lancelot, *Je veux regarder Dieu en face: Vie, mort et résurrection des Hippies* (Paris: Albin Michel, 1968); Morin, *Journal de Californie;* Bernard

Plossu, *Pourquoi n'êtes-vous pas hippie?* (Paris: Editions La Palatine, 1970); Henri Cartier and Mitsou Naslednikov, *L'univers des hippies* (Paris: Fayard, 1970); and the final chapter of Jean-François Revel, *Ni Marx ni Jésus: De la seconde révolution américaine à la seconde révolution mondiale* (Paris: Laffont, 1970). A summary of French attitudes toward the counterculture can be found in Richard Kuisel, *Seducing the French: The Dilemma of Americanization* (Berkeley: University of California Press, 1993), 198–201.

20. Theodore Roszak, *The Making of a Counter Culture: Reflections on the Technocratic Society and Its Youthful Opposition* (Garden City, NY: Anchor Books, 1969).

21. Compare Henri Cartier's description of the hippies as being "very much the children of America." Cartier and Naslednikov, *L'univers des hippies,* 8.

22. See, for instance, Alain Dister's comments in "Psychédelic, Qu'est-ce que c'est?" *Rock & Folk* 6 (April 1967): 39.

23. Patrick Thevenon, "Les hippies à Paris," *L'Express* 852 (16 October 1967): 134; Jacques Mousseau, "Ils veulent un monde spirituel," *Planète* 39 (March–April 1968): 117; and Morin, *Journal de Californie,* 138.

24. Chris Warne, "Bringing Counterculture to France: *Actuel* Magazine and the Legacy of May '68," *Modern & Contemporary France* 15, no. 3 (August 2007): 313.

25. Michel-Claude Jalard, in Plossu, *Pourquoi n'êtes-vous pas hippie?* 13. A similar sentiment is expressed in Dister, "Psychédelic, Qu'est-ce que c'est?" 39.

26. Editor's introduction to Stuart Hall, "La contre-société hippie," *Politique aujourd'hui* 5 (May 1970): 75.

27. Liner notes to *Les Fleurs de Pavot,* Underground Masters UM009.

28. Jean Chalvidant and Hervé Mouvet, *La belle histoire des groupes de rock français des années 60* (Paris: Fernand Lanore/Sorlot, 2002), 28.

29. For information on these two journals and their place in the musical press, see Mat Pires, "The Popular Music Press," in *Popular Music in France from Chanson to Techno: Culture, Identity and Society,* ed. Hugh Dauncey and Steve Cannon (Aldershot, UK: Ashgate, 2003), 90–93. On the origins of *Rock & Folk,* see Philippe Koechlin, *Memoires de rock et de folk* (Bordeaux: Le Castor Astral, 2007); and Christophe Quillien, *Génération Rock & Folk: 40 ans de culture rock* (Paris: Flammarion, 2006).

30. Jacques Barsamian, "Campus 70," *Rock & Folk* 33 (October 1969): 5.

31. Hennion and Vignolle observe that the resilience of the French chanson and *variétés* allowed the local record industry to "resist" English-language pop through the 1960s and '70s. Antoine Hennion and Jean-Pierre Vignolle, *L'économie du disque en France* (Paris: La Documentation Française, 1978), 43.

32. These observations are based on a survey of French sales charts published in the "Hits of the World" section of *Billboard* magazine and the "Hit Parade France" section of *Journal du Show Business.*

33. The last week of October 1968, for instance, saw six Anglo-American acts in the top ten. "Hit-Parade National no. 1," *Journal du Show Business* no. 3 (18 October 1968), 27.

34. On the differences between French and Anglo-American production techniques, see Thierry Nolan, "The Big Fashion for English Sound is Now Slowly Dying in France," *Journal du Show Business* 24 (14 March 1969): 17–18.

35. Rock's trajectory in France accords with the pattern of development of national rock styles that Roger Wallis and Krister Malm have outlined: an initial stage of Anglo-American dominance during the 1950s and 1960s was succeeded (circa 1970) by a second stage of "transculturation." Roger Wallis and Krister Malm, *Big Sounds from Small Peoples: The Music Industry in Small Countries* (New York: Pendragon, 1984), 297–311.

36. Christian Victor and Julien Regoli, *Vingt ans de rock français* (Paris: Albin Michel, 1978), 89–108; Looseley, *Popular Music in Contemporary France: Authenticity, Politics, Debate* (Oxford: Berg, 2003), 39–40; and Gilles Verlant, ed., *L'Encyclopédie du rock français* (Paris: Hors Collection, 2000), chapter 4.

37. Frederick Grasser, "La pop-music absente de la TV: le 'racisme anti-jeunes' se développe," *Journal du Show Business* 49 (7 November 1969), 1 and 17; Jacques LeBlanc, "Télé/Radio," *Pop 2000* 4 (18 March 1972): n.p. In addition to their paucity, television programs dedicated to rock were broadcast infrequently. See Gilles Pidard, "Rock et télévision: un rendez-vous manqué? Les émissions musicales pour la jeunesse," in Evelyne Cohen and Marie-Françoise Lévy, *La Télévision des Trente Glorieuses: Culture et Politique* (Paris: CNRS Editions, 2007), 145–61.

38. The band Maajun, for instance, complained that their debut album *Vivre le mort du vieux monde* was held back by the record company Vogue on account of its incendiary lyrics. See Philippe Koechlin, "Pop en France," *Rock & Folk* 48 (February 1971): 63.

39. Ibid., 64.

40. Gérome Guibert, *La production de la culture: Le cas des musiques amplifiées en France* (Paris: IRMA, 2006), 132.

41. Koechlin, "Pop en France," 64.

42. Jacques Panisset, in "Courrier," *Rock & Folk* 49 (February 1971): 27.

43. Philippe Paringaux, in "Disques du mois," *Rock & Folk* 31 (August 1969): 63.

44. Ibid.

45. Paul Alessandrini, "Pop français," *Rock & Folk* 43 (August 1970): 52.

46. P.-O. Seignon, "Où en est la pop music en France," *Pop Music/Superhebdo* 103 (6 April 1972): 14; see also "L'eur-rock est né," *Actuel* 12 (September 1971): 12, for a similar argument.

47. Jacques Chabiron, "Opération 666," *Rock & Folk* 37 (February 1970): 60.

48. Thierry Lewin, in "Dictionnaire de la pop music française," *Pop Music* 35 (26 November 1970): 13.

49. Philippe Constantin, "Pop et profit, le changement dans la continuité," *Musique en jeu* 2 (March 1971): 100; "Méchamment rock," *Charlie hebdo* 134 (11 June 1973): 11.

50. *Rock & Folk* 44 (September 1970).

51. Jean-François Bizot, "Pop en hausse," *L'Express* 969 (2 February 1970): 88; Anne Ginestou, "70% des ventes disquaires pour la pop music anglo-saxonnes

en France," *Journal du Show Business* 79 (19 June 1970): 1 and 15; and Monique Annaud, "Philips: 35% d'augmentation en 1 an pour la pop-music anglo-saxonne," *Journal du Show Business* 85 (4 September 1970): 1 and 11.

52. For instance, Pathé-Marconi (EMI) reported that twenty-five thousand direct imports were sold in France in October 1969 alone. Michael Way, "From the Music Capitals of the World: Paris," *Billboard* 81, no. 49 (6 December 1969): 62. See also "Le grand rush des disques d'importations," *Journal du Show Business* 94 (6 November 1970): 11.

53. Constantin, "Pop et profit," 97.

54. See, for instance, the Polydor advertisement in *Rock & Folk* 37 (February 1970): 10.

55. Philippe Koechlin, "De Coleman à Pink Floyd," *Nouvel Observateur* 268 (12 December 1969): 43; Chabiron, "Opération 666," 56–61; and Paul Alessandrini, "Pop aux Halles," *Rock & Folk* 37 (February 1970): 13–15.

56. "Le choc Woodstock," *Salut les copains* 96 (August 1970): 28–31; "Le cyclone Woodstock deferle sur Paris," *Pariscope* 113 (24 June 1970); Jean-François Bizot, "Au royaume de l'innocence pop," *L'Express* 989 (22 June 1970); "Woodstock—L'Extraordinaire Film Sur La Nouvelle Generation," *Nouveau Cinemonde* 1838 (2 June 1970); and Philippe Koechlin, "Woodstock contre Amougies," *Nouvel Observateur* 290 (1 June 1970): 45.

57. François Jouffa, "La salle de concert traditionnelle a éclaté," *Pop music* 5 (30 April 1970); reprinted in Jouffa, *La culture pop des années 70: Le pop-notes de François Jouffa* (Paris: Spengler, 1994), 1.

58. Paul Alessandrini, "Le public pop," *Rock & Folk* 41 (June 1970): 101.

59. Ibid., 67.

60. Serge Berstein and Jean-Pierre Rioux, *La France de l'expansion 2: L'apogée Pompidou (1969–1974)* (Paris: Seuil, 1995), 62–63.

61. On police repression of dissent during the *après-mai* period, see Maurice Rajsfus, *Mai 1968: sous les pavés, la répression: juin 1968–mars 1974* (Paris: Le Cherche midi éditeur, 1998).

62. Cited in Hamon and Rotman, *Génération*, 2: 188. See also Christophe Bourseiller, *Les maoistes: La folle histoire des gardes rouges français* (Paris: Plon, 2006), 277–79.

63. "Procès de *L'Idiot international*," *L'Idiot liberté* 7 (16 June 1971): 9.

64. *Journal officiel*, 9 June 1970, 5324.

65. Ibid.

66. François Jouffa, "Les festivals pop: L'avenir est sombre," *Pop Music* 14 (2 July 1970): 19.

67. Philippe Koechlin, "La chasse au pop'," *Nouvel Observateur* 299 (3 August 1970): 26.

68. "Les festivals pop' interdits," *Le Monde,* 25 July 1970, 24; and François Jouffa, "Tous les festivals interdits," *Pop Music* 17 (23 July 1970): 1 and 7.

69. Guillemette de Véricourt, "Les anti-pop," *L'Express* 995 (3 August 1970): 46.

70. Ibid.

71. Hamon and Rotman, *Génération*, 2: 187–88.

72. "Projet de manifeste du mouvement de la jeunesse: Pour que l'été soit chaud et la rentrée brûlante!" *La Cause du peuple* 25 (16 June 1970): 7.

73. Bourseiller, *Les maoistes,* 280; Jean-Pierre Le Goff, *Mai 68, l'héritage impossible* (Paris: La Découverte, 2002), 180.

74. "Projet de manifeste," 7.

75. "Marseille: A la Valbarelle le terrain de jeu est à nous, pas aux flics," *La Cause du peuple* 28 (September 1970): 5.

76. "Des groupes 'Alain Geismar est partout' . . . ," *La Cause du peuple* 28 (September 1970): 12.

77. "Les festivals pop' interdits," 24.

78. De Véricourt, "Les anti-pop," 46.

79. Claude Clément, *Faites l'amour et plus la guerre* (Paris: Fayard, 1971), 325.

80. "Les festivals pop': Le maire d'Aix-en-Provence s'explique sur l'arrêté d'interdiction," *Le Monde,* 26–27 July 1970, 16.

81. Michèle Manceaux, "La guerre du pop'," *Nouvel Observateur* 300 (10 August 1970): 20.

82. Jouffa, "Tous les festivals interdits," 7.

83. Martin Even, "Aix-en-Provence: la pop' music a manqué son entrée en France," *Le Monde,* 4 August 1970, 11; François Jouffa, "Le festival saboté," *Pop Music* 19 (6 August 1970): 1 and 3.

84. Manceaux, "La guerre du pop'," 20–21.

85. Paul Alessandrini, "Antibes, Valbonne, Saint-Paul-de-Vence, Biot ou la longue marche," *Rock & Folk* 44 (September 1970): 60.

86. "Les festivals pop' interdits," 24. According to Clément, the *harkis* were employed to clear the site, not provide security. Clément, *Faites l'amour,* 337.

87. Ibid., 339–40.

88. Ibid., 338; Jacques Vassal, "Aix-en-Provence ou la grande confusion," *Rock & Folk* 44 (September 1970): 62.

89. Clément, *Faites l'amour,* 339.

90. Claude Fléouter, "Les festivals de pop' music pourront-ils connaître le succès en France," *Le Monde,* 8 August 1970, 16.

91. Jean-François Bizot, "Été 70, Festival de Biot: Mais qui va payer la pop au peuple?" (1970), reprinted in *Underground: L'histoire* (Paris: Denoël, 2001), 108.

92. Ibid., 109.

93. Ibid.

94. Fléouter, "Les festivals de pop'," 16.

95. René François Cristiani, "L'histoire des festivals ou 'salauds de jeunes'," *Rock & Folk* 44 (September 1970): 55.

96. Ibid.; Vassal, "Aix-en-Provence," 62.

97. Fléouter, "Les festivals de pop'," 16. See also Jean-Noël Coghe and Jacques Barsamian, "Aix: un Woodstock à la française raté," *Pop Music* 19 (6 August 1970): 2–3.

98. Philippe Koechlin, "Le pop' et la fureur," *Nouvel Observateur* 304 (7 September 1970): 33.

99. See François Jouffa, "A Wight, heure par heure," *Pop Music* 23 (3 September 1970): 2–3; Catherine Claude, "J'accuse: on est en train de tuer la Pop Music française," *Pop Music* 25 (17 September 1970): 16.

100. "On nous écrit," *Pop Music* 27 (1 October 1970): 2.

101. Vassal, "Aix-en-Provence," 62.

102. "Courrier," *Rock & Folk* 45 (October 1970): 94.

103. Ibid.

104. Warne, "Bringing Counterculture to France," 319.

105. "F.L.I.P.," *Tout* 3 (29 October 1970): 3. The manifesto was also reprinted in Françoise Seloron, "La pop sauvage," *Rock & Folk* 52 (May 1971): 54–57.

106. Ibid.

107. Ibid.

108. Ibid.

109. Ibid.

110. "Rolling Stones: pas d'histoires d'argent entre nous," *Tout* 2 (8 October 1970): 8.

111. Ibid.

112. Philippe Paringaux, "La Ménagerie de verre, ou les confidences de Mick Jagger," *Rock & Folk* 45 (November 1970): 44.

113. "Rolling Stones: pas d'histoires d'argent entre nous," 8.

114. Ibid.

115. Seloron, "La pop sauvage," 57.

116. "Free, pop et politique," *Actuel* 6 (March 1971): 6–7.

117. "La jeunesse contre le vieux monde," *L'Idiot Liberté* 2 (January 1971): 21.

118. "La mouvement POP ça ne se recopie pas," *Tout* 1 (23 September 1970): 4.

119. Daniel Bensaïd, André Milos, and Camille Paulet, "Art et socialisme (II)," *Rouge* 105 (15 March 1971): 13.

120. Eugène Vincent, "Gimme Shelter: Le face sombre de la pop music," *Rouge* 125 (25 September 1971): 11.

121. On Vive la révolution, see Le Goff, *Mai 68, l'héritage impossible*, 154–56; Bourseiller, *Les maoistes*, 186–98 and 259–74; A. Belden Fields, *Trotskyism and Maoism: Theory and Practice in France and the United States* (New York: Praeger, 1988), 99–101; and Michel-Antoine Burnier and Bernard Kouchner, *La France Sauvage* (Paris: Editions Publications Premières, 1970), 185–93. For discussions that address *Tout!* specifically, see Le Goff, *Mai 68, l'héritage impossible*, 275–78; and Bercoff, *L'autre France*, 70–75.

122. "Lutte—Critique—Unité," *Vive la révolution*, 5 June 1970, 7.

123. "Vive les festivals POP ou à bas les festivals POP," *Tout* 1 (23 September 1970): 4.

124. Ibid.

125. "Rolling Stones: pas d'histoires d'argent entre nous," 8; and "F.L.I.P.," 3.

126. "Tout? Un nouveau journal," *Tout!* 1 (23 September 1970): 1–2.

127. "Mai 68 = Woodstock?" *Tout!* 4 (16 November 1970): 4.

128. Ibid.

129. "Je fais une disque," *Tout* 3 (29 October 1970): 6.

130. Le Goff, *Mai 68, l'héritage impossible,* 155. Le Goff attributes Vive la révolution's emphasis on the agency of the working class to the influence of Italian autonomist groups.

131. G.H., "Ici et maintenant," *Tout* 2 (8 October 1970): 3.

132. Helène, cited in "V.L.R.: Peut-on être heureux à la Courneuve?" *Actuel* 7 (April 1971): 5.

133. Roland Castro, cited in ibid.

134. "Libre disposition de notre corps," *Tout!* 12 (23 April 1971).

135. Fréderic Martel, *The Pink and the Black: Homosexuals in France since 1968,* trans. Marie Jane Todd (Stanford, CA: Stanford University Press, 1999), 22–23; Bourseiller, *Les maoistes,* 272–73.

136. Léon Mercadet, Jean-François Bizot, Michel-Antoine Burnier, Patrick Rambaud, and Jean-Pierre Lentin, *Actuel par Actuel: Chronique d'un journal et de ses lecteurs, 1970–1975* (Paris: Editions Stock, 1977), 33.

137. The dossier, entitled "Free, pop et politique," also included excerpts from Carles and Comolli's recently published *Free Jazz Black Power* and profiles of Country Joe McDonald and the French band Maajun. See *Actuel* 6 (March 1971): 6–20.

138. Paul Alessandrini, "L'Agit pop," *Actuel* 6 (March 1971): 14.

139. Ibid.

140. Ibid., 15.

141. Ibid., 13.

142. Peter Starr, *Logics of Failed Revolt: French Theory After May '68* (Stanford, CA: Stanford University Press, 1995), 27.

143. Guy Hocquenghem, "Le quotidien déprivatisé par 'Tout'," *Tout!* 1 (23 September 1970); reprinted in *L'après-mai des faunes: volutions* (Paris: Bernard Grasset, 1974), 77.

144. "La révolution pour le plaisir," *Actuel* 7 (April 1971): 2.

145. Ibid.

146. "Editorial," *Actuel* 10–11 (July–August 1971): 2.

147. Henri Weber, "Où en sont les maoïstes? (1): VLR," *Rouge* 87 (9 November 1970): 12.

148. Christiane Tillier, "Le groupe VLR se dissout," *Rouge* 111 (26 April 1971): 14.

149. Ibid.

150. "Le bonheur c'est la lutte," *Cause du peuple* 38 (8 April 1971): 10.

151. Ibid.

152. Ibid.

153. "Lyon: La voie de l'union," *Cause du peuple* 38 (8 April 1971): 10.

154. Ibid., 11.

155. Ibid.

156. Renewed fascination with the *fête* can be found in a range of scholarly books and articles, including Jean Duvignaud, *Fêtes et civilisations* (Paris: Weber, 1973); Jean Verger, "Fête et révolution," *Tribune socialiste* 579 (23 May 1973): n.p.; Jean-François Held, "La fête retrouvée," *Nouvel Observateur* 433 (14 July 1973): 41–43; Yves-Marie Bercé, *Fête et révolte: Des mentalités populaires du XVIe au XVIIIe siècle* (Paris: Hachette, 1976); *La fête, cette hantise!, Autrement*

7 (November 1976); and Jean-Jacques Wunenberger, *La fête, le jeu et le sacré* (Paris: Editions universitaires, 1977).

157. Cf. the remarks of Gérard Belloin in a roundtable discussion on the *fête:* "Aller à la fête, faire la fête, c'est introduire un temps de rupture dans le quotidien de la vie, qui le dépasse et peut anticiper sur son devenir." Gérard Belloin et al., "Dis-moi comment tu fais la fête," *France Nouvelle* 1589 (26 April 1976): 45.

158. This argument is made in Henry Skoff Torgue, *La Pop Music* (Paris: Presses universitaires de France, 1975), 85–86.

159. Ramon, "De festivals sans fête à fête sans festival," *France Nouvelle* 1299 (30 September 1970): 30–31.

160. "Incidents au Marché aux Puces: 86 personnes ont été interpellées," *Le Monde,* 23 March 1971, 28; Seloron, "La pop sauvage," 57; and "Vivre et vaincre ensemble: la révolution, c'est la vie," *Tout* 15 (30 June 1971): 8. Other such *fêtes* included a self-described *fête révolutionnaire* held at the Ecole normale supérieure in Paris and the aforementioned celebration organized by students in Lyon. See Antoine de Gaudemar in "Actes de vandalisme à l'Ecole normale supérieure à l'occasion d'une 'fête' révolutionnaire," *Le Monde,* 23 March 1971, 28; Jacques Paugam, *Génération perdue* (Paris: Robert Laffont, 1977), 209–11; and Hamon and Rotman, *Génération,* 2: 307–9.

161. Jean-Marc Pascal, "Le Bateau ivre," *Pop Music* 45 (11 February 1971): 4; Martin Even, "Concert pop' et guerilla," *Le Monde,* 2 February 1971, 23; and Philippe Paringaux, "Révolution au palais," *Rock & Folk* 50 (March 1971): 73.

162. Paringaux, "Révolution au palais," 74.

163. Even, "Concert pop' et guerilla," 23.

164. Pascal, "Le Bateau ivre," 4.

165. Paringaux, "Révolution au palais," 74.

166. J.-P.S., "Au Palais des Sports," *Tout* 9 (18 February 1971): 7. The initials J.-P.S. refer to Jean-Paul Sartre, who agreed to be designated the editor of *Tout!* as a way of protecting the publication against the threat of prosecution. It is unlikely that he participated in writing the article.

167. Ibid.

168. Pascal, "Le Bateau ivre." For a similar interpretation of the event, see Paringaux, "Révolution au palais," 74.

169. Benoît Gautier, "La Pop Music en danger," *Pop Music* 45 (11 February 1971), 4. Similar criticisms were aired by satirist Delfeil de Ton in "Au Palais des Sports, il pleuvait des gaufres," *Charlie-Hebdo* 12 (8 February 1971): n.p.; and in letters by Philippe Barjaud and Denis Seignez, in "Courrier," *Rock & Folk* 50 (March 1971): 27.

170. Jacques Chabiron, "Sac à pop," in "Courrier," *Rock & Folk* 51 (April 1971): 23.

171. See Jouffa, *La culture pop,* 132; and Koechlin, *Memoires,* 112.

172. Jean-Pierre Lentin, "Je hais les festivals," *Actuel* 24 (October 1972): 33.

173. On these crossover phenomena, see Victor and Regoli, *Vingt ans de rock français,* 136 and 129–30, respectively.

174. Alessandrini, "L'ouragan rock: une illusion éclatée," *La fête, cette hantise,* 98.

175. For the history of this event, see Noëlle Gérôme and Danielle Tarta-kowsky, *La fête de l'Humanité: Culture communiste, culture populaire* (Paris: Messidor/Editions Sociales, 1988); and Catherine Claude, *C'est la fête de l'Humanité* (Paris: Editeurs français réunis, 1977).

176. Gérôme and Tartakowsky, *La fête de l'Humanité*, 116–17.

177. Ibid., 138.

178. Paul Alessandrini, "Pop à l'Huma," *Rock & Folk* 45 (October 1970): 9; and Philippe Garnier, "Summertime Blues," *Rock & Folk* 81 (October 1973): 68.

179. Alain Dister, "Une fête populaire," *Rock & Folk* 57 (October 1971): 66.

180. Ibid.

181. Jean-Claude Gambert, "Des Musiciens à la chaine," *Pop Music* 114 (14 September 1972): 12.

182. On *fêtes contestataires* in 1970s France, see the essays by Paul Ariès and Noëlle Gérôme in Alain Corbin, Noëlle Gérôme, and Danielle Tartakowsky, *Les usages politiques des fêtes aux XIXe–XXe siècles* (Paris: Publications de la Sorbonne, 1994), 327–36 and 361–76, respectively.

183. "Printemps show," *Tribune socialiste* 578 (16 May 1973): 20.

184. Patrick Mignon, "Evolution de la prise en compte des musiques ampli-fiées par les politiques publiques," in *Politiques publiques et musiques ampli-fiées* (Adem-Florida: Conseil Régional d'Aquitaine, 1997), 24.

185. Verger, "Fête et révolution," n.p.

186. On the interdiction of the Ligue communiste révolutionnaire, see Hamon and Rotman, *Génération*, 2: chapter 14. On the disbanding of the GP, see Bourseiller, *Les maoistes*, 331–34.

187. Gérôme and Tartakowsky, *La fête de l'Humanité*, 120.

CHAPTER 5

The chapter epigraph is from François Delalande, "L'animation: une force au sein du système social de la musique," presentation given at the 1° Colloquio di Animazione Musicale: Animazione musicale: un binomio ancora fantastico?, Lecco, Italy (29 October 2005). Available online at http://musicheria.net/home/default.asp?id_testo=696&pagina=Studi%20e%20ricerche (accessed 4 May 2009).

1. "Création et diffusion musicale," *Développement culturel* 38 (June 1978): 1.

2. Pierre-Michel Menger, *Le paradoxe du musicien: Le compositeur, le mélo-mane et l'état dans la société contemporain* (Paris: Flammarion, 1983), 322. Statistics for record sales are given on page 323. See also Michel de Coster, *Le disque, art ou affaires? Analyse sociologique d'une industrie culturelle* (Grenoble: Presses universitaires de Grenoble, 1976), 44–45.

3. Maurice Fleuret, "Itinéraire sans horizon," *Nouvel Observateur* 471 (19 November 1973).

4. Gérard Mannoni, "Festival d'Automne: une semaine de déception," *Le Quotidien de Paris*, 2 November 1975.

5. Jean-Michel Damian, "La mode rétro," *Politique hebdo* 124 (18 April 1974): 26. For a similar critique, see Patrick Szersnovicz, "11e festival d'art contemporain de Royan," *Art Press* 12 (June–August 1974): 32.

6. "La musique contemporaine en question," *Musique en jeu* 25 (November 1976): 2.

7. "Les festivals et leur public," *Développement culturel* 28 (March 1976): 1.

8. Damian, "La mode rétro," 26.

9. Renato Poggioli, *The Theory of the Avant-Garde,* trans. Gerald Fitzgerald (Cambridge, MA: Harvard University Press, 1968), 8–12.

10. Sylvie de Nussac, "Les grande marché des contemporains," *L'Express* 883 (20 May 1968): 118.

11. "Les bruits du hasard: John Cage," *Actuel* 2 (November 1970): 42–45; "Là-haut sur la colline," *Actuel* 8 (May 1971): 48–51; "Musica Electronica Viva," *Parapluie* 2 (January–February 1971): 19.

12. Antoine Golea, "La Semaine de musique contemporaine de Paris," *Journal musical français / Musica disques* 176 (January 1969): 25; Michel Louvet, in "Les journées de musique contemporaine," *Courrier musical de France* 24 (1968): 223.

13. The program for the festival can be found in *La Revue Musicale* 265–66 (1969): 21, 43, 77, and 97–98.

14. Maurice Fleuret, "Bilan et leçon des journées de musique contemporaine," *La Revue Musicale* 265–66 (1969): 7.

15. Ibid.

16. Michel Granlet, "Le journal des journées," *La Revue musicale* 267 (1969): 9.

17. Fleuret, "Bilan et leçon," 7.

18. Christiane Duparc, "Un merveilleux scandale," *Nouvel Observateur* 208 (4 November 1968): 46.

19. For another evocation of May, see Fleuret, "Bilan et leçon," 10.

20. On the 1969 Royan festival, see Jacques Longchampt, "Nomos Gamma de Xenakis au Festival de Royan," *Le Monde,* 9 April 1969, 14. Henri Besançon notes that reduced ticket prices for students explains somewhat this increase in attendance. Henri Besançon, *Festival International d'Art Contemporain de Royan, 1964–1977* (Royan: Bonne Anse, 2007), 42–43.

21. Jean Lacouture, "Un nouvel art d'écouter?" *Le Monde,* 29 October 1969, 23.

22. An overview of the expanding range of aesthetic tendencies after 1968 can be found in Pierre-Albert Castanet, *Tout est bruit pour qui a peur: Pour une histoire sociale du son sale* (Paris: Michel de Maule, 1999), esp. 84–104.

23. François Madurell, *L'Ensemble Ars Nova: Une contribution au pluralisme esthétique dans la musique contemporaine (1963–1987)* (Paris: Harmattan, 2003), 331 ff.

24. For statistics on sales of contemporary music recordings, see Menger, *Le paradoxe du musicien,* 323. As for attendance at music festivals, the records for SMIP housed at the Médiathèque Mahler Musicale give some indication of the genre's declining popularity. SMIP's high point was 1970, with an average attendance of 820 per concert that year. By 1971 this number had dropped to 600, and by 1973 it had dropped yet again to 533. (After 1973 SMIP was absorbed into the newly founded Festival d'automne.) SMIP archives, Fonds Maurice Fleuret, Médiathèque Mahler Musicale.

25. Paul Alessandrini, "Les Outrances de Cage," *Rock & Folk* 46 (December 1970): 7–9.

26. Jean-François Hirsch, "L'oreille froide," *Musique en jeu* 1 (November 1970): 99.

27. Ibid., 99.

28. Ibid, 101.

29. Efforts to democratize access to music did not commence with the Fifth Republic, having long been an objective of state cultural policy in France. For examples of late-nineteenth-century policies that adumbrate those discussed in the present chapter, see Jann Pasler, *Composing the Citizen: Music as Public Utility in Third Republic France* (Berkeley: University of California Press, 2009), 201–2, 269–70, 319–24, and 328–30. For Popular Front–era initiatives for democratizing access to music, see Christopher Moore, "Music in France and the Popular Front (1934–1938): Politics, Aesthetics and Reception," Ph.D. diss., McGill University, 2006; and Jane Fulcher, *The Composer as Intellectual: Music and Ideology in France* (Oxford: Oxford University Press, 2005), 211 ff.

30. Menger, *Le paradoxe du musicien,* 118.

31. Commission nationale pour l'étude des problèmes de la musique, *Rapport générale 1963–4* (Paris: Ministère d'État des Affaires Culturelles, 1964), 12.

32. Ibid., 44–46.

33. Ibid., 12.

34. Ibid., 13.

35. Ibid., 78.

36. Ibid., 67.

37. Ibid.

38. On the controversy surrounding Landowski's appointment, see Joan Peyser, *Boulez: Composer, Conductor, Enigma* (New York: Schirmer, 1976), 174; Dominique Jameux, *Pierre Boulez,* trans. Susan Bradshaw (Cambridge, MA: Harvard University Press, 1991), 138–40; and Georgina Born, *Rationalizing Culture: IRCAM, Boulez and the Institutionalization of the Avant-garde* (Berkeley: University of California Press, 1995), 82–83. For Landowski's version of events, see Marcel Landowski, *Batailles pour la musique* (Paris: Seuil, 1979), 14–21; for Biasini's, see Emile Biasini, *Grands travaux: de l'Afrique au Louvre* (Paris: Odile Jacob, 1995), 156–60.

39. Pierre Boulez, "Why I Say No to Malraux" (1966), in *Orientations,* ed. Jean-Jacques Nattiez, trans. Martin Cooper (Cambridge, MA: Harvard University Press, 1986), 442.

40. Ibid.

41. Marcel Landowski, "Plan de dix ans pour l'organisation des structures musicales françaises," in *Les politiques culturelles en France,* ed. Philippe Poirrier (Paris: La Documentation Française, 2002), 265–68.

42. Ibid., 265.

43. Ibid., 266.

44. Ibid., 266–67.

45. Ibid., 267.

46. For overviews of Malraux's ideas on art's role in contemporary society, see David Looseley, *The Politics of Fun: Cultural Policy and Debate in Contemporary*

France (Oxford: Berg, 1995), 36–37; and Herman Lebovics, *Mona Lisa's Escort: André Malraux and the Reinvention of French Culture* (Ithaca, NY: Cornell University Press, 1999), 65–67 and 79–82.

47. On the Maison de la Culture of the Popular Front era, see Leslie Sprout, "Music for a 'New Era': Composers and National Identity in France 1936–1946," Ph.D. diss., University of California at Berkeley, 2000, 10–12; and Moore, "Music in France and the Popular Front," 98–100.

48. First popularized by Lucien Gravier in *Paris et le désert français* (Paris: Le Portulan, 1947), the term *cultural desert* was a commonplace of ministry discourse in the 1960s. See, for instance, Lucien Attoun, "M. Philippe Saint-Marc: Pour remédier au désert culturel français," *Nouvelles littéraires* 2195 (16 October 1969): 11.

49. Malraux, "Speech given on the occasion of the inauguration of the House of Culture at Amiens on 19 March 1966," in *French Cultural Policy Debates*, ed. Jeremy Ahearne (London: Routledge, 2002), 58.

50. Pierre Moinot, "Les Maisons de la Culture" (1961), reprinted in *André Malraux, Ministre: Les affaires culturelles au temps d'André Malraux 1959–1969*, by Comité d'histoire du ministre de la culture (Paris: La Documentation Française, 1996), 384.

51. Brian Rigby, *Popular Culture in Modern France: A Study of Cultural Discourse* (London: Routledge, 1991), 133–34.

52. Malraux, cited in J.C. Bécane, *L'Expérience des maisons de la culture* (Paris: La Documentation Française, 1973), 54.

53. Ibid., 6. The term *dirigisme culturel* is Bécane's.

54. Cited in Lebovics, *Mona Lisa's Escort*, 99.

55. The role of colonial administrators in the early years of the Ministry of Cultural Affairs is discussed in Lebovics, *Bringing the Empire Back Home: France in the Global Age* (Durham, NC: Duke University Press), 58–82; and Marie-Ange Rauch, *Le Bonheur d'entreprendre: Les administrateurs de la France d'outre-mer et la creation du Ministère des Affaires Culturelles* (Paris: Collection du Comité d'histoire du ministère de la culture et de la communication, 1998). Kristin Ross notes that the transfer of colonial "administrative techniques" to metropolitan France was not limited to cultural matters. Ross, *Fast Cars, Clean Bodies: Decolonization and the Reordering of French Culture* (Cambridge, MA: MIT Press, 1996), 7.

56. Rigby, *Popular Culture in Modern France*, 48.

57. Cited in Bécane, *L'Expérience des maisons de la culture*, 32.

58. Louis Althusser, "Ideology and Ideological State Apparatuses (Notes towards an Investigation)" (1970), in *Lenin and Philosophy*, trans. Benjamin Brewster (New York: Monthly Review Press, 1972).

59. Bernard Miège, Jacques Ion, and Alain-Noël Roux, *L'Appareil d'action culturelle* (1974), cited in Rigby, *Popular Culture in Modern France*, 150.

60. Jean Caune, *La culture en action: De Vilar à Lang, le sens perdu* (Grenoble: Presses universitaires de Grenoble, 1999), 198–201.

61. The statistics for Amiens are given in Bécane, *L'Expérience des maisons de la culture*, 23.

62. Pierre Bourdieu, "L'école conservatrice. Les inégalités devant l'école et devant la culture," *Revue française de sociologie* 7, no. 3 (July–September 1966): 344.

63. "Déclaration de Villeurbanne, 25/5/68," reprinted in Francis Jeanson, *L'Action culturelle dans la cité* (Paris: Seuil, 1973), 119. Translated in Alain Schnapp and Pierre Vidal-Nacquet, *The French Student Uprising, November 1967–June 1968: An Analytical Record,* trans. Maria Jolas (Boston: Beacon Press, 1971), 579–82; and Ahearne, *French Cultural Policy Debates,* 70–75. All translations here are mine.

64. "Déclaration de Villeurbanne," in Jeanson, *L'Action culturelle dans la cite,* 120.

65. Ibid.

66. On the paucity of musical offerings in the *maisons,* see Anne Rey, "Essais de définition d'une politique musicale," *ATAC-Informations* 41 (May 1972), 3. See also Lebovics, *Mona Lisa's Escort,* 114–15.

67. Data derived from "Programmes des Maisons de la Culture et des Centres Dramatiques," *ATAC-Informations* 2 (November 1966): 12–14.

68. Biasini, *Grands travaux,* 154–55.

69. Ferrari, in Jacqueline Caux, *Presque rien avec Luc Ferrari* (Paris: Main d'Œuvre, 2002), 171. In an interview with Charles Amirkhanian, Ferrari cited the militarization of France under de Gaulle as one reason for his politicization; Luc Ferrari, interviewed by Charles Amirkhanian, *Ode to Gravity,* KPFA radio, Berkeley, California, 11 April 1973. Another reason was the Algerian War of Independence; Brunhild Meyer-Ferrari, interview with the author, 7 June 2006.

70. Ferrari, in Caux, *Presque rien avec Luc Ferrari,* 56.

71. Interview with Brunhild Meyer-Ferrari, 7 June 2006.

72. Ferrari, in François-Bernard Mâche, "Entretien avec Luc Ferrari," *Nouvelle revue française* 232 (April 1972): 115. Reprinted in *La revue musicale* 214–15 (1977): 63–69.

73. Ferrari, in Hansjörg Pauli, *Für wen komponieren Sie eigentlich?* (Frankfurt: S. Fischer Verlag, 1971), 50.

74. Ferrari, in Denys Lemery, "Luc Ferrari: Entretien avec un jeune compositeur non-conformiste . . ." in *Actuel* 12 (1970): 16.

75. "Rencontres et discussions libres avec des personnalités invitées et les animateurs de la Maison de la Culture d'Amiens," *Maison de la Culture d'Amiens* 14 (1 January 1969): 4.

76. "M.C.A. Musique," *Maison de la Culture d'Amiens* 8 (1 October 1968): 4.

77. Ferrari, in Pauli, *Für wen komponieren Sie eigentlich?* 56–57.

78. Excerpts from the Villeurbanne declaration were published in the *maison*'s newsletter the same month that Ferrari began his residence. "Déclaration de Villeurbanne," *Maison de la Culture d'Amiens* 9 (15 October 1968): 1.

79. Luc Ferrari, *Tautologos III: oder, Darf ich sie bitten, mit mir zu tautologieren?* (Celle: Edition Moeck, 1970), 4.

80. Ibid.

81. Ferrari, in Pauli, *Für wen komponieren Sie eigentlich?* 58.

82. Ibid.

83. Ibid., 49. A more detailed discussion of Ferrari's use of photography as a model for the production of tape music may be found in Drott, "'Poor Man's Musique Concrète': Luc Ferrari's Tape Music after 1968," in *1968: Musik und Gesellschaftlicher Protest*, ed. Beate Kutschke and Arnold Jacobshagen (Stuttgart: Franz Steiner Verlag, 2007), 91–102.

84. Luc Ferrari, liner notes to *Hétérozygote/J'ai été coupé*, Philips, Prospective 21e siècle 836 885 DSY.

85. Translated as "Outline for a Sociological Theory of Artistic Perception," in Pierre Bourdieu, *The Field of Cultural Production*, ed. Randal Johnson (New York: Columbia University Press, 1993), 215–37.

86. Ibid., 220.

87. Ibid.

88. Ibid., 222.

89. *Pour* 18–19 (March 1971): 1.

90. "La formation des 'animateurs professionnels,'" *Développement culturel* 19 (September–October 1973): 1.

91. Georges Goubert, "L'animation," *ATAC-Informations* 40 (April 1972): 14.

92. L'Institut National d'Education Populaire, *Lexique de l'animation socio-éducative,* quoted in Denis Muzet, *L'Animation musicale, Cahiers Recherche/Musique* no. 7 (Paris: Institut National de l'Audiovisuel, 1979), 16.

93. Henri Théry, cited in Pierre Besnard, *L'Animation socio-culturelle* (Paris: Presses universitaires de France, 1985), 13.

94. Michel Simonot, *Les animateurs socio-culturels: Etude d'une aspiration à une activité sociale* (Paris: Presses universitaires de France, 1974), 29.

95. Jacques Duhamel, "L'ère de la culture," *La nouvelle revue des deux mondes* 9 (September 1972): 515.

96. Ibid., 518.

97. Ibid.

98. Jacques Chaban-Delmas, "Jalons vers une nouvelle société," *La revue des deux mondes* (January 1971): 6–16.

99. Pompidou's influence on cultural policy is discussed in Pascale Goetschel and Emmanuelle Loyet, "Les relations entre Georges Pompidou et les ministres des Affaires culturelles," in *Culture et action chez Georges Pompidou*, ed. Jean-Claude Groshens and Jean-François Sirinelli (Paris: Presses universitaires de France, 2000), esp. 317–21.

100. *Musique pour tous: Réalisations et perspectives d'une politique musicale française* (Paris: La Documentation Française, 1974).

101. Ibid., 3.

102. Landowski, *Mutation et organisation de la musique en France* (Paris: Académie des Beaux-Arts, 1972), 8.

103. *Réalisation et perspectives de la Direction de la Musique, de l'Art lyrique et de la Danse* (Paris: Ministère des Affaires Culturelles, 1973), 27–28.

104. Guy Herzlich, "Rendre la musique aux enfants," *Le Monde,* 24 February 1976, 21; "M. Haby veut faire chanter les petits français," *Le Quotidien de Paris,* 24 February 1976; and Pierre-Petit, "Marcel Landowski: Faire de la France scolaire une pépinière de musiciens," *Le Figaro,* 24 February 1976.

105. Cited in Muzet, *L'Animation musicale*, 55.

106. Jean Maheu, *Elements de politique de la musique, de l'art et de la danse* (Paris: Secrétariat d'Etat à la Culture, 1975).

107. Ibid., 19.

108. Ibid.

109. Ibid., 21.

110. Ibid., 48.

111. The development of *recherche musicale* has received considerable attention from scholars. See Pierre-Michel Menger, *Les laboratoires de la création musicale: Acteurs, organisations et politique de la recherche musicale* (Paris: La Documentation Française, 1989); Georgina Born, *Rationalizing Culture;* and Anne Veitl, *Politiques de la musique contemporaine: Le compositeur, la 'recherche musicale' et l'Etat en France de 1958 à 1991* (Paris: L'Harmattan, 1997).

112. Born, *Rationalizing Culture,* 71–72.

113. Maheu, *Elements de politique de la musique,* 37.

114. Ibid., 38. On the stakes involved in the division between "fundamental" and "applied" research, see Born, *Rationalizing Culture,* 90 and 218–22.

115. Ministère de la Culture et de la Communication, *Une politique de la musique pour la France, 1974–1981* (Paris, 1981), 41.

116. Muzet, *L'Animation musicale,* 139.

117. Ibid.

118. Brigitte Massin, "De la décentralisation avant toute chose," *ATAC-Informations* 100 (March 1979): 24–25.

119. The following discussion of *animation musicale* is based primarily on a survey of the journal *Cahiers de l'animation musicale,* published by the Centre national d'animation musicale (established in January 1976). Another invaluable resource is Denis Muzet's 1979 study of the profession; see Muzet, *L'Animation musicale.* Other useful surveys include Charles Scherer, *L'Animation musicale dans le cadre des Maisons de la Culture* (Mémoire de maîtrise de Musicologie, Université de Paris–Sorbonne, 1976); and Michel Poupet, *Les concerts éducatifs et l'animation musicale scolaire* (Paris: Centre National de Documentation Pédagogique, 1978).

120. The emphasis on ludic activities is evident in the pedagogical activities of the GRM and GMEB. For information on the GRM's pedagogical activities, see François Delalande et al., *Cahiers Recherche/Musique 1: Pédagogie musicale d'éveil* (Paris: Institut National de l'Audiovisuel, 1979); François Delalande, "Le jeu—la musique," *Forum de l'animation musicale* 2 (April 1978), 34–36; and François Delalande, *La musique est un jeu d'enfant* (Paris: Buchet-Chastel, 1997). For information on GMEB, see "Groupe de Musique Expérimental de Bourges," *ATAC-Informations* 41 (May 1972): 12; Françoise Barrière, "Le Gmebaugosse: Nouvelle technique de pédagogie musicale," *ATAC-Informations* 45 (December 1975): 20–21; and Roger Cochini, "Le Gmebogosse," *Faire* 2–3 (1974): 171–77.

121. See the entries for the Jeunesses musicales de France and the Centre France lyrique in Poupet, *Les concerts éducatifs,* 12–14 and 25–27, respectively.

122. Few *animateurs* used instruments from popular or folk traditions, an exception being the group Musicoliers. See Martine Palmé, "Les Musicoliers," *Panorama de la musique et des instruments* 22 (March–April 1978): 53–54.

123. "Un piano mobile," *Mobile* 1 (1972): 5.

124. Ibid.

125. As Muzet points out, the preference for contemporary music can be seen in the space the *Cahiers de l'animation musicale* dedicated to the genre, with 45 percent of articles in the journal focused on new music. Muzet, *L'Animation musicale,* 109–13.

126. Cited in ibid., 148.

127. Loïc Ruellan, quoted in Dominique Reffay, "L'Association pour la Diffusion et l'Animation Musicale en Gironde," *Action musicale* 1 (1977): 13.

128. Landowski, "Une politique de l'Education Musicale," *L'éducation musicale* 227 (April 1976): 6.

129. Madeleine Gagnard, *L'éveil musical de l'enfant* (Paris: ESF, 1977), 12–13 and 71.

130. Toby Miller and George Yúdice, *Cultural Policy* (London: Sage, 2002), 13–15.

131. Joëlle Goutal, "Comment est née la 'Galerie sonore,'" *Cahiers de l'animation musicale* 2 (December 1976): 2.

132. Ibid.

133. Fleuret, "Une idée en l'air," *Cahiers de l'animation musicale* 2 (December 1976): 5.

134. Ibid.

135. Ibid., 6.

136. For examples of the rhetoric of "nondirectivity," see Gagnard, *L'éveil musical;* and "L'Animation musicale: De nouveaux chemins vers la musique," *Panorama de la musique et des instruments* 21 (January–February 1978): 46–47.

137. Delalande, "Eveiller à quoi?" *Pédagogie musicale d'éveil,* 112.

138. "Dossier: L'Ile de la vieille musique," *Cahiers de l'Animation Musicale* 0 (October 1976): 2–5.

139. Igor, "Théâtre musical à l'école," *ATAC-Informations* 64 (January 1975): 33.

140. Ibid.

141. Yves Prin and Marie-Noël Rio, *L'Ile de la vieille musique.* A facsimile of the score is held at the CDMC in Paris.

142. Pierre Barrat, quoted in Dominique Darzacq, "Vous chantez . . . et bien jouez maintenant," *ATAC-Informations* 84 (March 1977): 43.

143. "Dossier: L'Ile de la vieille musique," 2–5.

144. Prin and Rio, *L'Ile de la vieille musique,* 40.

145. Maheu, *Elements de politique de la musique,* 21.

146. Tyler Stovall, "From Red Belt to Black Belt: Race, Class and Urban Marginality in Twentieth-Century Paris," in *The Color of Liberty: Histories of Race in France,* ed. Sue Peabody and Tyler Stovall (Durham, NC: Duke University Press, 2003), 351.

147. Georges Aperghis, "Le titre fait le tableau," in *Festival d'Automne à Paris,* ed. Jean-Pierre Léonardini (Paris: Temps Actuels, 1982), 239.

148. Vincent Colin, "Chercher le prolongement visible de la musique," *ATAC-Informations* 85 (April 1977): 25.

149. Philippe Urfalino, *L'invention de la politique culturelle* (Paris: Hachette, 2004), 309.

150. Ibid., 314–15.

151. Ibid., 328.

152. Ibid., 312.

153. Cited in Cyrille Guiat, *French and Italian Communist Parties: Comrades and Culture* (London: Frank Cass, 2002), 92.

154. Colin, "Chercher le prolongement visible," 26. See also Theodore Shank, "Atelier Théâtre et Musique: Structuring Everyday Gestures and Sounds," *The Drama Review* 23, no. 3 (September 1979): 4.

155. Colin, "Chercher le prolongement visible," 26.

156. Martin Even, "Le temps de souffler le verre," *Le Monde,* 21 October 1976, 17.

157. This incident is related in a radio program, *Calques Musique Travail,* broadcast on France Culture on 24 February 1976. A recording of the program is housed at the Institut Nationale de l'Audiovisuel.

158. Ibid.

159. Ibid.

160. Ibid.

161. A recording of this version of *La bouteille à la mer* was broadcast on *Calques Musique Travail* on the station France Culture on 24 June 1976. A copy is housed at the Institut Nationale de l'Audiovisuel. For accounts of the performance, see Jacques Poulet, "Théâtre musical en sous-sol," *France Nouvelle* 1598 (28 June 1976): 37–39; Even, "Le temps de souffler le verre"; and Chantal Mutel, "L'Atelier théâtre et musique ou comment les cailloux se mirent à chanter," *Nouvelle Critique* 107 (October 1977): 50–52.

162. Even, "Le temps de souffler le verre"; Sylvie de Nussac, "Aperghis: les rites de Bagnolet," *L'Express* 1320 (25 October 1976): 73.

163. This interpretation of the work conforms with one advanced by Jacques Poulet. See Poulet, "Théâtre musical en sous-sol," 38.

164. Georges Aperghis, "Pour une geste musicale," undated typescript in the dossier "Georges Aperghis, *La bouteille à la mer,*" CDMC.

165. Aperghis, in "Xenakis + pygmées + loubards + Sonacotra = Aperghis," *Libération,* 27 October 1976, 14.

166. Jacques Longchampt, "'La Bouteille à la mer' de Georges Aperghis," *Le Monde,* 20 October 1976.

167. Maurice Fleuret, "Une bouteille dans la tempête," *Nouvel Observateur* 628 (22 November 1976): 89.

168. "Xenakis + pygmées + loubards."

169. Ibid.

170. Aperghis, "Pour une geste musicale," 8.

171. Ibid.

172. The distinction between "cultural policy proper" and "cultural policy as display" is developed by Jim McGuigan in *Rethinking Cultural Policy* (Buckingham: Open University Press, 2003), 62–63.

173. Pierre Moulinier, *Dictionnaire des politiques culturelles* (Paris: Larousse, 2001), 20.

174. "Article envoyé au journal 'Le Monde,' " *Bulletin de l'Association des Professeurs d'Education Musicale* 78 (April 1977): 23.

175. Cited in Brigitte Massin, "Les cahiers de doléances de la musique," *Panorama de la musique et des instruments* 21 (January–February 1978): 44.

176. "Assises nationales de l'enseignement musical: texte de synthèse," *Bulletin de l'Association des Professeurs d'Education Musicale* 83 (June 1978): 21.

177. Ibid., 21–22.

178. Thomas Ferenczi, "La création contre l'animation," *Le Monde*, 20 October 1977, 19.

179. Renata Scant and Fernand Garnier, "Faux débat, vrais enjeux," *ATAC-Informations* 105 (November 1979): 5. See also Joël Dragutin, "Il arrive que le dialogue prenne un ton polémique," *ATAC-Informations* 85 (April 1977): 2–3; and Pierre Besnard, "La relation créateurs/animateurs: Une nouvelle dialectique maître/esclave dans le champ culturel," *Cahiers de l'Animation* 26 (Fall 1979): 47–54.

180. See, for instance, *Programme commun de gouvernement du parti communiste français et du parti socialiste* (Paris: Editions Sociales, 1972), 92–94. Ostensibly the joint platform of the PCF and PS, the Programme commun adhered largely to the Communists' positions on cultural affairs, reflecting the latter's ascendancy over the socialists at the time of its drafting.

181. Michel Simonot, "'A' comme animation," *France Nouvelle* 1591 (10 May 1976): 21.

182. "Orientations générales d'une politique d'action culturelle," *Nouvelle Revue Socialiste* 4 (1974): 18.

183. Cited in Caune, *La culture en action*, 215.

184. Looseley, *Politics of Fun*, 58.

185. "Bissons flute," *Action musicale* 5 (October 1978): 25.

186. Caune, *La culture en action*, 287.

187. Fleuret, "La création musicale comme école de la liberté," *Le Matin*, 21–22 March 1981, 23.

188. Ibid.

189. Anne Veitl and Noémi Duchemin, *Maurice Fleuret: une politique démocratique de la musique* (Paris: La Documentation Française, 2000), 153–54.

190. For more on the expanding range of genres addressed by French cultural policy, see Looseley, *Politics of Fun*, 113–34; and Kim Eling, *The Politics of Cultural Policy in France* (New York: St. Martin's Press, 1999), 128–48.

191. Fleuret, cited in Veitl, *Politiques de la musique contemporaine*, 171.

192. Veitl and Duchemin, *Maurice Fleuret*, 299.

193. Under Fleuret the Centre national de l'animation musicale was rechristened the Centre national de l'action musicale and assigned the task of encouraging the amateur practice of popular music. See Veitl and Duchemin, *Maurice Fleuret*, 148–49.

194. This information was obtained from the website of the Musicoliers, at http://pagesperso-orange.fr/musicolier/musicolierpartenariat.htm (accessed 3 December 2008).

195. From the website of the Fédération nationale des CMR, http://90plan .ovh.net/~cmrmusic/index.php?option=com_content&task=view&id=15&Ite mid=13 (accessed 3 December 2008).

196. Nadia Kiwan, "A Critical Perspective on Socially Embedded Cultural Policy in France," *International Journal of Cultural Policy* 13, no. 2 (May 2007): 153–67, esp. 159. David Looseley also notes the sociological (as opposed to aesthetic) rationale driving governmental support for popular music; Looseley, "Cultural Democratisation and Popular Music," *Modern & Contemporary France* 11, no. 3 (2003): 52.

197. Kiwan, "A Critical Perspective," 163.

CONCLUSION

1. Pascal Perrineau, "Strength through Disunity: The French Left from Defeat to Victory, 1978–1981," in *France at the Polls, 1981 and 1986: Three National Elections,* ed. Howard Penniman (Durham, NC: Duke University Press, 1988), 89 and 107.

2. Claire Brisset, "La nouvelle prise de la Bastille," *Le Monde,* 12 May 1981, 9.

3. Cited in Jean-Paul Liegeois, "Y a d'la joie," *L'Unité* 423 (16 May 1981): 12.

4. Keith Reader, *Intellectuals and the Left in France since 1968* (London: Macmillan, 1987), 136–40.

5. Yves Santamaria, *Histoire du Parti communiste français* (Paris: La Découverte, 1999), 90–91.

6. Pierre Milza, "Le Front national: droite extreme ou national-populisme?" in *Histoire des droites en France,* ed. Jean-François Sirinelli (Paris: Gallimard, 1992), 1: 691–729.

7. Jacques Fremontier, "Mai est enfin mort," *Libération,* 23–24 May 1981, 9.

8. Michael Scott Christofferson, *French Intellectuals Against the Left: The Antitotalitarian Moment of the 1970s* (New York: Berghahn, 2004), 89–112.

9. Peter Hall, "The Evolution of Economic Policy," in *The Mitterrand Experiment: Continuity and Change in Modern France,* ed. George Ross, Stanley Hoffmann, and Sylvia Mazacher (Oxford: Oxford University Press, 1987), 54–59.

10. "Les Nouveaux Partisans," *La Cause du peuple* 21 (8 May 1970): 2.

11. Gil Delannoi, *Les années utopiques, 1968–1978* (Paris: La Découverte, 1990).

12. See Eric Drott, "The *Nòva Cançon Occitana* and the Internal Colonialism Thesis," *French Politics, Culture & Society* (forthcoming).

Select Bibliography

Ahearne, Jeremy, ed. *French Cultural Policy Debates*. London: Routledge, 2002.

Aldrich, Robert. *Greater France: A History of French Overseas Expansion*. London: Macmillan, 1996.

Althusser, Louis. *Lenin and Philosophy*. Translated by Benjamin Brewster. New York: Monthly Review Press, 1972.

Anderson, Iain. *This Is Our Music: Free Jazz, the Sixties and American Culture*. Philadelphia: University of Pennsylvania Press, 2007.

Archer-Straw, Petrine. *Negrophilia: Avant-Garde Paris and Black Culture in the 1920s*. London: Thames and Hudson, 2000.

Aron, Raymond. *The Elusive Revolution: Anatomy of a Student Revolt*. Translated by Gordon Clough. New York: Praeger, 1969.

Artières, Philippe, and Michelle Zancarini-Fournel, eds. *68: Une histoire collective (1962–1981)*. Paris: La Découverte, 2008.

Atkin, Nicholas. *The Fifth French Republic*. New York: Palgrave, 2005.

Attali, Jacques. *Bruits: Essai sur l'économie politique de la musique*. Paris: Presses universitaires de France, 1977.

Barsamian, Jacques, and François Jouffa. *Vinyl fraise*. Paris: Laffon, 1993.

Barthes, Roland. *Image—Music—Text*. Translated by Stephen Heath. New York: Hill and Wang, 1977.

Baumol, William, and William Bowen. *Performing Arts—the Economic Dilemma: A Study of Problems Common to Theater, Opera, Music, and Dance*. New York: Twentieth Century Fund, 1966.

Bécane, J.C. *L'Expérience des maisons de la culture*. Paris: La Documentati Française, 1973.

Becker, Howard. *Art Worlds*. Berkeley: University of California Press, 1

Belleret, Robert. *Léo Ferré: une vie d'artiste*. Arles: Actes Sud, 1996.

Benjamin, Walter. *Illuminations*. Edited by Hannah Arendt. New York: Harcourt Brace Jovanich, 1968.

Bensaïd, Daniel, and Henri Weber. *Mai 1968: Une répétition générale*. Paris: Maspero, 1968.

Bercoff, André. *L'autre France: L'Underpresse*. Paris: Stock, 1975.

Berliner, Brett. *Ambivalent Desire: The Exotic Black Other in Jazz-Age France*. Amherst: University of Massachusetts Press, 2002.

Berstein, Serge. "L'historien et la culture politique." *Vingtième Siècle* 35 (1992): 67–77.

———, ed. *Les cultures politiques en France*. Paris: Seuil, 1999.

Bertrand, André. *Le droit d'auteurs et les droits voisins*. 2d ed. Paris: Dalloz, 1999.

Besançon, Henri. *Festival International d'Art Contemporain de Royan, 1964–1977*. Royan: Bonne Anse, 2007.

Besançon, Julien, ed. *Les murs ont la parole: Journal mural mai 68*. Paris: Tchou, 1968.

Besnard, Pierre. *L'Animation socio-culturelle*. Paris: Presses universitaires de France, 1985.

Biasini, Emile. *Grands travaux: de l'Afrique au Louvre*. Paris: Odile Jacob, 1995.

Boivin, Jean. *La classe de Messiaen*. Paris: Christian Bourgois, 1995.

Born, Georgina. *Rationalizing Culture: IRCAM, Boulez and the Institutionalization of the Avant-garde*. Berkeley: University of California Press, 1995.

Boulez, Pierre. *Orientations*. Edited by Jean-Jacques Nattiez, translated by Martin Cooper. Cambridge, MA: Harvard University Press, 1986.

Bourdieu, Pierre. "L'école conservatrice. Les inégalités devant l'école et devant la culture." *Revue française de sociologie* 7, no. 3 (July–September 1966): 325–47.

———. *The Field of Cultural Production*. Edited by Randal Johnson. New York: Columbia University Press, 1993.

Bourdieu, Pierre, et al. *Photography: A Middle-brow Art*. Translated by Shaun Whiteside. Stanford, CA: Stanford University Press, 1990.

Bourseiller, Christophe. *Les maoistes: La folle histoire des gardes rouges français*. Paris: Plon, 2006.

Bouyer, Christian. *Odéon est ouvert: Tribune libre*. Paris: Nouvelles Editions Debresse, 1968.

Brau, Jean-Louis. *Cours, camarade, le vieux monde est derrière toi: Histoire du mouvement révolutionnaire étudiant en Europe*. Paris: Albin Michel, 1968.

Brinton, Maurice. *For Workers' Power: The Selected Writings of Maurice Brinton*. Edited by David Goodway. Oakland, CA: AK Press, 2004.

Brunschwig, Chantal, Louis-Jean Calvet, and Jean-Claude Klein. *Cent ans de chanson française*. Paris: Seuil, 1972.

Burnier, Michel-Antoine, and Bernard Kouchner. *La France Sauvage*. Paris: Editions Publications Premières, 1970.

Calvet, Louis-Jean. "Changing Places of the French Song from 1945 to the Present Day." In *France and the Mass Media*, edited by Brian Rigby and Nicholas Hewitt, 195–99. London: Macmillan, 1991.

———. *Chanson et Société*. Paris: Payot, 1981.

————. *La Production révolutionnaire: Slogans, affiches, chansons* (Paris: Payot, 1976).

Carles, Philippe, and Jean-Louis Comolli. *Free Jazz Black Power.* Paris: Champs libres, 1971; reprint Paris: Gallimard, 2000.

Cartier, Henri, and Mitsou Naslednikov. *L'univers des hippies.* Paris: Fayard, 1970.

Castanet, Pierre-Albert. "1968: A Cultural and Social Survey of Its Influences on French Music." *Contemporary Music Review* 8, no. 1 (1993): 19–43.

————. "Les années 1968: les mouvances d'une révolution socio-culturelle populaire." In *1789–1989: musique, histoire, démocratie,* edited by Antoine Hennion, 145–52. Paris: Editions de la Maison des sciences de l'homme, 1992.

————. "Rêver la révolution: Musique et politique autour de Mai 1968." In *Résistance et utopias sonores,* edited by Laurent Feneyrou, 131–48. Paris: CDMC, 2005.

————. *Tout est bruit pour qui a peur: Pour une histoire sociale du son sale.* Paris: Michel de Maule, 1999.

Caune, Jean. *La culture en action: De Vilar à Lang, le sens perdu.* Grenoble: Presses universitaires de Grenoble, 1999.

Caux, Jacqueline. *Presque rien avec Luc Ferrari.* Paris: Main d'Œuvre, 2002.

Certeau, Michel de. *La prise de parole et autres écrits politiques.* Edited by Luce Giard. Paris: Seuil, 1994.

Chaban-Delmas, Jacques. "Jalons vers une nouvelle société." *La revue des deux mondes* (January 1971): 6–16.

Chalvidant, Jean, and Hervé Mouvet. *La belle histoire des groupes de rock français des années 60.* Paris: Fernand Lanore / Sorlot, 2002.

Christofferson, Michael Scott. *French Intellectuals Against the Left: The Antitotalitarian Moment of the 1970s.* New York: Berghahn, 2004.

Claude, Catherine. *C'est la fête de l'Humanité.* Paris: Editeurs français réunis, 1977.

Clément, Claude. *Faites l'amour et plus la guerre.* Paris: Fayard, 1971.

Cohen, Evelyne, and Marie-Françoise Lévy. *La Télévision des Trente Glorieuses: Culture et Politique.* Paris: CNRS Editions, 2007.

Comité d'histoire du ministre de la culture. *André Malraux, Ministre: Les affaires culturelles au temps d'André Malraux 1959–1969.* Paris: La Documentation Française, 1996.

Commission nationale pour l'étude des problèmes de la musique. *Rapport générale 1963–4.* Paris: Ministère d'État des Affaires Culturelles, 1964.

Corbin, Alain, Noëlle Gérôme, and Danielle Tartakowsky. *Les usages politiques des fêtes aux XIXe–XXe siècles.* Paris: Publications de la Sorbonne, 1994.

Coster, Michel de. *Le disque, art ou affaires? Analyse sociologique d'une industrie culturelle.* Grenoble: Presses universitaires de Grenoble, 1976.

Cotro, Vincent. *Chants libres: Le free jazz en France, 1960–1975.* Paris: Outre Mesure, 1999.

Coulomb, Sylvie, and Didier Varrod. *Histoire de chansons, 1968–1988: de Julien Clerc à Etienne Daho.* Paris: Balland, 1987.

Coulonges, Georges. *La chanson en son temps: De Béranger au juke-box.* Paris: Les Editeurs Français Réunis, 1969.

———. *La Commune en chantant*. Paris: Les Editeurs français réunis, 1970.

Dansette, Adrien. *Mai 1968*. Paris: Plon, 1971.

Dauncey, Hugh, and Steve Cannon, eds. *Popular Music in France from Chanson to Techno: Culture, Identity and Society*. Aldershot, UK: Ashgate, 2003.

Davis, Angela. *An Autobiography*. New York: Random House, 1974.

Delalande, François. "Le jeu—la musique." *Forum de l'animation musicale* 2 (April 1978): 34–36.

———. *La musique est un jeu d'enfant*. Paris: Buchet-Chastel, 1997.

Delalande, François, et al. *Cahiers Recherche/Musique 1: Pédagogie musicale d'éveil*. Paris: Institut National de l'Audiovisuel, 1979.

Delannoi, Gil. *Les années utopiques, 1968–1978*. Paris: La Découverte, 1990.

Deshayes, Éric, and Dominique Grimaud. *L'Underground musical en France*. Paris: Le mot et le reste, 2008.

Dillaz, Serge. *La Chanson française de la contestation: Des barricades de la commune à mai 68*. Paris: Seghers, 1973.

———. *Vivre et chanter en France*, vol. 1, 1945–1980. Paris: Fayard, 2005.

"Dominique Grange vs Jacques Tardi." *Barricata* 10 (June 2003).

Dommanget, Maurice. *Eugène Pottier, membre de la Commune et chantre de l'Internationale*. Paris: EDI, 1971.

Dorigné, Michel. *Jazz v. 1*. Paris: L'Ecole des loisirs, 1968.

Drott, Eric. "The *Nòva Cançon Occitana* and the Internal Colonialism Thesis." *French Politics, Culture & Society* (forthcoming).

———. "'Poor Man's *Musique Concrète*': Luc Ferrari's Tape Music after 1968." In *1968: Musik und Gesellschaftlicher Protest*, edited by Beate Kutschke and Arnold Jacobshagen, 91–102. Stuttgart: Franz Steiner Verlag, 2007.

———. "Spectralism, Politics, and the Post-Industrial Imagination." In *The Modernist Legacy: Essays on New Music*, edited by Björn Heile, 39–60. Aldershot: Ashgate, 2009.

Duhamel, Jacques. "L'ère de la culture." *La nouvelle revue des deux mondes* 9 (1972): 513–22.

Eling, Kim. *The Politics of Cultural Policy in France*. New York: St. Martin's Press, 1999.

Erismann, Guy. *Histoire de la Chanson*. Paris: Hermes, 1967.

Eudeline, Christian. *Anti-yéyé: Une autre histoire des sixties*. Paris: Denoël, 2006.

Eyerman, Ron, and Andrew Jamison. *Music and Social Movements*. Cambridge: Cambridge University Press, 1998.

Fabbri, Franco. "A Theory of Musical Genres: Two Applications." In *Popular Music Perspectives*, edited by David Horn and Philip Tagg, 52–81. Gothenburg and Exeter: IASPM, 1982.

Fabre, Michel. *From Harlem to Paris: Black American Writers in France, 1840–1980*. Urbana: University of Illinois Press, 1991.

Fall, Mar. *Le destin des Africains noirs en France*. Paris: L'Harmattan, 2005.

Ferniot, Jean. *Mort d'une révolution: la gauche de mai*. Paris: Denoël, 1968.

Ferro, Marc. *L'Internationale d'Eugène Pottier et Pierre Degeyter*. Paris: Editions Noêsis, 1996.

Ferry, Luc, and Alain Renaut. *French Philosophy of the Sixties: An Essay on Antihumanism.* Translated by Mary H.S. Cattani. Amherst: University of Massachusetts Press, 1990.

La fête, cette hantise!, *Autrement* 7 (1976).

Fields, A. Belden. *Trotskyism and Maoism: Theory and Practice in France and the United States.* New York: Praeger, 1988.

Fourastié, Jean. *Les trente glorieuses.* Paris: Fayard, 1979.

Frith, Simon. *Performing Rites.* Oxford: Oxford University Press, 1996.

Fry, Andy. "Beyond le Bœuf: Interdisciplinary Rereadings of Jazz in France." *Journal of the Royal Musical Association* 128 (2003): 137–53.

Fulcher, Jane. *The Composer as Intellectual: Music and Ideology in France.* Oxford: Oxford University Press, 2005.

Gagnard, Madeleine. *L'éveil musical de l'enfant.* Paris: ESF, 1977.

Gallant, Mavis. *Paris Notebooks: Essays and Reviews.* Toronto: Macmillan, 1986.

Gennari, John. *Blowing Hot and Cool: Jazz and Its Critics.* Chicago: University of Chicago Press, 2007.

Georgi, Frank. "'Le pouvoir est dans la rue'. La 'Manifestation gaulliste' des Champs-Élysées (30 mai 1968)." *Vingtième Siècle* 48 (October–December 1995): 46–60.

Gérôme, Noëlle, and Danielle Tartakowsky. *La fête de l'Humanité: Culture communiste, culture populaire.* Paris: Messidor/Editions Sociales, 1988.

Gervereau, Laurent. "Les chansons de mai–juin 1968." *Matériaux pour l'histoire de notre temps* 11, no. 11 (1988): 198–99.

Goetschel, Pascal, and Emmanuelle Loyet. "Les relations entre Georges Pompidou et les ministres des Affaires culturelles." In *Culture et action chez Georges Pompidou*, edited by Jean-Claude Groshens and Jean-François Sirinelli, 313–37. Paris: Presses universitaires de France, 2000.

Goffman, Erving. *Encounters: Two Studies in the Sociology of Interaction.* New York: Bobbs-Merrill, 1961.

Granotier, Bernard. *Les travailleurs immigrés en France.* 2d ed. Paris: Maspero, 1976.

Groys, Boris. *Art Power.* Cambridge, MA: MIT Press, 2008.

Guiat, Cyrille. *French and Italian Communist Parties: Comrades and Culture.* London: Frank Cass, 2002.

Guibert, Gérome. *La production de la culture: Le cas des musiques amplifiées en France.* Paris: IRMA, 2006.

Hall, Stuart, and Tony Jefferson, eds. *Resistance through Rituals: Youth Subcultures in Post-war Britain.* London: Routledge, 1993.

Hamon, Hervé, and Patrick Rotman. *Génération*, vols. 1 and 2. Paris: Seuil, 1987.

Hargreaves, Alec G. *Immigration, Race and Ethnicity in Contemporary France.* London: Routledge, 1995.

Hawkins, Peter. *Chanson: The French Singer-songwriter from Aristide Bruant to the Present Day.* Aldershot: Ashgate, 2000.

———. "Léo Ferré: Modernism, Postmodernism and the Avant-garde in Popular Chanson." *French Cultural Studies* 16, no. 2 (2005): 169–78.

Hennion, Antoine, and Jean-Pierre Vignolle. *L'économie du disque en France*. Paris: La Documentation Française, 1978.

Hesmondhalgh, David. "Subcultures, Scenes or Tribes? None of the Above." *Journal of Youth Studies* 8, no. 1 (March 2005): 21–40.

Hocquenghem, Guy. *L'après-mai des faunes: volutions*. Paris: Bernard Grasset, 1974.

Holt, Fabian. *Genre in Popular Music*. Chicago: University of Chicago Press, 2007.

Horne, Alastair. *A Savage War of Peace: Algeria 1954–1962*. London: Macmillan, 1977.

Huyssen, Andreas. *After the Great Divide*. Bloomington: Indiana University Press, 1986.

Jackson, Jeffrey. *Making Jazz French*. Durham, NC: Duke University Press, 2003.

Jameux, Dominique. *Pierre Boulez*. Translated by Susan Bradshaw. Cambridge, MA: Harvard University Press, 1991.

Jeanson, Francis. *L'action culturelle dans la cité*. Paris: Seuil, 1973.

Jones, LeRoi [Amiri Baraka]. *Black Music*. New York: William Morrow, 1967.

———. *Blues People: Negro Music in White America*. New York: William Morrow, 1963.

Jordan, Matthew. "Jazz Changes: A History of French Discourse on Jazz from Ragtime to Be-Bop." Ph.D. diss., Claremont Graduate School, 1998.

Jouffa, François. *La culture pop des années 70: Le pop-notes de François Jouffa*. Paris: Spengler, 1994.

Kallberg, Jeffrey. "The Rhetoric of Genre: Chopin's Nocturne in G Minor." *19th-Century Music* 11, no. 3 (Spring 1988): 238–61.

Kelly, Michael. *Modern French Marxism*. Baltimore, MD: Johns Hopkins University Press, 1982.

Kerbourc'h, Jean-Claude. *Le piéton de mai*. Paris: Juillard, 1968.

Kessel, Patrick, ed. *Le mouvement "maoïste" en France: Textes et documents*. Paris: Union générale d'éditions, 1972.

Khilnani, Sunil. *Arguing Revolution: The Intellectual Left in Postwar France*. New Haven, CT: Yale University Press, 1993.

Kiwan, Nadia. "A Critical Perspective on Socially Embedded Cultural Policy in France." *International Journal of Cultural Policy* 13, no. 2 (2007): 153–67.

Koechlin, Philippe. *Memoires de rock et de folk*. Bordeaux: Le Castor Astral, 2007.

Kramer, Lawrence. *Music as Cultural Practice, 1800–1900*. Berkeley: University of California Press, 1990.

Kravetz, Marc, ed. *L'Insurrection étudiante: 2–13 Mai 1968*. Paris: Union Générale d'Éditions, 1968.

Krims, Adam. *Rap Music and the Poetics of Identity*. Cambridge: Cambridge University Press, 2000.

Kuisel, Richard. *Seducing the French: The Dilemma of Americanization*. Berkeley: University of California Press, 1993.

Labro, Philippe, et al. *This Is Only a Beginning*. Translated by Charles Lam Markmann. New York: Funk and Wagnalls, 1969.

Laing, Dave. "Music and the Market." In *The Cultural Study of Music: A Critical Introduction*, edited by Martin Clayton, Trevor Herbert, and Richard Middleton, 309–20. New York: Routledge, 2003.

Lancelot, Michel. *Je veux regarder Dieu en face: Vie, mort et résurrection des Hippies*. Paris: Albin Michel, 1968.

Landowski, Marcel. *Batailles pour la musique*. Paris: Seuil, 1979.

———. *Mutation et organisation de la musique en France*. Paris: Académie des Beaux-Arts, 1972.

Lebovics, Herman. *Bringing the Empire Back Home: France in the Global Age*. Durham, NC: Duke University Press, 2004.

———. *Mona Lisa's Escort: André Malraux and the Reinvention of French Culture*. Ithaca, NY: Cornell University Press, 1999.

Lebrun, Barbara. *Protest Music in France: Production, Identity and Audiences*. Farnham: Ashgate, 2009.

Le Goff, Jean-Pierre. *Mai 68, l'héritage impossible*. Paris: La Découverte, 2002.

Lehman, Stephen. "I Love You with an Asterisk: African-American Experimental Music and the French Jazz Press, 1970–1980." *Critical Studies in Improvisation* 2 (2005): 38–53.

Léonardini, Jean-Pierre, ed. *Festival d'Automne à Paris*. Paris: Temps Actuels, 1982.

Lere, Pierre. "Free jazz: évolution ou révolution." *Revue d'esthétique* 23, nos. 3–4 (1970): 313–25.

Levaillant, Denis. *L'Improvisation musicale: Essai sur la puissance du Jeu*. Paris: Lattès, 1981.

Lewis, George. "The AACM in Paris," *Black Renaissance/Renaissance Noire* 5, no. 3 (Spring/Summer 2004): 105–21.

———. *A Power Stronger Than Itself: The AACM and American Experimental Music*. Chicago: University of Chicago Press, 2008.

Liauzu, Claude. "Le tiersmondisme des intellectuels en accusation: Le sens d'une trajectoire." *Vingtième Siècle* 12 (October–December 1986): 73–80.

Lipovetsky, Gilles. *L'ère du vide: Essais sur l'individualisme contemporain*. Paris: Gallimard, 1983.

Locke, Ralph. *Music, Musicians and the Saint-Simonians*. Chicago: University of Chicago Press, 1986.

Looseley, David. "Cultural Democratisation and Popular Music." *Modern & Contemporary France* 11, no. 1 (2003): 45–55.

———. *The Politics of Fun: Cultural Policy and Debate in Contemporary France*. Oxford: Berg, 1995.

———. *Popular Music in Contemporary France: Authenticity, Politics, Debate*. Oxford: Berg, 2003.

Louvier, Alain. "L'évolution des classes de composition et d'analyse depuis 1968." In *Le Conservatoire de Paris: Deux cents ans de pédagogie, 1795–1995*, edited by Anne Bongrain and Yves Gérard, 361–70. Paris: Buchet-Castel, 1999.

Madurell, François. *L'Ensemble Ars Nova: Une contribution au pluralisme esthétique dans la musique contemporaine (1963–1987)*. Paris: Harmattan, 2003.

Maheu, Jean. *Eléments de politique de la musique, de l'art et de la danse*. Paris: Secrétariat d'Etat à la Culture, 1975.

Mai 68 par eux-mêmes: Le mouvement de Floréal, An 176. Paris: Editions du
  Monde Libertaire, 1989.
"Mai 68, rue de Madrid." *Journal du Conservatoire* 30 (1998).
Marny, Jacques. *La chanson et ses vedettes*. Paris: Centurion, 1965.
Martel, Fréderic. *The Pink and the Black: Homosexuals in France since 1968*.
  Translated by Marie Jane Todd. Stanford, CA: Stanford University Press,
  1999.
Mason, Laura. *Singing the French Revolution*. Ithaca, NY: Cornell University
  Press, 1996.
McDonough, Tom, ed. *Guy Debord and the Situationist International*. Cam-
  bridge, MA: MIT Press, 2002.
McGuigan, Jim. *Rethinking Cultural Policy*. Buckingham: Open University
  Press, 2003.
McKinley, C. Alexander. "Anarchists and the Music of the French Revolution."
  Journal for the Study of Radicalism 1, no. 2 (2007): 1–33.
Menger, Pierre-Michel. *Les laboratoires de la création musicale: Acteurs, organ-
  isations et politique de la recherche musicale*. Paris: La Documentation
  Française, 1989.
———. *Le paradoxe du musicien: Le compositeur, le mélomane et l'état dans la
  société contemporain*. Paris: Flammarion, 1983.
Mignon, Patrick. "Evolution de la prise en compte des musiques amplifiées par
  les politiques publiques." In *Politiques publiques et musiques amplifiées*,
  23–30. Adem-Florida: Conseil Régional d'Aquitaine, 1997.
Miller, Toby, and George Yúdice. *Cultural Policy*. London: Sage, 2002.
Ministère de la Culture et de la Communication. *Une politique de la musique
  pour la France, 1974–1981*. Paris, 1981.
Monson, Ingrid. *Freedom Sounds: Civil Rights Call Out to Jazz and Africa*.
  Oxford: Oxford University Press, 2007.
Moore, Christopher. "Music in France and the Popular Front (1934–1938):
  Politics, Aesthetics and Reception." Ph.D. diss., McGill University, 2006.
Morin, Edgar. *Journal de Californie*. Paris: Seuil, 1970.
Morin, Edgar, Claude Lefort, and Jean-Marc Coudray. *Mai 1968: La Brèche*.
  Paris: Fayard, 1968.
Moulinier, Pierre. *Dictionnaire des politiques culturelles*. Paris: Larousse, 2001.
*Musique pour tous: Réalisations et perspectives d'une politique musicale fran-
  çaise*. Paris: La Documentation Française, 1974.
Muzet, Denis. *L'Animation musicale. Cahiers Recherche/Musique* no. 7. Paris:
  Institut National de l'Audiovisuel, 1979.
Negus, Keith. *Music Genres and Corporate Cultures*. London: Routledge, 1999.
Noblet, Jocelyne de, and Franc Lipsic, eds. *Spécial-Pop*. Paris: Albin Michel, 1967.
Nora, Pierre, ed. *Realms of Memory: The Construction of the French Past*,
  vol. 3. Translated by Arthur Goldhammer. New York: Columbia University
  Press, 1998.
"Orientations générales d'une politique d'action culturelle." *Nouvelle Revue
  Socialiste* 4 (1974): 12–31.
Ory, Pascal. *L'entre-deux-mai: Histoire culturelle de la France, mai 1968–mai
  1981*. Paris: Seuil, 1983.

———. "Une 'Révolution culturelle'?" In *Les Années 68: Le temps de la contestation*, edited by Geneviève Dreyfus-Armand, Robert Frank, Marie-Françoise Lévy, and Michelle Zancarini-Fournel, 219–24. Paris: Complexe, 2000.

Ory, Pascal, and Jean-François Sirinelli. *Les intellectuels en France: De l'affaire Dreyfus à nos jours,* 2d ed. Paris: Armand Colin, 1992.

Pasler, Jann. *Composing the Citizen: Music as Public Utility in Third Republic France.* Berkeley: University of California Press, 2009.

Paugam, Jacques. *Génération perdue.* Paris: Robert Laffont, 1977.

Pauli, Hansjörg. *Für wen komponieren Sie eigentlich?* Frankfurt: S. Fischer Verlag, 1971.

Peuchmaurd, Pierre. *Plus vivant que jamais.* Paris: Robert Laffont, 1968.

Peyser, Joan. *Boulez: Composer, Conductor, Enigma.* New York: Schirmer, 1976.

Plossu, Bernard. *Pourquoi n'êtes-vous pas hippie?* Paris: La Palatine, 1970.

Poggioli, Renato. *The Theory of the Avant-Garde.* Translated by Gerald Fitzgerald. Cambridge, MA: Harvard University Press, 1968.

Poirrier, Philippe, ed. *Les politiques culturelles en France.* Paris: La Documentation Française, 2002.

Poupet, Michel. *Les concerts éducatifs et l'animation musicale scolaire.* Paris: Centre National de Documentation Pédagogique, 1978.

Programme commun de gouvernement du parti communiste français et du parti socialiste. Paris: Editions Sociales, 1972.

Quattrocchi, Angelo, and Tom Nairn. *The Beginning of the End: France, May 1968.* London: Verso, 1998.

Quelle université, quelle société? Paris: Seuil, 1968.

Quillien, Christophe. *Génération Rock & Folk: 40 ans de culture rock.* Paris: Flammarion, 2006.

Radano, Ronald. *New Musical Figurations: Anthony Braxton's Cultural Critique.* Chicago: University of Chicago Press, 1993.

Raisner, Albert. *L'Aventure pop.* Paris: Robert Laffont, 1973.

Rajsfus, Maurice. *Mai 1968: sous les pavés, la répression: juin 1968–mars 1974.* Paris: Le Cherche midi éditeur, 1998.

Rauch, Marie-Ange. *Le Bonheur d'entreprendre: Les administrateurs de la France d'outre-mer et la creation du Ministère des Affaires Culturelles.* Paris: Collection du Comité d'histoire du ministère de la culture et de la communication, 1998.

Ravignant, Patrick. *L'Odéon est ouvert.* Paris: Stock, 1968.

Reader, Keith. *Intellectuals and the Left in France since 1968.* London: MacMillan, 1987.

Réalisation et perspectives de la Direction de la Musique, de l'Art lyrique et de la Danse. Paris: Ministère des Affaires Culturelles, 1973.

Revel, Jean-François. *Ni Marx ni Jésus: De la seconde révolution américaine à la seconde révolution mondiale.* Paris: Laffont, 1970.

Rigby, Brian. *Popular Culture in Modern France: A Study of Cultural Discourse.* London: Routledge, 1991.

Ritaine, Evelyne. *Les stratégies de la culture.* Paris: Presses de la Fondation Nationale des Sciences Politiques, 1983.

Robine, Marc. *Il était une fois la chanson française: des origines à nos jours*. Paris: Fayard, 2004.

Ross, George; Stanley Hoffmann, and Sylvia Mazacher, eds. *The Mitterrand Experiment: Continuity and Change in Modern France*. Oxford: Oxford University Press, 1987.

Ross, Kristin. *Fast Cars, Clean Bodies: Decolonization and the Reordering of French Culture*. Cambridge, MA: MIT Press, 1996.

———. *May '68 and Its Afterlives*. Chicago: University of Chicago Press, 2002.

Roszak, Theodore. *The Making of a Counter Culture: Reflections on the Technocratic Society and Its Youthful Opposition*. Garden City, NY: Anchor Books, 1969.

Santamaia, Yves. *Histoire du Parti communiste français*. Paris: La Découverte, 1999.

Scherer, Charles. *L'Animation musicale dans le cadre des Maisons de la Culture*. Mémoire de maîtrise de Musicologie, Université de Paris–Sorbonne, 1976.

Schlesser, Gilles. *Le cabaret 'rive gauche': De la Rose rouge au Bateau ivre (1946–1974)*. Paris: L'Archipel, 2006.

Schnapp, Alain, and Pierre Vidal-Naquet. *The French Student Uprising, November 1967–June 1968: An Analytical Record*. Translated by Maria Jolas. Boston: Beacon Press, 1971.

Seale, Patrick, and Maureen McConville. *Drapeaux rouges sur la France*. Paris: Mercure, 1968.

Seidman, Michael. *The Imaginary Revolution: Parisian Students and Workers in 1968*. New York: Berghahn Books, 2004.

Shack, William. *Harlem in Montmartre: A Paris Jazz Story between the Great Wars*. Berkeley: University of California Press, 2001.

Shank, Theodore. "Atelier Théâtre et Musique: Structuring Everyday Gestures and Sounds." *The Drama Review* 23, no. 3 (September 1979): 3–10.

Simon, Jacques, et al. *L'Immigration algérienne en France: De 1962 à nos jours*. Paris: L'Harmattan, 2002.

Simonot, Michel. *Les animateurs socio-culturels: Etude d'une aspiration à une activité sociale*. Paris: Presses universitaires de France, 1974.

Singer, Daniel. *Prelude to Revolution: France in May 1968*. New York: Hill and Wang, 1970.

Sirinelli, Jean-François, ed. *L'Histoire des droites en France*. 3 vols. Paris: Gallimard, 1992.

———. "La norme et la transgression. Remarques sur la notion de provocation en histoire culturelle." *Vingtième siècle* 93 (2007): 7–14.

Sklower, Jedediah. *Free jazz, la catastrophe feconde: une histoire du monde éclaté du jazz en France (1960–1982)*. Paris: L'Harmattan, 2006.

Smith, Owen. "Fluxus: A Brief History and Other Fictions." In *In the Spirit of Fluxus*, edited by Elizabeth Armstrong and Joan Rothfuss, 22–37. Minneapolis, MN: Walker Arts Center, 1993.

Sorum, Paul Clay. *Intellectuals and Decolonization in France*. Chapel Hill: University of North Carolina Press, 1977.

Sprout, Leslie. "Music for a 'New Era': Composers and National Identity in France 1936–1946." Ph.D. diss., University of California at Berkeley, 2000.

Stovall, Tyler. "From Red Belt to Black Belt: Race, Class and Urban Marginality in Twentieth-Century Paris." In *The Color of Liberty: Histories of Race in France,* edited by Sue Peabody and Tyler Stovall, 351–69. Durham, NC: Duke University Press, 2003.

———. *Paris Noir: African Americans in the City of Light.* New York: Houghton Mifflin, 1996.

Starr, Peter. *Logics of Failed Revolt: French Theory After May '68.* Stanford, CA: Stanford University Press, 1995.

Sweeney, Regina. *Singing Our Way to Victory.* Middletown, CT: Wesleyan University Press, 2001.

Tardieu, Marc. *Les africains en France: de 1914 à nos jours.* Monaco: Rocher, 2006.

Thornton, Sarah. *Club Cultures: Music, Media and Subcultural Capital.* Hanover, NH: Wesleyan University Press, 1995.

Tilly, Charles. *Contentious Performances.* Cambridge: Cambridge University Press, 2008.

Torgue, Henry Skoff. *La Pop Music.* Paris: Presses universitaires de France, 1975.

Tournès, Ludovic. "Amateurs de jazz français et mouvement noir américain." *Les années 68: événements, cultures politiques et modes de vie,* Lettre d'information 22 (February 1997).

———. *New Orleans sur Seine: Histoire du Jazz en France.* Paris: Fayard, 1999.

———. "La réinterpretation du jazz: un phénomène de contre-américanisation dans la France d'après-guerre (1945–1960)." In *Play it again Sim . . . : Hommages à Sim Copans,* special issue of *Revue française d'études américaines* (2001): 72–83.

Toynbee, Jason. *Making Popular Music: Musicians, Creativity and Institutions.* London: Arnold, 2000.

Urfalino, Philippe. *L'invention de la politique culturelle.* Paris: Hachette, 2004.

Vassal, Jacques. *Français, si vous chantiez.* Paris: Albin Michel, 1976.

———. *Léo Ferré: L'enfant millénaire.* Paris: Hors Collection, 2003.

Veitl, Anne. *Politiques de la musique contemporaine: Le compositeur, la "recherche musicale" et l'Etat en France de 1958 à 1991.* Paris: L'Harmattan, 1997.

Veitl, Anne, and Noémi Duchemin. *Maurice Fleuret: une politique démocratique de la musique.* Paris: La Documentation Française, 2000.

Verlant, Gilles, ed. *L'Encyclopédie du rock français.* Paris: Hors Collection, 2000.

Vernillat, France, and Jacques Charpentreau. *La Chanson française.* Paris: Presses universitaires de France, 1971.

Victor, Christian, and Julien Regoli. *Vingt ans de rock français.* Paris: Albin Michel, 1978.

Vienet, René. *Situationists and Enragés in the Occupation Movement, France, May '68.* New York: Autonomedia, 1992.

Vihlen, Elizabeth. "Sounding French: Jazz in Postwar France." Ph.D. diss., SUNY Stonybrook, 2000.

Vingtième Siècle no. 44, Numéro spécial: "La culture politique en France depuis de Gaulle" (October–December 1994).

Von Eschen, Penny. *Satchmo Blows Up the World.* Cambridge, MA: Harvard University Press, 2004.

Vovelle, Michel. "La Marseillaise: War or Peace." In *Realms of Memory: The Construction of the French Past,* vol. 3, edited by Pierre Nora, translated by Arthur Goldhammer, 29–74. New York: Columbia University Press, 1998.

Wallis, Roger, and Krister Malm. *Big Sounds from Small Peoples: The Music Industry in Small Countries.* New York: Pendragon, 1984.

Warne, Chris. "Bringing Counterculture to France: *Actuel* Magazine and the Legacy of May '68." *Modern & Contemporary France* 15, no. 3 (August 2007): 309–24.

———. "Music, Youth and Moral Panics." *Historia Actual Online* 11 (Fall 2006): 51–64.

Weiner, Susan. *Enfants Terribles: Youth and Femininity in the Mass Media in France, 1945–1968.* Baltimore, MD: Johns Hopkins University Press, 2001.

Willener, Alfred. *The Action-Image of Society: On Cultural Politicization.* Translated by A.M. Sheridan Smith. New York: Pantheon, 1970.

Willener, Alfred, and Paul Beaud. *Musique et vie quotidienne.* Paris: Maison Mame, 1973.

Yonnet, Paul. *Jeux, modes et masses: la société française et le moderne 1945–1985.* Paris: Gallimard, 1985.

Zegel, Sylvain. *Les idées de mai.* Paris: Gallimard, 1968.

Index

AACM (Association for the Advancement of Creative Musicians), 114, 116

"A bas l'état policier" (Grange), 72, 73

abortion, 189

Action, 161

action culturelle, 211, 217, 218, 222, 259–64. See also *animation culturelle;* Maisons de la Culture; state cultural policy

Action musique, 60–61, 66, 67, 111

Actuel (magazine), 151, 161, 189–92, 206

Actuel festival, 112–13, 114, 152, 156–57, 209

aesthetic experience, 217, 218, 221, 227–29. *See also* art

aesthetic transgression, 209–10, 272; in contemporary music, 204, 205–6; in free jazz, 113–15. *See also* avant-garde *entries*

African-American musicians, 60, 112–14, 115–17, 118, 135. *See also* free jazz musicians; *specific individuals and groups*

African-American radicalism, 122; Black Panther Party, 132, 141, 142, 150, 296n111; free jazz's link with, 16, 84, 90, 114–17, 120, 131–35, 152–54

African immigration, 120–21, 134, 251

age. *See* generation gap; youth *entries*

"The Age of Culture" (Duhamel), 231

Aix progressive music festival, 176–78, 187, 209

Al-Amin, Jamil (H. Rap Brown), 126

Alan Jack Civilization, 165, 167–68

Alessandrini, Paul, 113, 114, 151; on rock and rock festivals, 168, 169, 172, 177, 189–90, 194, 199–200

Algerian immigrants, 120–21, 134

Algerian War of Independence, 13, 23–24, 120–21, 124, 309n69

Algiers Pan-African Cultural Festival, 112

Alice (band), 164

alienation, 43, 47, 138, 157–58, 180

Almond, Gabriel, 276n17

Alpes (band), 201

Altamont festival, 172, 185

alterity, 5, 19, 85, 94, 104, 271–72; of jazz, 16, 117, 127, 272; of rock, 159; unconscious as, 138

alternatif rock, 272

Althusser, Louis, 122, 123–24, 220

amateur creative practice, 211, 233, 267, 270, 314n193; amateur/virtuoso opposition, 248; Atelier lyrique du Rhin's children's operas, 212, 243–50; ATEM's Bagnolet project, 251–59; creator/consumer distinction, 47, 67, 262; Ferrari's proponence of, 224–27; Galerie Sonore, 242–43; as threat to professional musicians, 58–59

American civil rights movement, 115–16

American contemporary music, 206, 208

American folk revival, 106

American jazz musicians, 60, 112–14, 115–17, 118, 135, 140

American race relations, 120, 133, 138
American rock. *See* Anglo-American rock
American youth culture, 17. *See also*
 Anglo-American youth culture
Ame Son, 178
Amiens Maison de la Culture: Ferrari's
 work at, 212, 222, 224–25, 227–29;
 Rosenfeld's work at, 239
Amougies festival, 112–13, 114, 152,
 156–57, 209
Amour Anarchie (Ferré), 93
amplification, 58
Amy, Gilbert, 53
Anglo-American rock: appeal for French
 youth, 158–59; French emulations of,
 161, 163, 168, 188; French pop and,
 103, 105; on French radio and
 television, 164, 166; French record
 industry and, 166, 300n52; jazz and,
 129, 130; live shows in France, 171,
 200; popularity in France, 114–15, 129,
 130, 164; press devoted to, 164, 167;
 transculturation of, 164, 299n31. *See
 also* rock *entries; specific artists and
 bands*
Anglo-American youth culture, 17, 159,
 160–63
animation culturelle, 17–18, 203, 211–12,
 219, 229–30, 241–42, 267; changing
 conceptions of, 229–32, 237; decline of,
 259–64; failures and critiques of,
 219–22, 235, 259–61; roles of the
 animateur, 219–20, 230, 232, 237, 244,
 260. See also *animation musicale;*
 Maisons de la Culture
animation musicale, 17–18, 203, 212, 216,
 240–41, 265, 271; Aperghis and the
 ATEM, 251–59; Atelier lyrique du
 Rhin's children's opera programs,
 244–50; educators' opposition to,
 259–60; experimental *animation*,
 238–39, 239–40, 242–43, 246–49;
 Ferrari's work at Amiens, 212, 222,
 224–25, 227–29; Galerie Sonore at the
 Grand Palais, 242–43; Landowski's
 ten-year plan, 216, 217, 233–34,
 264–65; post-1969 changes and decline,
 233–35, 237–38, 264–66; traditional
 animation, 238, 239, 240–41. See also
 animation culturelle; Ministry of
 Cultural Affairs; state cultural policy
anthems, 8. *See also* "The Internationale";
 "La Marseillaise"; "Les nouveaux
 partisans"

anti-casseur (antihooligan) law of 1970,
 173–74
anticolonialism. *See* colonialism; cultural
 colonialism; decolonization
Antoine, 85, 105–7, 163, 167
Aperghis, Georges, 208, 212, 251–59
L'Apocalypse de Jean (Henry), 206
Aragon, Louis, 65, 66, 95–96
Arc de Triomphe, "The Internationale" at, 34
ARFI (Association à la recherche d'un
 folklore imaginaire), 153
Armfield, Louis, 142
Aron, Raymond, 10–11, 19
art: political utility of, 124, 143; politicized
 contestations of, 25–26, 41–42, 50;
 spiritualized notions of, 217. *See also*
 culture *entries*
Art Ensemble of Chicago, 87, 112, 113,
 114, 116, 292n32
artistic identity: creator/consumer
 opposition, 47, 67, 262; demystification/
 despecialization impulses, 42–44, 48–49,
 67–68, 223–24, 225, 241, 264;
 specialization revalorized, 264
arts commerce: artworks as commodities,
 44–45, 281n71. *See also* music industry
arts education: popular education
 movement, 96, 219; in state cultural
 policy, 218, 221, 231–32, 237, 238,
 259–60. *See also* music education
arts policy. *See* cultural policies; state
 cultural policy
Assises nationales de la musique, 260
Association à la recherche d'un folklore
 imaginaire (ARFI), 153
Association des professeurs d'éducation
 musicale, 259, 260
Association for the Advancement of
 Creative Musicians (AACM), 114, 116
Atelier lyrique du Rhin, 211, 212, 243–44;
 L'Ile de la vieille musique, 244–50, 256;
 Un roi sans soleil, 244
Atelier théâtre et musique (ATEM), 211,
 251–59
Attali, Jacques, 87, 262
Aubin, Tony, 208
Aufray, Hugues, 106
Auric, Georges, 213
auteur-compositeur-interprètes, 93–94. See
 also *specific artists*
authenticity concerns, 8, 41, 85; French jazz
 practitioners, 135, 138–40, 296n108; in
 French rock culture, 159, 163, 170–71.
 See also cultural legitimacy

autogestion (self-management), 261–62
Auto Jazz: Le destin tragique de Lorenzo Bandini (Wilen), 87
automatic writing, 44, 93, 137–38
Auvers-sur-Oise rock festival, 198–99
avant-garde, as epithet, 9
avant-garde musical forms, 17; *animation musicale* and, 240, 242; appeal of, 114–15, 205–6; in contemporary music, 208, 223, 246–49; critiques of, 209–10; decline of, 264; linked with protest/contestation, 114–16, 207. *See also* contemporary (classical) music; free jazz
avant-gardes, 27, 41–42, 272; as inspiration for cultural agitators, 44–45, 47–48
"Avec le temps" (Ferré), 92
Ayers, Kevin, and The Whole World, 196
Ayler, Albert, 113, 115, 118, 119, 131, 138–39, 191

"Babylone USA" (Tusques), 150
Badiou, Alain, 122
Baez, Joan, 178
Bagnolet, 251; Aperghis's ATEM project, 251–59
Ballif, Claude, 224
banlieues, 251, 266; contemporary music projects in, 211, 212, 251–59
Baraka, Amiri, 115, 119, 132
Barclay records, 95, 166
Barrat, Pierre, 244
Barraud, Henry, 213
Barrault, Jean-Louis, 48
Barthes, Roland, 44, 122
Baumol, William, 55
Bayle, François, 53, 208
Béart, Guy, 71
beatnik movement and music, 100, 105–7
bebop, 119, 126, 130
Bechet, Sidney, 112, 130
Becker-Ho, Alice, 278n17
Beer, Ronnie, 296n111
Belloin, Gérard, 304n157
benefit concerts, 42, 53, 296n111
Benjamin (pop performer), 107
Benjamin, Walter, 44, 225
Bensaïd, Daniel, 32–34
Béranger, François, 19, 201
Berger, Daniel, 113
Berio, Luciano, 206, 207
Bertin, Jacques, 19
Best, 164

Biasini, Emile, 215, 216
"Bienvenue à . . ." (television show), 71
Bièvres rock festival, 199
Biot Popanalia festival, 174, 178–79, 209
Bizot, Jean-François, 178, 189
black nationalism, 115, 132–33
Black Panther Party, 132, 141, 142, 150, 296n111
black power, 132. *See also* African-American radicalism
blousons noirs, 103
Blues Convention, 164, 165
Blues People (Baraka), 120
Bluesy Mind (Alan Jack Civilization), 167–68
La Bohème (club), 118
Bosseur, Jean-Yves, 208
Bosson, Bernard de, 166
Boucourechliev, André, 208
Boulez, Pierre, 53, 136, 205, 208, 264, 282n101; at IRCAM, 233; and Landowski's appointment, 215–16; Semaine de la musique contemporaine lecture, 1–2, 4, 8–9
Bouquin, Jean, 198–99
Bourdieu, Pierre, 122, 129, 169, 184, 221; on aesthetic experience, 227–28; homologies notion, 85, 89
bourgeois culture: contestations/critiques of, 41, 123, 197, 221–22, 224, 232; embourgeoisement, 86, 117. *See also* cultural agitation
"La bourgeoisie périra noyée dans les eaux glacées du calcul égoiste" (Tusques), 142, 144*table*, 146, 147*ex.*
Les Bourgeois de Calais, 163
Bourseiller, Antoine, 119
La bouteille à la mer (Aperghis), 251–52, 253–58, 254*ex.*
Bowen, William, 55
Les Bowlers, 105
Brassens, Georges, 92
Brau, Jean-Louis, 46
Braxton, Anthony, 112, 114
Brel, Jacques, 92, 200
Brinton, Maurice (quoted), 38
British invasion bands, 105
British rock. *See* Anglo-American rock
Brown, H. Rap, 126
Brown, Marion, 112, 119
Bruits (Attali), 87, 262
Buin, Yves, 119, 122, 131, 137, 138–39
BYG/Actuel, 112, 117, 189; Actuel festival, 112–13, 114, 152, 156–57, 209

Cage, John, 206
Cahiers du jazz: "Ideology and Aesthetics in Free Jazz," 123–25
Caillois, Roger, 195
"Ça ira," 29, 97
Calvet, Louis-Jean, 83–84, 85, 95
Campus (radio program), 164, 165
CAR (Comité d'action révolutionnaire), 43, 46–50, 210
Carles, Philippe, 119; *Free Jazz Black Power,* 131–33
cartoons, 34–35, 35*fig.,* 108, 108*fig.*
Castanet, Pierre-Albert, 276n14
Caune, Jean, 263
La cause du peuple, 75, 80, 140, 153, 161, 173, 272
Caux, Daniel, 116
CBS records, 166, 171
Céline, Louis, 119–20
"Ce n'est qu'un début, continuons le combat," 28–29
Center for Action and Spontaneous Creation, 224
Centre démocratie et progrès, 231
Centre national d'art et de culture (Centre Georges Pompidou), 232–33
Ceremony (Henry), 87
Certeau, Michel de, 20, 70, 71, 195
"C'est extra" (Ferré), 92, 96
CFDT (Confédération française démocratique du travail), 61
CGT (Confédération générale du travail), 37–39, 61–62, 66, 75, 191
Chaban-Delmas, Jacques, 173, 232
Chabiron, Jacques, 169
Chailley, Jacques, 53, 208, 215
Chalon-sur-Saône Maison de la Culture, 222
Champs-Elysées march (7 May 1968), 32–36
chanson, 16, 18–19, 91–92, 104, 171, 298n31; as entertainment for striking workers, 3, 5; interactions with jazz, 87, 150; interactions with rock, 87, 199; Left Bank/Right Bank types, 94–95; literary values of, 93, 94, 95–96, 104, 110; press coverage, 167; in state cultural policy, 214, 265. *See also* revolutionary chanson; *specific artists and titles*
chanson artists, 54, 91–92, 200, 201. See also *specific artists*
chanson révolutionnaire. See revolutionary chanson

chanson rive gauche, 93–95
Chansons de mai-juin 1968 (Grange), 72–73, 73*fig.*
"Le chant des barricades," 21
"Le chant des partisans," 75
chants and slogans, 28–29, 38, 72–73, 97, 99
Charlan, Marc, 199
Charlie Hebdo, 198*fig.*
Le chat qui pêche, 118
Les Chats sauvages, 103
Les Chaussettes noires, 103
Chautemps, Jean-Louis, 137, 296n108
Cherry, Don, 113, 118, 136, 178
"Le Chien" (Ferré), 93
children: Atelier lyrique du Rhin's children's opera programs, 244–50; cultural innocence of, 241–42, 243, 244–45
China and Chinese communism, 121, 185, 270; Cultural Revolution, 73, 76, 142. *See also* Maoism
cinema, 129, 136; film music, 146
The Civic Culture: Political Attitudes and Democracy in Five Nations (Almond and Verba), 276n17
Claire, 19
Clapton, Eric, 178
Clarke, Kenny, 112
classical music, 58, 85, 89, 90; contemporary/classic-romantic opposition, 249; in state cultural policy, 214–16, 234, 235, 238, 239–40. *See also* contemporary (classical) music
Clément, Claude, 176–77
Cohelmec Ensemble, 111
Cohn-Bendit, Daniel, 10, 21, 32, 33*fig.,* 72
Cold War, 23
Coleman, Bill, 112
Coleman, Ornette, 118, 136
Colmar: Atelier lyrique du Rhin, 211, 212, 243–50
colonialism/anticolonialism, 273; allegorical images in *L'Ile de la vieille musique,* 246–48, 249; free jazz and, 8, 115, 120–22, 131–35; regionalism and, 297n129. *See also* cultural colonialism
Coltrane, John, 115, 125–26
Comité d'action du spectacle, 139–40
Comité d'action révolutionnaire (CAR), 43, 46–50, 210
Comité national de musique, 215
Comité révolutionnaire d'agitation culturelle. *See* CRAC
Comme à la radio (Fontaine), 87

"Comme une fille" (Ferré), 96–97
Commission nationale pour l'étude des
  problèmes de la musique, 213–15
communism: de Gaulle's invocation of communist threat, 63; "The Internationale"
  and, 31. *See also* Maoism; Marxism;
  specific organizations
Communist Party. *See* PCF
Comolli, Jean-Louis: *Free Jazz Black Power,*
  131–33; responses and critiques,
  123–25, 126–27; "Voyage au bout de la
  New Thing," 119–22, 124–25, 131
Compagnie européenne du disque, 171
Compagnie républicaine de sécurité (CRS),
  32, 50
composers: as *animateurs* and researchers,
  222, 236–37, 239–40, 265; responses to
  populist critiques, 210–12; revalorization of compositional craftsmanship,
  264. *See also specific composers*
composers' strike, 54, 57
composers' union, 43–44, 54
concerts: decline of live performance,
  55–58, 213–14; durying May '68, 28.
  See also cultural agitation; *fêtes*/festivals;
  rock concerts; rock festivals
Confédération française démocratique du
  travail (CFDT), 61
Confédération générale du travail (CGT),
  37–39, 61–62, 66, 75, 191
Connaître le jazz (radio program), 126–27
Conservatoire national supérieur de
  musique, 28, 51–53, 54, 68, 208, 213,
  282n92
Constantin, Philippe, 90–91, 122, 288n49
constructivism, 43
contemporary (classical) music, 19, 203–12,
  222–67; contemporary/classic-romantic
  opposition, 249; decline of experimentalism, 264; democratization impulses
  and practices, 17–18, 210–11; improvisation in, 87, 208, 264; interactions with
  jazz, 87, 88–90, 118, 126, 136–37;
  interactions with rock, 87, 90, 168;
  linked with cultural elite, 41, 84, 114,
  211; 1970s decline and stagnation,
  203–4, 208–9; politicized discourse
  about, 1–2, 4–5; post-May '68 vitality
  of, 204–8; production and sales, 203–4,
  206, 208–9; in the provinces, 219–20;
  recherche musicale, 235–38, 263–64,
  265; seen as youth music, 207, 209;
  state and municipal funding for, 6,
  211–12, 233, 236, 237–38, 252, 258–

59, 265, 267; as transgressive/contesta-
  tory, 204, 205–6, 207. *See also* state
  cultural policy; *specific composers,
  works, and groups*
contemporary music audiences, 204–5,
  206–7, 208, 306n24; audience
  expansion efforts, 211, 264–65
contemporary music festivals, 204, 205,
  206–8, 209, 306n24
"Contemporary Music in Question,"
  204–5
contraception, 189
Cording, Henry, 103
corporate sponsorship, regional arts groups,
  266
cost disease, 55–56, 57–58
Cotro, Vincent, 137
Coulonges, Georges, 104
counterculture, 152, 157, 160–63, 181,
  184–85. *See also* youth culture
counterculture press, 161
Coxhill, Lol, 196
CRAC (Comité révolutionnaire d'agitation
  culturelle), 55, 66, 71, 100–101;
  founding, 40–41; May '68 actions,
  43–46, 67–68, 210
Cream, 165
creation, in state cultural policy, 262–65
Cristiani, François-René, 179
Crocq, Jean-Noël, 282n92
CRS (Compagnie républicaine de sécurité),
  32, 50
Cuba, Ferrari's trip to, 223
Cuban revolution, 121
cultural agitation, 26, 27, 40–50, 55, 66–68,
  210; CRAC's founding and activities,
  40–41, 43–46, 67–68, 210; *gauchiste*
  interventions at rock performances, 175,
  177–84, 187, 196–97; Odéon theater
  occupation, 46–50
cultural colonialism, 219; free jazz and, 133,
  135, 139
cultural decentralization, 216
cultural democratization, 17–18, 20, 26,
  27, 267, 274; cultural agitators'
  democratic aims, 45–46, 67, 210;
  failures and critiques of state efforts,
  219–22; PCF's position on, 123; rock's
  potential for, 187–88; as state objective,
  211, 212, 233, 307n29. *See also action
  culturelle*
cultural deprivation, presumptions of,
  228–29, 241–42, 265
cultural diversity, 240, 265, 267, 270

cultural leftism, 160, 184–85, 191–92, 194; cultural interpretations of May '68, 11–13, 14, 195, 270–71, 274
cultural legitimacy, 8; jazz, 129–31, 136, 139–41, 296n108. *See also* authenticity concerns
cultural mediation, 17–18, 211–12; aesthetic experience and, 217, 218, 221, 227–29; Bourdieu on, 227–28; changing purposes of, 229–31; creator/mediator rift, 260–61; politicized critiques of, 219–20; presumptions of cultural deprivation/innocence, 228–29, 241–42, 265; social utility of, 217, 219, 266, 267. See also *animation culturelle; développement culturel*
cultural policies: as display, 258–59; political parties, 123, 210, 258–59, 261–65, 314n180; radical groups, 123, 185. *See also* state cultural policy
cultural production: creator/consumer boundary, 47, 67, 262; deprofessionalization of, 223, 262, 264; policy focus on artistic creation, 262–65; politicized notions of, 25, 123–25, 210. *See also* amateur creative practice; composers; musicians
cultural relativism, 240, 265, 267
culture: contestations of, 25–26, 41–42, 50; political utility of, 124, 143; social utility of, 231. *See also* art

Dadaism, 43
Dagon, 183
Damase, Jean-Michel, 208
Damian, Jean-Michel, 204
Les damnés de la terre (Fanon), 121–22
dance, 222
dance crazes, 105
dance music, 95, 104, 151
Daniel-Lesur, Jean-Yves, 208
Davis, Angela, 134
dazibao, 142; Tusques's *Piano Dazibao*, 141, 142, 143
Dear Prof Leary (Free Rock Band), 90–91
"Debout les damnés de Nanterre," 35fig.
Debré, Michel, 64
decolonization, 23–24, 86, 120–22, 218–19
Decoust, Michel, 208
Defaye, Jean-Michel, 95
de Gaulle, Charles, 11, 23, 62–63; SAMuP's letter to, 56, 57
de Gaulle government, 309n69; Grenelle accords and aftermath, 23, 61–69; May

'68 events and, 22, 23, 40, 50, 269; SAMuP's relations with, 60–61. *See also* state cultural policy
Degeyter, Pierre, 30
Delalande, François, 203, 243
Delannoi, Gil, 273
Delcloo, Claude, 112, 189
Deleuze, Gilles, 122
Delorme, Michel (quoted), 138
Denis, Didier, 204
Descendre dans la rue, 278n17
"Description automatique d'un paysage désolé" (Tusques), 137
développement culturel, 231–32
Devotion (band), 164
direct action. *See* cultural agitation
Direction de la musique (originally Service de la musique), 215–16, 233–38, 252, 263. See also *animation musicale*
Disc'AZ, 101
Dister, Alain, 200
diversity. *See* cultural diversity
Dolphy, Eric, 136
Domaine musical, 208
Dorigné, Michel, 128
"D'où viens-tu Billy Boy?" (Gérard), 103
Downbeat, 119
Drogoz, Philippe, 208
Drouet, Jean-Pierre, 136
Duchamp, Marcel, 44
Dufourt, Hugues, 264
Duhamel, Jacques, 230–31
Dumesnil, René, 213
Durkheim, Emile, 195
Dutchman (Baraka), 119
Dutilleux, Henri, 53, 57, 204, 208, 213
Dutronc, Jacques, 107, 167
Duvignaud, Jean, 195
Dylan, Bob, 106, 167
Dynastie Crisis, 165

Ecole des Beaux-Arts, 25, 32, 33fig.
economic context, 23, 24
écriture, seen as utopian space, 12, 264
Edouard (pop performer), 107
education: cultural attitudes and, 220, 221; popular education movement, 96, 219. See also arts education; music education
egalitarianism: in rock, 187–88. *See also* cultural democratization
electroacoustic music, 52, 68, 203, 264; *recherche musicale* programs, 235–38, 263–64, 265; tape compositions,

224–25, 226–27, 228. See also *specific composers, groups, and works*
"Éléments d'une théorie sociologique de la perception artistique" (Bourdieu), 227–28
elite culture: contemporary music linked with, 41, 84, 114, 211; state cultural policy and, 218–19
Eloy, Jean-Claude, 265
"Les Elucubrations" (Antoine), 106
English-language pop, French resistance to, 164, 298n31. *See also* Anglo-American rock
L'Enragé, 30, 65–66
Ensemble Ars Nova, 208
Ensemble Intercontemporain, 238
Erismann, Guy, 80
Estienne, Charles, 96
établissement, 74
Etats généraux du cinéma, 43
L'été 68 (album) (Ferré), 93, 96–100
"L'été 68" (song) (Ferré), 93, 96, 97–100, 99*ex.*, 110
l'été chaud, 175, 177–84, 187, 196–97
l'été pop, 171, 172–80
"Et moi et moi et moi" (Dutronc), 107
Evariste, 41, 100–102, 107–10
ex-Gauche prolétarienne, 71, 74–75, 184, 186, 191, 192–94; rock festival actions, 175, 177, 178, 179, 180–81, 182–83. *See also* GP
existentialism, 130
Exposition 60/72, 232, 233
L'Express, 107
expression, liberation of *(prise de parole)*, 11, 12, 20, 68, 273–74; as goal of cultural agitation, 45–48; through rock, 187–88
Eyerman, Ron, 27

factory concerts, 3, 72
factory occupations, 37–39, 50
Fanon, Frantz, 121–22
Fauré, Gabriel, 204
"La Faute à Nanterre" (Evariste), 100
Favors, Malachi, 113
Fechner, Christiane, 106
Fédération anarchiste, 28, 43
Fédération de la gauche démocrate et socialiste (FGDS), 62
Fédération des étudiants révolutionnaires (FER), 36
femininity, in *yéyé*, 104, 105
feminist movement, 186, 192, 273
FER (Fédération des étudiants révolution-naires), 36

Ferrari, Luc, 53, 136, 208, 222–29, 264, 265; Amiens *musique concrète* project, 212, 222, 224–25, 227–29; *Hétérozygote*, 226; politicization, 223–24, 309n69; *Presque rien*, 225–26, 226–27, 228, 229; proponence of amateur musical practices, 212, 224–27; *Tautologos III*, 225
Ferrat, Jean, 92, 200
Ferré, Léo, 19, 87, 92–100, 167, 283–84n119; anarchist politics of, 28, 43, 92; background and early career, 93–96; May 10 concert, 28, 42–43; as poet, 95–96; political festival performances, 200, 201; post-May '68 work, 92–93, 96–100, 110; radicals' criticisms of, 42–43, 92
Ferry, Luc, 12, 270
Festival d'Amougies, 112–13, 114, 152, 156–57, 209
Festival d'automne, 204, 232, 233, 252, 256–58
Festival de Royan, 205, 207–8
Fête de l'Humanité, 200–203
fêtes/festivals, 20, 194–202, 270, 304n157; convivial/collective spirit of, 172–73, 194–95, 197; *gauchiste fêtes sauvages*, 195–96, 304n160; party-organized political festivals, 200–202; politicized understandings of, 193–95, 201–2; Sorbonne occupation celebration, 2; state-supported music festivals, 232, 234. *See also* rock festivals; *specific festivals and locations*
FGDS (Fédération de la gauche démocrate et socialiste), 62
Fille qui mousse, 183
film. *See* cinema
First Pan-African Cultural Festival (Algiers), 112
First World War, 80
Fléouter, Claude, 178–79
Fleuret, Maurice, 28, 53, 90, 206, 242–43, 257; as head of Direction de la musique, 263–65, 314n193
Les Fleurs de Pavot, 163
FLIP (Force de libération et d'intervention pop), 181–84, 187, 194
Fluxus, 44, 281n71
folk music and folksingers, 100, 102, 106, 172, 190; Antoine, 85, 105–7, 163, 167; regional and world musics, 153–54, 274; state views of, 214
Fontaine, Brigitte, 19, 87, 167, 201

Force de libération et d'intervention pop (FLIP), 181–84, 187, 194
"Les forces réactionnaires" (Tusques), 143, 144*table,* 145–46
foreign musicians: concerns about, 56–57, 58, 59–60, 135. *See also* American jazz musicians
Foucault, Michel, 122
France Nouvelle, 261
François, Claude, 105, 200
Franco-Prussian War, 29, 30
Freedom Now Suite (Roach), 150
Free Jazz (Tusques), 118, 137–38
free jazz, 111–54, 271, 272, 274; arrival in France, 19, 118–19; BYG/Actuel's recordings and festival, 112–13, 114, 152, 156–57, 209; and contemporary music, 87, 88–90, 118, 126, 136–37; critical advocacy of, 118–25, 131; in the French cultural landscape, 111–17, 129–31, 151–54; immediacy, power and physicality valorized, 113, 114; indigenous French scene, 118, 135–41; interactions with chanson, 87, 150; interactions with rock, 90, 113, 165, 168, 178; legitimacy and authenticity concerns, 129–31, 135, 136, 138–40, 296n108; linked with African-American radicalism, 16, 84, 90, 114–17, 120, 131–35, 152–54; linked with anticolonial struggle, 8, 115, 120–22, 131–35; linked with French social struggle, 26, 111, 139–41; in the media, 112, 114, 116, 118–19; at political festivals, 201; record labels devoted to, 112, 117. *See also* jazz criticism; Tusques, François; *other artists and groups*
Free Jazz Black Power (Comolli and Carles), 131–33
free jazz musicians: Americans in France, 60, 112–14, 115–17, 118; French practitioners, 60, 111, 118, 135–41, 296n108. See also *specific artists*
Free Rock Band, 87, 90–91
French cultural patrimony, 130; state cultural policy and, 211, 214, 222, 231, 235
French economy, 23, 24, 70–71, 86
French government: antihooligan law of 1970, 173–74; before May '68, 23; 1981 elections, 268–69; repression of radical groups and media, 173–76, 201; rock festival concerns and prohibitions, 173–74, 176. *See also* de Gaulle government; state cultural policy; *other specific politicians and parties*
French politics: before May '68, 23–24. See also *gauchisme; specific groups and parties*
French Revolution: allusions in Ferré's "L'été 68," 97, 98; revolutionary festivals, 194; songs of, 29, 97
French rock, 104, 272; emergence and maturation of, 19, 103, 160, 163–65, 168, 170–71; Léo Ferré's shift to, 92–93; live music scene, 171; at political festivals, 200–201; in the press, 167–69, 171; progressive rock, 165, 168–69, 172, 287n37; on radio and television, 165–66, 299n37; record industry and, 163, 164, 171, 299n38; reliance on Anglo-American models, 161, 163, 168; transculturation of Anglo-American styles, 164, 299n31. See also rock *entries; specific artists and works*
French rock bands: emulation of Anglo-American bands, 161, 163, 168, 188; on Fête de l'Humanité programs, 200–201; politicized underground bands, 183–84; problems faced by, 165–69; progressive bands, 165, 168–69, 172, 287n37. See also *specific groups*
French rock culture, 12, 17, 271; authenticity concerns in, 159, 163, 170–71; contemporary music's decline and, 209; and failure of *l'été pop,* 178–80; FLIP's activities, 181–84, 187, 194; fragmentation/divisions in, 84–85, 85–86, 172, 199–200, 287n37; politicization of, 160, 171, 177–78, 180–81, 184–92, 194; Queÿsanne's study of, 156–59, 170, 271; radical leftist views of, 184–92. *See also* rock audiences
Front de libération de la jeunesse, 186
Front homosexuel d'action révolutionnaire, 186
Front nationale, 269
funding: corporate, 266. *See also* state funding
fusion musics. *See* generic interactions
Futura, 117
futurism, 43

Gagnard, Madeleine, 241
Gagneux, Renaud, 52, 282n101
Gainsbourg, Serge, 167
Galerie sonore, 242–43
Gall, France, 70, 100

Gallant, Mavis (quoted), 62–63
Gallois-Montbrun, Raymond, 52, 213
garage rock, 105
Garaudy, Roger, 123
Gauche prolétarienne. *See* GP
gauchisme, gauchistes (radical leftism), 68,
71, 160, 184, 201–2, 269–71; and the
counterculture, 17, 158–59, 185–91;
critiques of, 191–92; government repression, 173–76; and the institutional left,
26, 32, 37, 66, 124–25. See also *specific
individuals and organizations*
Gaulle, Charles de, 11, 23, 62–63; SAMuP's
letter to, 56, 57. *See also* de Gaulle
government
Gaullist counterdemonstrations, 31, 63–64,
279n33
Geismar, Alain, 173, 175
gendered critiques of *yéyé*, 104–5
general strike (May–June 1968). *See* strikes
generation gap, generational conflict, 89,
102, 107–9, 119, 170
generic interactions, 87–91, 88*fig.*, 270,
288n49; Bourdieu's homologies and,
89–90; jazz/chanson, 87, 150; jazz/
contemporary music, 87, 88–90, 118,
126, 136–37; at party-organized
political festivals, 200, 201; rock/
chanson, 87, 199; rock/contemporary
music, 87, 90, 168; rock/jazz, 90, 113,
165, 168, 178; rock/*variétés*, 199
Genet, Jean, 48
Gennari, John, 127
genre cultures, 6, 7–8, 16, 82–86, 271–72,
274. See also *specific genres*
genres. *See* musical genres; *specific genres*
Georgakarakos, Jean, 113, 174
Georgi, Frank, 64
Gérard, Danyel, 103
GERM (Groupe d'étude et réalisation
musicale), 208, 264
Gérôme, Noëlle, 202
Gimme Shelter, 185
Giscard d'Estaing, Valéry, 262, 268
Globokar, Vinko, 136
Godard, Jean-Luc, 72, 119
Goldman, Pierre, 11
Gong, 178, 196
Gounod, Charles, 28
government actions and policies. *See* French
government; state cultural policy
GP (Gauche prolétarienne): government
crackdown and dissolution, 173, 175,
201; and "Les nouveaux partisans,"

79–83, 272. See also *La Cause du
peuple;* ex-Gauche prolétarienne
Grange, Dominique, 9, 41, 71–81, 110;
background and early career, 71; fall
1968 record, 72–73, 73*fig.;* government
prosecution of, 173; May '68 participa-
tion, 71–72; turn to Maoism, 73–75. *See
also* "Les Nouveaux partisans"
graphic scores, 208, 211, 223, 247–48, 264
Grateful Dead, 199
Grenelle accords, 23, 61–62
grève du silence, 54. *See also* musicians'
strike
Grisey, Gérard, 264
GRM (Groupe de recherches musicales),
223, 243
Groupe d'étude et réalisation musicale
(GERM), 208, 264
groupuscule epithet, 2, 8–9
Groys, Boris, 8
Guem, 150
La Guepe (Vitet), 87
Guérin, Beb, 118, 135, 142, 150, 296n111
Guibert, Gérome, 166
Gulag Archipelago (Solzhenitsyn), 270
Les Gypsys, 105

Haley, Bill, 103
Hallier, Jean-Edern, 173
Hallyday, Johnny, 103, 106, 130, 163, 164,
167, 200
hard rock, 287n37
Hausser, Michel, 59–60
Hawkins, Peter, 95
hedonism, 12, 184
Helffer, Claude, 53
Hendrix, Jimi, 167
Hennion, Antoine, 298n31
Henry, Pierre, 19, 87, 114, 205, 206, 265;
Journées de musique contemporaine
concert, 206, 207
Hétérozygote (Ferrari), 226
Higelin, Jacques, 199
hippies and hippie movement, 157, 158,
161, 162–63, 176; French emulations of,
179–80; *gauchiste* views of, 185, 187
Hirsch, Jean-François, 209–10
Hodeir, André, 119, 126–27, 128–29, 130
Hoffman, Abbie, 184
Hommes et problèmes du jazz (Hodeir),
128–29
homologies, 85, 89–90
homosexuality and homosexual groups,
186, 189

Howard, Noah, 112
Huggins, Erika, 144
L'Humanité, 72, 200
"The Hunting of the Snark" (Carroll), 143

idealism. *See* utopianism
identity and identity articulations, 7–8,
    27–28; through musical genres, 7–8, 16,
    82–86, 271, 274. *See also* genre cultures;
    "The Internationale"; *specific genres*
"Ideology and Aesthetics in Free Jazz,"
    123–25
L'idiot international, 80, 92, 173, 189;
    Queysanne interviews, 155–56, 170, 271
L'idiot liberté, 189
L'Ile de la vieille musique (Prin), 244–49,
    247*ex.*, 250*ex.*, 256
L'Image-action de la société (Willener), 152
immigration, 120–21, 134, 251
improvisation, 111, 152; in contemporary
    music, 87, 208, 253, 264; in free jazz,
    137–38, 152
individualism, 12, 20, 44
institutional left: *gauchistes* and, 26, 32, 37,
    66, 124–25. *See also* political parties;
    trade unions; *specific organizations*
Institut national d'éducation populaire,
    230
intellectualism: in French jazz, 138; in rock,
    169
Intercommunal Free Dance Music
    Orchestra, 150–51, 153
Intercommunal Music (Tusques), 142,
    143–50, 144*table*, 145*ex.*, 147*ex.*,
    149*ex.*; musical structure and analysis,
    144–50; "Portrait d'Erika Huggins,"
    144, 148–50; track titles, 142, 143–44
"The Internationale," 8, 30–32, 34–40,
    121–22, 191; as symbol of student-
    worker solidarity, 36–39, 85; as symbol
    of working-class identity, 8, 31, 35–36,
    39; at Mitterrand's inauguration, 269;
    counterpoint with "La Marseillaise," 29,
    30, 80; in PCF rhetoric, 65, 66; May '68
    students' adoption of, 15, 26–27, 30–32,
    34–37, 65, 85; sung at 7 May march,
    30–32, 34–36
IRCAM, 233, 236, 238
Iron Butterfly, 196
Isle of Wight rock festival, 172, 179

Jackson, Jeffrey, 117
Jagger, Mick, 182
Jalard, Michel-Claude, 119

Jamison, Andrew, 27
Jarman, Joseph, 116
jazz, 26, 58; alterity of, 117, 127; in the
    French cultural landscape, 116–17,
    118–22, 127–31, 151–53; interactions
    with chanson, 87, 150; interactions with
    contemporary music, 87, 88–90, 118,
    126, 136–37; interactions with rock, 90,
    113, 165, 168, 178; race and, 127,
    131–35, 138, 295n94; SAMuP and,
    59–60; at Sorbonne occupation, 2, 5,
    41; state cultural policy and, 214, 265;
    in the U.S., 127–28, 130; universalist
    views of, 127–29, 130–31. *See also* free
    jazz entries
Jazz (Dorigné), 128
"Jazz, Poésie et Pouvoir Noir" concert,
    296n111
jazz criticism, 112, 118, 122–27, 151, 152,
    274; *Free Jazz Black Power*, 131–33;
    on French jazz practitioners, 138–39;
    "Ideology and Aesthetics in Free Jazz,"
    123–25; in the U.S., 127–28; universal-
    ism in, 127–29, 130–31; "Voyage au
    bout de la New Thing," 119–22,
    124–25, 126, 131
Jazz et jazz (Hodeir), 126
Jazzex (Parmegiani), 137
Jazz-Hot, 111, 112, 122–23; Hodeir at, 126;
    Le Bris at, 122, 140, 153; reviews and
    articles, 90, 118, 122, 151
Jazz Magazine, 112, 118, 123; articles,
    88–89, 90, 119–22
JCR (Jeunesse communiste révolutionnaire),
    10, 32–34, 71, 124
Jeanneau, François, 165
Jefferson Airplane, 199
Jenkins, Leroy, 114
Jenny-Clark, Jean-François, 136
Jeune Afrique, 90
Jeunesse communiste révolutionnaire (JCR),
    10, 32–34, 71, 124
Jeunesses musicales de France, 237, 239,
    266
Jolas, Betsy, 224
Jones, LeRoi. *See* Baraka, Amiri
Jouffa, François, 172
Journées de musique contemporaine, 206–7,
    209
juvenile delinquency, 103
Juvet, Patrick, 199

Kandahar, 201
Kant, Immanuel, 228

Kessel, Joseph, 75
The Kinks, 200
Kiwan, Nadia, 266
Koechlin, Philippe, 114
Kofsky, Frank, 115
Komintern (band), 183
Kopelowicz, Guy, 119

labor unions. *See* trade unions
Lacy, Steve, 112, 118
Lafitte, Guy, 59–60
Lancelot, Michel, 164
Landowski, Marcel, 208, 215–16, 233–34, 237, 238, 240–41, 264–65
Lang, Jack, 262–63, 264, 274
Lapassade, Georges, 41
Lavilliers, Bernard, 199
Le Bris, Michel, 119, 122, 140, 153
Le Dantec, Jean-Pierre, 153
Led Zeppelin, 165, 197, 199
Lefebvre, Henri, 184, 188
Le Forestier, Maxime, 19
Left Bank chanson, 94–95
leftism and leftist groups. *See* cultural leftism; *gauchisme;* institutional left; *specific organizations*
legislation: antihooligan law of 1970, 173–74
Le Goff, Jean-Pierre, 75
Lehman, Stephen, 116
leisure, 175, 177–78, 184
Lemery, Denys, 88–89, 90, 288n49
Lentin, Jean-Pierre, 199
Le Pen, Jean-Marie, 269, 295n106
"Lettre d'un socialo," 80
Lettres françaises, 31
Lévinas, Michaël, 282n101
Lewin, Thierry, 169
Lewis, George, 119
Libération, 201, 257–58
libertarian leftism, 185–90
"Liberté! Liberté!" (Queysanne), 156–59, 170, 271
Ligeti, György, 204
Ligue communiste révolutionnaire, 185, 191, 192, 201
Lipovetsky, Gilles, 12, 270, 274
literary chanson. *See* chanson
literature, 136
live performance, decline of, 55–58, 213–14
Logos (Wakhevitch/Triangle), 87
Longchampt, Jacques, 257
Looseley, David, 94, 262

Lutte ouvrière, 201
Lyon *fête,* 193–94
lyrics. *See* song text and titles

Maajun/Mahjun, 183, 201, 299n38
Mâche, François-Bernard, 53, 224
Macherey, Pierre, 124
Maciunas, George, 281n71
Magma, 87, 164, 165
Magny, Colette, 19, 87, 92, 140, 150, 201
Maheu, Jean, 234–38, 251, 253, 265. See also *animation musicale*
Mahjun/Maajun, 183, 201, 299n38
Maisons de la Culture, 217–22, 239, 252; Ferrari's work at Amiens, 212, 222, 224–25, 227–29
Maka, Jo, 150
The Making of a Counter Culture (Roszak), 161
Malcolm X, 120
Malec, Ivo, 208
Malherbe, Didier, 196
Malm, Krister, 299n35
Malraux, André, 60–61, 64, 213, 215, 218–19, 230; views of art and aesthetic experience, 217, 218, 221
Malson, Lucien, 119, 125, 126, 129
Mannoni, Gérard, 204
Maoism and Maoist groups, 32–33, 124, 186, 192; *l'été chaud,* 175, 177–84, 187, 196–97; Grange's turn to, 73–74; Tusques and, 141, 142; Vive la révolution, 186, 188–89, 192, 196, 201. *See also* China and Chinese communism; GP; UJCML
Marcellin, Raymond, 174
Marchais, Georges, 39
marches, 22, 32–36, 37–39, 63–64, 279n33
Marcus, Gérard, 220
Mariétan, Pierre, 208
Marly, Anna, 75
Marre, Michel, 150
"La Marseillaise," 29–30, 31, 64–66
Martenot method, 240
Martin Circus, 164, 165, 166, 168
Marxism and Marxian theory, 7, 47, 86, 192, 270; Marxist cultural policy, 123, 185; revolutionary subjects, 86–87, 117, 121–22, 153, 192
Marxist groups. See *specific organizations*
Masculin/Féminin (Godard), 119
masculinity, in rock, 104, 105
mass culture critiques: of beatniks, 106; of rock and roll, 103; of *yéyé,* 104–5

mass media, 231, 233, 239, 243, 261; rock
on radio and television, 164, 165–66,
299n37; as threat to musicians, 213. *See
also* radio; television
Masson, Diego, 136
Le Matin, 263
May '68, 3–4, 21–69; arts and music in,
25–28; de Gaulle's invocation of
communist threat, 63; in Evariste's "La
Révolution," 101–2, 109–10; Gaullist
counterdemonstrations, 31, 63–64,
279n33; government response, 22, 23,
40, 50, 269; Grenelle accords and
aftermath, 61–69; immediate aftermath
of, 70–71; outside Paris, 72; overview
of events, 21–23; as political failure,
10–11, 269–70; romanticized in Ferré's
"L'été 68," 97–100; sociopolitical context
of, 23–24; student-worker relations, 25,
36–39, 85; violence in, 12. *See also*
cultural agitation; May '68 legacy;
musicians' strike; strikes; *specific
participants*
May '68 legacy, 9–14, 19–20, 68–69, 195,
268–74; cultural interpretations, 11–13,
14, 195, 270–71, 274; political interpretations, 10–11, 12–14; scholarly investi-
gations, 276n14; utopian conceptions
of, 20, 24–25, 71, 269
McGhie, Noël, 150
McKenzie, Scott, 163
meaning: music's semiotic limitations, 143,
148–49
media. *See* mass media; radio; television;
underground press; *specific
publications*
Mendès-France, Pierre, 62
Menger, Pierre-Michel, 204, 212
Messiaen, Olivier, 53–54, 204, 208,
282n101
Michel Portal Unit, 87
Miereanu, Costin, 208
Mignon, Patrick, 201
Miller, Toby, 241
Ministry of Cultural Affairs: Duhamel's
hiring and programs, 230–31, 233;
initial staffing, 218–19; Malraux's
departure, 230–31; Mitterrand era,
263, 264–65; Service de la musique
establishment, 215–16; surveys
conducted by, 161, 220. See also
*animation culturelle; animation
musicale;* Malraux, André; state
cultural policy

Mitchell, Eddy, 130, 164, 200
Mitterrand, François, 18, 62, 264, 268–69
Mitterrand government: cultural policy,
263, 264–67, 274
Mollet, Guy, 121
Le Monde, 112, 125, 178–79, 207, 257,
260
Monson, Ingrid, 115
Montéhus, 80
Montels, Aline, 278n17
moral critiques of musical genres, 103, 106,
130
Morin, Edgar, 287n40
Morisse, Lucien, 101
Mothers of Invention, 165
Mouloudji, Marcel, 118, 201
Moustaki, Georges, 92
Mouvement de libération des femmes,
186
Mouvement du 22 mars, 10
Mouvement jeune révolution, 39–40
Moving Gelatine Plates, 168
municipal cultural policy and funding,
252–53, 262, 266
Murail, Tristan, 204, 264
Murray, Sunny, 112, 113, 135, 142, 145,
296n111
musical genres, 5–8; differential impacts of
technology on, 57–59; "genre" defined,
5; popular genres in state cultural policy,
214, 218, 228, 265, 266, 314n193;
stratification in state cultural policy,
214, 266–67. *See also* generic interactions; genre cultures; *specific genres*
musical instruments: Galerie sonore,
242–43
musical taste, 7, 89, 90, 214–15
music education, 210, 211, 213, 234, 235;
Conservatoire reforms, 52–53, 68;
educators' critiques of *animation
musicale,* 259–60; Ferrari's programs at
Amiens, 224; Landowski's primary
school program, 234, 237, 238, 240–41;
nontraditional pedagogies, 238–39,
239–40, 242–43; state funding for, 260;
traditional pedagogies, 238, 239,
240–41, 260
Music Electronica Viva, 206
Music Evolution (club), 176
music hall tradition, 94, 95
musicians, professional, 26, 27, 28;
economic/employment situation,
55–58, 213, 236–37, 283n113;
economic issues, 57–58; foreign

competition, 56–57, 58, 59–60, 135; in state cultural policy, 215, 216. *See also* composers; *specific genres*
musicians' strike, 53–61; Action musique's positions, 60–61, 67; background, 53–54; composers in, 54, 57; end and gains of, 67–68; Grange's participation, 71–72; record industry and, 57, 283n115; SAMuP's demands, 56–60, 67
musicians' unions, 26, 44. *See also* SAMuP
music industry: commercialization of rock, 158, 171, 177, 181–84; contemporary music sales, 204, 206, 208–09; early pseudo-hippie music releases, 163; musicians' strike and, 57, 283n115. *See also* rock concerts; *specific genres and labels*
Musicoliers, 266
musique concrète, 87, 126, 137, 208; Ferrari's Amiens project, 212, 222, 224–25, 227–29
Musique en jeu, 204–5, 209
Musique et vie quotidienne (Willener), 152
Musique pour tous, 233
Musique vivante, 136
La Mutualité, 28, 42–43, 118, 139–40
Muzet, Denis, 237

Nantes Festival de Saint-Gratien, 199
nationalism, 7, 64, 80; black nationalism, 115, 131, 132–33; "La Marseillaise" and, 29, 30, 31, 64–65
Nazi occupation, 75–76
Negus, Keith, 6
New Phonic Art, 87, 136, 208, 264
New Society program, 232
Newton, Huey P., 142
new wave cinema, 136
Night of the Barricades (10 May 1968), 22, 28, 46
Noël, Gérard, 288n49
noise music, 246–48
nondirectivity, 243
North African immigration, 120–21, 134
Nougaro, Claude, 92, 136, 140
nouveau roman, 136
"Les nouveaux partisans" (Grange), 75–81, 76*fig.*, 78*ex.*, 79*ex.*, 173, 272; Calvet's critique of, 83–84, 85; GP's adoption of, 79–83
Le Nouvel Observateur, 112, 114, 207, 215, 257

Nouvelles littéraires, 113
Nussac, Sylvie de, 107

Occident (political organization), 21, 31
occupations (May '68): Conservatoire, 50–53, 54; factories, 37–39, 50; Sorbonne, 2, 5, 22, 40; theaters and concert halls, 45–50, 54, 223
Odéon theater occupation, 46–50, 223
Office de radiodiffusion-télévision française (ORTF), 57
Ohana, Maurice, 224
"Oink Oink" (Magny and Tusques), 150
Opéra, 50, 51*fig.*, 67–68
Opéra-Studio de Paris, 244
Opus N, 208
orchestras and symphonic music, 95; decline of live performance, 55–58, 213–14; in state cultural policy, 215, 216, 234, 237, 239. *See also* classical music
Ordre Nouveau, 201
"L'oreille froide" (Hirsch), 209–10
Orff method, 240
Organisation armée secrète, 176
Ortega, Sergio, 244
ORTF (Office de radiodiffusion-télévision française), 57
Ory, Pascal, 114

Palais des Sports, 103, 182, 196
Palais Garnier. *See* Paris Opéra
Panassié, Hugues, 119, 126
Parapluie, 161, 206
Paringaux, Philippe, 167–68
Paris *banlieues*, 251, 266; contemporary music projects in, 211, 212, 251–59
Paris Commune, 22, 27, 29, 30, 80
Paris Commune commemoration (1971), 196
Paris Jazz Festival (1966), 118, 131
Paris Opéra, 50, 51*fig.*, 67–68
Parker, Charlie, 137
Parmegiani, Bernard, 137, 208
parody and satire, 103, 107, 109–10
Parti communiste français. *See* PCF
Parti socialiste (PS), 9–10, 121, 201–2; cultural policy, 261–65, 267, 274, 314n180; 1981 elections and aftermath, 264–66, 268–71
Parti socialiste unifié, 62, 201
Pascal, Jean-Marc, 197
Pathé/Marconi/EMI records, 166, 300n52
patriotism: "La Marseillaise" and, 29, 30, 64–65

Pauli, Hansjörg, 224, 226
PCF (Parti communiste français), 23;
colonialism and, 121, 124; cultural
policy and funding, 123, 252–53, 261,
314n180; declining support for, 269;
Fête de l'Humanité, 200–201; GP and,
75; and Grenelle accords, 62; and "La
Marseillaise," 30, 64–66; May '68
aftermath, 62, 63, 64–66; and May '68
strike, 37; and Parti socialiste, 201–2;
radical views of, 31–32, 34, 61, 124;
rallies, 34, 64–65; and state cultural
policy, 220
pedagogy, in state cultural policy, 218, 221,
231–32, 237, 238, 259–60. *See also*
music education
"La pègre" (Grange), 72–73
Pékin Information, 74
Perception, 201
"Les Percussions de Strasbourg," 206
performance ensembles: state support for,
213, 216. *See also* orchestras; *specific
groups*
performers. *See* musicians
petitions, 42
Peuple et culture, 96
Philips records, 166
Phillips, Barre, 150
photography, 129
physicality: in free jazz performance, 113;
in rock, 169, 188, 189
Piano Dazibao (Tusques), 141, 142, 143
pieds noirs, 120–21
Pink Floyd, 113, 165, 171, 178, 197,
199, 200
Pinot-Gallizio, Giuseppe, 281n71
Plaisance, Eric, 123–25
pleasure, and political struggle, 184, 188–93
Poète, vos papiers! (Ferré), 95
Poètes d'aujourd'hui, 96
poetry and poetic conventions: in chanson,
93, 94, 95–96; Ferré's "L'été 68," 93, 96,
97–100
Le Point, 34–35
police, 22, 71, 176, 196–97
political parties: cultural policies, 123, 210,
258–59, 261–65, 314n180; party-
organized political festivals, 200–202;
responses to rejection of Grenelle
accords, 62; union of the left, 201–2. *See
also specific parties*
political songs, 278n17; "Le chant des
barricades," 21; "La Marseillaise,"
29–30, 31, 64–66; revolutionary

chanson, 16, 80–81. *See also* "The
Internationale"; slogans and chants;
specific artists and titles
politicization of music: genre and, 5–8, 15–16,
81–83. *See also* cultural agitation; *specific
genres*
politicized aesthetic discourse, 1–2, 4–5, 8–9
Politique hebdo, 83, 201
Polnareff, Michel, 107
Polydor, 171
Pompidou, Georges, 2, 40, 232–33
Pompidou government, 193
Popanalia festival (Biot), 20–29, 174,
178–79
pop music, 16, 102, 272–73; French pop in
the press, 167; French popular music
market, 166–67; generic subdivisions in,
85–86; negative images of, 103–5, 107.
See also *specific subgenres*
Pop Music (magazine), 179, 197
popular culture, 228–29; state cultural
policy and, 214, 218, 228, 265, 266,
314n193
Popular Front, 30, 217
Portal, Michel, 87, 135, 136, 139, 141, 153
Porter, Eric, 115, 132–33
"Portrait d'Erika Huggins" (Tusques), 144,
148–50
posters, 25, 32, 33*fig.*
poststructuralism, 12
Pottier, Eugène, 30
Potts, Steve, 112, 142, 144, 145, 149
Pour en finir avec le travail, 278n17
Presley, Elvis, 103
Presque rien (Ferrari), 225–26, 226–27,
228, 229
Pretty Things, 113
Prey, Claude, 208
Prin, Yves: *L'Ile de la vieille musique,*
244–49, 247*ex.,* 250*ex.,* 256
prise de parole. See expression, liberation of
Prix de Rome, 68
Les Problèmes, 106
professional licensing for musicians, 56, 57,
58–60, 67
professional musicians. *See* composers;
musicians
progressive rock, 165, 168–69, 172, 287n37
"Projet d'association internationale de
dissolution culturelle" (CRAC), 44–46
proletariat. *See* revolutionary subjects;
working class
propaganda, 25
Protestant ethic, 191

protest song. *See* beatnik movement and music
provincial Maisons de la Culture, 217–22
PS. *See* Parti socialiste
psychedelic music, 163–64
Puig, Michel, 208
punk rock, 272

Quand le son devient aigu, jeter la girafe à la mer (Thollot), 87
Queysanne, Bruno, 156–59, 170, 271

R&B, 148, 150
race and race relations: in France, 121, 134–35, 151, 251; jazz and, 127, 131–35, 138, 295n94; in the U.S., 120, 133, 138. *See also* African-American radicalism
radical leftism. See *gauchisme; specific organizations*
radio, 283n113; *Connaître le jazz,* 126–27; contemporary music on, 206; and decline of live performance, 55, 56, 57, 213; de Gaulle's May 30 speech, 11, 63; rock programs, 164, 165. *See also* mass media
Radzitsky, Carlos de, 125
raï, 272–73
Raisner, Albert, 105
rap, 266, 272–73
Ravignant, Patrick, 47–48
Rawson, Jean-Pierre, 163
Recasens, Manuel, 60–61
recherche musicale, 235–38, 263–64, 265
recorded music: impact on musicians and live performance, 55–57, 58, 213, 283–84n119. *See also* electroacoustic music; music industry
recording technology, 248–49
record production and sales, 57, 283n115; contemporary music, 204, 206, 208–9
Red Noise, 87, 111, 165, 168, 169
regional cultural institutions: music research entities, 236; in state cultural policy, 216, 236, 252, 264–65. *See also* Maisons de la Culture; orchestras
regionalism, 153, 273–74, 297n129
Reibel, Guy, 208
Reid, Bob, 142
religion, 187, 217
Renault factory (Boulogne-Billancourt), 3, 37–39, 50, 61–62
Renaut, Alain, 12, 270
repetition (in music), 225, 253, 257

Répression (Magny and Tusques), 87, 150
revolutionary chanson, 16, 80, 82–84, 85, 191, 255. *See also* "The Internationale"; "Les nouveaux partisans"
revolutionary festivals, 194; post-May '68 *fêtes sauvages,* 195–96, 304n160
revolutionary subjects, 86–87, 117, 121–22, 153, 192
"La Révolution" (Evariste), 100, 101–2, 107–10, 108*fig.,* 109*ex.*
rhythm and blues, 148, 150
Ribeiro, Catherine, 201
Rigby, Brian, 219
Right Bank chanson, 94–95
Riley, Terry, 206
Rio, Marie-Noël: *L'Ile de la vieille musique,* 244–49, 247*ex.,* 250*ex.,* 256
Roach, Max, 150
Roche, Jean, 22
Rochet, Waldeck, 65
Rock & Folk, 164, 167, 171, 179, 180, 200; contemporary music coverage, 206
rock, 155–202; commercialization of, 158, 171, 177, 181–84; French counterculture's adoption of, 152; interactions with chanson, 87, 199; interactions with contemporary music, 87, 90, 168; interactions with jazz, 90, 113, 165, 168, 178; interactions with other genres, 87, 199; moral critiques of, 103; physicality of, 169, 188, 189; and the record industry, 163, 164, 166–67, 171, 299n38, 300n52; SAMuP and, 58, 59, 284n120; in state cultural policy, 265, 266; as youth music, 84, 90–91, 102, 158–59. *See also* Anglo-American rock; French rock
rock and roll, 103, 159, 164–65, 200
rock audiences: at festivals, 172, 177, 178, 179–80, 202; press condemnations of, 179–80; Queysanne's interviews, 156–59, 170, 271; sense of community, 172–73, 180, 187, 195
rock concerts, 171, 196–98; *Charlie Hebdo* death notice, 198*fig.; gauchiste* interventions, 182–83, 187, 196–97; live rock in France, 171, 182–83; at party-organized political festivals, 200–202. *See also* rock festivals
rock culture. *See* French rock culture; rock audiences
rock festivals, 17, 20, 161, 172–80, 181; Actuel festival, 112–13, 114, 152, 156–57, 209; after 1970, 198–200; Aix,

rock festivals *(continued)*
176–78, 187, 209; Altamont, 172, 185;
Biot Popanalia festival, 178–79, 209;
financial problems, 177, 178; as forges
of collectivity/community, 172–73, 180,
187, 195, 197, 199–200; *gauchiste*
interventions, 175, 177–83; government
concerns and prohibitions, 173–74,
176; press reaction and recriminations,
178–80, 185; Troisième festival de rock
(1961), 103; Valbonne, 176; Woodstock, 172
rock press, 164, 167–69, 171; *Actuel,* 151,
161, 189–92, 206; contemporary music
coverage in, 206; reaction to festival
failures, 178–80
Un roi sans soleil, 244
Rolling Stones, 167, 182, 183, 185, 191, 199
Ronfard, Jean-Pierre, 278n17
Roques-Alsina, Carlos, 136
Rosenfeld, Edmond, 239
Ross, Kristin, 11, 12–14, 20, 24, 122
Rostand, Claude, 213
Roszak, Theodore, 161
Rouge, 201
Rouget de Lisle, Claude-Joseph, 29
Rovere, Gilbert, 137
Roy, Camille, 222
royalties, 56, 283n113
Royan contemporary music festival, 205,
207–8
Rubin, Jerry, 184
Russia. *See* Soviet Union

SACEM (Société des auteurs, compositeurs
et editeurs de la musique), 203
Salvador, Henri, 103
SAMuP (Syndicat des artistes-musiciens de
Paris), 44, 56–61, 66–67, 213,
283–84n119; rock/pop and, 58, 59,
284n120; strike demands, 56–60, 67
Sanders, Pharaoh, 119
San Francisco (Hallyday), 163
Sarkozy, Nicolas: on May '68, 9–10
Sartre, Jean-Paul, 45, 68, 86, 121, 153,
304n166
satire and parody, 103, 107, 109–10
Saudrais, Charles, 137
Sauvage, Catherine, 200
Savouret, Alain, 282n101
Schaeffer, Pierre, 208, 223
Schoenberg, Arnold, 136
The Screens (Genet), 48
Seale, Bobby, 144

Séchan, Renaud, 41
Second World War, 75–76
Secrétariat nationale des affaires culturelles
(SNAC), 261–62
Séguy, Georges, 61–62, 191
self-expression, 187–88, 231. *See also*
expression, liberation of
self-management *(autogestion),* 261–62
self-realization, 158; *animation culturelle* as
instrument of, 230, 231–32, 235, 240
Semaine de la musique contemporaine:
Boulez lecture, 1–2, 4, 8–9
Semaine musicales internationales de Paris
(SMIP), 206, 242–43, 306n24
serialism, 136, 204
Service de la musique (later Direction de la
musique), 215–16, 233–38, 252, 263.
See also animation musicale
sexual politics, 189, 191, 192
Shandar, 117
Sheila, 105, 136
Shepp, Archie, 113, 115, 118–19, 178
Shorter, Alan, 142, 144, 149
Siffer, Roger, 269
Silva, Alan, 112, 135, 142, 146, 201,
296n111
Simonot, Michel, 230
Siné, 34–35, 35*fig.*
singer-songwriters, 93–94. *See also* chanson;
specific artists
Siohan, Robert, 213
situationism, 25, 42, 62, 184
The Slave (Baraka), 119
slogans and chants, 28–29, 38, 72–73, 97,
99
SMIP (Semaine musicales internationales de
Paris), 206, 242–43, 306n24
Smith, Wadada Leo, 114
SNAC (Secrétariat nationale des affaires
culturelles), 261–62
SNAM (Syndicat national des artistes-
musiciens), 56
social change, 269, 272–73; culture's role in,
230, 231; festivals as glimpses of, 195;
genres and genre changes as reflections
of, 86–91, 288n49. *See also* cultural
policies; decolonization; immigration
social inequalities: and authenticity in jazz,
138–39; cultural attitudes and, 221;
cultural inequalities and, 217; cultural
policy and, 230, 231, 233, 263. *See also*
race
socialist parties. *See* Parti socialiste; Parti
socialiste unifié

Société des auteurs, compositeurs et editeurs de la musique (SACEM), 203

Soft Machine, 113, 165, 178, 196, 200

solfège, 240

Solleville, Francesca, 3, 15

Solzhenitsyn, Alexander, 270

song text and titles: Antoine's lyrics, 106; chanson, 93, 94, 95–96, 104, 110; French resistance to English-language pop, 164, 298n31; revolutionary songs, 255; rock, 190; Tusques's titles, 142, 143–44; *yéyé,* 104. See also *specific songs*

Sorbonne demonstrations and occupation, 2, 5, 21–22, 40, 45; CRAC founding, 40–41; music at, 2, 5, 41, 203

sound installations, 223

"Souvenirs de l'oiseau" (Tusques), 137

"Souvenirs souvenirs" (Hallyday), 103

Soviet Union, Soviet communism, 44, 121, 123, 124, 185, 217

Spanish Civil War songs, 80

specialization: critiques of, 15, 43, 45, 47–48, 53, 55, 224; revalorization of, 264

spectralism, 204, 264

spirituality, 187, 217

Spooky Tooth, 87

Stalin, Josef, 123

Starr, Peter, 10, 12, 191

state cultural policy, 211–22, 307n29; *action culturelle,* 211, 217, 218, 222, 259–64; *développement culturel,* 231–32; as display, 259; failures and critiques of, 219–22, 224, 259–61; genre stratification in, 214, 266–67; history and objectives, 211–12, 307n29; individual right to culture, 211, 214, 217; Ministry of Cultural Affairs establishment, 211; municipal policy and funding, 252–53, 262, 266; music policy, 213–16, 217, 233–38; pedagogy in, 218, 221, 231–32, 237, 238, 259–60; politicization of, 252–53, 258–59; Pompidou's influence, 232–33; popular culture and, 214, 218, 228, 265, 266, 314n193; post-1969 changes in, 229–32; *recherche musicale,* 235–38, 263–64, 265; under Mitterrand's socialist government, 263, 264–67, 274. See also *animation culturelle; animation musicale;* Maisons de la Culture; Ministry of Cultural Affairs

state funding, 48; audience expansion as goal of, 237–38, 264–65; for contemporary music, 6, 211–12, 233, 236,

237–38, 252, 259, 265, 267; for creation vs. *animation,* 260–61, 263; current funding for regional arts groups, 266; municipal arts funding, 252, 262, 266; for popular music genres, 265; SAMuP's calls for, 56, 57, 68, 213–14; tax breaks, 56, 57, 68. See also state cultural policy

Stearns, Marshall, 127–28

Sternheimer, Joël (Evariste), 41, 100–102, 107–10

Stockhausen, Karlheinz, 136, 205

Stovall, Tyler, 251

strikes, 2, 3, 22–23, 26, 57; de Gaulle's denunciation of, 63; Paris Opéra, 50, 51*fig.;* rejection of Grenelle accords, 23, 61–62; strike-related concerts, 3, 5, 26, 42, 53, 72. See also musicians' strike

structural repetition, 191, 192

student militants: contemporary criticisms of, 11, 39–40; immediately after May '68, 71; and the PCF, 31–32, 34; role in May '68 events, 2, 3–4, 9, 13, 21–22, 24; student-worker relations and solidarity, 25, 36–39, 85, 194. See also *specific schools and student groups*

students, in contemporary music audiences, 207

suburban communities, 251, 266; contemporary music projects in, 211, 212, 251–59

surrealism, 43, 44; automatic writing, 44, 93, 137–38

symphonic music. See classical music; orchestras and symphonic music

Syndicat des artistes-musiciens de Paris. See SAMuP

Syndicat national des artistes-musiciens (SNAM), 56

Tac Poum Système, 164, 165, 168

"T'aimer follement" (Hallyday), 103

tape compositions, 224–25, 226–27, 228

Tartakowsky, Danielle, 202

Tautin, Gilles, 111

Tautologos III (Ferrari), 225

Taylor, Cecil, 118, 136

techno, 272–73

technology, 237, 248–49; as challenge for professional musicians, 55–58, 216; *recherche musicale,* 235–38, 263–64, 265; recorded music, 55–57, 58, 283–84n119. See also electroacoustic music; recorded music

television, 71, 165–66, 299n37. *See also* mass media
Terroade, Kenneth, 296n111
Terronès, Gerard, 151
Texier, Henri, 165
text. *See* song text and titles
text compositions, 208, 211, 223, 225, 264
theater, 213; creator/*animateur* rift in, 260–61; as focus of *action culturelle*, 222; musical accompaniments, 143
theater occupations, 45–50, 54, 223
Théâtre de l'Odéon, 46–50, 223
Théâtre de Poche, 119
théâtre musical, 208
Théâtre nationale populaire, 96
Théry, Henri, 230
Third Stream, 118
Thollot, Jacques, 87, 118, 135, 136
Thornton, Clifford, 140
tiers-mondisme, 8, 121–22
Tixier-Vignancour, Jean-Louis, 139, 295n106
Tomb of the Unknown Soldier, demonstrations at, 34, 64
Tortelier, Paul, 53
Total Issue, 165
total person ideal, 47–48
Tournès, Ludovic, 130, 133–34
Tout!, 186–89, 191, 195, 197, 304n166
trade unions, 27, 44; artists' unions, 43–44, 46, 54–61; and Grenelle accords, 23, 61–62; worker response to Odéon occupation, 48–49. *See also* strikes; *specific organizations*
Traité des objets musicaux (Schaeffer), 208
transgression: of creator/consumer boundary, 47–48, 67, 262; "The Internationale" as symbol of, 36–39. *See also* aesthetic transgression
Travail et Culture, 3
Triangle, 87, 161, 165, 168, 169
Troisième festival de rock (1961), 103
Trotskyist groups, 124, 185, 192; JCR, 10, 32–34, 71, 124
Tusques, François, 118, 135, 136, 139–40, 141–51, 296n111; Black Panther influences and allusions, 141, 142, 144, 150; *Free Jazz*, 118, 137–38; Intercommunal Free Dance Music Orchestra, 150–51, 153; *Intercommunal Music*, 142, 143–50; Maoist influences and allusions, 141, 142; *Piano Dazibao*, 141, 142; *Répression*, 87, 150

UJCML (Union des jeunesses communistes (marxistes-léninistes)), 74, 124, 186
unconscious, 44, 93, 137–38
underground press, 161; *Actuel*, 151, 161, 189–92, 206; *Tout!*, 186–89, 191, 195, 197, 304n166
UNEF (Union nationale des étudiants de France), 36, 52
Union des Arts plastiques, 43
Union des compositeurs, 43–44, 54
Union des écrivains, 42, 43–44
Union des jeunesses communistes (marxistes-léninistes) (UJCML), 74, 124, 186
Union nationale des étudiants de France (UNEF), 36, 52
union of the left, 201–2
unions. *See* trade unions
United States: jazz in, 127–28, 130; race relations in, 120, 133, 138. *See also* African-American *entries*; American *entries*; Anglo-American rock
universalism, universalist rhetoric, 8, 16, 115, 127–29, 130–31, 240–41
Urfalino, Philippe, 252, 267
utopianism, 12, 269–73; cultural agitation as, 27, 45–46, 47–48, 55; festivals, 180, 202; *gauchiste* revolutionary aspirations as, 71, 82, 192; genres and generic convergence seen as harbingers of change, 86–91, 288n49; May '68 and utopian aspirations, 14, 18, 20, 24–25, 53, 269–70; rock's potential to forge community/collectivity, 172–73, 180, 187, 195, 197, 199–200

Valbonne rock festival, 176
Valoaz, Juan, 150
Vander, Christian, 165
Vander, Maurice, 165
Varèse, Edgar, 136, 206, 207
Les Variations, 165, 168, 287n37
variétés, 92, 94, 136, 199, 214; in the music market, 166, 171, 298n31; production standards, 104, 165
Vassal, Jacques, 27, 179, 180
Vautours, 103
Venice Biennial, 256–58
Verba, Sidney, 276n17
Vian, Boris, 103, 165
Vian, Patrick, 165
Vietnam War opposition, 21, 114, 121, 139–40
Vignolle, Jean-Pierre, 298n31

Vincent, Bruno, 122
Vincent, Eugène, 185
violence, 12, 75, 103, 138
virtuosity, 59, 245–46, 248
visual arts: cartoons, 34–35, 35*fig.*, 108, 108*fig.*; May '68 posters, 25, 32, 33*fig.*; working-class iconography in, 75–76, 76*fig.*
Vitet, Bernard, 118, 135, 139; collaborations with Tusques, 150, 296n111; engagement with contemporary music, 87, 136, 137
Vive la révolution, 186, 188–89, 192, 196, 201
Vogue records, 299n38
"Voyage au bout de la New Thing" (Comolli), 119–22, 124–25; responses and critiques, 123–25, 126–27

Wadleigh, Michael, 172
Wagner, Jean, 119
Wakhevitch, Igor, 87
Wallis, Roger, 299n35
Warne, Chris, 162, 181
Weber, Henri, 10, 32–34
Webern, Anton, 136
The Who, 171, 200
The Whole World, 196
Wilen, Barney, 87, 90–91, 135, 296n108
Willener, Alfred, 111, 152
Winkler, Adolf, 150
Wolinski, 108, 108*fig.*
women's movement, 186, 192, 273
Woodstock, 172
workers: artists reconceptualized as, 43–44, 48–49; May '68 worker-student relations and solidarity, 25, 36–39, 85, 194; Odéon workers' responses to occupation, 48–49
workers' movements, 13, 29. *See also* strikes
working class: chanson and, 5; economic conditions before May '68, 24; embourgeoisement, 86, 117; French, French free jazz and, 141; "The

Internationale" as symbol of class identity, 8, 31, 35–36, 39; in Maoist views of class struggle, 74, 81, 186; musical genres associated with, 5, 156–58, 172; popular culture and education movements, 219; portrayed in Aperghis's *La bouteille à la mer,* 257–58; postwar arts education initiatives, 96; revolutionary chanson linked with, 27, 82–84, 85; rock and, 156–58, 172; seen as culturally deprived, 228–29, 241–42
world music, 153–54
Wright, Frank, 112, 113, 116, 134, 201

Xenakis, Iannis, 19, 28, 114, 224; Journées de musique contemporaine concert, 206–7; record sales and audiences, 204, 205

The Yardbirds, 165
Yes, 113, 196
yéyé, 12, 94, 167, 200; lack of topicality in, 92, 100, 104; in the musical landscape, 85–86, 102, 103–5, 107, 115
Yonnet, Paul, 159
Young, Jean-Luc, 113
Young, La Monte, 206
youth: in Ferré's "L'été 68," 98–99; as revolutionary subject, 86–87, 90–91, 192
youth culture: American, 17, 161–62; Anglo-American, 17, 159, 160–63; commercialization of, 162–63; French, 105–7, 160–63; *gauchiste* ideas of, 177–78. *See also* counterculture; French rock culture; generation gap
youth music: contemporary music seen as, 207, 209; New Orleans jazz as, 130; rock and roll as, 84, 90–91, 102, 130
Yúdice, George, 241

Zhdanov, A. A., 123, 125
Zoo, 92, 93, 161, 165, 168, 169

TEXT
10/13 Sabon
DISPLAY
Sabon
COMPOSITOR
Westchester Book Group
INDEXER
Thérèse Shere
PRINTER AND BINDER
Sheridan Books, Inc.